25 —

D1393643

INVENTING THE INDUSTRIAL REVOLUTION

INVENTING THE INDUSTRIAL REVOLUTION

The English patent system, 1660–1800

Christine MacLeod

Research Fellow, Clare Hall, Cambridge

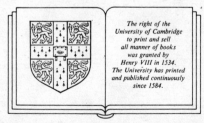

The right of the
University of Cambridge
to print and sell
all manner of books
was granted by
Henry VIII in 1534.
The University has printed
and published continuously
since 1584.

CAMBRIDGE UNIVERSITY PRESS

Cambridge

New York   New Rochelle   Melbourne   Sydney

Published by the Press Syndicate of the University of Cambridge
The Pitt Building, Trumpington Street, Cambridge CB2 IRP
32 East 57th Street, New York, NY 10022, USA
10 Stamford Road, Oakleigh, Melbourne 3166, Australia

First published 1988

Printed in Great Britain at
the University Press, Cambridge

British Library cataloguing in publication data
MacLeod, Christine
Inventing the industrial revolution,
1. England. Patent system, 1660–1800
1. Title
608.742

Library of Congress cataloguing in publication data
MacLeod, Christine.
Inventing the Industrial Revolution: the English patent system.
1660–1800/Christine MacLeod.
p.   cm.
Bibliography.
Includes index.
ISBN 0 521 30104 1
1. Patents – Great Britain – History – 17th century.   2. Patents –
Great Britain – History – 18th century.   1. Title.
T257.P2M33   1988
346.4104′86–dc19
[344.106486]   87-37406CIP

ISBN 0 521 30104 1

For my parents, Jean and Roderick MacLeod

Contents

Tables and figure

Acknowledgements

My greatest debt is to Donald Coleman, who not only supervised the Ph.D. thesis that provides the foundation for the present work, but also took a keen interest in the subsequent research and development of the project, generously giving advice, criticism and encouragement. John Harris and Roy Porter, who examined the thesis, urged me to publish it and made valuable suggestions to improve it.

Mark Goldie has borne the completion of both thesis and book with constant support and enthusiasm. By discussing my ideas, offering insights of his own and, not least, sharpening my prose, he has enhanced both immeasurably.

Since the history of patents and inventions is not a well-populated field, I have been exceptionally fortunate to discover two colleagues working in close proximity and deeply saddened to lose one of them. I learned a great deal from conversations with the late Harry Dutton, whose book on the English patent system has broken new ground, and from Liliane Perez, who is currently making a comparative study of French and British inventors in the eighteenth century that will greatly extend our understanding of the area. Peter King has shared with me his wide knowledge of the eighteenth century and made incisive comments on the text. I am also grateful to Wilfrid Prest for many helpful discussions during his stay in Cambridge.

There are many others whose help I am glad to be able to acknowledge. The Royal Society of London, the Royal Society of Arts, and the Wellcome Institute for the History of Medicine have kindly permitted me to consult their archives. The staff of the Cambridge University Library, the British Library and the Public Record Office have furnished me with most of my working materials, and the Cambridge University Computing Service, particularly Maggie Carr, has taught me how to operate the new technology on which the data was analysed and the text typed. The President, Fellows, students and staff of Clare Hall have provided a congenial and supportive environment in which to write. To the Open University I owe the opportunity to tutor students whose enthusiasm for the history of technology in particular and higher education in general has been an inspiration. Last, but not least, my thanks are due to the British taxpayers whose financial support was essential to the completion of the thesis. I hope that any reading this book will consider the money well spent.

Abbreviations

B.I.H.R.	*Bulletin of the Institute of Historical Research*
B.L.	British Library, London
Bodl.	Bodleian Library, Oxford
B.R.L.	Birmingham Reference Library
H. of C. Jnl	*Journals of the House of Commons*
H. of L. Jnl	*Journals of the House of Lords*
C.S.P.D.	*Calendar of State Papers Domestic*
C.S.P.V.	*Calendar of State Papers Venetian*
C.U.L.	Cambridge University Library
D.N.B.	*Dictionary of National Biography*
E.H.R.	*English Historical Review*
Ec.H.R.	*Economic History Review*
Econ. Jnl	*Economic Journal*
H.M.C.	Historical Manuscripts Commission
J.H.I.	*Journal of the History of Ideas*
Jnl Econ. Hist.	*Journal of Economic History*
L.Q.R.	*Law Quarterly Review*
P.R.O.	Public Record Office, London
R.S.A.	Royal Society of Arts, London
R.S.L.	Royal Society of London
S.C.L.	Sheffield City Library
S.R.O.	Scottish Record Office, Edinburgh
T.N.S.	*Transactions of the Newcomen Society*
V.C.H.	*Victoria County History*

Notes on style

Spelling in quotations has been modernized and initial letters, where necessary, altered to conform syntactically with the sentence in which they appear. Old-style dates are used, but the year is taken to begin on 1 January. Unless otherwise stated, the place of publication is London.

The serial numbers of English patents correspond with those in the indexes prepared by Bennet Woodcroft (see Introduction, n. 3), their dates corrected where necessary following A. A. Gomme, 'Date corrections of English patents, 1617–1752', *T.N.S.*, 13 (1932–3), 159–64.

In the tables, numbers have been calculated to one decimal place; in the text, decimals have been rounded to the nearest whole number.

INTRODUCTION

The English patent system is both older and younger than we tend to think. Patents for invention have been granted regularly since the middle of the sixteenth century, but it was not until 1852 that the first major legislation on patents was enacted by parliament and the Patent Office established. Between 1660 and 1800 the 'patent system' was something of a misnomer. It was not the orderly protector and promoter of inventions that one steeped in the patent law of the twentieth, or late nineteenth, century might imagine. Yet neither was it the corrupt dispenser of Court patronage that one whose perspective was the early-Stuart monopolies controversy would perhaps expect. This study starts by explaining how a recognizable patent *system* emerged from the monopoly muddle. The Statute of Monopolies (1624), enacted in an attempt to curtail the crown's abuse of patents, exempted from its general proscription those granted for new inventions. Contrary to the impression often given, this essentially negative piece of legislation was insufficient by itself to produce an institution at all capable of meeting the needs of the inventors of the industrial revolution. Development was gradual and quiet: there was no legislation, little activity in the law courts, and only muffled sounds to be heard from a few books and pamphlets. For a long time, the system's survival was precarious: invention took place outside it and often in ignorance of it. It survived, in the first place, because enough people found a use for a patent beyond simple protection of an invention and, eventually, because in using it they created an institution that took on a life of its own, which they could not ignore. Soon after the middle of the eighteenth century the system developed its own momentum and promoted a first-strike mentality among its users: one neglected to patent at one's peril. Change came through the initiative of its 'customers' and the response of its administrators to the uses and abuses discovered for it.

This book is not concerned simply to provide an administrative history of the patent system. It explores the relationship between patents and inventions in seventeenth- and eighteenth-century England, and suggests a more fruitful role for the patent records than those to which they have usually been reduced. Invention and its contribution to economic growth are slippery

1

subjects to grasp. To the historian grappling with the elusive problem of productivity growth in the eighteenth century, patents for invention have seemed to offer a firmer grip, a quantitative supplement to inconclusive, qualitative evidence. But danger notices have been posted; we have been repeatedly warned away and told not to put too much weight on patent statistics.[1] Marshalled into serried ranks of gross figures, as a crude index of either inventive activity or technical change, the patent statistics are, at best, misleading. Used with appropriate historical sensitivity, however, they can illuminate a range of economic and social developments. If this book does nothing else, it should finally undermine all attempts to build tall superstructures on the fragile foundations of the patent statistics. But I hope it will do more, of a more positive nature. For the patent records remain one of the few consolidated sources of information about inventors and their activities, before the nineteenth century, that we possess. It is not my intention to dismiss the patent system, but to explore it: to demonstrate how it worked and was used; to discover who the patentees were and how they exploited their grants; to assess the extent of inventiveness both inside and outside the scope of its records; to investigate how it was regarded by contemporaries and what we may learn about their attitudes to invention. In the words of Jacob Schmookler, 'we have a choice of using patent statistics cautiously and learning what we can from them, or not using them and learning nothing about what they alone can teach us'.[2]

Patents for invention were, until the late eighteenth century, a small minority of all letters patent filed (letters patent being a regular administrative instrument for the granting of lands, titles, offices, and other privileges). This complicates the task of tracing them. Fortunately, it has already been done. All researchers are indebted to Bennet Woodcroft, the first head of the Patent Office, who undertook this Herculean labour, tracked down the vast majority of them, and in 1854 published his work in three indexes. They and the blue books containing the texts of these patents, published by the new Patent Office shortly afterwards, must be the starting point for all subsequent research.[3] To understand the workings of the patent system, however, one must delve, beyond these printed registers with their deceptively regular appearance, into the morass of documents which trace the labyrinthine course through the government bureaucracy that a would-be patentee had to steer. Together, these petitions, warrants, reports, and dockets, held in the Public Record Office, amplify the barely audible tread of administrative development. Sadly, however, their impressive bulk is misleading: it is chiefly bureaucratic replication, revealing little about patentees and their inventions or projects. In this period the English patent system was one of registration, not examination.[4] Scrutiny of applications for patents was minimal, and information about them is accordingly sparse. Before the introduction of written specification in the early eighteenth century, and sometimes also after it, even the subject of the patent is shrouded in secrecy and only briefly described. And it is only from the same period that patentees regularly recorded their occupation and place of residence. There is a sharp contrast here with, say, the French archives, which contain a wealth of detail about the personal backgrounds, inventions, and enterprises of those seeking a *privilège*. The difference arises from the fundamental distinction between the two institutions: while the French government needed to know which applicants were worthy of its financial and other assistance, the English government was issuing a permission in which it had no further stake and whose value rested entirely on market forces.[5]

Researchers into the English patent system have to look more widely than the system's own records. There is no other consolidated source: it is a matter of tracing individual patentees and inventors. If a patentee suffered the unhappy fate of a legal case, court records sometimes reveal further material about him and his invention. A case law on patents only begun to develop in the second half of the eighteenth century. Earlier cases and those in which no precedent worth recording was established are not easy to unearth. I have chanced on a number, most of them in the equity courts, which are discussed in chapter 4. A systematic search of the indices to Chancery and King's Bench would doubtless reveal more. Parliament occasionally discussed individual patents, when the patentee sought an extension of his term or a private Act to give him stronger powers: reports are to be found in the journals of the two Houses, and abbreviated debates in Cobbett's *Parliamentary history*.[6] Pressure for reform of the patent system in the early nineteenth century was finally released through the safety valve of a select committee inquiry: since the system was still essentially the same as the eighteenth century's, some information can be gleaned from the evidence given to the committee.[7] For the rest, one is dependent entirely on literary sources. A very few patentees, like John Wyatt and James Watt, left letters and business records. Some, Thomas Savery for instance, wrote tracts to promote their inventions; others were attacked in print by rivals and victims of their monopolies and failed projects.[8] The seventeenth and eighteenth centuries did not see inventors in the heroic light characteristic of the nineteenth. Contemporary accounts of either enterprises or personalities are consequently rare, while the next century's retrospective hagiography is often inaccurate. Fortunately, there is a growing secondary literature, both biographical and technological, which often produces valuable nuggets of information. Indeed, I have been dependent throughout on the careful researches of many historians who have shed light on the technologies and industries to which patents referred.

Most of the existing 'standard histories' of the patent system were written by lawyers or economists with present-day causes to plead. J. W. Gordon in 1897 was anxious to defend 'the public against the abuse of patent right'; fifty years later, H. G. Fox thought that judges were being too harsh on patentees, demanding some mysterious component of 'inventive genius', unintended by those who originated the system. Both looked to the Statute of Monopolies

(1624) for clarification of patenting's historical function, and largely ignored the late seventeenth and eighteenth centuries. In 1906 William Hyde Price investigated the history of monopolies and patents under the Tudors and early Stuarts from an economic standpoint. Again he ended the story in 1640, drawing some timely conclusions about monopolies, no doubt in the light of current anti-trust legislation in the United States.[9] Allan A. Gomme, of the Public Record Office, in 1946 produced a straightforward, if brief, administrative history of the patent system from the late middle ages to the twentieth century.[10] This succeeded a series of articles in the *Law Quarterly Review*, by E. Wyndham Hulme and D. Seaborne Davies, which made an important contribution to the administrative and judicial history of the subject.[11] In 1967 Boehm and Silberston, researching 'the economic effects of the British patent system', found it necessary to devote considerable space to elucidating not only the legislative position but also the history of the patent system.[12] Their synopsis of the early history, however, is brief and concentrates again on the Statute of Monopolies; their historical emphasis is on the reform of the patent system in the nineteenth century and its subsequent sophistication.

If historians of the patent system have failed to account for what happened to it between 1640 and 1852, historians of the industrial revolution have not been deterred from speculating on its economic consequences – and reaching widely variant conclusions.[13] It is only recently that an economic historian has studied this question in depth. Harry Dutton went beyond administrative and legal history to look at inventive activity for its own sake and 'to see what effect patents had on those who used the system'.[14] With an ingenious model of an 'infant invention industry', he reached the conclusion that the very imperfections of the system 'paradoxically, created something close to the ideal'. Inventors used it because it was the only protection available to them, yet it was insufficiently watertight to prevent the fairly rapid diffusion of new techniques.[15] Dutton's work illuminates the late eighteenth century, and I make frequent references to it here, but his emphasis was on the first half of the nineteenth. There remains more to be said about the earlier period, which is perhaps only visible if it is approached travelling forward from the seventeenth, rather than in reverse from the nineteenth century.

Otherwise, early patent records have usually been treated either as a source to be mined for names and dates to attach to inventions, or as a shabby but serviceable index of inventive activity. The former has its dangers, in encouraging an heroic view of technical change,[16] the latter, which I shall examine more closely, has been a false trail. Now econometric history has taken the pressure off patents.[17] Its far more sophisticated calculations are at hand to investigate the rate and direction of technical change during the industrial revolution. There is the further advantage that econometric studies, by focusing on productivity increase, take us more surely into the economic consequences of technical change. Inventive activity, to which patents provide only an approximate guide, is itself but the raw material; the economic historian is usually more interested in the extent and rate of an invention's diffusion and its consequences for productivity. No definitive answers have yet been produced: historians using similar econometric methods have reached quite different conclusions about the extent and nature of productivity growth.[18] It is possible that a consensus will be reached; it is also possible that historians will finally conclude that calculation of 'the residual' (total factor productivity) is no more helpful than counting patents. As the term implies, the residual is what is left unaccounted for once inputs of land, labour, and capital have been deducted from output – 'a "best guess" and no more than that'.[19] Both are attempts to quantify qualitative change. While they provide a valuable perspective, the historian is forced, in the end, to move back from measurement to judgement. In the case of the residual, it is necessary to assess how large a role was played by technical innovation *vis-à-vis* other externalities, such as organizational improvements or education of the labour force.[20] In that of patents, we are forced to enquire which inventions, caught in the system's net, were the crucial ones, and to estimate whether there were economically important inventions, or indeed other externalities, unrecorded by a patent. There is no short cut.

The temptation to seize on the patent statistics as an indicator of inventive activity remains largely because the graph does exactly what our historical 'common sense' tells us it should. It shows a marked upward trend from the third quarter of the eighteenth century. From an average of 60 patents per decade in the century after the Restoration, the decennial total jumped to over 200 in the 1760s, to nearly 500 in the 1780s, and continued doubling every two decades to the mid-nineteenth century. The obvious explanation is that this rise expressed a sudden blossoming of inventive talent; it was the 'wave of gadgets' that notoriously swept the country in the late eighteenth century.[21] That wave itself remains a source of controversy. Historians of technology disagree over whether there was a discontinuity in techniques sufficient to constitute a technological revolution; economic historians debate the role of technical change in economic growth. Akos Paulinyi has recently made the case for regarding the introduction of 'material-forming working machines' in manufacturing industry, particularly the invention of machine tools, as *the* technological revolution.[22] His thesis challenges those who, like McCloskey and Von Tunzelmann, believe that technical progress in this period consisted, not in the famous new machines and engines, but in a host of small improvements – 'more like a gentle (though unprecedented) rain, gathering here and there in puddles' – and was evolutionary rather than revolutionary.[23] Emphasis on the diffusion of inventions, rather than their initial appearance, also tends to minimize the importance of the 'revolutionary' factory technologies of steam and cotton before the second half of the nineteenth century. Raphael Samuel, in particular, has stressed the size of the unrevolutionized sector and its continuing dependence on human muscle power.[24]

A gradual, evolutionary development starting in the sixteenth century, or earlier, is also espoused by those who follow Nef in regarding, not factories and their machinery, but the long-running shift from a wood-burning to a coal-burning technology as the crucial innovation.[25] Moreover, there has long been doubt among economic historians whether a bundle of striking technical inventions has not been mistaken for industrialization. Although important to a few industries, their economic impact was perhaps slight before the middle of the nineteenth century; the English economy grew fast, but did not achieve the sustained rise in per capita real incomes that may be taken as the defining characteristic of 'industrialization'. Recently 'the first industrial revolution' has been depicted as the concatenation of two distinct phenomena. Crafts, for instance, recognizes the major technical changes occurring in the 'modernized' sectors – the cotton and iron industries – but doubts their overall economic significance, at least before the 1830s: the revolution was chiefly in the structure of the economy, not in manufacturing productivity.[26] Wrigley argues even more strongly for expansion within a traditional economic and technical framework: the remarkable growth of England's eighteenth-century economy was based on 'organic' resources (the produce of the land); the full switch to an 'industrial inorganic' economy, based on coal and steam, was a post-1830 phenomenon.[27] Both Crafts and Wrigley regard agricultural productivity as the key to eighteenth-century growth, and technical change in industry as contingent and fortuitous. In Crafts's view, it was by chance that cotton-spinning machinery was invented in England rather than elsewhere; for Wrigley, England's coal seams were 'an uncovenanted blessing'.[28] The patent statistics cannot be employed to decide between these interpretations and none of these historians have called on their support. The answer, if there is one, lies elsewhere, in more detailed but also more wide-ranging, comparative and counterfactual investigations.

Yet the phenomenon represented in the graph persists and requires explanation. As the various series of figures which supported a 'cataclysmic' interpretation of the industrial revolution have been reworked and smoothed out,[29] patents' rapid late-eighteenth-century climb has remained one of the few steep ascents in a landscape of now gently rising hills. One might rework the patent series too, perhaps eliminating all but the 'technologically significant' inventions and taking note of important, unpatented ones.[30] This might of itself be a valuable exercise, but it would not provide a historically valid new series; we would simply be back in the realm of qualitative evidence. The patent statistics have to stand. The printed records are not complete and they contain some errors, but the omissions and inaccuracies are trivial: they provide no basis for any new insight.[31] An imperfect series of statistics is not the difficulty. The problem is two-fold. It is first that the patent system was a rag-bag institution: it contained many dubious minor improvements, variations and designs, while some of the most important inventions (for example, Newcomen's atmospheric engine, Huntsman's crucible steel, and Crompton's mule) were never patented. It is secondly that inventions themselves are not reducible to units to be totalled. They are 'fuzzy objects', like the peaks in a mountain range: it is difficult to determine where one ends and another begins. Attempts have been made to measure them in a variety of ways, none of them simple or straightforward. (Can technical achievement be put in the same scales as economic potential, for example? Which was more important, the initial breakthrough or the host of later, minor improvements that made it technically and economically feasible? How far was that breakthrough an illusion, the cumulation of many small steps? How does one count failed prototypes or the multiple inventions of the same product or process?)[32]

An individual patent may mark a technical achievement. The significance of patents as a group, however, must be considered in economic terms. Collectively, eighteenth-century patents are indicative of points of economic growth in a competitive, capitalistic context. The patent statistics need reinterpreting, not recalculating. We have been asking them the wrong questions. If we cannot trust them very far as a guide to invention, let alone productivity increase, we can trust them completely as an index of patenting. This is not the tautologous dead end it appears to be. The timing and distribution of patents *qua* patents is suggestive of tensions within the economy, some acute, others chronic: the pressure of costs to be cut or of opportunities to be seized. Sometimes, but not always, these were pressure points amenable to technological relief; often they indicate a fashion for some consumer good, where technology's role was minor or nonexistent.

Whether inventors were motivated chiefly by the search for profit or by noneconomic factors, such as curiosity or 'an instinct of contrivance', has been the subject of a long debate, which has largely revolved around the work of Jacob Schmookler.[33] Whichever view of inventors in general is correct, patentees provide a special case. There was no glory attached to being a patentee. The purchase of a patent was a commercial transaction. Patents were expensive to obtain, and nobody sought them without an economic end in view. This aim might have been to protect and exploit an invention; or it might have been to impress potential customers or investors; to escape the control of a guild, or to replace a guild's protective cloak, when that began to grow threadbare and competition to increase. The connection between inventing and patenting is historically tentative; it only started to be firmly established in the second half of the eighteenth century.

The first four chapters examine how the patent system developed between the Restoration and 1800: the residual influences of Elizabethan practice and the monopolies controversy; the administration of patents by government officials; the patentee's strengths and weaknesses when trying to defend his claims in the law courts. Chapters 5 and 6 draw out the implications of the system's idiosyncratic operation for the way in which patents were (or were not) used. They demonstrate how patents were sought, and granted, for a variety of reasons beyond the obvious one of protecting an invention from unlicensed imitation. The other side of this coin was that many genuine inventions were not patented. Although long recognized, it has not been fully appreciated that this varied considerably between different industries and different technologies, and that it changed over time. There were some spheres in which patenting was not cost-effective, and some types of invention less suited to patent protection. As the structure of industry changed, particularly as it became more centralized and more heavily capitalized, these factors could alter and prompt a higher ratio of patenting to inventing. An analysis of the distribution of patents by the place of residence and the occupation of patentees, in chapter 7, makes this apparent. Chapter 8 draws these findings together, to explain both the short-term fluctuations of the patent figures and their late-eighteenth-century 'take off'. The final three chapters are distinct from the exploration of the patent system in the first eight. In chapter 9, by examining the rationales offered by patentees for their inventions, I offer a new perspective on the goals of eighteenth-century inventors, and suggest that there was less interest in saving labour than is often thought. Chapters 10 and 11 move from economic activity to economic ideas, first to explore what contemporaries thought about the patent system and why they promoted alternative schemes of reward for inventors; secondly, to chart the change in perception of inventors and invention that occurred as Englishmen grew in technological confidence.

'English' patents covered England, Wales, Berwick-on-Tweed and, on request, the colonies and plantations. Scotland and Ireland maintained separate patent systems until 1852, and no attempt has been made to include them in this study. Union, in 1707 and 1800 respectively, led to the extension of the Statute of Monopolies to both.[34] Prior to Union, the crown was restrained only by prudence from granting unregulated monopolies in inventions as in other things. In seventeenth-century Scotland, however, private Acts of Parliament, giving limited terms of monopoly over inventions and new industries, were issued under the Act for Encouraging Trade and Manufactures of 1661.[35] Few Scottish patents were issued before 1760, and the subsequent acceleration in their use was largely produced by holders of English patents seeking to close this back door to infringement. Only seven patents were obtained for Scotland alone in the eighteenth century; 37 people with Scottish addresses took out one both north and south of the border, as did 106 people with English addresses; a further 22 resident Scots obtained solely an English patent.[36] Irish patents aroused less interest, especially before the Union. Eager projectors sought to extend their grants to Ireland in the wake of William III's victories, during the stock-market boom of the 1690s, but they appear to have been exceptional.[37] The engineer, Robertson Buchanan, wrote from Glasgow to his agent in London, in 1813, to enquire 'whether a patent for Ireland be now advisable and if so the expense. Before the Union I recalled Mr [James] Watt told me that a patent for Ireland was of no use'. Presumably Buchanan was advised that the expense still outweighed the risk, since his next letter requested Mundell 'to obtain an English and Scotch patent. I do not suppose we shall meddle in one for Ireland.'[38] It became a major complaint that protection for all three countries had to be purchased separately and was secured only at the expense of over £300.

Although the focus of this study is England and I have accordingly used the adjective 'English', it should be remembered that several of the major protagonists were Scottish, not least the inventor-engineers James Watt and John Rennie, and the economists David Hume, Adam Smith and Dugald Stewart.[39] The male gender is used throughout in referring to patentees, not through inadvertence, but because ninety-nine per cent of them were indeed male.[40]

I

PATENTS 1550–1660: LAW, POLICY AND CONTROVERSY

Over the last two centuries, the word 'patent' has come to have a precise and technical meaning: a grant of monopoly powers over the commercial exploitation of an invention for a limited period. This conceals its origin. William Blackstone, the jurist, writing in 1768, was still familiar with the broader understanding of the word, in which a patent for invention was but one type of royal 'letters patent':

The king's grants are also a matter of public record . . . These grants, whether of lands, honours, liberties, franchises or ought besides are contained in charters, or letters patent that is, open letters, *litterae patentae*, so called because they are not sealed up, but exposed to open view, with the great seal pending at the bottom: and are usually directed by the king to all his subjects at large.[1]

Thus letters patent were simply the document by which special privileges were conferred. Grants for invention were a relatively late arrival on the administrative stage, and were regarded as just one more instrument of royal policy. This meant that they were recorded indiscriminately on the patent rolls, among grants of land, office, honours, and other perquisites in the royal gift.

1.1 ELIZABETHAN AND EARLIER PATENTING PRACTICE

There are records since the reign of Edward III of 'letters of protection', given by the English crown to named foreign craftsmen, mainly weavers, salt-makers and glassmakers, with the intention of encouraging them to settle in England and transmit their skills to native apprentices.[2] These grants did not confer any exclusive privilege or monopoly. The practice was revived on a larger scale in the middle of the sixteenth century, again with the purpose of encouraging the introduction of Continental manufactures and skills. This time exclusivity was a major feature, through the influence of mainly Italian ideas.

The notion of creating property rights in technical achievements had arisen in the Italian city states.[3] In the early fourteenth century the Venetian republic rewarded inventors of corn mills who submitted their designs to practical tests with long-term credits and free sites for their mills. Florence granted an exclusive monopoly patent in 1421 – to the architect Brunelleschi for a barge with hoisting gear, used to transport marble. But Venice was the first to regularize in law the award of monopoly patents, the Senate ruling in 1474 that inventions should be registered when perfected: the inventor thereby secured sole benefit for ten years, with a penalty of 100 ducats for infringement, while the government reserved the right to appropriate registered inventions. Emigrant Italian craftsmen, seeking protection against local competition and guild restrictions as a condition of imparting their skills, disseminated knowledge of their patent systems around Europe. Six of the first nine patents in the Archives of Brussels, for example, were issued to Italians. It is no coincidence that the first recorded patents in several countries at this time were for glassmaking, a skill in which the Venetians excelled. German merchants trading with Venice also returned with the idea, and the petty German states were among the first in Europe to grant patents. Indeed, 'one way or another, Italian influence shows like a thread in all incipient patent systems'.[4]

England was no exception. Writing to Thomas Cromwell from Naples in 1537, Sir Antonio Guidotti proposed a scheme to bring Italian silk weavers to England:

one only grace I demand from your lordship in this affair, which is to be intermediator to the king's majesty to one privilege for fifteen of twenty years [so that] no man may within the realm make or let make any such kind of work, but under me and my name.[5]

There is no indication that the request was granted, but the Venetian practice was becoming known and alluded to with some admiration. 'In Venice, as I heard, and in many places beyond the sea, they reward and cherish every man that brings in any new art or mystery whereby the people may be set to work', wrote Sir Thomas Smith in 1549.[6] Then in 1552 a patent was granted for glass, apparently to an Englishman, Smyth, the next in 1561 to two immigrants for making Castile soap. The first Scottish patent was issued in 1565 to Francisco Berty, a Florentine, for saltmaking and the first Irish patent in 1586, again for glass.

Acquisition of superior Continental technology was the predominant motive for the issue of patents under the guidance of Elizabeth I's chief minister, William Cecil, later Lord Burghley. The shaping of patents to serve his policy of importing and improving technology left a lasting imprint, one which they bore for most of the period under review. Encouraging foreign artisans to settle in England remained the most apposite way of introducing new technology for so long as the English lagged behind their competitors. It was particularly successful in the fields of textiles, mining, metallurgy, and above all ordnance. Burghley took full advantage of the opportunity offered by the persecution of Protestant textile workers in the Low Countries to help establish the 'new draperies'. Religious differences and regulations such as the Statute of Artificers were not allowed to obstruct their immigration, and the Council was solicitous in attending to problems that arose between them and established interests. During the 1560s, twelve patents were granted for chemical processes and six for mechanical devices, and extensive privileges in mining and metallurgical enterprises were allowed; companies formed to exploit mineral resources with the aid of German technicians were given extensive rights of monopoly.[7]

Burghley had in mind, first, the expected national benefit – in assuring the supply of some necessary commodity or the creation of employment – and secondly, the rewarding of inventors for their labour and expense 'agreeable with justice', in order to encourage others. He was particularly eager to promote the introduction of those industries that had figured most prominently in the list of imports (alum, glass, soap, and saltpetre, for example) and the exploitation of native resources previously untapped for lack of the requisite skills.[8] Patentees were required to implement their 'invention' without delay and ensure its continuance by communicating the necessary skills to native workmen. The grant was revocable if these conditions were not met. It was regularly stipulated that the goods produced should be cheaper than their imported equivalents, and sometimes that they should be inspected periodically for quality.[9] The government was careful not to jeopardize the success of established industries. Its decisions were informed by the need to prevent unemployment and to respect the preserves of trade guilds, which were valued for their role in regulating industry. Sometimes Burghley personally altered clauses in the interests of precision and the safeguarding of established artisans and landowners.[10]

There is further evidence to show that early-Elizabethan patents were by no means granted on demand: the nature of the invention and its potential effects on the fortunes of interested parties were investigated. For example, a group of French glassmakers petitioned the crown in 1567 for a twenty-one-year patent to produce Normandy window glass. The government consulted the Chiddingford glassmakers, enquiring whether they had made, or could make, that type of glass. Only when they replied in the negative, was a patent granted. In 1589 a patent for saltmaking was refused to German artisans on the grounds that many of the queen's subjects were already making salt from brine. Further indicative of Burghley's close interest is a case reported by Stow. Henry Newell and Sir Thomas Mildmay were refused a patent for refining sugar. Their business, they claimed

[would] cause no hindrance to her majesty's customs, no prejudice to any Merchant Adventurer, no damage to the Grocers of London, no inconvenience to the commonwealth although it might be called a monopoly: but the Lord Treasurer (who would never consent to such things without hearing what could be said by others against it) received reasons why the refining of sugar should not be granted to one, two or three persons private only.[11]

It was of great significance in the development of the patent system that the primary goal of Burghley's policy was the introduction of entire industries or manufacturing techniques from abroad. The rights of the first inventor were understood to derive from those of the first importer of the invention.[12] This had two important ramifications for what the government required of the patentee (our present principle of publication was not established until the late eighteenth century). First, the consideration or quid pro quo originally demanded was not the disclosure of his secret, but 'the furtherance of trade' through the effective introduction of a new technique or industry. It followed that the patenting of mere improvements was frowned upon – whether to an existing trade or a patented invention – since they were liable to interfere with the livelihoods of established workers.[13] This is the force of the dual judgement in Bircot's case (1572).[14] As expressed by Sir Edward Coke, half a century later, it meant that 'a new invention is that which brings to the commonwealth [what] they had not before', whereas '[a]n addition to an old invention' was 'but a new button' on 'an old cloak'.[15] Employment was sacrosanct, and the inventor who threatened it was denied official recognition and protection by patent.[16] In 1571 the Council rejected Matthey's petition for a patent to protect his new knife-handles, on the Cutlers' complaint: by a monopoly of superior handles, they alleged, he would bring all the Company's members to ruin.[17] It was not until the last quarter of the eighteenth century that this criterion was abandoned in the law courts, Lord Justice Mansfield deciding in *Morris* v. *Branson* (1776) that the objection to improvement, if held valid, 'would go to repeal almost every patent that was ever granted'. As Mansfield's statement implied, the principle had not prevented the granting of numerous patents for what were technically no more than improvements. The citation of Bircot's case had procured the subsequent disallowance, however, of patents whose enforcement threatened existing livelihoods or which had been judged mere improvements.[18]

Secondly, the original consideration lost its rationale as fewer patents were granted to foreign artisans. In 1624 Sir Edward Coke fell back on Burghley's subsidiary justification:

the inventor brings to and for the commonwealth a new manufacture by his invention, cost and charges, and therefore it is reason that he should have a privilege for his reward (and the encouragement of others in the like) for a convenient time.[19]

Petitions for patents after 1660 regularly opened with mention of 'the great charge, labour, cost and pains' (or similar sacrifices) that the petitioner had expended on his invention, and usually offered some platitudinous potential benefits aimed at the government's social and economic prejudices – employing the poor, developing native resources, or saving vast sums on imports. Putting the invention into practice had obviated the disclosure of it to the public by other means, such as by written description. Late-seventeenth-century patents, still reclining on the older practice, required in effect neither form of publication. It was rare to demand anything of the patentee. The condition imposed on the Lustring patentees and White Paper Company in the 1680s, that they should instruct native apprentices, was exceptional: significantly, both were established by Huguenot refugees.[20] The early eighteenth century witnessed the emergence of the written specification, but it was only much later, through the decisions of common-law judges, that the specification was legally required to carry the weight of informing the public.[21]

These and other issues of the patent's proper function and format, which arose in the adaptation of the patent system to changing economic and technical conditions, hung fire throughout the seventeenth and much of the eighteenth centuries.[22] They were decided *ad hoc*, by officials and judges, as the occasion arose. The consideration demanded of the patentee was long left undetermined: sometimes a clause to implement and instruct, sometimes (and increasingly) a written specification were required. Improvements to inventions were awarded patents although officially disallowed. The judicial determination of infringements and patent validity cases consequently rested on shifting and uncertain ground.

1.2 POPULAR HOSTILITY TO MONOPOLIES

Burghley had worked hard to make his industrial policy a success, but most newly planted industries had not flourished as expected. Even by 1569 he had gloomily, if irresolutely, decided 'not to move her h[ighness] any more to make grants whereof nothing did grow, wherein her honour was touched'.[23] Worse, without a committed, firm hand guiding the system to well-defined ends, malpractices began to creep in that were to bring it into disrepute and ultimately endanger its existence. Although no longer instruments of a deliberate policy of importing technology, patents could still be obtained for the introduction of foreign (and native) inventions; influence at Court was, to say the least, advantageous. More controversially, monopolies based on no new industry or invention were granted to courtiers and their clients who had a purely fiscal end in view.[24] Since they interfered with established trades, protests were raised almost immediately by those whose interests, as producers or consumers, were in jeopardy.

Grievances concerning the crown's use of letters patent to regulate manufactures and trade were voiced in several of Elizabeth I's parliaments. They culminated in 1601 in a concerted attack on what was deemed an abuse of the royal prerogative. To forestall the passing of 'an act for the explanation of the common law in certain cases of letters patent', the queen promised to revoke the more objectionable patents by proclamation and to relinquish the remainder to the jurisdiction of the common law.[25] Yet under her successor, despite the establishment of the Commission for Suits to investigate the claims of patentees and James's declaration of self-restraint in the *Book of bounty* (1610), the Commons found increasing cause for complaint.[26]

For proclamations and patents, they are become so ordinary that there is no end, every day bringing forth some new project or other. In truth, the world does ever groan under the burden of perpetual patents, which are become so frequent that whereas, at the king's coming in there were complaints of some eight or nine monopolies then in being, they are now said to be multiplied by so many scores.[27]

In 1621 the Commons launched another attack on monopolies. Giles Mompesson, the chief agent of the 'Buckingham ring', which operated the monopolies of gold and silver thread and the licensing of inns and ale-houses, fled the capital, and parliament ordered the cancellation of eighteen patents and the submission of seventeen others to the test of common law. But matters did not rest there: a bill, passed by the Commons but rejected by the Lords in 1621, was reintroduced in 1624 and this time enacted as the Statute of Monopolies (21 Jac. I, c.3).

The dramatic story of this Act has often been told, usually in the context of the constitutional crisis of the early seventeenth century in which, according to whiggish interpretations, it marked a major blow struck by the Commons against the royal prerogative.[28] Intended to proscribe the crown's abuse of its dispensing powers, the Statute's role as the legal basis for the patent system was a curious side-effect, a quirk of history.[29] It exempted letters patent for new invention from the general proscription.[30] Its targets were rather the abuses of patents of registration (for example, of ale-houses), the various sharp practices that had grown up around industrial patents, and the licences issued to circumvent the restrictions of older corporations and companies, particularly in the export trades.[31] Control of an entire industry had some-times been established on the basis of a patent for invention in one part of the process: Mansell's patent for glassmaking was criticized for this in 1621 – it was if 'a man for the invention of galoshes should have the sole making of shoes'.[32] Courtiers who extorted large sums from petitioners as the price of advancing their claims were roundly condemned. But most offensive of all was the granting of monopoly powers in established industries, as a form of patronage, to courtiers whom the crown could not otherwise afford to reward. This was to the detriment of consumers and established manufactur-ers alike.

Projects of all kinds, many ridiculous, many scandalous, all very grievous, were set on foot; the envy and reproach of which came to the king, the profit to other men, in so much as of £200,000 drawn from the subject by these ways in a year, scarce £1,500 came to the king's use and account.[33]

These abuses parliament sought to eradicate in 1624 by the restriction of letters patent, conferring monopoly powers, to first inventors alone. The validity of royal licences would henceforward be liable to trial at common law, and anyone aggrieved by them could sue for relief in the courts of King's Bench, Common Pleas or Exchequer, and be recompensed, if successful, with three times the damages he had sustained and double costs.[34]

But there were loopholes in the Act which the crown, desperate for new sources of patronage and revenue in the 1630s, was able to exploit. Industrial corporations were created or transformed to operate patents that conferred monopoly powers, at the price of an annual rent or pro rata payment to the crown. Major items of consumption – salt, soap, starch, coal, for example – rose dramatically in price, as monopolists sought to recoup the rents and premiums demanded by the government and to exact high profits while their political luck held. The practitioners of some trades were barred from exercising their legitimate occupations except on the payment of fines, or they paid harsh penalties for refusal.[35] In consequence the patent system was totally discredited. It was effectively dismantled by the Long Parliament's calling-in of patents, in 1640, amidst a general outcry against monopolies.[36] Only a very few patents – all hedged round with restrictions – were issued during the Interregnum.[37]

'Monopoly' had become, more than ever, an emotive word, and it retained its pejorative force long after 1660. There was clearly still much animosity towards predatory courtiers and any fiscal exploitation of patents by the crown. In 1654 the mayor and corporation of Norwich, angered by a proposed postal monopoly, had warned Cromwell: 'having bought our liberties at vast expense of blood and treasure we hope not again to be troubled with distasteful monopolies, but to have liberty to convey our letters freely'.[38] An anonymous writer (apparently a disappointed royalist) warned Charles II in 1664 against 'dissolute and covetous courtiers who sell places of trust, ingross grants and hunt after patents and new inventions until the kingdom is impoverished and the prince hated'.[39] In the same year it was reported to the government that a wiredrawer, Simon Urlin, at a meeting summoned by him to oppose John Garill's application for a patent, 'said in passion that the late king lost his head by granting such patents'.[40] The doggerel of *Vox et lacrimae anglorum* (1668) made the same point:

> Tread all monopolies into the earth
>   And make provision that no more get birth,
> In this a prince's danger chiefly lies
>   That he is forced to see with others' eyes,
> From hence our troubles rose in Forty One
>   When that Domestic War at first began.[41]

The abuse of monopolies had entered popular mythology as a major cause of the Civil War. Indeed monopolies had headed the Committee of Grievances' list of abuses of the prerogative relating to property in 1640.[42]

The Case of Monopolies, a dispute in 1684 over the East India Company's rights to exclude interlopers, brought the issue fully into the public view again. 'The word monopoly, or engrossing, generally spoken of is odious in the eye of the law', pronounced Justice Withins.[43] From two parliamentary debates in 1692–3, it is clear that accusations of monopoly were a ready weapon: William Walcot's 'Sea water fresh' bill was passed despite such charges; not so the bill to grant the proprietors of the Convex Lights' patent a longer term. Opposed by much stronger interests, it was thrown out as a monopoly and thus 'directly against the interests of the public'.[44] Aaron Hill, the poet, when promoting his beech oil project in 1714, felt it necessary to preempt accusations that patents were 'very burthensome prerogatives of the crown, and an encouragement to monopoly'. He reassured landowners that,

when the queen gives me a patent to make oil from mast, she gives me nothing that was others' property, neither does she force you to sell me your mast; for if you think it more your interest, you are certainly at liberty to let it alone.[45]

The Commons was reminded in 1732 of the unhappy genesis of the patent system's statutory foundation, on the occasion of Thomas Lombe's attempt to renew his patent by private Act of Parliament. One of his supporters argued that since there had been no unlawful monopoly 'we are not confined by the former law'. He recalled 'the bubbles and monopolies which were erected, and the many enormities which were committed about that time' which led to the enacting of that law 'to prevent the setting up of any such bubbles or monopolies for the future'.[46] The memory, so entangled with the liberties of the House of Commons, died hard and Restoration governments forgot it at their peril. Josiah Tucker appreciated this a century later:

When King Charles II was restored he not only revived all the former monopolies relating to foreign trade, but created as many new ones, foreign and domestic, as the times would then admit; I say *then* admit: for the arbitrary proceedings of Charles I in relation to these things, were too odious, and too recent for the son to proceed immediately to the same exorbitant lengths.[47]

I.3 THE STATUTE OF MONOPOLIES

What then did the Statute of Monopolies allow? Various types of grants and privileges were explicitly exempted from its purview. These included grants made or confirmed by Act of Parliament, warrants under the privy seal to justices of the courts of law and of the peace, patents for printing, making ordnance, gunpowder and alum, and the manufacturing patents granted to four named individuals; also exempted were charters to towns, corporations and companies. The latter proved a major loophole through which the crown continued to drive its monopolies until 1640. Then there were letters patent for invention. Section 6 of the Statute merits quotation in full as the clause on which the patent system came to rest:

Provided also and be it declared and enacted that any declaration before mentioned shall not extend to any letters patent and grants of privilege for the term of fourteen years or under, hereafter to be made, of the sole working or making of any manner of new manufactures within this realm, to the true and first inventor and inventors of such manufactures, which others at the time of making such letters patent and grants shall not use, so as also they be not contrary to law, nor mischievous to the State, by raising prices of commodities at home, or hurt of trade, or generally inconvenient; the said fourteen years to be accounted from the date of the first letters patents, or grant of such privilege hereafter to be made, but that the same shall be of such force as they should be if this Act had never been made, and of none other.

Evidently, the law was little more than declaratory of preceding practice and common law, but it converted previous prudential restraints into statutorily binding codes of practice.[48] It became the standard by which the crown's law officers tested applications for patents. Its only innovations were the limitation of the term to fourteen years, and the declaration that cases concerning monopolies, letters patent, licences, and so forth, should be tried and determined at common law.

The new law was expounded and some of its immediate ramifications drawn out by Sir Edward Coke (1552–1634), who may be accredited as an expert on the Statute of Monopolies. Not only had he served as a law officer and Chief Justice, but he had appeared for the plaintiff in *Darcy* v. *Allein* (1602) – in which a monopoly of importing playing cards was set aside and the common law on patents hotly debated – and had investigated many patent and trade disputes since 1593. As an M.P., he had introduced (with William Noy) the 1621 bill against monopolies and served on the committee that considered the bill of 1624.[49] The Statute, in Coke's view, permitted letters patent for the sole working of new manufactures, provided seven conditions were fulfilled.[50] First, that the term was limited to fourteen years maximum. This limit was not chosen entirely at random: it was twice the statutorily prescribed, seven-year term of trade apprenticeship. Coke deliberated whether, as such, it was not still too long, for the first apprentices would be restricted by their master's patent for a further seven years and consequently discouraged. Secondly, 'it must be granted to the first and true inventor', and thirdly, 'it must be of such manufacture, which any other at the making of such letters patent did not use'. Coke did not anticipate any difficulties in the interpretation of these clauses. He followed Elizabethan practice in understanding 'inventor' to include the importers of manufactures and technical devices.[51] Similarly, it was not a question of whether the manufacture or device concerned had *ever* been used in England before, but whether it was in use at the time the patent was applied for. Fourthly, 'the privilege must not be contrary to law', that is, it had to be 'substantially and essentially newly invented: but if the substance was *in esse* before, and a new addition thereunto, though that addition make the former more profitable, yet it is not a new manufacture in law'. Coke here referred to the precedent of Bircot's case, decided in the Exchequer Chamber in 1572; it informed legal thinking on patents until the late eighteenth century, when it was cited in several cases only to be overturned. In Bircot's case it was also 'resolved, that if the new manufacture be substantially invented according to law, yet no old manufacture in use before can be prohibited'. Fifthly, it should not lead to a rise in the price of commodities at home: in every new manufacture deserving of a patent there must be '*urgens necessitas, et evidens utilitas*'. For, it was held that the establishment of industries to substitute native for imported goods should not be at the expense of the consumer. There was in effect little regard paid to this: prices were generally only considered when they became issues of law and order, as with grain.[52] This obeisance towards utility was strictly in line with the Elizabethan policy that fostered the patent system, as befitted a one-time client of Burghley's. Sixthly, it should not be 'to the hurt of trade', to Coke apparently a self-evident proposition. Finally, and vaguely, it should not be 'generally inconvenient'. To illustrate this clause, Coke gave the example of a fulling mill that could replace the labour of eighty men: it would fall foul of a sixteenth-century statute (7 Edw VI, c.8) which ordained 'that bonnets and caps should be thickened and fulled by the strength of men, and not in a fulling mill, for it was holden inconvenient to turn so many labouring men to idleness'. Otherwise, where no statute stood in the way, it was left to the discretion of the Privy Council to determine 'inconveniency'.[53]

The 1624 Act looked back to the exacting operation of a patent system, designed to further an enlightened industrial policy in the early decades of Elizabeth I's reign, and to common-law precedents. Its importance lay in crystallization, in giving letters patent for invention statutory recognition and hence legal status; perhaps it even allowed them a new lease of life when the crown might have lost interest in issuing them. But in thus codifying, the Act made barely perceptible alterations in the administration of the patent system, and in practice left jurisdiction over it with the Privy Council, where it remained until 1753. The early Elizabethan experience had defined for posterity – as the 1624 Statute confessed – the 'proper' function of the patent system. It took a long time and extensive experience of economic conditions to which that system was not well suited to redefine its function and remodel the system accordingly.

2

THE LATER-STUART PATENT GRANT – AN INSTRUMENT OF POLICY?

Patents for invention survived the Commonwealth and Protectorate, reemerging in 1660 barely scarred by the experience.[1] As this chapter will show, they were still regarded by the crown as rewards for service and as instruments for subcontracting its business – one of the resources at hand for administering the realm. But something had changed. The hostility towards monopolies that had helped destabilize the government of Charles I was still alive and menacing. The restored king could not afford to give it cause to surface. Charles II attempted to use patents covertly as grants of monopoly during the first few years of his reign, but apparently recognized that it entailed too great a risk. On the whole, allegations of unjust exercise of monopoly powers by patentees received swift investigation and, where necessary, action by the government. There was no regular fiscal exploitation of the patent system and little systematic patronage of courtiers, although they and office-holders received preferential treatment. Nor is there any evidence for an industrial policy such as Burghley's. Yet the government remained an interested party in the patenting of inventions until the early eighteenth century.

2.1 GOVERNMENT REVENUE

Despite a chronic shortage of funds during the first half of Charles II's reign and the recourse to heavy taxation and deficit finance to pay for William's and Anne's Continental wars, the patent system was only minimally exploited as a fiscal device. At least £70, and perhaps twice that amount, entered the coffers of the crown and the pockets of its officials every time a patent was steered through the maze of writs, seals and docquets to enrolment.[2] Annual rents were demanded only occasionally before 1688 and never, it seems, after the Revolution. Lord Treasurer Southampton, when asked to recommend a fair rent for William Chapman's saltmaking patent in 1661, reported that 'small rents are usually reserved in such cases, therefore I think thirty pounds per ann[um]. Or a fourth part of the clear profits at your majesty's choice, to be reasonable if you choose within three years.'[3] Thirty pounds was exceptionally high: 13s 4d (66p) to £5 was the apparent range of all other rents imposed in this period. Small rents were required in virtually all patents granted in the two years from February 1671: although this was a period of acute financial stringency for the government, it is hard to believe that these small sums were viewed as necessary contributions to its relief.[4] In 1664 Timothy Fulthorpe, whose patent had been obstructed by a similar previous invention, attempted to bribe the Secretaries of State to let it pass. He offered each fifty pieces of gold 'as a token of gratitude' and tendered a bond of £2,000 against it subsequently emerging that 'I have had the discovery from any other person'. His offer was not accepted.[5] Of course, this is not conclusive evidence against the efficacy of bribery: there may have been much on a less ostentatious, indeed unselfconscious, scale.[6]

In a number of other cases the patentee agreed to admit the crown to a share in any profits made by working the patent. This was the regular procedure for patents which were concerned with the recovery of wrecks and treasure from the sea. Whether or not the crown shared the optimism of the common investor in such projects, it claimed a risk-free tenth or sometimes fifth of any profits.[7] Outside this highly speculative sphere in which no established interests or livelihoods were concerned, the crown demanded no stake in the outcome. But it was not immune to offers of a potentially lucrative share. In 1680 Sir Clement Clerke requested a patent for metallurgical processes; his petition was rejected. Six years later he sought a patent for ostensibly the same invention, but this time offered 'a proviso of one half to the king after six years and in case the term be enlarged by Act of Parliament then two thirds'. The patent was issued on this basis.[8] (Clerke's religious sympathies may have been more influential than this offer in securing it: a partner in his patent was Robert Brent, possibly the Roman Catholic lawyer who gained notoriety as James II's 'electoral agent'.)[9] Furthermore, to secure its interest and perhaps to reward a loyal supporter at the expense of men too closely associated with the previous regime and its religion, the new government transferred the patent to Richard Lord Coote in 1689 on the same terms. Coote's claim was based on the assertion that the patentees were unable to implement the invention, and the new grant repeated it, in justification of Clerke's deprivation:

the patentees . . . have not hitherto made any considerable advance in their said invention nor are certain they shall until their workhouses and other materials are finished which must be very great expense.[10]

Non-implementation did not normally give cause for voiding an English patent.

After 1660 the crown did not attempt to augment its income by granting exclusive rights to particular interests at the expense of the public at large. Even where it exacted a rent or a percentage of the profits, it did not convey monopoly privileges to further its own and the patentees' interests. Its policy in this respect contrasts sharply with that of the first two Stuarts, and Allan

Gomme's view that 'in spite of the Statute of Monopolies, Charles I and *the later Stuart sovereigns* continued for revenue purposes to issue monopolies that were flagrantly contrary to its provisions' must be modified accordingly.[11]

While profiting to only a minimal extent from the fees and perquisites arising from the issue of patents, the crown was careful not to prejudice its hard-won revenue by improvident grants. It proved very jealous of its customs and excise revenues, especially the latter once they constituted a major element in post-Revolution finance. In consequence, patents for invention which might diminish these revenues were scrutinized with unusual care. Inventions were frequently recommended to the crown as a means to improve the 'balance of trade' by establishing the manufacture of a previously imported item. The negative side of this boon was the threat posed to its customs revenue, and petitioners were consequently at pains to reassure the government that the duties paid on imported raw materials and exported finished products would more than compensate for the initial loss.[12] In 1687 Paul Decloux, a French silk worker, and his two English partners, Paul Clowdesly and William Sherard, requested a patent for 'the sole making of certain silks called alamodes, renforcies and lustrings, heretofore made at Lyons in France'. The Treasury Commissioners were asked to consider how it might affect the customs revenue. Three months later, having heard the petitioners and representatives of the Weavers Company and examined samples of the silks, the Commissioners recommended the grant be made, with the proviso that the patentees should pay two shillings (10p) on each piece not exceeding 60 ells that they produced, and submit a quarterly account to the Exchequer of the number and length of pieces woven, the number of looms employed, and the names and addresses of all their weavers. This fee together with the duty on imported, unwrought silk would, they calculated, sufficiently recompense the crown for the lost import duties on wrought silk.[13]

There is no evidence that the government ever refused a patent because it posed a threat to the customs revenue. The excise, however, was another matter. Levied on a widening range of home-produced commodities at steadily increasing rates from the early 1690s, the excise was one of the corner-stones of post-Revolution finance. The wars of William and Anne were won on credit: income from taxation was mortgaged for years in advance to repay the sums invested in the Bank of England and other loans to the government. It was vital that the yield of the excise should not be (nor be thought to be) jeopardized in any way.[14]

One of the most important and lucrative excises was that on salt. In 1698 the government negotiated a loan of over £2,500,000 with the New East India Company on the security of the salt duties. These were accordingly doubled from 20d (8p) to 3s 4d (16p) on native salt, and made perpetual.[15] Any subsequent invention that appeared to threaten the yield of the salt duties was subjected to severe scrutiny. In 1709 Samuel Schmettau petitioned that he had discovered a better method of boiling salt, by means of which 'it might be made at less charge and afforded at lower rates than formerly', leading to an export trade 'to the prejudice of France'. The Salt Commissioners were prepared to accept these claims but withheld their approval. They were anxious lest the patentees improve their method and produce a stronger salt, which would 'very much prejudice the revenue'. An accommodation was, however, reached: Schmettau agreed to covenant that 'the nature of the salt shall not be altered by the said invention', which satisfied the Lord Treasurer – an early example of revenue taking precedence over productivity.[16]

Others were not so fortunate. George Campbell and Alexander Inglis, Edinburgh merchants with a new process for making salt, applied a second time for a patent in 1713, protesting that fiscal considerations should not be allowed to override their legal rights. The Salt Commissioners, again fearful of the fiscal implications of stronger salt, rejected their claim, since 'it may be prejudicial to the revenue, which, if so, may possibly alarm many persons who have advanced money on the credit of those duties'.[17] Thomas Slyford received similarly short shrift the following year.[18] In contrast, William Guy's petition in 1722 for a new method of salting provisions, accompanied by the certificates of five London traders attesting that it used *more* salt than usual, was enthusiastically received.[19]

The case of William Cowpland further demonstrates the care taken to protect crown revenues to the detriment of innovation. Cowpland, a London soapmaker, claimed in 1718 to have invented 'an art of making liquid soap . . . [valuable] for its sweetness and delicacy in washing the finest laces, muslins, cambricks and other fine linens, preserving their strength and beauty and making them curiously clear and white'. His invention would actually increase the revenue, he assured the Attorney General, who was not convinced and referred the petition to the Excise Commissioners. They sent one of their officers 'to see the operation of the said liquid soap, without enquiring into its ingredients', to ascertain how a duty on it (if chargeable) might be secured. The Commissioners confessed they were doubtful whether the liquid could be deemed soap under the terms of the Act; the amount equivalent to one pound of soap would vary according to the strength at which the liquid was made and would be very difficult to gauge. Furthermore, although Cowpland had spent twelve hours over the operation for the benefit of the investigating officer, they were 'not satisfied that so much time was necessary for that purpose, . . . some of our officers having informed us, that they have in less than one hour's time made a like sort of liquor', which opened a route to tax evasion. That is, one of the invention's chief commercial advantages, its speed of production, counted most heavily against its securing a patent.[20]

Three attempts to patent candles similarly came to grief at the Excise Commissioners' hands in the early eighteenth century. In 1728 they considered that Nicholas Mandale's substitute for tallow candles ('more clean, sweet and lasting and very near as good as wax') might prove so successful that they would be used instead of wax: since tallow candles were charged only 1d (0.4p) per pound duty and wax ones 8d (3.2p), the revenue would be seriously affected.[21] Six months later John Lewis Milot, admitting that Mandale's petition had been submitted on his behalf, protested that it would be beneficial to grant the patent rather than 'let it come to be practised by every tallow chandler, which if not prevented by granting the said letters patent, it is likely to happen.' The Commissioners apparently preferred to take that risk and (another divergence from pre-1640 practice) let their own officers, rather than the patentee, police the chandlers' activities.[22] The Commissioners became entangled again in the differential duties on wax and tallow candles when John Thorpe, a London apothecary, attempted to patent spermaceti candles in 1738. They decided that Thorpe should not be allowed a patent unless he paid the full duty as for wax. Attorney General Dudley Ryder demurred: the king had no power to lay such a duty on the candles and it would be improper to insert such a clause in the patent without statutory authority. Eighteen months after his first petition, Thorpe again approached the crown, requesting that the steps necessary to effect Ryder's judgement should be taken: bureaucratic inertia apparently defeated him shortly afterwards.[23]

It was not until the late 1760s that patents for candles – or for oil lamps, which threatened to replace them – began to appear. Other excised commodities were similarly absent or very sparse before the last quarter of the eighteenth century.[24] Their appearance suggests that revenue was losing its veto over technical innovation in the administration's thinking.[25] Nervousness about the funds' creditworthiness decreased with time, while Pitt's financial reforms in the early 1780s also helped promote a less defensive approach.

2.2 PATRONAGE AND MONOPOLY

Charles II was inundated, on his return in 1660, with petitions requesting grants of land and office, benefices and fellowships, all of which stressed their loyal service and often great sacrifices for the royalist cause. Their claims had to be balanced against the political necessity to retain the support of those who had served the Commonwealth and had benefited accordingly.[26] It was by partnership with individuals and groups that the crown had executed much of its business in the past and the granting of such requests was unexceptional.[27] Vociferous opposition to the interference of crown licensees in the regulation of trade and manufactures before the Civil War had been raised, for the most part, because they had abused their powers in pursuit of profit. Charles II was not unduly hindered by any recollection of that opposition, and warrants were issued for such licences, including the reestablishment of some rescinded by the Long Parliament. Robert Horton and Humphrey Buckner, for example, were permitted to revive their office for examining the quality of dyed silk.[28]

In the light of this, Charles II might be expected to have employed the patent system as a fund of patronage to reward loyal supporters. And this he did, but with some significant changes from the policy of his father and grandfather. Some risks were taken during the first few years of the Restoration but good sense prevailed, perhaps prompted by the murmurings and warnings already noted.[29] Courtiers and their clients remained the chief beneficiaries throughout the century. Patents did not, however, entail monopoly powers – with one certain, and a few possible, exceptions. The one certain exception which proves the rule was the virtual monopoly over the manufacture of high-quality glassware conferred on George Villiers, second Duke of Buckingham.[30] This case merits attention since it shows the Court's concern to avoid any appearance of monopoly and patronage of courtiers. Moreover, the available evidence suggests that Buckingham treated the manufacture of glass as a serious business venture and sought his profit through its improvement; he did not attempt to exploit his monopoly at the public expense.

The reversion of Sir Robert Mansell's highly profitable pre-Civil-War monopoly over the glass industry was eagerly sought. No application was received and no patent enrolled in the duke's name, but his control of the trade gradually became known. In June 1663 Buckingham requested that his grant for making crystal glass should be renewed 'with a clause shown for the sole making of looking glass plates, glasses for coaches', and other glass plates. On 21 August next, the petition of Bryan Leigh and others for a patent to protect their new way of making looking glasses and crystal glassware was referred to the Attorney General with the disingenuous remark, 'his majesty remembering something of this nature to be already passed' in favour of the Duke of Buckingham.[31] It appears that the patent for making crystal glass issued in November 1662 and surrendered by Martin Clifford and Thomas Paulden on 4 August 1663 was the one mentioned in Buckingham's petition; it was then reissued, to include the new clauses, in the name of Thomas Tilson 'merchant'. Martin Clifford and Thomas Paulden were both clients of the duke; neither was a glassmaker. That Tilson had been Buckingham's nominee was alleged by another of the duke's employees, John Bellingham, in 1676.[32]

Without any shadow of a doubt the crown was conniving at this subterfuge, and it continued careful of Buckingham's interests. 'Thomas Tilson' was specifically exempted from the jurisdiction of the Glass Sellers Company in their charter of 1664.[33] In July 1664 the importation of 'any manner of glass plates, either rough or wrought . . .' was prohibited by proclamation.[34] Care was taken that Buckingham should not be publicly associated with this measure: a petition had been submitted by the London glass-plate and spectacle makers, who also stood to gain by it. That it had been granted primarily at Buckingham's request was revealed in 1668, on its revocation.[35] Having immediate access to the king's favour was invaluable. An order, granted to the inhabitants of Lambeth, staying the erection of a glass house was reversed when it was revealed in Council that the owner was Buckingham.[36]

Although the duke's control of certain sectors of the glass industry became common knowledge, there is no evidence that it was attacked as a monopoly. First, his patents were granted and operated within the terms of the Statute of Monopolies. While extensive, they were not exclusive: in comparison with early-Stuart patents, their powers were limited. Nobody should be restrained from making glass 'which is and has been formerly made in such manner as the same has been so made . . . within this realm', and there was even another patent for glassware granted three years before Buckingham's expired.[37] Although no new invention was involved, his patents were legally sound on the count of novelty according to the conventional interpretation, since no such industry was then operating in England. Thus Mansell's earlier production of the same types of glass did not invalidate the duke's claim. Despite the legality of the grant to Buckingham, the crown recognized it would be politic to keep the affair as quiet as possible. The association of the name of Buckingham with a monopoly would have been particularly unfortunate, given the unpopular activities of the first duke in James I's reign.

Secondly, by most accounts, English drinking glasses and looking-glass plates improved in quality and fell in price during the time of the duke's monopoly. Venice's prohibition on the export of unfinished glass plates had presented a great opportunity to capture the home market which Buckingham seized. In anticipation of a patent he signed a contract with John de la Cam of Ventiaou, in August 1660, to set up a glass works at Rutland House: the duke provided the initial capital of £6,000; in return Cam would communicate to him 'the art and mystery of melting of cristall de roach or Venice crystal'.[38] In 1671 Buckingham secured the services of John Bellingham who described himself as 'expert in the art or mystery of making looking-glass plates and the same being a great secret and at that time known to few or none in England besides [himself]'.[39] Buckingham was operating his patent in conjunction with men who possessed the necessary technical skills but lacked the capital to work on a similar scale. Contemporary accounts indicate that by the early 1670s the plate glass produced in Buckingham's works could compete successfully with the Venetian. If he had rather less success with drinking glasses, the Venetian ambassador was, nonetheless, extremely worried by their improvement.[40] This suggests that the consumer did not suffer by Buckingham's monopoly. Neither, of course, was such glassware an item of common consumption or necessity. Although the granting of the patent and the royal favour subsequently shown the duke in its operation might suggest a patronage of courtiers in the pre-Civil-War style, to consider it as such would be misleading.

In general, the crown held rigidly to the principle that a patent for an invention should not confer monopoly powers over the whole industry to which it related. This was wise both economically and politically. Colenett and Holden in 1661 and Dallowe in 1689 offered to standardize the sizes of glasses and bottles in return for glassmaking patents: neither received the desired commission, redolent of pre-Civil-War monopoly powers, but they did get their patents.[41] The government was quick to respond to any suggestion that patentees were exceeding or abusing their rights. In 1662 the Cutlers Company of Hallamshire had complained of Charles Tucker of Rotherham. 'Upon false suggestion that he and one Morrossey had discovered a new art and invention of making steel never before used', he had obtained a patent from Cromwell 'for the sole making of steel within this kingdom with a restraint on all others', yet steel as good, if not better, had been made in the area for the past forty years. Tucker's aim, they said, was 'to monopolize the making of steel' and thus force inflated prices on them. The Council ordered that no new patent be issued to Tucker and any extant ones be revoked.[42] The Hallamshire smiths' problems were not over. In 1667 they had to petition the king again to stay Tucker's monopolizing hand: for £100 he had engaged Sir John Reresby and Thomas Strickland to procure a patent on his behalf. Although Reresby, the newly appointed high sheriff of Yorkshire, was a client of the Duke of Buckingham, he and Strickland were summoned to attend the Solicitor General and the patent was revoked.[43]

In 1675 Captain Thomas Gilbert petitioned Charles II for the payment of his salary as Provost Marshall of London, Westminster and Middlesex over the past fifteen years. He also requested, for his maintenance, a patent for making indigo powder. A counter-petition was soon submitted by four men who claimed that they had made indigo powder for 'above four score years' [sic], and prayed relief from further harassment by the patentee. The government's response was a compromise: the petitioners should proceed in the exercise of their trade; further disturbance would result in the patent's revocation. If the patent had been issued in lieu of the salary owed Gilbert, the crown had a financial incentive to prevaricate in this case.[44] Gilbert was left with an enabling, but not controlling, patent.

The wording of patents made it clear that 'the sole use and benefit' of an invention was not to disallow the employment of other methods of producing the same article. When the objection was raised to Sir Philip Howard's bill (to confirm his patent) in 1670, 'that many others did already use lead to that purpose', it was emphasized that the bill restrained others 'only from making use of those materials so prepared as by Sir Philip Howard is invented.'[45] This was not so, however, in the case of an entirely new product, 'all of which had been previously imported'.[46] Such instances of import substitution became increasingly rare, but the practice continued in respect of totally novel inventions. The steam engine provides an example: Newcomen's unpatented engine, although quite different, was able (and had little option but) to shelter under the wide umbrella of Savery's patent and subsequent Act for generating power 'by the impellant force of fire'.[47]

The crown was markedly less cautious in its grants to courtiers that were to be operated in the colonies, where there were fewer organized interests and any opposition would not directly affect it. A patent for 'a new way of making and framing of sugar mills', invented by David Mercato, was granted for twenty-one years to Lawrence Hyde, son of the Lord Chancellor, and Francis, Lord Willoughby, the governor of Barbados. It blatantly contravened the Statute of Monopolies in two respects: it was not granted to the inventor, and it exceeded the statutory term of fourteen years.[48] In 1687 the Duke of Albemarle, recently appointed to the governorship of Jamaica, petitioned that for want of saw mills many acres of land lay waste and unimproved. He was granted a patent for the sole 'erecting saw mills to move by wind or water' in the American colonies and plantations excluding New England. There was no pretence to an invention beyond the introduction of a piece of machinery supposedly unknown there, and the patent appears to be a monopoly of importation or licensing.[49]

Immigrant Protestant tradesmen and artisans continued to obtain a significant, but dwindling, share of patents.[50] The other recipients of Restoration patents for invention were, however, almost exclusively courtiers and officials or their clients. Patents provided the crown with a cheap source of patronage for those who could be satisfied with such things. Several petitioners referred to their deserts as loyal supporters of the king and his father during the Civil War. Thorness Franke, for example, detailed his service in both the royalist army and James I's navy, and explained that an earlier patent had proven of little benefit because of the war. His case did not rest entirely on presumed royal gratitude: he described his invention in some detail, annexed certificates to its worth, and offered the crown a rent of one-tenth 'of all such clear yearly value' after three years. The patent granted him the exclusive right of 'building furnaces *his own way*' to smelt mineral ores.[51] The certificate accompanying John Lillie's application in 1660 attested, however, to neither the value nor the novelty of his invention, but to his loyalty and wounds during the war.[52] Allegiance did not guarantee success. Despite extensive military service in the royalist cause, as a result of which his estate was sequestered and his ironworks destroyed during the Commonwealth, Dud Dudley failed to get his patent for smelting iron with coal restored in 1660. It was given instead to a Colonel Proger and three associates who petitioned for it, although they seem to have had little knowledge of ironmaking.[53]

A few patentees found their rights in jeopardy after the Revolution, as opportunists approached the new monarchs for favours at the expense of those loyal to James II. The ruse by which Richard, Lord Coote took over Clement Clerke's patent has already been mentioned.[54] Coote was a vigorous supporter of the new regime both in parliament and on the battlefield, while Clerke may have been a Catholic.[55] James Delabadie's patent for a napping engine was claimed by Sir John Guise, in June 1689, to have been obtained 'by means of his wife being nurse to the pretended Prince of Wales' and he was now disqualified from enjoying it 'being a papist and at this time in open rebellion to your majesty in Ireland'.[56] Six months later the patent was revoked, less, however, on account of Guise's allegations than on the representation of two denizened merchants, John Auriol and Peter Fauconnier, that Auriol's father had invented the engine in France and was the first who brought it to England.[57] Their patent was, in its turn, cancelled before receiving the great seal, on the emergence of Sir Simon Leach and others announcing their interest in Delabadie's patent.[58]

While the patent system was not used systematically as a fund of patronage, it was most accessible to courtiers; friends at Court were a major asset – as some discovered to their cost. Andrew Yarranton was engaged in the manufacture of tin plates in Worcestershire, using methods learned in his travels through Saxony. He made no attempt to secure a patent. But his enterprise aroused a 'sleeping' patentee, William Chamberlain, who proceeded to seek the renewal of an earlier patent, on the grounds that imprisonment for debts incurred in royal service during the Civil War had prevented his working it.[59] Yarranton wrote later that a patent was 'trumpt up . . . the patentee being countenanced by some persons of quality', and he was prevented from further manufacture.

What with the patent being in our way and the richest of our partners being afraid to offend great men in power, who had their eye upon us, it caused the thing to cool, and the making of tin plates was neither proceeded in by us, nor possibly could be by him that had the patent, because neither he that had the patent, nor those that countenanced him can make one plate fit for use.[60]

There is no evidence that Chamberlain's service in the royalist cause held sway over Yarranton's in the parliamentary.[61] It was apparently determined in ignorance (on the crown's part) of Yarranton's enterprise. Not only did he lack a spokesman at Court, but he was also deprived of information about Chamberlain's case until the patent had been issued. The government made no investigation of the feasibility of Chamberlain's 'invention' nor of the tin-plating industry.[62]

Most seventeenth-century patentees had some lifeline to the Court. William Sherwin, for example, a portrait engraver who patented a method of printing calicoes in 1676, was connected by marriage with the Duke of Albemarle.[63] Jacob Richards and Thomas Phillips were both military engineers at the Board of Ordnance.[64] Several were fellows of the Royal Society.[65] Samuel Pepys, as Secretary to the Navy, was instrumental in securing several patents. In June 1676 he entered an agreement with Lewis

Bayly, who had invented an engine to dredge ballast from the Thames.[66] Pepys was required to secure a patent in Bayly's name and to pay half its cost as well as £50 'for his half part of building and fitting each other engine' and £62 10s per annum towards the running and management costs. He also succeeded in procuring a contract with the Ballast Office for the sale of Bayly's dredged sand.[67] Pepys was disappointed of his profit when shareholders in one of Bayly's earlier patents successfully petitioned that this latest patent covered the same engine as theirs (in which they had invested over £3,000), 'to his own separate profit . . . without any material alteration'.[68]

Many members of the Court and landed classes found in the projecting mania of the early 1690s an opportunity to indulge their gambling fancies in a new sort of speculation – everything from wreck-fishing to glassmaking. Peers often lent their names to chartered joint-stock companies as governor or deputy-governor, while some courtiers (most notoriously, Thomas Neale) acted as regular patent-brokers.[69] But, with the founding of the National Debt, safer avenues of investment were opened and patents, now tainted with the reputation of stock-jobbed projects, largely lost their attraction as courtly perquisites.[70] The shift in investment strategies is epitomized by the activities of two generations of the Lowther family. Sir John (1643–1706) 'was a pioneer with a finger in most industrial pies': he was governor of the Company for Making Iron with Pit Coal, and had interests in salt-panning.[71] In contrast, his son Sir James (1673–1755), although fully involved and innovative in the mining of coal on his Cumbrian estates, was notorious for his parsimony: at the time of his death, he had £150,000 invested in the Bank and East India Company, £140,000 in the South Sea Company and £130,000 lent on mortgage and bonds.[72]

Yet patenting was not entirely immune from the 'influence' that was such a major component of eighteenth-century political life. Under-Secretary of State, Charles Delafaye was caught up in several ventures, including one in 1722 that involved exploiting Jacob Rowe's patented diving machine. He recommended the project to William Stanhope, then ambassador in Madrid, and sought his assistance.[73] When John Payne of Bridgwater found his application for a patent obstructed by William Wood's rival ironmaking concern, he wrote to Delafaye asking advice: whether 'I have any occasion to use the interest of my friends with his majesty. Which the Duke of Montague, Lord Chancellor Mr Dodington and several of my friends in town, have promised me.'[74] The grant of a patent to Samuel Simpson, a Leeds butcher, became entangled in the whig electoral machinery in 1734. Sir William Milner, M.P. for York, and the Speaker, Edward Thomson, wrote to the Duke of Newcastle stressing the urgency of processing the patent: 'we beg the favour of your grace to get it signed by the king as soon as you can, because it is of some consequence to the county election that Mr Simpson should go down as soon as possible'.[75] But such interference in patents was on a downward trend.

2.3 INDUSTRIAL POLICIES

Traces of the Elizabethan rationale for patents lingered. Even apart from the revenue aspect, there are a number of indications that the individual's claim to protection for his invention was subordinate to the interests of the state. In February 1686 the Customs Commissioners were required by Lord Treasurer Rochester to report on John Finch and partners' invention of a 'woven wire engine', specifically on its advantage to the king's service and the public. The Commissioners could not envisage the invention being of any benefit to either, but nonetheless 'as they have been at great cost in inventing the same', a patent might be granted.[76] It was on the grounds of greater serviceability that Solicitor General Yorke, in 1721, preferred Brown and Wright's application to a similar one (although this was discounted by the Privy Council). At the behest of the Clockmakers Company, the Privy Council examined Clay's application in 1717: one reason given for rejection was that it was unlikely to prove beneficial to the public.[77] The same year, an application was turned down because parliament had considered its subject – the determination of longitude – too important to be left to free enterprise and was offering premiums instead: the Attorney General ruled that the public interest required the invention be submitted for a premium and disclosed, not reserved under a patent.[78] Yet, while the individual's stake in his intellectual property was not fully acknowledged, the 'benefit of the public' was slipping further into the background, becoming a minimum standard rather than a guiding light of patenting policy. It reappeared, controversially, on the judicial bench in the late eighteenth century.[79]

As will be shown, the scrutiny accorded to most patent applications was cursory and the benefits promised in them conventional.[80] Sometimes, however, the government expressed greater interest in a project for which a patent was sought. These cases shed a little light on economic thinking in official circles. There is no evidence for a concerted policy, such as Burghley's, to foster native industries and encourage the introduction of foreign technology. But the concern to replace imports that was evinced by Tudor Commonwealthsmen, supplemented by anxiety about employment and strategic supplies, was still evident in the late seventeenth century. Though doubtful of its prospects of success, the Attorney General, George Treby, was impressed by the potential benefits of Dupin and Million's linen business:

if brought to perfection it would be very beneficial in employing many thousands of poor, taking them off the parish, improve the land by causing great quantities of hemp and flax to be sown; some would be consumed at home, some exported at great profit – thereby preventing importation of linen from France and obstruct its trade and manufacture which has so long overbalanced this kingdom in trade.[81]

It promised to fulfil every wish the government could have in this sphere.

In 1680 Du Fresne, a French emigré, recommended his invention in the terms of a crude theory of particular balances of trade, and received a ready hearing. 'Having found out a more exact and easy way of making salt here, much stronger and in greater quantities, and [with] less charge and trouble than now practised', he could produce sufficient to import Baltic metals and naval stores 'for mere exchange of salt'. The Committee of Trade was enthusiastic: Du Fresne's project, it surmised, would not only be of great use for salting fish and flesh, but also would 'produce a beneficial trade between your majesty's dominions and . . . Sweden and other northern countries, enough being made to pass in exchange for copper'. It was all that rival saltmakers could do to secure a hearing.[82] A raw nerve had been touched: the Baltic had long been a clear case of an 'unfavourable' trade, and the opportunity to 'balance' the trade was eagerly seized. The project, however, was entirely at the patentee's risk; the extent of government commitment was the patent grant.

Another project which caught officialdom's eye was John Garill's scheme in 1664, based on his discovery of the 'art of casting and preparing gold and silver ingots of the goodness of the standard of the Mint to be drawn down' into wire. The great advantage of his new method, he stressed, was that it would 'be a preservation and increase of the bullion – which is not to be melted down, the operation being supplied with silver to be brought into the kingdom'. Lord Treasurer Southampton noted on the reverse of Garill's petition, '. . . it would preserve and increase bullion', and reported that 'I cannot conceive but it may redound to the public profit.' A far more extensive scrutiny than usual was, however, ordered. The London craftsmen and traders who tested the wire reported that it would be to the king's and the public's advantage, principally because 'there will be that done with eleven ounces of silver which is not now done under twelve'. Everything seemed in Garill's favour. Only the last minute intervention of the London Gold and Silver Wire Drawers, who feared Garill's monopoly would exclude them from their own trade, halted the patent.[83] Subsequently it was discovered that Garill's scheme would have operated *against* the interests of crown and kingdom. The officers of the Mint, consulted for the first time, put the Council straight both on a point of law and on its economic reasoning. Further arguments, advanced by the Goldsmiths and Wiredrawers, clinched the case against Garill: they could not imagine how he hoped for any profit except through malpractice and abuse.[84] Garill's case demonstrates not only the tenuous grasp of economic mechanisms held by government officers in the seventeenth century (highlighted again in the recoinage of 1696),[85] but also the fascination that bullion still held for them.

The crown was prepared to intervene, on request, in attempts to protect embryonic native industries sanctioned by letters patent. The seventeenth-century patentee who could provide reasonable assurances of his ability to supply the country's total requirements without loss of quality, at the same or lower price than the commodity was imported, stood a good chance of protection. For example, three months after receiving a patent for the sole

production of blue paper, Charles Hildeyard petitioned the crown to prohibit its importation. He claimed he had 'given good testimony of the reality
of his invention by the goodness of the paper he lately has, and daily does
make'; its manufacture could be increased, to the benefit of consumers and
the relief of many poor employed in it, provided the importation of Dutch
paper did not frustrate 'that good work'. The Privy Council consulted the
Stationers Company, which provided some information about qualities and
prices; Hildeyard affirmed he could produce 4,000 reams per year, more if
necessary, which the Company believed to be in excess of current national
sales (one-third, or 1,000–1,500 reams, being imported). The proclamation
was issued, 'his majesty being willing to give all due encouragement to the
industry and ingenuity of his subjects'. Hildeyard, however, was unable to
exploit this opportunity; only 189 reams were imported in the first year, 1667,
but the total rose again to 1,026 in 1668–9.[86] By claiming that it had not
enjoyed the benefit of its patent through the smuggling of great quantities of
silk, the Royal Lustring Company was able to secure, by private Act, a
renewal of its patent and restrictions on imports.[87]

Sometimes assistance of other kinds was given, if it cost the government
nothing. In 1687, for instance, the Company of White Paper Makers represented that their best workmen were being enticed away by French agents
and they suspected that one of their managers was sabotaging his mill. In
response the government issued a proclamation taking the Company into
royal protection. It prohibited the inveigling away of any employee on pain
of strict punishment and gave the Company authority to appoint a person as
constable at each mill; it also banned the exportation of linen rags and other
papermaking materials.[88] Others prompted the crown to prohibit the exportation of certain machinery.[89] There are no examples of assistance to particular patentees after 1700, although Thomas Thwaites, a London weaver who
patented a thread-spinning engine in 1723, evidently thought it worth
applying for 'some allowance towards enabling him to work the same': his
petition was firmly rejected.[90] Continuing competition for skilled labour led
to government attempts to control the outflow of both artisans and machinery in patented and unpatented manufactures alike. Applications were
frequently made to the government for tighter controls over the emigration of
workmen, and English embassy officials abroad were active in encouraging
their return.[91]

Late-seventeenth-century governments pursued no systematic policy of
protecting native industries. They were prepared to consider the requests
presented to them and, if there were no obvious reasons against it, implement
the control that was sought. In doing so, ministers worked with only the
vaguest economic notions: that it was beneficial to substitute native manufactures for imports and reduce bullion exports – provided always that the
revenue and, to some extent, the interests of consumers and extant industries
could be safeguarded.[92]

2.4 THE PARTNERSHIP OF CROWN AND PATENTEE

The patent system was neither a major source of revenue nor an instrument of industrial policy. But it was an arm of the royal prerogative, expressly sanctioned by statute, through which the crown could conduct its business, and it provided at the same time a limited fund of patronage. For, on the whole, late-Stuart patents had less to do with technological developments than with franchises and the validation of enterprises which impinged on the rights of other bodies, particularly the guilds.[93]

Patents for invention were often incidental to the real business in hand. Many of those with inventions to promote did not bother to request a patent. Their interest lay only in securing a government contract, and if it could be achieved by some method cheaper than a patent, that was all to the good. Others proceeded no further with a patent once their invention had been rejected by the Admiralty or Ordnance Office. Some applicants seemed more concerned to secure employment in the royal service, honorary titles or the equivalent of a royal warrant for their goods, than protection for their inventions.[94] Joseph Moxon was made Royal Hydrographer in 1662 on the basis of his newly designed globes and charts; Philip Dallowe wished to become 'Glassmaker in Ordinary' in 1689; and John Cowley, Geographer to the King, sought a commission as Lieutenant of Marines, in 1741, on the strength of his gunnery inventions.[95] Yet, while in some cases an application was no more than a means of attracting official attention, in others an enrolled patent was the medium for cementing business arrangements between crown and patentee.

The major spheres of crown interest were the currency and, above all, military and naval supplies. The patent granted to Pierre Blondeau to mint gold and silver coins most certainly represented a major technical innovation, though not strictly a new one. Blondeau had been brought to England by the Commonwealth in 1650, and had produced coins by pressing and milling machines to a standard unachievable by the old method of hammering. Not only were these coins aesthetically superior but, with their standard weight and milled edges, they also went a considerable way to prevent counterfeiting.[96] Soon after the Restoration the Master of the Mint, Henry Slingsby, persuaded the king to recall Blondeau. A patent was issued authorizing him to coin all silver and gold money 'after his new invented way, with letters about the edges according to an agreement made with Mr Slingsby'. The terms of the agreement went far beyond the simple protection of an invention. Blondeau was appointed 'Engineer of the Mint' for life, with an annual pension of £100 for twenty-one years; he was also accorded, at his request, a pro rata payment for the money he coined and exclusive rights over his machinery (including the imposition of an oath of secrecy on his workmen).[97] In a related area, George Tomlyn, a London stationer who had lost £200 in 'vellum texted with the late king's name', received two successive patents at the Restoration. The first was for a new way 'to text and flourish in vellums and parchment in black and white'. The second was made more explicit after Tomlyn had prosecuted two stationers who defied his patent: 'for the sole printing with a rolling press and engraven plates onto vellum and parchment of the name and title of his majesty, his heirs and successors, and also of his royal consort the queen, with the imperial arms and badges'.[98]

The one area of inventions in which Stuart governments showed a consistent, positive interest was in naval and military matters, including navigational instruments and the maintenance of dockyards and inland waterways. Naval and military inventions provided the largest category of patents in the late seventeenth century (and there were many other inventions in this sphere submitted besides). Patentees recognized this as a lucrative field, thanks both to the increasing scale of warfare and to the Stuart kings' well known fascination with such inventions.[99] With the Royal Navy steadily expanding in size and cost, devices to improve ships and ordnance were all likely to attract official attention and perhaps secure a reward for the inventor without the hazards of commercial development; and if the government did not take up the idea, there was always the merchant marine to fall back on.[100]

Inventors addressed most of their efforts to a limited range of problems, ones which can be independently identified as of great concern to the Navy. Numerous devices were offered to improve the manoeuvrability of warships, from changes in rigging to horse-driven paddles and, in 1736, steam power.[101] Most were tried out on the orders of an interested, if sceptical, crown. The sheathing of ships for protection against 'the worm' was another area of inventive activity. Various bituminous substances were tendered for the crown's approval, resulting in seven patents, between 1681 and 1695.[102] Intense excitement was generated by the invention of 'mill'd lead' as a covering for ships' hulls. The company set up by the patentees, Sir Philip Howard and Francis Watson, was ordered by Charles in 1670 to sheathe a number of ships for trial. Favourable reports secured it royal approval and a potentially lucrative contract, but the company's hopes were soon dashed by the discovery of rusted ironwork on several of the sheathed ships, which was blamed on the lead. It made repeated but vain attempts over the next twenty years for the case to be reconsidered.[103] It was successful, however, in its bid for a contract to use milled lead in scuppers for the Navy, following a contest with the Plumbers Company, in which each made thirty trial scuppers.[104]

Most viable-sounding inventions in the naval and military sphere were given serious consideration, but it is unclear how many were implemented, or how many inventors ever received any reward.[105] Thomas Savery complained bitterly that, despite royal approval of his engine to propel ships in a calm, further progress had been blocked by one of the Surveyors of the Navy who claimed it was impracticable. He could not afford to continue the trials, since 'although the engine did not cost much, yet the continual charge of the yacht was considerable'. He turned instead to the merchant navy, offering to install his engine gratis for the first captain who applied.[106] Colonel Jacob Richards, His Majesty's Third Engineer, secured a patent in 1694 for a 'new invention of several small engines of divers kinds' to prevent boarding. Twelve months later the Lords of the Admiralty requested the opinion of the Navy Board regarding the 'allowance fit to be made' to Richards for fitting his devices on H.M.S. *Coventry*. The Navy Board decided the Ordnance Office should bear the charge: the prospects for Richards did not look good. He, meanwhile, had been taking the financial precaution of fitting his 'engine' into several merchant vessels.[107] Tendering for contracts to supply the Navy or Ordnance with new devices was a high-risk activity.

Inventors were lured into these expensive ventures by the prospect of large rewards, which were usually as illusory as most of the inventions themselves.[108] The crown was in general unwilling to invest money in their trial and development (in stark contrast to today, when over half of government research and development funds are spent on military research). It became even less willing in the eighteenth century. During the War of the Spanish Succession, military inventions disappeared from the patent records; they were received in profusion, nonetheless, by the Ordnance Office.[109] The Ordnance Board's report on Charles Pingstone's request for a trial and reward, in 1738, was categorical: it 'observes that experiments of this or the like nature which are attended with expense have usually been made at the sole risk and charge of the proprietor – not of your majesty'.[110] After a decade of indecision, the Admiralty ordered a trial of Stephen Hales's ventilators in 1751, to see whether they would prevent ships' timber from rotting, but the Commissioners of the Dockyard reported against them and recommended that 'Dr Hales should be at the expense' of the trial.[111] When, after another unsuccessful trial in 1754, Hales proposed doubling the number of ventilators, the Admiralty ordered an end to the experiment as too costly. Finally in September 1756, following the obviously beneficial installation of ventilators into naval hospitals, gaols and slave ships, the Admiralty gave orders 'to fit ventilators into all his majesty's ships'.[112]

In those areas where its interests were directly involved, the crown was quite unscrupulous in its administration of patents. Patents were neither secure nor were they endowed with as full powers as usual.[113] An Act of 1690, imposing excise duties on low wines and spirits, voided any existing or future charters or patents made in this sphere, in favour of encouraging production.[114] One notorious case was that of the rival 'sea water fresh' patents. William Walcot had been awarded a patent for his invention in 1675, the Attorney General reporting that 'the invention (if perfected) may be of great use . . . for your majesty's service'.[115] Eight years later Richard Fitzgerald, a nephew of Robert Boyle, F.R.S., procured a patent for a similar invention and offered Charles II favourable terms for installing his device in garrisons and ships. Walcot's patent was revoked on the petition of Fitzgerald and his partners.[116] Although the crown did not install any of Fitzgerald's engines, it favoured the party which promised the best deal should it ever take up the option. Fitzgerald's connections at Court also helped weight the decision in his favour, while Walcot may have been handicapped by kinship with Captain Walcot, one of the Rye House plotters.

The crown was even more careful not to inhibit inventors' activities and enterprise in strategically vital areas. Patent grants were worded with the specific intention of guaranteeing the crown freedom of action in securing naval and military supplies, unhindered by the rights of patentees.[117] Military operations in Ireland and the declaration of war against France in 1689 were the signs for a rash of petitions tendering for contracts to supply saltpetre. The government was clearly reluctant to commit itself exclusively to any one supplier, and was anxious that any patent it granted should be effectively exploited. Robert Price and partners offered to furnish the king after six months 'with such quantities as shall be sufficient from time to time to serve all his occasions'. They were granted a patent for the sole making of saltpetre 'in the said new way'.[118] In 1691 the Attorney General recommended the charter of incorporation requested by a number of London merchants (who, it was later alleged, had bought Price's patent) but, he stressed, it was not to exclude others from making saltpetre.[119] A syndicate led by William Tyndall, applying for incorporation shortly afterwards, acutely stated that it did not seek to exclude others. Stringent conditions were nonetheless laid down: the company was obliged to supply 200 tons of the best white saltpetre at £70 per ton in the first year of its operation, and subsequently with as much as the government desired, up to 1,000 tons at £70 or the market rate, whichever was less. It was to vacate the charter if it did not immediately set about making and refining saltpetre or could not meet its commitments, and it was to contribute £1,000 per annum towards the projected hospital for seamen.[120]

This remained an area in which the usually *laissez-faire* attitudes of eighteenth-century administrations regarding patents were compromised.[121] In 1779, John Wilkinson found his patent for a cannon-boring machine revoked by the Privy Council when he alleged its infringement by the royal arsenal. Since it had contracted with others for cannon at £16 per ton and Wilkinson was demanding £20, the Ordnance Office proposed revocation: the patent would be 'prejudicial to his majesty's subjects' and detrimental to the Treasury since production of the best ordnance would 'become a monopoly'. It claimed the invention was not new, but had been introduced to Woolwich by two Dutch founders, the Verbruggen brothers.[122] A few years later, when David Hartley, M.P., proposed to secure his patent for fire plates by Act of Parliament, the government drafted a clause permitting their use in the royal dockyards 'without leave obtained' from the patentee.[123] During the French wars of the 1790s, a new clause was inserted into patents covering naval inventions, that the grant would be avoided if the patentee declined to enter a contract to supply the government with the patented product 'in such manner and at and upon such reasonable price and terms as shall be prescribed' by the Navy or Ordnance Board.[124]

Such clauses as these and the retrospective action taken in Wilkinson's case demonstrate how far the patent system had moved away from its Stuart role of cementing a crown–patentee business partnership. Since the early eighteenth century it had been made increasingly clear that the business transaction and the patent were quite separate.[125] Also symptomatic of the patent's separation from government business was the award of premiums to those whose invention was regarded as of immediate public importance and unsuitable for either monopoly or commercial exploitation.[126] But it was parliament rather than the crown to which suggestions or petitions were addressed, and several Acts were passed in the eighteenth century that gave large monetary rewards to inventors.[127] Parliament also offered rewards for inventors who resolved certain intractable problems. The first was for the accurate determination of longitude, and many received small awards for their attempted solutions, before the main prize was finally awarded to John Harrison for his chronometer in 1773.[128] By the Act of 1713 Commissioners were appointed to judge all proposals, experiments and improvements relating to the longitude, with provision for awarding bounties of up to £20,000, according to the degree of accuracy achieved.[129] In 1717 a patent was refused to John French, who declined to reveal his method to the Commissioners, 'apprehending . . . he shall be defeated of the benefit'. Attorney General Northey's response was that, since the purpose of the Act was 'to encourage persons to use their endeavours for making so useful a discovery and that whatever should be proposed in order thereunto should be made public to be improved for making the discovery perfect', a patent would be contrary to the public interest. *Laissez-faire* had, as usual, its limits. There was no absolute right to a patent.[130]

While the patent system in this period was not moulded by any government's using it as a major source of patronage or revenue, nor as an instrument in any industrial policy, it was still heavily shackled by the interests of government and its bureaucracy. Seventeenth-century patents were relatively few in number, but they tended to disappear altogether at times of political crisis: the Exclusion Crisis is marked by the issue of no patents in the eighteen months from March 1680, the Glorious Revolution by but four patents between November 1688 and February 1691. Whether royal preoccupation, or courtier hesitancy to start new projects at times when the regime was endangered were to blame is a matter for conjecture. Government interference decreased during the course of the eighteenth century, but the system continued to bear the stamp of its origins in the royal prerogative. A sharp reminder came in the winter of 1788–9, when George III was incapacitated by illness and therefore unavailable to sign the necessary documents. No patents were issued between November and March. Any inventor fearful of his secret being stolen and preempted had to sweat it out with the king.[131] As the next chapter will show, securing a patent was a major operation, especially in the seventeenth century for those who had no access to Court patronage. With its maintenance of this complicated and expensive system, the government cannot be said to have actively encouraged inventors.

3

THE DEVELOPMENT OF THE PATENT
SYSTEM, 1660–1800

The routine management of the English patent system was left to government officials acting within the wide scope allowed by the common law and, after 1624, by the Statute of Monopolies. No statutory changes interrupted their habits of administration before the Act of 1852 (15 & 16 Vict. c. 83), yet 1660–1800 was a period of considerable discontinuity and development. Indeed, to find a watershed for the patent system we should look not to 1640–60, when it was in abeyance, but to the quieter years, 1700–20. The Restoration patent system embodied no new administrative features and, while shorn of its worst abuses, it was still a creature of courtly circles. Change came in with the new century: there was an ebb in patenting and, largely in reaction to speculative financial booms which exploited and discredited patents for invention in 1691–4 and 1717–20, new restrictions were placed on them. Partly as a result of these controls, and partly because of new market forces and opportunities, patents ceased to be the perquisite of courtiers, office-holders and immigrant tradesmen. They began to assume a more distinct and recognizable form as instruments of protection and competition among native inventors and entrepreneurs and, increasingly, if hesitantly, to leave London for the provinces.

3.1 ADMINISTRATION AND SCRUTINY OF PATENTS

The route to a patent was laid down by the Clerks Act of 1535, which applied to all grants of the crown under the great seal and was intended, as stated ingenuously in its preamble, to finance unsalaried government clerks.[1] To achieve this end it made the journey from petition to enrolment unnecessarily lengthy and tortuous. The petitioner was responsible for transmitting the documents for each of the procedure's ten stages through the corridors of Whitehall. There were no professional patent agents before the early nineteenth century.[2] At each office there were fees and gratuities to be paid. This circuitous route has been rehearsed in some detail by Allan Gomme, but it will be useful to summarize it here.[3]

The would-be patentee prepared a petition to the crown, briefly outlining the nature of his invention, its economic or social benefits, and his particular claims to preferment. He took the petition to one of the Secretaries of State, who endorsed it and referred it to either the Attorney or Solicitor General. If the law officer approved the application, the petitioner returned the petition plus the law officer's report to the Secretary of State's office, where a warrant was prepared. This warrant, countersigned by the sovereign and the Secretary of State, required the law officers to draft a bill employing the exact final wording of the patent which, in its turn, would receive the signatures of both sovereign and Secretary. The petitioner then transmitted this king's bill to the Signet Office. There a signet bill was prepared and sealed, authorizing the Lord Privy Seal to issue a writ of privy seal to the Lord Chancellor; the king's bill was retained in the Signet Office and a note of it entered in the docquet book. Carrying his signet bill to the Lord Privy Seal, the petitioner was now in sight of his patent; he would emerge with the writ that authorized the Lord Chancellor to engross the patent on parchment and seal it with the great seal. The new 'patent' was placed in a box and handed to the patentee. To record the grant, it was copied from the writ onto the patent roll, and both were kept in Chancery. From the early eighteenth century, the patentee had one further task to perform before the patent was secure: to file a specification (a more detailed description of the invention) within a limited period, of usually two to four months.

The English patent system was one of simple registration. Extensive scrutiny was not expected of the law officers administering it. This approach contrasts sharply with that of the Netherlands and France. A committee appointed by the States General of the United Provinces inspected all applications for patents: in the sixteenth and seventeenth centuries, one containing men with relevant technical expertise was appointed for each individual case; in the eighteenth, a permanent committee was constituted, although petitions might be forwarded to another expert body, such as the Admiralty. A full drawing or written specification had to be submitted with the application, and tests were often conducted on a prototype.[4] In France, the Académie des Sciences was set to work by Colbert, shortly after its inception, to examine applicants for *privilèges*. The examination was supposed to be thorough, with regard to both the technical viability of the invention and its likely economic and social consequences; (nonetheless, some unrealistic inventions slipped through). This practice was regulated by statute in 1699, and in 1735 reports began to be issued of abridged specifications, supplemented by half-yearly *Memoirs* of the Académie, containing accounts of discoveries.[5]

In the English system, unless a patent was challenged, all the stages except one were mere formalities. This was when the law officers were first required to examine the application: to determine whether the patent would be legal under the Statute of Monopolies. Neither the viability nor the utility of an invention was their concern, while novelty was generally taken on trust. Its potential economic and social effects were, however, part of their brief, in considering whether the patent would be 'contrary to law, . . . mischievous to the State, by raising prices of commodities at home, or hurt of trade, or generally inconvenient'. But their responsibility for exercising this minimal safeguard was itself eroded by knowledge of the Privy Council's powers of revocation on these same grounds. Where closer attention was expected of them, was in recognizing any threat to the royal revenue or other, related interest.[6]

In his report, the law officer drafted any additional clauses he considered necessary. Otherwise, he used a conventional formula. No report was made if he rejected the application.[7] As a result, there is usually no way of discovering the criteria informing the law officers' decisions. They cannot be inferred with any certainty from the types of petition that lapsed, since it may have been the petitioner's decision not to proceed further.[8] A few clues emerge, however, from the more controversial applications.

By the 'non-obstante' provision in royal grants the patentee was absolved from making public the exact nature of his invention.[9] Specification, introduced in the early eighteenth century, still allowed the grant to be sealed before any details need be revealed. The onus lay with objectors to prove the patent covered no new invention or was otherwise invalid. Normally, the scrutiny of a petitioner's claims went no further than hearing his verbal assurance of novelty – supplemented, from around 1707, by the presentation of a sworn affidavit (or affirmation by Quakers) to that effect. This is apparent from those cases where a fuller investigation was deemed necessary, for instance, where priority of invention was contested: the law officer then reported that he had heard the interested parties separately and required them to reveal the exact nature of their respective inventions. Also suggestive is the Secretary of State's rare, explicit instruction to the law officers in 1681, to examine 'particularly whether letters patent have not been already granted for the same engine mentioned in the petition'. He may have been unnerved by the plethora of water-raising engines being presented for patents.[10] The inference one draws, that all this went beyond the normal procedure, is supported by the evidence of John Farey and others to the select committee on patents in 1829.[11] As a satirist jibed in 1776, 'patents are obtained as fancy wills'.[12]

Further illustration is provided by the Privy Council's investigation into the patent for gold and silver wire that slipped from John Garill's grasp after the Wire Drawers' last-minute protest in 1664.[13] The issue was reopened by Garill's second petition six months later. A Privy Council committee was ordered by the king 'to inform themselves, which way he prepared his silver etc. to be cast into ingots; and thereupon requiring him to reveal his secret unto them, under their oaths of secrecy'. Garill offered instead to declare his secret once the patent had been sealed, and to raise no objection to its revocation if 'it be not found to be a new invention and no fraud in it', but this anticipation of the specification clause was not deemed acceptable and Garill's petition lapsed.[14] Only as a last resort, when various 'expert' opinions had been canvassed and an impasse reached, was the exact nature of Garill's invention thus probed. Investigations had been comparatively thorough in the first place because bullion supplies were involved. They had been limited, however, to testing the finished wire for its quality and consideration of its utility to the crown (which was misjudged);[15] the actual process had not been scrutinized, and the grant had been recommended subject to the tentative qualification, 'that if gold and silver can be prepared as claimed'.[16]

Occasionally petitioners volunteered further information about their inventions, appended a diagram or offered a demonstration. This typically was the case when an inventor was working in a heavily subscribed area, such as water pumps or, in the 1690s, diving engines.[17] Edmund Blood, a London merchant seeking a patent for a new fabric, attached a sample of it to his petition and enclosed the affidavits of five trading mercers to the effect that they had never seen or heard of any such manufacture before.[18] References and affidavits signed by members of relevant trades or, where pertinent, by eminent mathematicians or physicians, were more frequently appended to petitions in the early eighteenth century – perhaps because more petitioners lacked Court connections and hence personal recommendation. Charles II and James II were renowned for their fascination with clever inventions and the new science. If an invention caught their eye or was potentially useful in the naval or military spheres, they might request its demonstration. Charles II had James Ward bring his pump into St James's Park 'for trial', and was already sufficiently informed of 'the folly' of Thomas Smith's 'extraordinary pump' in 1677 to reject it out of hand.[19]

A scrutiny more searching than normal was most often made at the prompting of an individual or group (usually a regulated or joint-stock company) who feared their interests were endangered. The Clockmakers Company was particularly anxious. With considerable expense of effort and money, it opposed at least three patents and two private Acts during the late seventeenth and early eighteenth centuries.[20] Opposition from interested parties may have obstructed more applications than is apparent from official records. Henry Oldenburg's attempt to patent watch springs, for example, was halted by opposition within the Royal Society, but it is only through private papers that one learns of this.[21]

To insure against a damaging patent being passed without their knowledge, anyone could enter a 'caveat' with the law officers; this was valid for three months, renewable on payment of a further small fee. They would then be informed of any application for a patent relevant to their interests, and could make their case at any stage up to and including the great seal, though usually and most cheaply before the law officer reported to the crown. Without a caveat, it was most unlikely that they would hear of the patent before its enrolment was announced, in the *London Gazette*, for there was no publication of applications.[22] In at least one seventeenth-century case a caveat was obtained, *instead of* a patent, to protect an invention: a cheaper, if less secure, device. A petition describing a water engine, invented by one Thomas Hatton, gentleman of Blanckney (Lincolnshire), requested in 1676 that Sir Stephen Fox (the financier) should be informed if anyone sought letters patent for that or a similar engine.[23] A century later Jeremy Bentham, concerned that his brother Samuel's invention had been discovered, wrote from Russia to a friend in London, 'begging you to tell us whether a caveat would answer in any, and what respect, the purpose of securing the property of the invention in the meantime. . . . I have all along understood that the taking out a caveat costs but a guinea'.[24] By this time, if not before, caveats seem to have been a regular recourse for anxious inventors unable or unwilling to go to the expense of a patent until pushed by imminent preemption.[25]

A caveat was already a valuable precaution in the Restoration because the law officers were generally unaware of the established interests that might be jeopardized by the new patent rights they were granting. Neither were they (more than most other laymen) apprised of the state of native industries and their techniques, nor possessed of any systematic record, for ready reference, of patents already in force. The enrolment of patents for invention on the single run of comprehensive patent rolls made consultation extremely difficult. There are references to books kept by Burghley and Walsingham in which manufacturing patents may have been registered systematically, but nothing of a similar kind in this period has come to light. A few lists of grants are extant for limited periods, but they give the appearance of being later compilations of entries from docquet books.[26] The Clerk of Patents kept a docquet book of all grants passed under the great seal, which may have been some help.[27] Specifications were no easier to trace, being enrolled in three offices, each of which held a large class of records, not always indexed.[28]

Much depended on how conscientiously the individual law officer chose, or was able, to perform his office. An illuminating complaint was made by Secretary Sydney to the Solicitor General, Sir John Somers, in February 1692:

About a week since I signed a reference to you upon the petition of one Anthony Forester Smith for a new invention of heating liquors. Now therefore being fully satisfied by the examination of that matter that the same is a new invention as the petitioner does set forth I hope you will for once take my word for it, and let the petitioner have a favourable report from you without giving yourself the further trouble of enquiring thereinto, or obliging the petitioner to so great a loss of time as he must necessarily be at to give you the usual satisfaction in such cases.[29]

Somers appears to have been unusually meticulous in applying the criteria prescribed by the Statute of Monopolies, a trait that Sydney clearly thought eccentric. Uniquely in this period, Somers had a petitioner's claim, that his invention would 'employ vast numbers of poor people', investigated – in a way that even Burghley would have approved.[30] (Such assertions were normally copied verbatim into the patent grant, apparently unquestioned, though perhaps sceptically nonetheless.) John Sherbrook and his partners sought incorporation on the basis of a patent for a silk-winding engine. Somers wanted further information, in particular about the effect it would have on employment and the business of English silkmakers: ostensibly, it would require less, not more, labour. The silk throwers were able to confirm, however, that 'that sort of silk can be wound no otherways but by the engine mentioned in the petition'; it was all imported from Italy, but winding it in England would increase employment in the throwing sector also. Satisfied with this, Somers allowed the patent and charter of incorporation, provided the patentees were restrained 'absolutely from throwing any manner of silk' or winding any Turkey silk, in order to protect the winders and throwers.[31]

On several other occasions Somers and his protégé and successor as Solicitor General, Sir Thomas Trevor, gave fuller than normal reports, on the basis of interviews where petitioners were made to describe their inventions more closely.[32] During Somers's term as a law officer (April 1689–April 1693), 24 per cent of petitions for patents lapsed. Not all of these can be laid at Somers's door, of course, but the proportion may be compared with an average of 17 per cent for the period 1660–99, and 20 per cent for 1700–50. Only during Sir Edward Northey's second term as Attorney General (1710–17) was a higher proportion, 36 per cent, of lapsed petitions recorded. Somers's stringent attitude towards patents for invention may have been shaped by early association with Andrew Yarranton, the projector, a strident critic of the system.[33]

Normally it was only when powerful interests were likely to be concerned, or when several patents were sought for similar inventions within a short space of time, that the law officers demanded further information on their own initiative. The interests of the Duke of Buckingham in the glass industry, for example, were sufficiently well known and respected for Francis North not to hesitate in inquiring more closely into the nature of George Ravenscroft's invention.[34] He was able to report: '[I] find that the glass mentioned in the petition is of a finer sort, and made of other ingredients, than any other glass-house in England have used, and in that respect may well be esteemed a new invention'.[35] Nor is it surprising to find a patent application for preparing pepper, a major commodity in the East India Company's trade, attracting the attention of Sir Creswell Levinz in 1680. He advised 'that the merchants might be heard, as to what inconveniences may thence arise to the pepper trade which is very considerable', and directed the Committee of Trade to hear all the parties concerned. Bolstered by the London Grocers Company's view of the invention as potentially valuable, the Committee overruled the East India Company's (unspecified) objections, with the proviso that the patentees should consent to trial at law with anyone who opposed their patent.[36] When George Treby received Thomas

Hutton's petition for a papermaking patent in 1692, he was sufficiently aware of the Company of White Paper Makers' rights (secured by a private Act in 1690) to order an inquiry. Hutton was allowed a patent, on condition that his mill be used only for making the low-quality types of paper not reserved to the Company.[37]

On the rare occasions when an application was challenged, the law officers were prepared to make extensive enquiries to ascertain whether a patent could legally be granted and to whom. Close investigation was required to sort out the wrangle over a patent for a fire extinguisher, disputed by Ambrose Godfrey and Charles Povey in 1723. Povey was alleged to have taken advantage of the miscarriage of Godfrey's first public demonstration to pirate his extinguisher and preempt his patent application. The Attorney General, Robert Raymond, summoned numerous witnesses to testify concerning Godfrey's failed demonstration, Povey's approaches to Godfrey's assistants, and the differences between the two devices. He concluded that the patent was rightfully Godfrey's, as the first introducer of the device into England.[38]

In 1722 a dispute over priority led to the rejection of *both* parties' claims. The most remarkable point about the case is that Thomas Forrest's petition would have been granted, unquestioned, if a counter-petition had not been received from Jonathan Brown and William Wright. Instead, the rival inventions were investigated, 'and it not being made appear that either of the petitioners have found out any new invention, but only made some improvements in the manner of melting iron ore', the Privy Council decided that neither was entitled to a patent. Solicitor General, Philip Yorke's report, that Brown and Wright had developed their invention further and were in a better position to implement it effectively, carried no weight: it was decided on a strict interpretation of the Statute of Monopolies.[39] The applicants were unfortunate in their timing, since the Council was being particularly cautious in the wake of the South Sea Bubble.[40]

It was rare for the law officers to seek advice outside their office, except where the revenue was directly concerned. The various councils and committees for trade established after the Restoration were occasionally asked to consider applications.[41] But the members of these advisory bodies had little or no specialized knowledge of manufacturing and were too preoccupied with wider questions of policy ever to have the time to scrutinize particular inventions. The tentative nature of the advice that was given is instructive. In 1669 George Herriot claimed to have discovered 'the way of cold pressing of cloth' which, as Attorney General Palmer perceived, could be of great value for England's major export industry. To hand was the standing committee of the Privy Council for trade and plantations, which had been investigating the cloth trade.[42] At Palmer's request, the committee, composed of leading political figures, civil servants and merchants, interviewed Herriot, who said that he had learned the Dutch method of cold pressing; this was more effective than the common way and so would obviate the efficient, but often damaging, hot press. It advised a patent:

although this cold press should not be attended with all those advantages to the woollen manufacture of this nation, which the petitioner suggests, yet in as much as the granting his request will be an encouragement to other ingenious inventions, and so may be introductory to the improving the present fabrics to a greater perfection, and the inventing of new, and also he does not propose to hinder any man from using other kinds of cold press which have hitherto been made use of in the kingdom.[43]

The committee had learned sufficient of the woollen industry and its problems to appreciate the potential value of Herriot's invention, but his new process was not subjected to any detailed examination with a view to actively promoting its widespread adoption. Herriot was given the opportunity of testing it on the market, and no closer scrutiny was deemed necessary when a monopoly of all cold pressing was out of the question. Moreover, there was no hint of any pretension to impose the new press on the woollen industry. The lessons of the disastrous Cockayne project in James I's reign had been well taken.[44] This decision reflects the more disinterested use of patents after the Restoration. As interference was limited, so was investigation.

Twice, in 1664 and about 1709, it was proposed that the Royal Society should examine all inventions submitted for patents. The second time was at the government's instance, possibly prompted by the example of the French government, which from 1699 referred all applications to the Académie des Sciences, or through closer acquaintance with the Dutch system. Neither request – to Charles II or from Queen Anne – was acted upon.[45] The Royal College of Physicians was approached more frequently by the Admiralty to recommend medical supplies than it was by the law officers to comment on medical or chemical patents.[46] It would certainly have rejected the majority of the proprietary medicine patents which blossomed in the middle years of the eighteenth century, and it gave some indications of general hostility to patenting.[47] The City Companies also were consulted more for the sake of their vested interests than for their professional opinions on an invention's technical feasibility.[48]

Such minimal consultation declined even further with time. Increasingly the government's approach to administering the patent system was one of *laissez-faire*. The view was taken that, if an invention proved a technical failure or unprofitable, the only loser was the patentee; if it were at odds with other interests, injured parties could take their case to the Privy Council or the law courts. Lord Treasurer Southampton explicitly took into account this safety-net in recommending John Garill's application in 1663: he concluded, 'I cannot conceive but that it may redound to public profit', especially since 'in case any unseen abuse be found out' it could be rescinded by the Council.[49] This was in sharp contrast with the paternalistic control exercised by Burghley. In 1681 the Committee for Trade overruled the objections of several saltmakers to Du Fresne's patent, on the basis that it would be advantageous to the kingdom if successful – and no harm if it failed.[50] Solicitor General Finch recommended the renewal of Chamberlain's patent for tin-plating in 1672, since the 'petitioner is willing to run the hazard how far a new patent will be good'.[51] When Richard Newsham's application to patent his fire-engine was opposed in 1721, Attorney General Raymond examined 'models' (probably drawings) of the engines of Newsham and his rivals, and decided that Newsham's 'appears to me to be differently made'; he recommended the patent, since it was at Newsham's 'own hazard' both as to its novelty and its success.[52] He reached a similar decision after hearing Thomas Billin and his opponents, Holt and London (themselves already patentees), who in 1722 contested his title to a patent for earthenware: the cups made by Billin were aesthetically far superior to Holt and London's, they seemed 'different and preferable', but Raymond's confidence in recommending the grant rested on it being Billin's risk whether the earthenware was really new and different according to the Statute of Monopolies.[53]

This denial of ultimate responsibility came to be enshrined in the law officers' reports at this time, in the conventional formula that the grant of a patent was to all appearances legal and could be forwarded, 'since it is at the hazard of the petitioner both as to his expense and trouble . . . whether the said invention is new and whether it will have the success he expects or not'. The formula is to be found first in Edward Northey's report on Timothy Byfield's petition in September 1711.[54] At the same period, new demands were being made on patentees that assisted this transition from the Court to the courts. The petitioner was required to produce a sworn affidavit (or affirmation) to his being the inventor and to the invention's novelty. With increasing frequency he also had to be prepared to enter a specification describing the invention more closely.

3.2 SPECIFICATION AND CONTROL

Modifications to the patent system in the century after 1660 were all introduced by the law officers in the course of reporting on inventors' petitions. Two were of particular long-term importance and influence on the development of the patent system – specification, and the restriction of shareholding in patents. Both helped systematize patenting of inventions and take it out of the realms of Court patronage and stock-market speculation. In the later eighteenth century the influence of the administrators was superseded by that of the judiciary, who began to mould the system both by stricter interpretation and enforcement of the law officers' clauses, and by determining ambiguities left by law officers and Privy Council alike. Lord Mansfield was particularly influential in this, as in other areas of commercial law, establishing common-law precedents to bring more certainty into areas notoriously bereft of statutory guidelines.[55]

Specification – the enrolment of a separate, more detailed description of the invention within a certain time of the patent's issue – was at first exceptional.[56] There are a few instances of it in the seventeenth century: for example, the private Acts which confirmed the patents of the Marquis of Worcester in 1663 and of Howard and Watson in 1670, while the Lustring patentees were required to submit a written description, such as a native master could understand, on their patent's expiry.[57] From 1711, when John Nasmith was required to detail his method of distilling spirits, it was more common, featuring in approximately 20 per cent of patents enrolled before 1734. It became the standard practice after 1734, although particularly full recitals in the petition seem to have exempted the patentee from appending a further description even then.[58] A novel wording was introduced in 1723, which voided the grant in the event of a specification not being enrolled within the given time.[59] This penalty clause was usual from 1730 and standard from 1734 to 1883, but in effect the specification was of limited legal significance in the first half of the eighteenth century. (Two patentees may even be found, around 1730, offering to communicate their respective secrets to the public 'on reasonable terms'.)[60] The immediate precedent for standardizing the practice was perhaps the Act of 1732 which awarded £14,000 to Thomas Lombe, on condition that he deposit a model of his silk engines in the Tower of London with a full description of their manner of working.[61]

Increasing emphasis by the judiciary on accurate and full specification culminated in Lord Mansfield's decision in *Liardet* v. *Johnson* (1778). This stipulated that the specification should be sufficiently full and detailed to enable anyone, skilled in the art or trade to which the invention pertained, to understand and apply it without further experiment. For the first time, the recognized quid pro quo for the award of a patent was the disclosure of the invention.[62] It was perhaps indicative of growing skill in technical drawing and description at that time, visible in the increasing sophistication of diagrams appended to specifications. For most of the period under discussion such skills were fairly rudimentary.[63] Technical handbooks were a rarity, and the acknowledged way of disseminating technical information was through personal demonstration.[64]

This may help account for the fact that little attention had been paid to the quality of the specifications filed; they could be as informative or as evasive as the patentee saw fit. Captain Robert Hamblin, for instance, was granted a patent in July 1730 for 'a new method for distinguishing of lights whereby one light erected for the guidance of shipping may be perfectly known from another'. His specification gave no clearer picture of the method he proposed, but was not queried at the time. When Trinity House, jealous of its rights, petitioned four months later for the patent's revocation, the law officers agreed: 'the instrument enrolled by him not ascertaining the nature of this invention or the method by which it is to be carried into execution'.[65] This was again typical of the administration's policy regarding patents: action was taken only on the initiative of interested parties. Despite increased emphasis on correct specification, neglect of the requirement to specify appears to have been frequently overlooked.[66] This was possible because, while patents were announced in the *London Gazette*, specifications were not published. Interested parties could obtain a copy, on request and on payment of a small fee, from the three offices – Petty Bag, Rolls Chapel and Enrolment – where specifications were filed. Commercial publication of specifications, secured by this means, only began in the 1790s with Wyatt's *Repertory of Arts*.[67] The administration's supervision became no tighter after 1778, but patentees were forced to recognize their increased vulnerability at law, when drawing up their specification. They might still decide, nonetheless, to risk an obfuscatory one.[68]

Since official and judicial guidance was lacking for most of the eighteenth century, it is doubtful whether patentees had any clear idea what the function of a specification was or how full and accurate it ought to be. Like most other things about the system, it was left to the patentee's discretion. The type of invention being patented was fairly influential in directing a patentee's decision regarding how much to reveal in his specification. Mechanical inventions were usually described quite clearly and often accompanied by a simple diagram. The patentee thereby staked his claim to what could, in any case, be discovered relatively easily. Jedediah Strutt, for example, was prepared to go to the expense of a second patent for his Derby-rib machine when he was unable to file an accurate specification in time to secure the first.[69] Specifications for chemical processes, in contrast, gave little away: not only were they harder to describe accurately, but a patentee could be reasonably sure that even the most devious espionage would fail to spring his secret.[70] Samuel Ashton confessed in 1794 that,

it is unnecessary to observe that the above preparation and proportions are specified upon the supposition that the various materials therein mentioned respectively contain the utmost degree of strength or astringency which they in general possess; but as the same are variable, according to circumstances, . . . the strength of the tan liquor must ultimately, in all cases, be determined by the taste.[71]

Moreover, as a witness to the 1829 select committee testified, 'especially in chemical processes', specifications were often 'made imperfect with a view to concealing the process'.[72] The most obscurantist specifications were to be found among the recipes for medicines: for example, 'the cordial mixture . . . is of a cordial nature, being a large compound of the most valuable cordial productions of nature, together with other specific ingredients extracted and combined both by chemical and Galenical preparation'. One which vaguely claimed the nostrum was 'extracted from a hard substance, of which there are several sorts of equal virtue and efficacy', went on to prescribe the precise dosage![73] Indeed, while allowing for self-interested hyperbole,[74] it is worth noting David D'Escherny's account in 1760:

I imagined that a person, who did design to get a patent was obliged to bring proofs of the efficacy and inoffensiveness of his nostrum; but the Solicitor [General] laughed, when I asked him such a question, and told me that provided the empiric swore that the thing was his own invention it was sufficient; . . . the remedy is never known; for in the place of the genuine recipe, an absurd and nonsensical one is filed at the office four months after the patent is published.[75]

Why was specification introduced? It was certainly not for the purpose of disseminating inventions by disclosure. Davies endorsed Hulme's view that 'the practice arose at the suggestion and for the benefit of the grantee with a view to making the grant more certain'.[76] It seems more likely, however, from the wording of specification clauses in numerous patents and law officers' reports that it was introduced on the government's initiative, to make discrimination between superficially similar inventions easier.[77] Ideally, it might be thought, the law officer needed this information at the time of making his report. That would imply, however, movement towards a different system – of examination, not simple registration. On the contrary, specification helped shift responsibility from the law officers to the courts. It established the terms of any dispute between a patentee and those accused of infringement.

Seventeenth-century demands for specification indicate a concern to prevent attempts by patentees to monopolize an industry or trade under cover of vagueness, or to extend their control to others' methods and ingredients discovered subsequent to enrolment. When an M.P. objected to Sir Philip Howard's bill to strengthen his patent in 1670, 'that it does not appear what the invention is, and that it may be said if anyone hereafter does find out any other new invention relating to the better dressing of ships, that this is Sir Philip Howard's invention', Howard was required to enter a written description within six weeks.[78] The grants where specification was stipulated in the two decades before it became compulsory all covered inventions that involved a new method of making known products. Among them, for example, was a series of patents starting in 1713 for extracting oil from 'certain seeds', following one issued in 1708 for 'green oil' (probably linseed).[79] Each in the series simply specified a different plant, thereby marking out his own territory but limiting it at the same time. Fears of monopoly continued to increase the workload of the law officers. The Company of Copper Miners of England objected to the patent being sought by Benjamin Lund and Francis Hawksbee in 1727–8: because the petitioners gave no full description, the Company was rendered incapable, through ignorance, of offering proof of its not being a new invention. They brought forward experienced refiners, who testified that furnaces varied in design and that they did not confine themselves to any one sort, 'but order the building of them as the artist judges proper for the ore'; further, that although every master refiner 'goes upon the same principles in refining, yet scarce any two exactly pursue the same method and form in practice'. Lund and Hawksbee sought to reassure the Company that they were not applying for a grant of the sole privilege of making brass without pots but only of making it *in a particular*

furnace, which had never been used before, without pots. On the basis of
detailed, written descriptions of the respective furnaces, Philip Yorke decided
that the petitioners had a new invention worthy of a grant. He required a
specification clause in the new patent.[80]

Applicants preferred to keep their inventions shrouded in secrecy until
their rights were safeguarded by the enrolled patent, and this was respected
(except where the entitlement was in dispute and the law officers heard the
respective parties *in camera*).[81] Early-eighteenth-century law officers' reports
often mention that the petitioner thought it 'not safe to specify' but agreed to
provide a fuller description once the patent had been sealed. This was the
case with Nasmith, who also succeeded in extending the time limit from the
one month mentioned in the king's bill to six months.[82] Nasmith was clearly
reluctant to specify. And the initiative was definitely the Solicitor General's
when he inserted a specification clause in Sybilla Masters's warrant.

That in regard the petitioner has not described the method or engines in which the
invention consists that therefore it will be requisite that she shall describe such method
and engines . . . to make the grant therein certain.

He allowed Masters a year's grace since she had returned home to America
(leaving her husband to complete the formalities).[83] In 1737 James Peyn, a
London merchant, secured exemption from specification: in partnership
with two Zealanders, he had erected 'a worm pitch factory', and had entered
a reciprocal bond for 20,000 guilders not to reveal their commercial secrets.
Moreover, pleaded Peyn, taking refuge in 'the national interest', if he
enrolled a specification in Chancery, any foreigner might 'have recourse to
his said invention and to set up a worm pitch fabric', which would lessen the
consumption of British colonial pitch.[84]

Specification became the norm in 1734 after a decade in which the law
officers had been finding their duties overburdened with disputed applications for patents. The 1720s had witnessed renewed, heavy use of the system,
with numbers more than doubling over the previous decade. It may also have
been a more aggressive use, since patents began to be increasingly regarded as
instruments of protection and competition rather than royal perquisites.[85]
Several cases have already been mentioned in which extensive research and
probing was required to determine who, among a number of applicants for a
similar-sounding patent, was most entitled to it.[86] The system seemed almost
in danger of becoming one of examination. An unusually long tenure as
Solicitor, then Attorney General, at this time (1719–33) may have helped
force such a perception on Philip Yorke, who was bearing the brunt of these
disputes. To assist Yorke in reaching a decision when several patents for
ironmaking were being sought, John Payne of Bridgwater submitted a list of
the ingredients he used:

And as this is a secret I desire it may not be exposed until my patent is ingrossed and
passed by reason I fear some other person when they know what it is will out of

opposition to my invention pretend to the knowledge of it although not in practice anywhere in England.[87]

Payne's claim, that his invention was quite different from the other petitioners', was accepted and his patent authorized. But Yorke did not leave the matter there: as in Lund and Hawksbee's case, he inserted a clause demanding the written specification of those ingredients. No specification was required of the other two inventions covered by the patent, which were not subjects of dispute.[88] The point at issue was thereby clarified for future reference, in case the problem arose again, and Payne, having reluctantly risked the piracy of his secret, now had the unlooked-for consolation of a well-defined stake in the invention.

If the patent's validity was to be left to 'the hazard of the patentee', something had to be done to relieve the law officers of the charge of irresponsibility. Specification offered a mechanism whereby the system could be self-policing and the law officers be spared much tedious investigation. Several hard-fought prosecutions of patent infringements at the same period further emphasized the value of knowing what *exactly* had been patented.[89] When in 1731 Robert Barlow, a millwright from Reading, sought an extension of the time allowed him in which to file a specification, Yorke permitted it, with a hint of paternalism, 'in regard his enrolment of the said description of his machine was intended only for his benefit, by securing to him with greater certainty his said invention'.[90] This was not to say that the initiative to introduce specification belonged to patentees. Rather, that they might be reluctant to reveal anything about their inventions, but doing so could save them trouble later, if their title were challenged or they wished to prosecute infringements. By 1829 John Taylor could describe it as a 'principle' of the English system 'that the risk of the patent is upon the patentee, who must defend it at great expense'.[91] He and other witnesses stressed the cursory investigation given even contested applications brought before the Attorney General, who was likely to grant both or several, rather than take the trouble to discriminate between their entitlements.[92]

Another contemporary innovation was the affidavit. The applicant for a patent was required to swear (or, if a Quaker, to affirm) before a Master in Chancery or a Justice of the Peace that the invention was his own and, to the best of his knowledge, not already in use in England. There is reference to an affidavit in Shallcrosse's petition in 1701, but the first one extant in the State Papers is John Cole's, appended to his petition of August 1707 to patent a new design of coaches.[93] Evidence which suggests that the affidavit was treated seriously, by some patentees at least, is provided by John Kay's reference to the patent he secured in 1745 for the powered tape looms that he had built for a manufacturer, Joseph Stell: it was 'got in my name because Mr Stell could not make oath that he invented it'.[94]

It is surely not coincidental that the same short period (about 1705–15) witnessed the more frequent requirement of written specification, the sworn affidavit, and the 'hazard of the petitioner' formula – as well as the revived proposal to submit all applications to the Royal Society's examination.[95] They were introduced in the wake of the first wave of stock-market specula- tion, during which patents for invention were badly tarred with the 'projecting' brush.[96] Notoriously, a number of the inventions and schemes for which patents had been issued had proven chimerical. Administrative ad- justments were made to tighten the reins on patenting. Collectively these developments reflected a tacit admission by the government that it was unwilling (and lacked the technical competence) to intervene directly in the promotion of invention and industry. Since the currency of patents for invention had been devalued as patronage, the crown had little interest in keeping immediate control over their issue. With some securing of the moorings, the patent system could be allowed to float out into the mid-stream of commerce. It was pushed further out after 1734 when specification was required on a regular basis. In this context, these new measures may be regarded as part of a more general restructuring of Augustan financial institutions, designed to strengthen the fabric of deficit financing, in the wake of the first stock-market crash.[97] As Daniel Defoe remarked, to keep fickle Credit, 'you must preserve sacred all the foundations, and build regular structures upon them'.[98] The reforming hand seems to have belonged to Sir Edward Northey. Not only were these innovations all made during his terms as Attorney General (1701–7 and 1710–17), but an unprecedentedly high proportion of applications also lapsed during that time.[99] Northey appears to have found a like-minded successor in Sir Philip Yorke.

Longer-term influences should also be considered. It was indeed becom- ing more difficult for the law officers to recognize innovations, as the focus shifted from entire, new industries to changes in products and processes. Late-seventeenth-century entrepreneurs still looked to the Continent for bright ideas and the techniques needed to implement them. Consequently one finds patents to protect a product and the entire means of manufacturing it, as with 'Normandy' and cast glass, tin plates, or 'alamodes and lustrings', for example. In contrast, by the third decade of the eighteenth century patents were much more specific, covering improvements *within* existing industries – new looms or improved reeds for them, springs for carriages, regulators for windmills – and new products were largely of native devising. The timing of this shift varied between industries, but by the mid-eighteenth century British manufacturing had lost much of its technological inferiority complex; the direction of industrial espionage was being reversed. There was no longer any call for the government to encourage the establishment of new industries, and it confined itself to instituting regulations at the behest of interested parties. Written specification helped to chart manufacturing de- velopments, to keep track of change. The shift towards patenting constituent parts that made specification feasible – to have required detailed descriptions of total processes would have entailed lengthy treatises – also made them necessary, if any check at all was to be kept on which particular improvements had been patented.

3.3 PATENTS AND THE BUBBLE ACT

The other major modification made by the law officers was definitely introduced in response to the fear of stock-jobbing. Between 1720 and 1832 a clause was regularly inserted into patent grants rendering them void if the benefits were divided between more than five persons (twelve from 1832 to 1852). In the late spring of 1720 the government pushed a panic measure through parliament, in an attempt to curb the wave of wild stock-market speculation that came to be known as the 'South Sea Bubble'.[100] Under the 'Bubble Act', projects unsanctioned by a royal charter or an Act of Parliament and which had begun operations since June 1718 were deemed public nuisances and their sponsors rendered subject to the penalties of the Statute of Praemunire.[101] It was an ambiguous, ill-drafted piece of legislation, whose main effect was further to confuse business law over the next century. In the event, *scire facias* proceedings were started against four projects, but allowed to drop by 1722.[102] It also affected the patenting of inventions. Without restraint, it is possible that patents would have mushroomed as they had in the early 1690s (when more patents were enrolled in two and a half years than was normal for a whole decade). In July 1720, however, the Lords Justices (acting in the king's absence) ordered the law officers to consider a clause to be inserted in patents 'for preventing the illegal use made of such patents to raise subscriptions contrary to the late Act of Parliament'. The result was the uniform limitation of shares in patents to five. The Lords Justices' concern had been such that they had rejected wholesale all the petitions before them, reporting that, 'during your majesty's absence by reason of the great abuse that was then made of several charters and patents [they had discouraged] all applications of that nature'.[103] They also ordered that a committee of the Privy Council meet to consider 'of the most effectual means to prevent the present method of buying up old charters or patents, which have been disused, and under colour thereof, to make use of them to purposes different from what they were originally intended'.[104] The Bubble had been the immediate cause of their action, but it played on existing anxiety regarding the abuse of patents.

The law officers were intractable in administering this clause.[105] Patentees occasionally sought its overruling in their particular case, but without success. In 1725 James Christopher Le Blon contended that his tapestry-weaving invention would only be successful with the assistance of more partners and a large stock. He desired authority to raise up to £100,000 by 10,000 shares, offering to abide by any limitations imposed by the government on the employment of the capital, as testimony to his intention 'not to make it a mere stock jobbing project'. Attorney General Yorke reported that, having heard Le Blon, he could discover no good reason for acceding to his request, and doubted whether the manufacture would either require or support such a capital stock as he proposed. Yorke recommended an ordinary patent 'with liberty to take in a greater number of partners than five, but . . . [it was] advisable to restrain it to some certain number'. The matter held fire for eighteen months, when Yorke was told by the Under Secretary of State that,

Mr Le Blon's petition for a patent is so strongly recommended, that I doubt he must have it his own way. He says he cannot carry on his invention with fewer partners than a hundred: and what I must beg your commands upon is whether the restrictive proviso in that respect should be quite left out; or the number 100 mentioned in it instead of 5?

Yorke's view now was that the mention of any number might be construed 'as licence to take in so many by subscription'; he stressed his preference for a general proviso to restrain Le Blon from doing anything contrary to the Bubble Act, a clause which might make potential investors more cautious. Le Blon seems, in fact, to have settled for limitation of the partners to five in the patent issued in June 1727. Six years later he was refused leave to bring in a bill to incorporate the partnership and raise share capital.[106]

Yorke and Talbot advised against allowing William Wood and his partners a charter to raise £100,000 by 10,000 shares on his ironmaking patent in 1730, after hearing of shady financial deals and doubts expressed whether any amount of money would produce merchantable iron by Wood's methods. They concluded wryly that if Wood could make good, cheap iron by his new method, then his gain would be so great that he would not need a larger share capital. They drew attention to the partnership clause and expressed disapproval that it should be circumvented by charter.[107] One is left wondering whether this was an expression of commercial naïvety or an astute judgement on Wood's technical abilities. Joseph Foljambe's plea, that to disseminate the benefits of his new plough through the country in fourteen years would require at least one person to manage it in each county, was discounted by Yorke the same year; he could see no cause for setting a precedent in waiving the partnership clause.[108] One of the charges brought against Robert Hamblin that led to him losing his patent in 1730 was that he had 'left parchments as he calls them (not books) for public subscription at several places mentioned in the public papers and has drawn several unwary persons to become subscribers therein . . . although by the said letters patent he is in no way warranted therein'.[109]

The 'Bubble' clause was a blanket response to events largely extraneous to the patent system and invention. It complemented, however, other recent developments through which the law officers had been removing themselves as far as possible from responsibility for the day-to-day supervision of the system. Together with regular specification, it helped confine patents to particular processes and mechanical devices, and exclude most over-ambitious projects and chimerical schemes. This was the last major internal reform of the patent system and it set the course for the next 130 years. Rapidly the patent system was outgrowing its original functions, but it was left to the courts and, ultimately, to parliament to make further adaptations. The more nicely tuned instruments necessary for a much more complex technological situation had begun to be forged. That it was still in many ways a sledgehammer was evident in the late-eighteenth-century reformers' complaints and the judiciary's continuing confusion.[110]

4

THE JUDICIARY AND THE ENFORCEMENT
OF PATENT RIGHTS

Complex as the procedure was, the purchase of a patent was but the preliminary step in protecting an invention against competition. The security it afforded against alleged interlopers was contingent upon the respect accorded to the authority it professed or the force of the threat it was seen to pose. It is necessary therefore to consider what sort of protection was offered by the law courts. Ideally, a patentee would find the threat of prosecution sufficient to suppress infringements; where his title was genuinely in dispute, arbitration would be simple, quick and cheap. A form of arbitration was available, in the Privy Council, until the mid-eighteenth century, but to secure damages was a different matter, exposing patentees to the delays, expense and uncertainty of equity jurisdiction. It is not hard to imagine that this would have a deleterious effect on the patentee's capacity to deter interlopers. These interrelated questions, of the legal process and the patentee's extra-legal authority, are the subject of this chapter. Its focus is the period 1660–1750. The major patent cases of the late eighteenth century are relatively well known, and Harry Dutton recently examined the century after 1750 from a perspective similar to mine.[1] Dutton found not merely judicial confusion and inconsistency in patent cases, but also considerable prejudice against patentees; this persisted from the late eighteenth century to the mid 1830s, when commentators noted the 'decided turn which the feelings of *judges, jurors and the public* have taken in favour of inventors'.[2] Prior to the mid-eighteenth century, there is no evidence that judges held any anti-patent prejudices, but confusion and inconsistency were already rife.

4.1 THE LEGAL FRAMEWORK

Patents for invention were usually announced in the government organ, the *London Gazette*, where patentees took the opportunity to give their wares a brief 'puff', advise where they were to be contacted and threaten interlopers with prosecution. To implement their threats, prior to 1753, patentees could have interlopers summoned by the Privy Council to face a charge of contempt of the royal prerogative. Francis Watson and Sir Philip Howard had recourse to this in 1669: the king in person warned the infringing Company of Painter Stainers that they 'presume not to . . . do anything which might violate, or infringe the privilege'.[3] When George Tomlyn, the holder of a patent for embossing parchment, tried to exert his authority against two interloping stationers, they 'slightingly said [they] valued the patent at nothing and refused to obey it'. At a hearing before the Privy Council in June 1661, the Attorney General was instructed to prosecute them.[4] This was unusual. More often, the Council referred patent cases to the civil jurisdiction of the common-law courts – and it was open to either party to take their case direct to common law. Few subsequent suits have been traced; a settlement was presumably reached out of court. The alternative, generally preferred by patentees seeking damages, was equity jurisdiction – Chancery and occasionally Exchequer.[5]

The Privy Council also heard the grievances of tradesmen and manufacturers against patentees. The Statute of Monopolies had established a mechanism for challenging a patent: a quorum of six Privy Councillors could summarily rescind a patent for an invention that was shown to be either harmful or already in use.[6] For instance, John Chater's patent for marble mantlepieces was voided in 1687 when the Privy Council accepted the Joiners Company's case that it was not a new invention.[7] And in 1745 Edmund Darby and Samuel Boden of Colebrookdale, makers of 'an oil commonly called British Oil', were successful in their appeal to the Privy Council for the revocation of a three-year-old patent for a medicinal oil, held by their Salopian neighbours, Michael and Thomas Betton.[8] The Council also arbitrated in cases where partners to patents disputed their respective titles.[9]

In the mid-eighteenth century a distinct break occurred in the development of patent law, when the Privy Council finally ceded its jurisdiction in patent-validity cases to the common-law courts.[10] In the light of earlier controversies, it was a curiously unremarked transference of authority. Walter Baker's challenge to Robert James's patent in 1752 was the watershed. The Privy Council dismissed Baker's charge, but he then presented it with an unprecedented request: to allow the clerk of the Council to testify in the case that he was bringing against James for perjury in his earlier affidavit to the Council. According to Hulme, this led to 'a reconsideration, from a constitutional standpoint, of the Council's jurisdiction', and 'as a result, the Council decided, under the advice of the law officers, to divest itself of its functions' in this regard. It was now for the law courts exclusively to determine whether a patent had been violated: the patentee's normal procedure was to prove infringement in a common-law court, and then to seek damages in an equity court.[11] Before resorting to litigation, however, he could attempt to restrain interlopers simply by obtaining an injunction in Chancery against named parties.[12] Complaints against patentees continued to be received by the Privy Council, but its way of resolving them was now to order patentees to take their common-law remedy, threatening revocation in case of refusal.[13] A common-law court might also be called upon to decide a patent's validity, subsequent to the failure of a prosecution for infringement. This latter action, on a writ of *scire facias*, put the patentee into the position of a defendant in a criminal cause, 'in having obtained the king's patent fraudulently'.[14] Such a course, however, was exceptional: defeat was usually sufficient to annul a patent *de facto*.[15]

4.2 PROSECUTION – AN 'UNCERTAIN AND PRECARIOUS' BUSINESS

The strength of a patent depended ultimately on the patentee's willingness and financial capacity to prosecute infringements in the law courts. Apart from the cost, there were several major problems in enforcing a patent at law. One – common to all litigants – was the intricacy and slowness of court proceedings; another, the judiciary's ignorance of industrial techniques (which prompted several witnesses in 1829 to propose a tribunal or commission of experts to judge patent cases); and, most harmfully, the lack of any positive law (other than the sparse Statute of Monopolies) or judicial precedents by which to predict the likely outcome of a prosecution with any degree of certainty.

Chancery, the butt of Samuel Butler's wit in *Hudibras*, provided a common cause for complaint for the next two centuries.[16] Writing of Lord Keeper Guildford's harsh criticism of 'the prodigious injustice and iniquitable torment inflicted upon suitors by vexatious and false adversants', his brother, Roger North, remarked that the unreasonable delays in Chancery suits 'often made the suitor quit his right, rather than live upon the rack in pursuing it'.[17] John Kay, for example, complained of weavers continuing to infringe his patent,

choosing rather to wait the issue of a number of law suits (well knowing that might overcomes right) which the defendants so prolonged that [Kay] had spent his all without being able to bring his affairs to issue . . . at which time he made his case known to several Members of Parliament, thinking either to get a premium and let his invention go free, or an Act *which would enable him to come at his rights otherwise than by tedious Chancery suits*.[18]

Patentees' attitudes were encapsulated by John Crosbie, writing to one of his agents in 1755:

although we have a patent from the king for the whole making pot and pearl ashes all over America for fourteen years . . . yet I recommend it to you not to divulge the secret to anybody because there is [*sic*] some people in the world . . . would be so daring as to set up a work, and then we should have the trouble and charge of a law suit against them which may as well be avoided.[19]

Litigation was undoubtedly expensive. Gravenor Henson made numerous references to patentees in the hosiery industry who were prevented by poverty from prosecuting infringements. Implicitly he contrasted them with

'Mr Morris, who from long experience, had become quite a veteran in law [and] was too formidable, from his successes, to be infringed with impunity', and 'the Messrs Haynes who, joined to a large personal property, had a considerable knowledge in law affairs and received credit for more than they actually possessed'.[20] The costs of enforcement informed the decisions of those most knowledgeable about the system, at an early stage. In 1758 Jedediah Strutt reported to his partner, William Woollat, advice he had received regarding his newly invented 'Derby-rib machine':

we may readily have the patent for money enough but then he is sensible we shall have innumerable enemies that will endeavour to disturb us and afraid we shall not be able to contend with 'em. (This I think is very just reasoning.) Therefore he thinks that if Mr Bloodworth would heartily engage in it and come into such measures as he and I have talked of, his character and fortune would bear down all opposition.[21]

Subsequently, the partners took interlopers to court and, after a demonstration of the machine, won convincingly.[22] James Watt considered James Keir's 'purse too shallow for Westminster hall from which Good Lord deliver us' to make his obtaining a patent worthwhile.[23] Such counsel as Strutt and Keir received was not, however, universally available.

Fears of the expense involved were compounded by the arbitrariness of the courts.[24] The success of a prosecution turned on two points: one was a point of fact – whether the invention protected by the patent was, or was not, already in use in England – the other, a problem of law, to determine what constituted an 'invention' entitled to a patent under the Statute of Monopolies. The legal situation was highly uncertain. The equity courts were rarely guided by precedent:

it is a common objection against our courts of equity, that their power being absolute and extraordinary, their determination must consequently be uncertain and precarious . . . the unhappy suitor must enter into a court of equity with doubts and fears.[25]

And, where patents were concerned, the common-law courts were no better. It was only from the time when the Privy Council relinquished jurisdiction that a case law on patents began to develop. The first major patent case at common law since the early seventeenth century was Dollond's in 1766, in which the judiciary began to address the thorny problem of the proper consideration for a patent.[26] But it was a slow process and even the spate of hard-fought patent cases at the end of the eighteenth century did little to establish a solid core of judicial wisdom.

For whether it has happened that questions between patentees have commonly been questions of fact and not of law, which I take to be the case, or that the general questions of law on the subject have never been brought forward on any important trial, or from whatever cause it has arisen, it may with truth be said that the books are silent on the subject and furnish no clue to go by, in agitating the question 'what is the law of patents?'[27]

This quandary, expressed in 1785 by James Watt's solicitor, Abraham Weston, was echoed ten years later by Chief Justice Eyre in the case of *Boulton and Watt* v. *Bull*; he objected that 'patent rights are nowhere accurately described in our books'.[28] Two of the four judges trying this case even denied that a process or method of manufacture could be patented, leaving it to Eyre to point out that the majority of patents since 1624 had been for processes, rather than products.[29] In 1829 Marc Isambard Brunel told the select committee that 'I might as well toss for the fate of a patent' in the courts, and another witness more soberly considered, 'there being no existing basis of law, the dictum of the judge is one thing one day and another thing another'.[30] The late-eighteenth-century judiciary struggled to accommodate outdated legislation and precedents, designed with a view to stimulating a relatively backward economy, to situations precipitated by the new technical and competitive conditions of industrialization. Little agreement could be reached over what properly constituted a patentable invention, on what grounds it was entitled to this special protection and privilege, and how wide ranging the powers conferred by patent should be. The first legal treatise specifically on patents was not published until 1803.[31]

It was a situation notoriously full of pitfalls for patentees, and James Watt and his contemporaries found there was still all to play for.[32] Two judicial decisions had, however, played a major role in relocating the point at which the patentee was weakest. Lord Mansfield's judgements, in 1776 and 1778 respectively, made a new addition or improvement to an existing manufacture patentable, and made the specification bear the weight of instructing the public in the invention.[33] Previously, the patentee's Achilles heel at law had been whether his 'invention' was no more than a mere improvement on extant technology. The definition of 'invention' as against 'improvement' had provided the fulcrum of judicial uncertainty. Following Mansfield's decisions, this difficulty receded and the question of correct specification came to the fore: incorrect or insufficient specification made the patent more vulnerable than ever. As Chief Justice Eyre pronounced in 1795, 'the modern cases have chiefly turned upon the specification, whether there was a fair disclosure'.[34]

It was generally accepted that a patentee was entitled to improve his invention between enrolment and specification.[35] Before 1778, however, there was no clear principle in law that the patent covered only the invention as described, at the time of either enrolment or specification. Sir William Jones, as Attorney General in 1676, gave his opinion that it was not necessary for an invention to be described in the patent: it could be constructed as the patentee pleased, but once set up and used, that was the sole model protected by the patent.[36] Indeed, with patents so vague in wording, it is hard to see how he could have given a stricter interpretation. Robert James, in the 1750s, was forthright on this question:

in my specification I mention no particular salt, but reserve to myself the choice of whatever salt I find by experience to answer my purposes best . . . I cannot determine precisely which is best for these purposes, but apprehend I am at liberty to use any, or either, or several at the same time, in preparing my powder.

Furthermore, he regarded himself 'at liberty to improve my medicine by all possible means, and have done it at a very great expense'.[37] Clearly James did not think he was prejudicing his case by this declaration. Nonetheless, the allegation of improvement to the invention subsequent to specification was one made by the defendants in the cases brought by Stanyforth in 1741 and Kay in 1737.[38] Prior use seems similarly to have occupied an ambiguous position in judicial thinking. Grew's patent of 1698 was one of several known to have been granted in the face of prior commercial use of the invention.[39] Yet, evidence given for the plaintiff in Stanyforth's case – that the patented ploughs had been made and sold 'upwards of twenty years before obtaining the said patent' – was apologetic in tone, the deponent believing it was 'in order to be made use of for experiments only to try whether the same deserved a patent or not'.[40]

Specification was a problem which patentees had faced on a more pragmatic level before 1778. Their dilemma was how many details of the invention to reveal. The fuller and more exact the patentee's description, the simpler he made any future defence of the patent at law by having an agreed, dated statement to refer to as evidence of first invention, and the more avenues he officially sealed off to rivals.[41] This was the strategy of Michael Menzies in 1750. Himself an advocate, Menzies described, in a twenty-page specification, all the variations to his colliery winding gear he could imagine:

[so that] none may pretend, when they make these or such circumstantial variations, that they have discovered a new machine, or are not using my machine when they use one with such variations, the principal thing in my machine being the drawing up of solids by the descent of water.[42]

On the other hand, there were advantages in a more secretive strategy, particularly when the invention was chemical rather than mechanical:[43] it extended the patentee's scope for subsequent adjustments and improvements; it was hard to imagine *all* the possible variations; and, of course, it kept competitors ignorant of the precise invention. Moreover, parsimony of detail was unavoidable if an invention was still little more than a concept when the time allowed for specification expired. Wyatt and Paul took two years in patenting their first spinning machine, partly through lack of money, and partly through the difficulty of bringing it to a degree of completion where a specification could be settled on. There was a further problem. 'It will be impossible', protested Wyatt, 'to describe the invention through all its varieties which will always differ so much in proportion to the quantity of work proposed to be done or the number of bobbins in any particular engine.'[44] Even when they finally submitted a specification, it was, as Hills has said, 'probably designed to protect a half-finished machine and stop others from developing similar ones', and there was much (legally dubious) post-specification development.[45] Another strategy was to patent a principle of operation rather than a particular engine. In 1720, for instance, Joshua Haskins petitioned for a patent 'for the sole use of quicksilver for raising water'; J. T. Desaguliers had forcefully pointed out to him that there were several methods of utilizing the principle Haskins had thought of – reducing friction by the introduction of mercury.[46] Notoriously, this was also James Watt's course when patenting the separate condenser in 1769. Its legal status was much discussed in the harsher climate that prevailed after 1778, when courts regularly overturned patents for incorrect or insufficient specification.[47]

4.3 DWIGHT'S CASE, 1693–8

Examination in some detail of two relatively well-documented prosecutions for infringement in an equity court before 1750 will illustrate some of the difficulties encountered by both plaintiffs and defendants in patent suits. Both cases turned on the distinction between an invention and an improvement, where neither the exact nature of the patented invention nor the state of the art was at all clear. The legal murkiness induced by lack of case law and of strict specification is amply demonstrated. These cases also indicate the hesitancy of patentees to use the law courts and, in Dwight's case in particular, the difference that one successful defence of the patent could make in inspiring a determined pursuit of interlopers.

For John Dwight, a patent represented an offensive weapon with which to fight off competition in manufacturing salt-glazed stoneware and new types of earthenware. It cannot be sheer coincidence that this most litigious of patentees had been a lawyer before establishing his pottery-making business at Fulham in 1671.[48] Soon after his arrival in the capital, Dwight secured a patent for 'the mystery of transparent earthenware commonly known by the names of porcelain or China and Persian ware as also the mystery of the stone ware vulgarly called Cologne ware'.[49] His porcelain-like pottery did not prove commercially viable, and he concentrated his resources on stoneware and statuary, for which he quickly acquired a good reputation.[50] Dwight, like the glass patentee Ravenscroft, strengthened his rights by an exclusive agreement with the London Glass Sellers Company, who agreed to discourage imports of stoneware.[51] In 1684 he secured a second patent, two years before his first was due to expire, extending protection to the wares he had begun producing since 1672.[52] John Stearne, a Lambeth potter who claimed to have been deterred from starting a stoneware manufacture in Kent by this patent, said Dwight had told him it was prompted by his threatened competition 'and . . . had put him to £100 charge'.[53] There seems, however, to have been a general feeling among potters that Dwight's second patent was invalid, and many of them produced similar wares in spite of it. The number of stoneware potteries had grown to 3 by 1685, 13 by 1690, and 17 by 1695.[54]

For nine years, however, Dwight took no action against them. It may have been the difficulty of securing the necessary evidence,[55] or consciousness of rival claims to the invention that held him back. Possibly he felt the market could support competition, and it was only the increase in stoneware potteries combined with wartime interruption of trade in the early 1690s that induced him to reconsider.[56] The success of his first action – an injunction obtained in Chancery against James Morley of Nottingham in 1693 and subsequently upheld by the court of Common Pleas – no doubt encouraged Dwight to proceed against others. This he did almost to the day of the patent's expiry.[57] The judgements are not extant, but other evidence points to varied success both in and out of court. A member of the Wedgwood family was reported in 1698 as saying that:

[Dwight] is now (or has lately been) in suit with several p[er]sons for infringing his patent, and particularly with W[edgwood]'s brother for making the ordinary glazed drinking pots in the form (or imitation) of those which Mr D. makes of stoneware. He says further that there are a company of Dutchmen who (by licence from Mr D.) make the fine ware in Staffordshire.[58]

Whether or not the Wedgwoods' activities had actually been curtailed by Dwight is unclear, but they bridled under what they considered to be unreasonable restrictions. It is evident that Dwight was exacting royalties from the Elers brothers (the 'Dutchmen'), whom he had prosecuted in 1693: they claimed to have themselves discovered (in Cologne) the secret of stoneware and unglazed red earthenware.[59] Even those who successfully defended themselves in court could nonetheless be ruined. Luke Talbot and Matthew Garner blamed their bankruptcy on both 'the very great expense and loss of time in trade' occasioned by the Chancery suit and Dwight's intimidation of shopkeepers to deter the sale of their goods.[60]

The most striking point which arises from Dwight's Chancery suits is the inadequacy of patents in industries, such as ceramics, where the definition of 'invention' was even more arbitrary than usual and was largely a matter of variations in design (shapes, clays and glazes). Stoneware and porcelain, the subjects of Dwight's patents,[61] were made of clays that assumed their distinctive features by firing at temperatures over 400° farenheit higher than earthenware. There was no material difference in the methods of working these clays.[62] Early stonewares were commonly salt-glazed, a technique signally different from the usual method of glazing with metallic oxides. Dwight has been credited with the first commercial production of salt-glazed stoneware in England. This was questioned by several defendants to his suits, and certainly the technique had been outlined by Glauber in *A description of new philosophical furnaces*, translated into English in 1651.[63]

The thorniest legal problem lay in those defences that protested they were producing only earthenware which happened to look something like Dwight's stoneware. They generally sought justification in the rights and privileges of their trade – not in the niceties of the term 'invention'. Dwight understood his patent to cover such imitations. His complaint against Talbot, White and Johnson in 1694 was that their wares,

are the very same in *figure form and outward appearance* with those made by your orator though far inferior in intrinsic value and service, and that if there be any alteration or variants therein as to outward appearance it is only by some addition to or subtraction from your orator's said invention'.[64]

Talbot admitted making only some earthenwares which were similar to Dwight's. Full of righteous indignation, he contended that they were 'made with clay and coloured with such ingredients as usually was and is by this defendant and others used . . . in the said trade of a potmaker'; even if some of his pots did resemble Dwight's, he should be allowed to follow his trade without hindrance.[65] Talbot also implied that since Morley was a brick-maker, not a potter, the judgement which Dwight had secured against him at common law was not applicable in his own or other potters' cases. Moses Johnson indeed opened his defence with his credentials: he had served his apprenticeship as a potter and plied his trade for fourteen years. He had made earthenware in imitation of stoneware and even porcelain, in forms and figures as the fancy took him or as his customers 'should bespeak or request to be made for them or according to such fashion and forms as was most in use and fittest to accommodate or please the customer'. Although some of his pots might resemble Dwight's 'being of the same shape and after the same form and fashion and . . . for the same use', they were not made in imitation of Dwight's, nor were they ever put on sale masquerading as Dwight's, nor sold at undercutting rates or prices. He was doing no more than what belonged to his trade.[66] This assertion of the right to pursue one's trade unhindered was echoed by a group of Staffordshire potters, led by three of the Wedgwood family, who petitioned the Privy Council in 1695 to restrain Dwight's interference 'under pretence of a patent'.[67]

It was a principle to which the defendants in a number of cases other than Dwight's also appealed. John Ffowke contrasted his 'two several seven year apprenticeships' as a plumber and engine-maker and his long experience in the trade, with the patentee, Richard Newsham's, background as a buttonmaker; it was Newsham's sheer ignorance of the trade that allowed him to think his fire engines were new inventions.[68] Lancashire weavers and shuttlemakers objected that John Kay tried to 'hinder and prevent many persons from following the employment wherein they were educated and brought up'.[69] It seems, however, to have been a principle that was losing its force, especially as apprenticeship declined. Unlike Burghley or Coke, eight-eenth-century Chancellors and judges showed little respect for the conven-tions of craft fellowship, guild solidarity or protection of traditional ways of working, if they obstructed the path of innovation and efficiency.[70] A defen-dant protested vainly in 1766, against Morris's patent, that there should be no restraint on use of the stocking-frame – it being a major manufacture of national interest.[71]

The lack of any clear definition of what constituted an 'invention' and of any mechanism for isolating the novel features in an extant instrument, machine or process were at the heart of many disputes. In industries like ceramics, where design was the chief variant, this problem was at its most acute. Most potters respected this and refrained from patenting. Both Dwight and Ralph Shaw, in trying to enforce patents, found themselves entangled in intricate litigation.[72] In another case, as we have seen, the Attorney General allowed two similar patents both to stand, having nothing more than aesthetic grounds on which to decide between them.[73] Such problems were not resolved until design copyright and registration were introduced. 'Hogarth's Act' instituted a measure of protection for artists and printmakers in 1735, as did the Copyright Act of 1787 for cotton textile printers, but it was not until 1839 that protection of design was extended to ceramics and articles of manufacture in general and a system of registering designs established.[74] Attention was drawn by W. Kenrick, in 1774, to the disparity between the degrees of protection offered different types of intellectual property. He considered that 'so little idea of copyright have [potters] in their respective labours, that they disregard even the privilege of a patent in the hands of other artists, under pretence that their manufacture is not of new invention'.[75]

4.4 STANYFORTH'S CASE, 1741

Stanyforth's case illustrates the problems of this conceptual weakness even in areas where artistic design did not intrude. Joseph Foljambe, the inventor of the Rotherham plough, had assigned his patent rights to his partner, Disney Stanyforth. In 1741 the latter's widow took legal action against William and John Bashforth, alleging that they were producing ploughs in imitation of hers.[76] The following year she prosecuted sixteen farmers for using the 'imitation' ploughs.[77] The verdict went against Mary Stanyforth and she was ordered to pay costs.[78] Her husband had apparently turned a blind eye to interlopers, collecting modest annual sums for the use of the plough – eight shillings (40p) was mentioned by one defendant – and presumably taking some premium from the ploughwrights he licensed to produce it.[79] Despite infringements, the business had flourished in the twelve years since the patent was obtained. Among several Yorkshire ploughwrights testifying on Stanyforth's behalf, one claimed to have made over fifty ploughs in the previous year, another to have made 'several hundreds of them and has taught several ploughwrights in divers counties of England to make them', while a third had also been employed 'to go up and down the country to instruct people in making and using the said patent ploughs'.[80] This last witness reckoned that he had laid out £2,300 of Stanyforth's money in this employment 'over and besides the charge of obtaining the patent', and Mary Stanyforth protested that evasion of the patent had cost them £5,000.[81] It was perhaps the coincidence of her widowhood with the patent's imminent expiry that prompted the attempt to recoup some of these losses at law.

The defendants rested their case on the well-established precedent of Bircot's case. They argued that all ploughs must necessarily imitate one another in order to perform their function, so that the patent plough could be no more than an improvement; the Bashforth's plough was similarly but an improvement on older ploughs. Several deponents even testified that the patent plough was *less* efficient than traditional models.[82] Naturally the plaintiff's witnesses deposed that there were material differences, and these were said to make it a third more efficient than other ploughs. By the time of the second suit they concurred in pinpointing the use of particular moulding boards as the superior feature: one testified that nobody except the patentee, Foljambe, could make them without the exact dimensions and moulds for that purpose, although they might imitate them superficially. This was the point on which the case turned. The decree summarized the successful defence: the patent plough 'was not substantially and absolutely a new invention but barely and only a small additional improvement on an old invention, such as was frequently made on many other utensils in husbandry'.[83] This must have left not only the patentee with a sense of grievance, but also the ploughwrights and farmers who had been paying royalties for the past thirteen years.

4.5 BLUFF AND COUNTER-BLUFF

Both Dwight and Stanyforth tolerated what they considered to be infringements for most of the term of their respective patents. The threat of prosecution had not proven a sufficient deterrent and at the last (for reasons we can only guess at) they each ventured into the courts. A similar course was pursued by Boulton and Watt. They were weighing up the risks of prosecution in 1784: 'we had better bear with some inconvenience than lose all [in a law suit], yet if we do not vindicate our rights we run a risk of losing all that way'.[84] They tolerated infringements for a further eleven years until, finally, 'the impudence of some aggressors and the powerful party which supported them' drove the partners to court.[85] The reluctance of patentees to go to court is hardly surprising. But how many actually did? Could interlopers rely on the initial hesitancy of these examples being more typical than their ultimate resort to law? Was it necessary to prosecute, or was the threat normally sufficient?

Unfortunately, the records are recalcitrant. Prosecutions in any court were relatively infrequent before 1815, especially before 1770. The compilations of judicial precedents are totally silent on patents for the period 1614–1766, except for brief reference to *Edgebury* v. *Stephens* (1691),[86] and searches through the records of Chancery and Exchequer have produced few instances. Cases in Chancery are particularly hard to unearth because of their poor indexation. It is possible, therefore, that a number have slipped the net. This disquieting reservation is especially necessary in the light of remarks by two judges in 1684: Chief Justice Jeffreys spoke of 'all the actions that have been brought upon that Statute of Monopolies, by the patentees of new inventions, as there have been multitudes in my Lord Hale's time, and at all times'; Justice Withins referred to 'the cause of new inventions, upon which letters patent actions are brought by every day's experience'.[87] It remains possible that the bulk of such actions did not come to court. Yet the sparsity of patents granted in this period itself gives cause for scepticism about these two remarks. A century later, Lord Mansfield, summing up in *Liardet* v. *Johnson* (1778), stated that he had deliberated in several but not many cases. And Dutton counted only twenty-two reported cases coming before the superior courts in London in the second half of the eighteenth century, involving less than one per cent of patents granted in that period.[88]

The paucity of such cases, if it can be taken at face value, could be indicative of either of two contradictory situations – or indeed of both, in different times and circumstances. On the one hand, the system may have functioned in practice as in theory: the threat of prosecution normally deterring interlopers without the case coming to law. On the other, a patent may often have not been worth the parchment it was written on: patentees had great difficulty in detecting infringements, or felt it wiser to let matters slide, rather than chance a prosecution with its attendant expense. There is evidence for both situations but the balance of it supports what we have seen in Dwight's and Stanyforth's cases – that the threat of prosecution was rarely sufficient to suppress infringements.

The problem of enforcement is demonstrated in the case of Nehemiah Grew, F.R.S., botanist and physician, who discovered a method of producing Epsom Salts (magnesium sulphate) out of spa water. Grew showed his salts to the Royal Society in 1679 and had begun commercial production of them by 1699.[89] He was soon beset, however, by extensive imitation of the salts, 'some so unwholesome, that they have been sent back out of the country to the seller, as a vile cheat', which damaged both his trade and his professional reputation. He advised physicians of the 'only effectual method I can think of at present' to prevent the abuse: they should buy their supplies direct from his overseer, 'a citizen of good substance and great honesty'.[90] Finally, in July 1698 he resorted to a patent.[91] Grew's troubles, however, were by no means over. The chief interlopers were George and Francis Moult, chemists in the City of London, whom Grew accused of attempting to bribe his operators to divulge the process. Francis Moult had issued an inaccurate English translation of Grew's Latin treatise, audaciously claiming that his intention was to prevent abuse of the salts.[92] After taking legal advice, Grew served them with the patent 'and showed them the words wherein obedience to his majesty's authority is specified and required'. They were not deterred: Francis Moult published an advertisement in four London newspapers stating that he had prepared the 'bitter purging salt' for some years past 'and continues to do so, notwithstanding any power or authority of Dr Nehemiah Grew to the contrary'. Grew's next move was to solicit the opinion, among others, of the Lord Chancellor, John Somers, who declared the advertisement 'very impudent and saucy', and had it suppressed with a reprimand to Moult and the four printers. He recommended Grew to prosecute. Grew preferred, however, to settle out of court. The Moults stalled and, eventually, 'for peace sake', Grew offered to sell them his patent rights. When negotiations again broke down, he sold them instead to Josiah Peter, who proceeded to write a detailed defence, not only of the patent, but also of Grew's personal and scientific integrity. Peter did not indicate why Grew chose not to prosecute. He may have felt unsure of the patent's validity. Peter twice referred to Somers's opinion having been sought: that the patent was not invalidated by previous laboratory production of mineral salts.[93] Also, Grew, as a physician and fellow of the Royal Society, may have been embarrassed by the patent and the secrecy of his production.[94] Peter had no more success than Grew in suppressing competition: he referred to the Moults' producing 150–200 pounds of salts per week and to other interlopers. Final testimony is provided by a report to the Royal Society in 1723 which, while crediting Grew with the first attempts to make the salts, referred to 'those two ingenious chemists Mr George and Mr Francis Moult' who were producing over 200 pounds of salts per week at Shooters Hill, Kent, in about 1700.[95]

Richard Newsham seems to have curtailed John Ffowke's infringements of his fire-engine patent for four years by the threat of prosecution. Ffowke, who had been blatantly cashing in on Newsham's success, was pressured into an agreement with Newsham in May 1725. But in January 1729 Newsham found it necessary to begin a suit in Chancery, with the complaint that Ffowke had made 'great numbers of the like engines' and 'declares he will not discontinue the same although he had notice of the said letters patent'.[96] That Newsham failed to quash his rival is suggested by the reference in 1747 to 'the struggle that has subsisted many years between our two eminent fire-engine makers' in 'the invention and improvement of them, for the several uses they are designed'.[97]

In 1764, thirty-five London opticians and instrumentmakers petitioned the Privy Council to revoke a patent granted to John Dollond in 1758 for achromatic lenses.[98] For five years the patent had lain dormant, but Peter Dollond, the son of the late patentee, had recently prosecuted an ex-partner for making telescopes that contained the patented lenses, and threatened others who failed to pay royalties with the same treatment. The opticians contended that not Dollond, but Chester Moor Hall, a barrister who had produced achromatic lenses over thirty years before, was the true inventor and, because he was aware of this, the elder Dollond had 'permitted them to enjoy the benefit thereof in common with himself rather than risk a contest with them'.[99] John Dollond may indeed have had grave doubts about the legitimacy of his patent or preferred to respect the trade fraternity among his fellow instrumentmakers.[100] His son was able to press his case to a satisfactory conclusion – it was decided that the earlier production of such lenses did not obstruct the patent since it had not been taken beyond the laboratory – but litigation had been essential to secure the compliance of his competitors.

A few years later, Josiah Wedgwood reached a reluctant compromise with a potter who was infringing his two-year-old patent for 'encaustic vases', on the strength of their mutual desire to avoid the expense of litigation and to uphold the patent against the mass of other potential interlopers. He resolved to have no further truck with patents.[101] And it was claimed that Edmund Cartwright was compelled, 'by the exigency of his affairs in 1793, to desist from a suit, and enter into a compromise with another person who had taken out a patent, which . . . was not a valid patent, but an infringement' of his own.[102]

The evidence for patentees' successful intimidation of interlopers prior to court action is sparse. There is John Stearne's testimony that he and his partner bowed before Dwight's patents and abandoned their plan to establish a stoneware pottery.[103] Yet the existence of sixteen other stoneware potteries by 1695 indicates that others were less intimidated, and Dwight eventually initiated legal proceedings. Andrew Yarranton deferred to the authority of the patent granted – unjustly, in his view – to William Chamberlain in 1673 for tin-plating.[104] The threat of a Chancery action was sufficient in 1757 to deter John Baskerville, the printer, from infringing Tonson and Co.'s patent for publishing Milton's works.[105] Printing patents, however, with their clearly defined subjects, were much more easily defended than were patents for invention. John Stedman of Birmingham, in 1785, used the advertisement of one successful threat of prosecution to deter others – with what success is unknown.[106] Boulton and Watt appear to have pressured Jonathan Hornblower into paying them royalties, but had to take other 'pirates' to court, and reluctantly tolerated many.[107]

The legal action was not all one way. A patentee's intimidating threats could go disastrously wrong. Wise patentees did not press their claims too officiously, unless they were sure of their ground, their financial resources, and the sympathy of the judiciary. Burslem potter Ralph Shaw's patent for decorating earthenware covered apparently nothing more than the use of a thick slip (clay) of flint and pipe-clay, in its combination perhaps novel, but certainly not so in its elements, and therefore likely to trespass on the practices of many of his neighbours.[108]

[Ralph] Shaw . . . unwilling to admit the customary practices of the business, and to brook any appearance of competition, . . . was constantly objecting to every trifling improvement, as an infringement on his patent, and threatening his neighbours with suits in equity, to protect his *sole* rights; till at length self-defence urged them to bear the expenses of a suit he had commenced against John Mitchell, to try the validity of the patent, at Stafford, in 1736.[109]

The defence brought in evidence of Astbury's prior inventions that employed flint, and the Stafford jury decided against Shaw. This was signalled locally as a major victory.[110] Matthew Boulton speculated in 1781 that, if Arkwright 'had been quiet, he might have gone on and got £40,000 p.a. by all the works he has now erected, even if there be some interlopers', instead of intimidating the cotton spinners to the point where they felt it worth the expense of demonstrating the illegality of his patent.[111] He passed a similar judgement on Parker's exploitation of Argand's lamp patent, also lost in the courts.[112] Indeed Dutton concluded that the attitude of common-law judges, for about fifty years before 1830, was largely hostile to patents. Sixty-one per cent of the cases he examined went against the patentee in the second half of the eighteenth century.[113]

The relative paucity of examples of patentees successfully intimidating interlopers may simply be a function of enforcement's unspectacular routine. As Geoffrey Tookey has remarked of present-day patents,

it is always to be remembered that a minimal proportion of patents or of patent applications come before the court, and those that do so represent border-line cases. . . . in order to judge the general state of health of a country you do not look only in the hospitals.[114]

On the other hand, that infringement was a common problem for a substantial minority of patentees is suggested by a number of contemporary remarks deploring the ease with which patent rights could be invaded. Richard Holt, who held a patent for a decorative plaster that he called 'artificial stone', claimed that 'a certain pretending architect' threatened to set up in competition,

vowing and swearing . . . that no patent should protect me from his attempts, for by ways and means, he knew how to elude, or set aside any patent whatsoever. In a country of so much liberty as England, patents were easily broken through, under the pretence of setting up some other affair; or even the same thing, under another name.[115]

Similar criticism had been voiced in the wake of the projecting mania of the early 1690s:

if any one man gets considerably by a happy and useful invention, abundance run immediately into it, and, in spite of the patent, take with little alteration a copy, and then out come the proposals in print.[116]

George Sylvanus found neither the patent nor his trade-mark of a 'falcon and spear' sufficient to prevent unlicensed competition. An advertisement he placed in Houghton's *Collections*, six months after obtaining the patent, protested that he was having great problems with counterfeits and offered a reward to anyone who helped detect the plagiarists.[117] In 1756, entrepreneurial failure was blamed on the fallibility of patent protection:

[the patentee's] apprehension of not being properly secured in the advantage that may redound from the undertaking . . . by his majesty's letters patent, which are oftentimes greatly abused . . . has at present deterred him from carrying it into execution.[118]

It may have been a lame excuse for commercial incompetence, but it suggests that patents were so generally acknowledged not to provide much security against interlopers that it was a tenable one.

The weaknesses of patents were also highlighted by the powers some inventors sought from parliament. Private Acts of Paliament offered inventors a longer term of protection and specified penalties for infringement, enforceable in a court of record. That obtained by William Walcot in 1695 allowed him exclusive use of his desalination furnaces and process and all improvements to them for thirty-one years. No one was to use anything similar 'if principally the same' without his licence, under penalty of the forfeiture of their equipment and heavy fines.[119] Thomas Savery was able to extend his patent to thirty-one years by an Act of 1699; its strength lay chiefly in its inclusiveness, for it covered all employments of 'the impellent force of fire'.[120] John Hutchinson's petition to parliament in 1712 was explicit in its criticisms:

Patents are also defective in never describing the essential parts of the invention to secure it, and the improvements thereon, to the inventor; and that for want of assigning a penalty, the damages to be recovered for making a thing of this value will not be worth suing for; and that for want of a power to discover the maker or seller, these [watches and clocks] may be made, and carried away privately and so used at sea.[121]

The other advantage Hutchinson was seeking was a longer term than the statutorily limited fourteen years of the patent, in which to recoup what he considered to be abnormally high development costs. Not surprisingly, the Clockmakers Company, notoriously jealous of the freedom of its members, mounted a campaign to quash the bill; and it succeeded. Most such bills, in fact, fell foul of anti-monopoly sentiment in parliament, much of it prompted by the fears of vested interests. In the eighteenth century, a patentee's powers were rarely enhanced by an Act, beyond the prolongation of his term of protection. Four patentees, including James Watt, secured Acts to extend their patents in 1775-7, and four in 1785-95, with two (Hornblower and Bramah) withdrawing their petitions when failure looked probable. Such extensions were said in 1829 to be 'very difficult to obtain and very expensive to solicit'.[122]

Patentees dreaded the law courts: financial costs were ruinous, while the outcome seemed random and too often dependent on a technicality. Undoubtedly this was a serious weakness in the system. It penalized those who made genuine and valuable inventions, for only at great risk and expense could they inhibit piracies. Knowledge of this weakened the authority of patents: a threat to prosecute was rarely effective. Indeed, by the late eighteenth century, it was becoming a dictum that a patent was of little commercial value until it had been successfully defended in the courts.[123] On the other hand, uncertainty of enforcement complemented laxity of administration. When patents were issued with so little attention to novelty and viability, the difficulties of litigation offered some protection to those who might be harassed by fraudulent patentees. What was needed was an inexpensive system of arbitration. Until 1753 this was, to some extent, provided by the Privy Council. It was an inexpert body in an area where technical competence was required, but was in that regard no worse than any law court. Once it withdrew from the arena, the patentee and his opponents were left with no recourse except litigation – or compromise. Mounting competition among patentees and manufacturers turned patent litigation into a bear pit in the closing decades of the eighteenth century, and the odds were stacked against patentees.

One might be left wondering why, if enforcement was so difficult, inventors continued to obtain patents. As subsequent chapters will show, the patentee's calculus was complex. For many of them, exclusivity was not a major preoccupation: they sought enabling rather than monopolizing powers, defence rather than offence, kudos rather than control. And where control *was* deemed important and secrecy not a viable option, a potentially weak patent was the only alternative to no protection at all.

5

THE DECISION TO PATENT

It is evident that numerous inventions went unpatented and, conversely, that many patents were taken out for apparently unworkable or trivial devices. For what reason did some inventors decide to patent their inventions, and others not? What were patentees doing when they patented inconsequential, mundane, or technically unfeasible devices? A patent will be shown to have served several functions beyond the straightforward protection of an invention. The system's clients discovered a variety of uses for their expensive pieces of parchment. As a royal grant, a patent conferred prestige on an enterprise; it also afforded a degree of immunity from the regulation of craft guilds and other corporate bodies. With the decline and dissolution of the guilds in the eighteenth century and the concomitant intensification of competition, the former benefit grew at the expense of the latter. This shifted the balance of the system's usage towards established tradesmen and manufacturers. For a few decades at the end of the eighteenth century, prior to the emergence of professional inventors and the attendant 'invention industry', the patent system offered more to those inside manufacturing than to those on its periphery. This trend was reinforced by the growth of defensive patenting. To a large extent, the patent system created its own market: as its existence became more widely known, not only were inventors and manufacturers more willing to use it, they also became more fearful of not using it. This chapter concentrates on the elements in the decision confronting the potential patentee at the level of individual motivations. The subsequent three chapters will take up the question on a broader scale to an analysis by industry, culminating in an explanation of the growth of patenting as a phenomenon, both geographically and over time, that will draw these threads together.

5.1 DISINCENTIVES TO PATENTING

First, however, it is worth considering some common reasons for *not* seeking a patent. Not all inventions were equally suitable for patenting, whatever the use envisaged for the patent. This varied considerably according to industry, but there were also significant differences within industries.[1] The present chapter proceeds on the assumption that the potential patentee had gone beyond this preliminary stage in his calculation, to the recognition, rightly or wrongly, that his invention was suitable for patenting.

The major deterrent to patenting was the expense. The purchase of a patent was costly both in time and money. This changed little between 1660 and 1852. Official fees and stamp duties (introduced in 1694) amounted to approximately £70, but the gratuities payable to everyone concerned – from doormen to high-ranking officials – usually added another £10 to £30 to this cost and might double it in some cases.[2] Witnesses to the 1829 select committee mentioned £120 as the normal cost for an English patent; protection in Scotland and Ireland would raise it to approximately £350.[3] The expensive manoeuvring that might be involved is vividly illustrated by the diary kept by Samuel Taylor of Manchester. He itemized his expenses during the six months of 1722–3 he spent in London procuring a patent for his thread-winding machine. Official and solicitors' fees, gratuities, inn charges and the entertainment successively of the Secretary of State's, the Solicitor General's and the Lord Chancellor's servants cost Taylor and his associates nearly £130. It was three months after he arrived in London and lodged his petition that Taylor managed to secure a warrant; on several occasions he had waited in vain to see the Solicitor General. Taylor was unfortunate, since local rivals entered a caveat and, although overruled, they attempted to obstruct the patent's subsequent progress.[4]

One or two months was the normal period between petition and enrolment. Yet even this was a major commitment of time for those not normally resident in London. (Davies thought the 'loss of time . . . [was] often a greater object with inventors than the expense'.)[5] Personal attendance was required. An inventor might retain the services of a solicitor or be helped by a patentee who had already navigated the tortuous Whitehall route. Taylor mentioned meeting a Dr Eaton – probably the medicinal patentee, Robert Eaton – who introduced him to a solicitor.[6] The complex procedure, the enforced sojourn in London, and the exactions of the crown and its officials surely deterred many inventors from securing a patent, and probably account for many of the applications for patents which fell before enrolment.[7] John Dickens, who finally secured a patent for his water engine in 1723, provides an insight. He referred to two earlier applications when, because his estate was in the hands of mortgagors, 'your petitioner . . . has been disabled from raising the necessary charges for the passing the said patent.'[8] At least two schemes were mooted in the early eighteenth century to assist poor inventors with the cost of patenting.[9] Early letters to the Society of Arts also bear witness to the difficulties experienced by poor inventors. Anthony Goude asked the Society in 1756, for example, to 'allow him a premium for his projection towards enabling him to obtain a patent for it'.[10]

Indeed, the patent costs came on top of whatever sums had already been spent on experimenting, constructing and testing the invention. Several patentees stressed this expenditure as an argument for their being granted a patent. John Watlington, a London skinner, mentioned £1,000 as the cost of inventing his fur-cutting machine,[11] and Sir Richard Steele calculated a similar outlay on his 'fish pool sloop'.[12] Such sums were astronomical in contemporary terms, when even the basic £70 for a patent was out of the reach of most artisan inventors.[13] Sir William Jennens convenanted £150 in 1685 'for taking out of the letters patent . . . and for making such liquors and proofs hereof as shall be judged requisite', to be reimbursed him from the projectors' first profits.[14] Fifty years later, Jonathan Hulls was lent £160 by a local gentleman to patent and develop his steam boat.[15] Such heavy expenditure placed an immense burden on patentees. Thomas Benson, who introduced important flint-crushing machinery into the pottery industry, was said to have been ruined by 'the sums he borrowed to carry out his improvements and secure his patents', and died impoverished.[16] To put an invention into commercial production required still more capital. Yet once a patent had been secured, an inventor was in a better position either to sell the invention to a manufacturer or to attract partners. Unable to afford one, some refused to risk their invention being stolen and so left it unworked; others were able to develop theirs with some success. A patent was a heavy investment, not to be undertaken capriciously.

Many inventors remained ignorant of the patent system's very existence and some perhaps thought of it as a dispenser of Court patronage, unrelated to their interests. As late as 1834 Henry Bessemer, by his own admission, 'knew nothing of patents or patent law', even after three years' residence in London, and consequently sold his unprotected, early inventions for paltry amounts.[17] Patents were a novelty that spread only slowly into the provinces. It may often have been the example of a neighbour who took out a patent, or indeed his competition, which induced an inventor or manufacturer to secure his own. It was not until 1749 that any inhabitant of Derbyshire obtained a patent, and then there were three patents in two years, all from the small town of Bakewell: two taken out by John Baker, a whitner and hosier, the third by Henry Watson, a stonecutter and carver, who filed his petition just three months after Baker's second patent was enrolled.[18] Baker's business sometimes took him to Manchester; one of his partners in the patent was a Liverpool merchant who had London agents. It was probably by this metropolitan route that Baker, then Watson, discovered the patent system.[19] The year 1749 also witnessed Suffolk's first patent. It was granted to Daniel Jewes, a Bury St Edmunds builder, in partnership with William Lodge, gentleman. Lodge had arrived in Bury only recently from Bristol, the city with the highest concentration of patentees outside London at that time.[20] Patents show a marked degree of geographical concentration, in which such

accidental disseminations of information into the provinces presumably
played a part. The closer an area's commercial links with London, the more
opportunity its inhabitants had to learn of the patent system.[21]

Anxiety regarding the difficulty and cost of enforcing patent rights also
acted as a deterrent of unknown magnitude. William Murdoch is said to have
been dissuaded from patenting gas lighting in 1792 by James Watt jun., who
was disenchanted by repeated infringements of his father's patents for the
steam engine.[22] It is unlikely, however, that such long-term considerations
normally carried much weight with first-time patentees. And indeed, seven
years and several successful court cases later, Watt offered Murdoch quite
contrary advice.[23] Celebrated cases that went against patentees – even the
successive defeats of Arkwright and Argand in 1785 – appear not to have
dampened the demand for patents. Of course, we cannot know how much
further the already high totals for 1785–6 would otherwise have climbed. A
witness before the 1829 select committee believed that 'the difficulty and
uncertainty attending patents and their specification is a cause why the
government do not receive at least three or fourfold the amount they would,
of revenue from that particular department'.[24] Whether this speculation can
be read back into a period ending thirty or forty years before is seriously open
to question: the intervening three decades were marked by a particularly
high rate of failure for patentees in both common-law and equity courts.[25]

5.2 VARIETIES OF PATENT AND PATENTEE

Three broad categories of patentee are discernible throughout the period,
but each had their particular heyday. Two contained 'outsiders' to the
business world, one 'insiders'. The first was the amateur inventor, a complete
'outsider', for whom mechanics or chemistry was an amusing diversion that
might one day open up a lucrative sideline. For some such men a patent
perhaps represented nothing more than a mark of recognition and establishment of priority; for others among them it secured their property in a
commercial proposition or entry into a gildated trade. They rarely took out
more than one patent, and their inventions were often ambitious: for instance, Ducrest's for pasteboard houses and bridges, or Lord Stanhope's for
steam boats.[26] Alternative forums for their activities were, in the Restoration,
the Royal Society and, more important, after 1754, the Society of Arts.
Richard Lovell Edgeworth is a good example of the type. A Berkshire
gentleman with political and philanthropic interests, Edgeworth was an
active member of the Lunar Society of Birmingham, and a prolific inventor of
mechanical devices. 'I amused myself with mechanics', he wrote. His inventions ranged from the mundane (a turnip cutter) to the speculative (a
telegraph system, intended to convey information from race meetings) to the
outlandish (a man-sized barrel for transportation). Most were submitted to
the Society of Arts.[27] There is nothing to indicate why he obtained one (and

only one) patent – for a form of caterpillar traction – in 1770, but James Watt and Josiah Wedgwood, manufacturing colleagues in the Lunar society, were very patent-conscious at that particular time. If he saw commercial possibilities in it, he took no action.[28] Another Lunar Society member, Dr William Small, also took out a single patent, in 1773, reporting to Watt that 'a patent has been taken out for my clocks and watches, and *there is reason to hope they may become an article of commerce*'.[29] The amateur inventor made regular appearances in the patent records throughout the period, but he was numerically overwhelmed by 'business' patentees after the mid-eighteenth century. Clearly not all gentlemen patentees fell into this category: Lord Dundonald's six patents between 1781 and 1798 were directly related to his attempts to revive his family's fortunes through industrial enterprise.[30]

The second category comprised the amateur's mirror image, the professional inventor – yet he was also an 'outsider'. Inventing was for him not a hobby but a livelihood. Typically he obtained a large number of patents across a wide field of industries, with a view to selling his inventions to manufacturers. His existence and activities have been well documented by Harry Dutton, but I shall argue that the heyday of the professional inventor (and the 'invention industry' which he generated) did not dawn until the early nineteenth century.[31] A few such inventors were operating in the second half of the eighteenth century, for instance, Bryan Higgins who held four diverse patents and, by lecturing, analysing chemical samples, and selling chemical and pharmaceutical preparations, managed to make a living from his technical and scientific interests.[32]

The third and catch-all category is that of the businessman – the artisan or manufacturer and the millwright or machine-maker – who appeared in force after 1760 and dominated the system for the rest of the century. It is sharply differentiated from the two former categories since it contained 'insiders', those who were ready to engage in manufacturing or a trade.[33] Such men wished to protect any novel products or processes they might devise (or purchase from the inventor) and to boost their business's image by the kudos that a patent could lend. While they sometimes obtained more than one patent, these usually related only to their own branch of business. This category would include, for example, John Dwight, Jedediah Strutt, Joseph Bramah and James Watt. Not all patentees fit neatly into one of these three categories. Hardest to place are the upper-class entrepreneurs, men like Dundonald, the second Duke of Buckingham and the late-seventeenth-century projector, Thomas Neale. Probably the third category should be stretched to encompass them since, while not strictly 'businessmen', their patents were obtained to protect commercial enterprises; and neither Buckingham nor Neale were themselves inventors.

Since patentees had such markedly different characteristics, it is not surprising that patents were used in a variety of ways, some of which we would not now consider legitimate or orthodox. Before proceeding, however, to a separation of heterodox from orthodox uses for patents, the anachronism of such a distinction should be fully recognized. Certain abuses of patents were ruled out by statute and the force of public opinion. Otherwise there was nothing to say that one use was more valid than another. The Statute of Monopolies and the crown's lax administration of the patent system gave inventors and others much room for manoeuvre. Nonetheless, the distinction is maintained here in order to emphasize the differences that make the seventeenth- and eighteenth-century institution barely comparable with that which developed in the nineteenth century.

The patent system's function was evolving throughout this period. As we have seen, the thirty years from 1690 to 1720 were transitional between the Restoration ghost of patenting as Court patronage and the eighteenth-century development of patents as instruments of industrial competition.[34] In the first phase from 1660 to the 1690s the patent was, on the whole, an enabling instrument, giving its holder royal authority to evade or override the regulations of trading and manufacturing monopolies. The second, transitional, phase was marked by the decline of crown and Court involvement and the emergence of new functions. In the 1690s patents were used by entrepreneurs to lend a gloss of respectability to their projects, in order to attract both investors and customers. The third phase began after 1720 when the Bubble Act sharply curtailed the new stock-market potential of patents. Their value as an attraction to customers persisted throughout the century, however, providing a major reason for patenting: 'patent' became virtually a brand name for a host of products. They began to be used more aggressively as instruments of competition, by artisans and manufacturers who sought to carve out limited monopolies of production and sale. Patents varied enormously in the degree of novelty they covered. Increasingly the patent system generated its own logic: as patent protection became the norm, so it became harder to ignore the threat of preemption. The pressure on inventors to secure their title by patent mounted, as did the pressure on artisans and manufacturers to cover their products with kudos equal to that obtained by their patenting rivals. Cipolla points to a similar psychological momentum developing in clock and watch ownership: the more that society was regulated by the clock, the more those without an accurate timepiece were disadvantaged, even excluded.[35]

The several functions of patents outlined here were not exclusive to a particular phase in the system's development. Orthodox and heterodox uses coexisted side by side, sometimes within a single patent. It is rarely possible to ascertain which motive predominated, and one must assume that inventors were not always rational agents acting in their own best interests. The picture is also clouded by broader economic developments: old forms of industrial organization were in decline and new ones hesitantly emerging. A patent could put the inventor in an unassailable position *vis-à-vis* his commercial rivals: alternatively, it might prove an expensive white elephant and belie his expectations.

5.3 HETERODOX USES: PRESTIGE AND INTRUSION

Seventeenth-century patents were often equally concerned with subcontracting government business and authorization of potentially controversial activities, as with protecting invention.[36] The second largest type of inventions patented in the period 1660–1700 was of water-pumping machinery. Several of these were sought with a particular water supply or river in mind: for instance, Thomas Neale's for Shadwell, James Van Daalen's for the Exe, and Thomas Povey's to dredge the River Ouse in Norfolk.[37] Laying the pipes for a water supply would usually mean digging up public roads and crossing private lands; the machinery might be noisy or interrupt the course of a river. A royal warrant in the form of a patent could help smooth the projectors' path. That issued to Francis Williamson and Ralph Wayne in 1663, for example, empowered them to carry water to Piccadilly and its environs. Ten years later Wayne and his new partner, Ralph Bucknall, sought permission to change the source of supply from 'certain springs' to the Thames. Christopher Wren, as Surveyor General, viewed the site and engine, and the patentees were granted a 99-year lease at York Buildings on the Strand. After a fire at the waterworks in 1684, it came to light that they 'were not built answerable to the engine first proposed by the said undertakers and approved of by his majesty's surveyor'. The king ordered that the new waterworks incorporate neither a chain pump nor a windmill, whose clatter had infuriated residents; a new patent was to be issued 'according to a model to be agreed upon . . . which said model shall be included in the patent'.[38] Throughout this episode there was remarkably little interest in the novelty of the water-raising methods, much more in mediating between various interests.

Patents for invention were a means by which the crown granted franchises. Other clear examples were the patents for diving engines in the early 1690s. The new diving bell or suit was often no more than 'window-dressing' to reassure investors and to provide the basis for a patent whose real value (if any) lay in the exclusive share of the sea-bed it assigned. By his patent of 1689 Francis Smartfoot (an aptly named projector) was authorized to fish for wrecks anywhere on the British coasts, except from the North Foreland to westward of the Lizard.[39] Andrew Becker, in 1714, requested that his patent for a wreck-raising engine be redrafted to grant him certain latitudes off the American coast, 'this being the only place left for your petitioner where any considerable wrecks are lying'.[40] The holders of patents for street-lighting disputed their areas of operation. Andrew Vernatty accused a rival patentee of overstepping the boundaries of his patent: Edward Wyndus was erecting street lights 'under pretext of a grant to him since obtained, for lighthouses, ships and mines.'[41] Since London had been catered for, several entrepreneurs petitioned in the early 1690s to erect their 'newly invented' lights in Dublin. Two patents granted in the next decade contained clauses that specifically prohibited their exercise in London, where the Convex Lights Company had leased exclusive rights from the Corporation by a controversial Act of 1694.[42] Until the mid-eighteenth century, special licences were granted under cover of a patent for invention for a variety of enterprises which, although new or relatively so, were not technical inventions. These included banking and insurance schemes, lotteries, navigational aids, and whaling and fishing licences.[43]

Patents might also be used to cut a swathe through restrictive legislation – unless sufficiently vociferous opposition was raised. This, one suspects, was the advantage expected by Joseph Bacon, whose attempts to introduce a version of the outlawed friezing mill were resisted by local clothworkers.[44] Charles Howard's patent for tanning leather without bark may have been prompted by the mass of regulations surrounding the leather industry.[45] This incentive to patent disappeared when the Bill of Rights finally removed the crown's prerogative power to override statute laws in 1689.[46] (When doubts arose concerning the validity of Samuel Ashton's patent for tanning leather in 1794 because of statutory restrictions, he resorted to parliament for an Act, 'that nothing in any previous Act' should obstruct his patent.)[47]

Virtually all patentees in the first two decades after the Restoration had some claim of service, performed or promised, on the crown.[48] They were joined from about 1675 by a steady influx of craftsmen and merchants from the Low Countries and France, where the Revocation of the Edict of Nantes in 1685 turned the trickle of Huguenot refugees into a flood.[49] Thirty-one immigrants applied for a patent between 1675 and 1700, twenty-two of them successfully.[50] This was, of course, a traditional role of patents, but it was its last flourish. Its demise is evident in Attorney General Yorke's hesitant report on the application of two immigrant weavers in 1730: 'it appears to me that patents of this kind for the sole use of manufactures newly brought into England and never before made here have formerly passed'.[51]

The interests of immigrants and Court nominees often clashed with those of established groups and individuals in the business world, and a patent could ease their way. Recent research, by Michael Walker, suggests that the thirty years following the Restoration witnessed a reinvigoration of guild control. Hostility to 'unfree' craftsmen remained a cause for anxiety to outsiders (by place or trade) who wished to seek their fortune in a corporate town.[52] It drove some of them to seek a patent and thereby royal protection. But the government had to tread carefully: it dare not trample too roughshod on guild preserves. Thomas Vahan requested a patent in 1670 for 'keeping common ovens' to provide neighbourhood baking facilities, promising to undertake nothing against the privilege of any corporation. Attorney

General Heneage Finch was not satisfied: the patent would be opposed by both bakers and lords of the manor, who had the privilege of common ovens, and Vahan would be indicted for not having served an apprenticeship as a baker; in addition, it would be invalid, 'for baking or baking cheap cannot pretend to a patent of privilege of a new invention'. Vahan replied that he did not seek a privilege to restrain others, but only a *permission* for baking as well as others did, in order 'to secure himself better' since he was 'a foreigner born'.[53]

Some awareness of guild sensitivities was shown by Francis Watson in a statement of 1669 accusing members of the Painter Stainers Company of infringing his patent. Using his varnish without fully understanding it, they produced shoddy work; he had offered them a licensing agreement, 'they being the proper persons to use it', but they had continued its clandestine use. Watson won his case before the Privy Council and deposited at the Company's hall 'a copy of the Order in Council forbidding the painters to intermeddle in the business of lacquering'.[54] John Greene was in a position shared by many gentlemen who put their minds to improving coach travel and wished to exploit their ideas commercially. Without the patent that he secured in 1692, the Coachmakers Company would presumably have suppressed Greene's enterprise. With it, he was able to advertise that the patented coach could be viewed at his house in Westminster, 'where coachmakers may have licence to make or alter, and Hackney and stage-coaches to drive and use [them] on reasonable terms'.[55] Exemption from guild regulation as a motive for patenting should not be overestimated, but there was clearly some advantage in it for amateur inventors and courtier and immigrant businessmen.

Guilds, not surprisingly, distrusted patents for invention, which created independent pockets in their midst. This loosened their control and maintenance of standards. Patents also undermined their ethic of unrestricted communication of trade secrets between the freemen of a company.[56] Doubtless this represented an idealized situation and most guildsmen were as secretive and possessive of their innovations as the average patentee, but it was an ethic which helped bolster the solidarity on which guild authority rested. The position taken by the Weavers Company on the introduction of 'alamodes and lustrings', types of fine silk cloth, is indicative of this concern for control. In 1684 it granted its own 'patent' to a Huguenot: 'the [Company's] court . . . being willing to give all just and reasonable encouragement for the bringing in . . . of those works here (which have not at any time been used here)', it allowed a six-week experimental period. On the production of a piece of alamode, the court admitted Jean Llarguier of Nimes a free master *gratis*, conditional upon his employing English weavers in making the new silks for at least one year.[57] Four years later, the Company closely followed the application for a royal patent by other Huguenots, Paul Decloux and his associates, and spent approximately £250 in protecting its interests.[58] The Weavers declared that they had no objection to the patent, provided it was restricted to black hoods and scarves, and the manufacturers were under the Company's regulation. In July 1688, the Company petitioned the king: it had learned that the patent covered 'improvements' to the silk which, it feared, 'will include the weaving all figured, flowered, striped and spotted silks', thereby threatening a substantial part of its members' trade. Both parties were heard and the Attorney General duly removed the offending clause. Moreover, it was stipulated that all who wove the silks within a twenty-mile radius of London must have served apprenticeships in the trade and be members of the Weavers Company.[59]

Before the second quarter of the eighteenth century, patentees who described themselves by a trade were usually branching out into new enterprises. There were, for example, four drapers who requested patents between 1661 and 1731: for a fulling mill, iron bolts, marbled paper and a 'double-writing' machine respectively, of which only the first was remotely connected with their trade.[60] But some guildsmen seem to have sought the crown's protection when breaking their guild's restrictions. They attracted particular odium. Not only did the Clockmakers Company fight Daniel Quare's application to patent a portable barometer but, defeated at the first hurdle, it promised assistance to any of its members who defied it.[61] Quare may have wished to hire unskilled labour: demand for barometers (which were marginal to his clockmaking trade) was such that mass production was perhaps viable.[62] In 1716 the London Court of Aldermen heard the complaints of William Harding, a blacksmith who had been refused his guild's permission to employ 'foreign' journeymen although 'he could get no freemen to do his work, being engine work of new inventions'. It was probably not coincidental that in January 1717 he petitioned for a patent to produce sugar mills. Perhaps a temporary accommodation was reached with the Blacksmiths, but in 1721 he again sought, and this time secured, a patent.[63] Guild authority over the majority of trades, in both London and provincial corporate towns, remained strong until the 1720s. It was generally between 1720 and 1740 that membership of the manufacturing craft guilds collapsed, although there were some important exceptions which maintained their control until late in the century.[64]

Other regulatory bodies were also jealous of their rights. Patents were twice taken out for erecting lighthouses, which impinged on Trinity House's monopoly, producing strongly worded complaints. Justinian Angell's patent, which apparently covered no invention, authorized him to levy a farthing (0.1p) per ton on every laden ship passing the lighthouses he planned to build at the mouth of the Humber, 'in as ample a manner as the masters of Trinity House . . . do hold their licence'.[65] Under cover of a patent for a method of distinguishing between existing lights, Robert Hamblin set about erecting new ones on which he would charge tolls.[66] The eighteenth century saw a sudden boom in patents for compound medicines. One possible reason was to avoid the regulation of the Royal College of Physicians, and at the same time to give the nostrum a status equivalent to that of the medicines authorized by the College in the *Pharmacopoeia Londinensis*, which were often of exactly the same composition.[67]

It was not only from the traditional authorities, of course, that patentees sought protection. From the 1690s, the patent's function as an instrument of competition began to emerge more strongly. It was used to protect an inventor against his rivals in trade and to secure a competitive edge through the kudos it lent. Patents began to be used in a way similar to that in which registered trade-marks are now applied to products – to establish one particular brand as the original, genuine and, by implication, best – at first with goods that fell outside guild control and protection. (Enforcement of trade-marks was one of the functions of the craft guilds, its primary purpose being to maintain standards of workmanship by making bad work traceable. It provided a form of corporate brand name.)[68]

Proprietary medicines provided the main sphere in which patented names were first cherished, although it is visible in other consumer products, such as 'Record Ink Powder' in 1709 – 'that no other persons may presume to counterfeit the same in this name or by any title whatsoever' – and 'German Balls' for leather in 1693.[69] Such patentees discovered that a patent was in itself no guarantee against counterfeit labels.[70] Following the death in 1726 of patentee Richard Stoughton, a Southwark apothecary, battle was joined in the advertisement columns of the *London Journal* between various relatives of the deceased, each professing to sell the genuine elixir, and one Susannah Wilkinson, who unashamedly announced, 'as for me, I am no upstart, but am the widow of William Wilkinson, who prepared the elixir some years ago, but was restrained by the late Lord Chancellor'.[71] Stoughton had successfully prosecuted Wilkinson in 1721. He had been less concerned, it seems, about Wilkinson's possessing his recipe than with his imitation of Stoughton's publicity materials and his taking a warehouse in the same vicinity, outside which he even hung a similar sign.[72] Again problems were arising from the use of patents in areas where copyright over a design or a registered trade-mark would have been more appropriate.[73]

In 1711, Timothy Byfield, 'M.D., Fellow of the College of Physicians in Dublin', set the pace when he patented 'Sal Oleum Volatile' (by no means a new product), and published a pamphlet puffing his practice.[74] Six months later, Stoughton patented his 'Great Cordial Elixir', announcing that it had been produced and widely distributed for twenty years. He was among the first to dispense in distinctively shaped bottles, and he advertised regularly in *The Spectator*.[75] Such patentees were keenly attuned to the value of publicity. This new use for patents began at the same time as did commercial advertising on an unprecedented scale, with the birth of the provincial press and, in London, the daily newspaper. Proprietary medicines took up a major share of the advertising space, which itself soon began to crowd out the news.[76] A patent helped direct the consumer's choice among the plethora of remedies for sale: it lent a gloss of respectability and authority to a nostrum. (An alternative was to elicit the sanction of a member of the royal family or, failing that, of the Royal Society or College of Physicians.) Of the ten proprietary medicines advertised more than 160 times in Bath newspapers between 1744 and 1800, five had been patented. Since the ratio of patented to unpatented proprietary medicines was approximately one to six, this suggests that patents were acquired by the more publicity-conscious proprietors.[77]

Handbills and newspaper advertisements were headed with the formula 'By the King's Royal Patent . . .', labels and seals were printed and bottles moulded with it, and the royal coat of arms was prominently displayed. A royal guarantee was implied.[78] David D'Escherny was unfavourably impressed by the advantage a patent gave:

Shall we not pity the misfortunes attending too often those, who are dazzled by the illustrious name made use of? . . . These permissions give as great a privilege to practise physic as any degrees from the university, or the admission into the Royal College of Physicians.[79]

As for the 'Liquid Shell', a rival remedy for the stone patented by Walter Baker, its 'excellency consists chiefly, and I believe very nearly only, in the patent the person who disposes of it has obtained'.[80] Baker himself challenged the validity of Robert James's patent for fever powder. He complained it had seriously damaged his trade in 'Schwanberg's Universal Powder' (an unpatented remedy). Mary Schwanberg, Baker's partner and widow of the original producer, confirmed that 'the demand for the same has greatly decreased . . . wholly owing to James having obtained such letters patent'.[81] A successful proprietary medicine was often the magnet which built up a doctor's or apothecary's practice, but his reputation with his peers frequently suffered in inverse correlation with his popular success.[82]

A patent sanctioned the creation of various ephemeral enterprises that fell outside the respectable circle of guild-controlled trades, and might be confused with the shady dealings of hawkers and chapmen. Contemporary advertisements offer some idea of their operations: the patentees could be contacted at a coffee house or inn, or their goods inspected at a warehouse. The patentees of 'the new invented engine for making and twisting whips' announced that merchants and shopkeepers could obtain the whips at a warehouse in Upper Moorefields (London) and at the next Exeter, and other major, fairs.[83] Some operated a service, such as the business which Philip Bertie and his partners opened in Thames Street, London, in 1695: the patented engine 'which fulls all sorts of stuffs by hand or man's labour' would wash, scour and full all sorts of cloth, stockings, quilts and hangings 'with expedition and at reasonable rates'. It sounds to have been little more than a laundry.[84] Similarly, Edward Hurd offered a lacquering service,[85] and William Sutton a waterproofing service.[86] Others sold direct to the public. In 1723 a visiting Swede described a newly invented 'swimming engine', presumably that patented by Benjamin Habakkuk Jackson the previous year, a rather clumsy life-jacket made of thin iron cylinders: at a public demonstration it was sold for a guinea.[87] Such patents appear to have been the direct ancestors of the mail-order businesses which place small advertisements with large claims in today's newspapers.

The publicity value of these patents was not lost on established city tradesmen, who, as the cloak of guild protection grew threadbare, were increasingly feeling the chill winds of competition. The 'insider' began to appear in relatively large numbers from the 1720s, and arrived in force after 1760, patenting improvements to his stock items of trade.[88] One must allow that some of these patents covered technical improvements, even significant inventions, but many were for nothing more than a variation in design. Similar products tended to bunch, over the space of one or two years, suggesting that tradesmen felt it unwise to allow a rival a monopoly of kudos.[89] The patent was used extensively as an advertising device. For instance, 'Beetham's Royal Patent Washing Mill' and the royal crest are emblazoned across a plate showing the machine and announcing where it could be bought.[90] Others were so keen that 'By the King's patent' was already stamped on the item portrayed in the specification. It probably permitted a significant premium on an article's price.[91]

Contemporaries were well aware of this use for patents. *The patent, a poem* (1776) reserved its venom for 'patent-placemen' and corruption in high places, but not before lampooning the patenting practices of various London tradesmen, helpfully identified in the notes:

> Hail to the Patents! which enables Man
> To vend a folio . . . or a warming-pan
> This makes the windlass work with double force,
> And smoke-jacks whirl more rapid in their course.
> Hail to the patent! that at Irwin's shop
> Improves the flavour of a currant drop.

Here the satirist neatly targeted the *reductio ad absurdum* of late-eighteenth-century patents, Irwin's simple recipe for boiled sweets, sold from his confectioner's shop in Berkeley Square. The crux of the matter was that 'patents are obtain'd as fancy wills'.[92] Lord Chief Justice Kenyon, who expressed reservations regarding the equity of patents, was said to have remarked that, 'we could not look into the newspapers of the day, without being astonished at the numerous advertisements of articles for which patents had been granted'. Yet his anonymous reporter, who favoured (and perhaps held) patents, also commented that 'the number of frivolous articles for which patents are obtained is, indeed, matter of surprise'.[93] Craftsmen seem to have accommodated themselves to these patents, recognizing them for what they were. They were not the stuff of which lawsuits were made, not least because they rarely covered important inventions.

It was not only with the consumer that the patent's gloss of respectability was valuable. It also helped attract the investor. This was a major use discovered for patents between 1690 and 1720. 'Oh, a patent gives a reputation to it, and cullies [i.e. dupes] in the company', wrote the author of *Angliae tutamen* in 1695, condemning the craze for unsound 'projects'.[94] In his opinion patents had been abused to an unprecedented extent in the previous few years as the bases for stock-jobbing chimeras. The prestige of patents fell in the late 1690s: they had been tainted with the odium of projecting in general and were worse than useless for some time. By the second decade of the eighteenth century, however, the memory had faded and again people were investing in schemes to which a patent seemed to impart a 'gilt-edged' guarantee of security.[95] In its success lay its downfall, for this speculative use of patents was made obsolete by the Bubble Act. The Act allowed more sober relationships between patentees and their financial partners to continue.[96]

5.4 ORTHODOX USES: PROTECTING AN INVENTION

Vital as it is to recognize the ingenious ways in which patents were used, the importance cannot be doubted, from at least the second quarter of the eighteenth century, of the motive we perceive as orthodox – that of securing one's property in an invention. Applicants for patents expressed their fears. Richard Baddeley wanted to patent his thimble-making engine in 1709, 'least others when he makes it public should counterfeit it to the petitioner's damage, before he be reimbursed his expenses'. John Payne, of Bridgwater, referred to harassment from spies and would-be partners. Many inventors, he thought, had been deprived of the benefit of their discoveries 'by others in almost a lazy manner'.[97] Aaron Hill reassured potential investors in 1715 that 'the patent secures the whole benefit of the beech-oil to its proprietors, whereas the cider trade lies open, and has many thousand rival sharers to divide and lessen its profits'.[98] Several remarked that the capital outlay necessary to implement the invention would not be worthwhile without protection, 'otherwise their expense might be thrown away and defeated at [the] last'.[99]

While escape from the control of a guild may have motivated some early patentees, the unbridled competition in trades which grew up outside the guild structure, or in which the guild's control was crumbling, provided an increasingly potent motive for seeking a patent. Protection of an invention and kudos were closely linked motivations and, at this distance of time, hard to disentangle. The scramble for patents in plate-glass manufacture in the late seventeenth century was probably related to the unusual degree of competition already existing in the London glassmaking trade, which had never been organized into a guild, and to the tradition of patenting established by Mansell's and then Buckingham's monopolies.[100] In the second half of the eighteenth century trade rivalry stimulated patenting particularly in the centres of close, unregulated competition, for instance, the Nottingham hosiery trade and the Birmingham metalware industries, and among certain

London trades, such as the clock, instrument, and coach makers.[101] It was often the immediate threat of competition, sometimes when the invention had already been stolen, that drove an inventor to patent, and this pressure grew with the century. 'Two villains' had betrayed John Wyatt's projects (for a button lathe) to a rival: 'this, Sir, makes it absolutely necessary to take out a patent with the utmost expedition'.[102] In 1748 Wyatt and his partner, Lewis Paul, finally raised the money to patent a carding machine invented some seven years before. This postdated by seven months, and presumably was prompted by, the patent secured by Daniel Bourn of Leominster, one of their licensees for the spinning machine. They had felt threatened by Bourn's patent to the point of offering him £600 to suspend the spinning licence.[103]

Increasingly, the fear was less that of competitors free-riding on one's invention, more that of the patent's preemption. Richard Arkwright was said to have been eager to patent the water-frame since he was 'fearful lest Hayes should hear what he was about and find a friend to push his prior claim at the patent office'.[104] And Sir John Dalrymple explained to a House of Commons committee in 1798 that, 'having been careless in talking of our contrivances, I was afraid that some person might steal out a patent against us, use it as a monopoly, and turn it into a restraint against the government itself', and so had rushed to secure a patent.[105] A cheaper alternative in the short term for those who feared preemption was to pay for a caveat, an insurance policy used, for example, by James Keir to protect his discoveries in making synthetic alkali in 1771, and by Boulton and Watt to secure their chlorine-bleaching process in 1787. On the former occasion Keir expressed his anxieties to Watt:

I was afraid lest some persons might prevent our obtaining a patent, if we should think it necessary, by entering a caveat in general against all patents for obtaining alkali from sea-salt, especially as I found upon inquiry that you and Dr Black had not taken that precaution.[106]

Indeed, Dutton has suggested that the increased use of caveats is an indication of the rising temperature of competition among inventors.[107] Part of that was a growing nervousness about preemptive patenting. Another indication is the readiness of inventors to go to the expense of a succession of patents in order to secure improvements – the original patent perhaps having been taken out too hastily in a bid to preempt preemption – for, if they failed to, someone else probably would.[108]

Beyond the monopolization of a new product or process, a patent opened up several ways of exploiting an invention. It was a piece of alienable property: although, according to the Statute of Monopolies, to be granted only to the first inventor, patents were bought, sold, bequeathed and divided into shares.[109] A patentee could transfer the risks of manufacturing by selling the patent for a lump sum or by licensing any number of manufacturers to use the invention. Alternatively, he might decide to share the risks and enter manufacturing: a patent, or the prospect of one, could be used to attract creditors or partners.[110] A patent had fewer positive attractions for an established manufacturer–inventor, but the pressures generated by the patent system itself and by the expanding national market drew in more and more after the mid-century.[111]

Partnership was a financial necessity forced on reluctant inventors. John Houghton greeted the first great wave of speculation in company shares in the 1690s with enthusiasm, since he believed 'many good undertakings fail for lack of money'.[112] The Stock Exchange released inventors from direct and close dependence on their financial supporters, but the Bubble Act's restriction of partners to five returned them to it. The laws of partnership and liability were both uncertain and discouraging.[113] The larger his own resources, the greater was an inventor's chance of securing his invention by patent before trusting his secret to an outsider. On the other hand, if he could interest others at an early stage, then the financial burden of development could be more evenly spread. In such cases a patent might be obtained partly to cement the partnership and secure the financial partners' investment. James Watt was first financed by John Roebuck in return for a two-thirds share of the steam-engine patent. Following Roebuck's bankruptcy in 1773, this was taken over by Matthew Boulton, and when the patent was extended by Act of Parliament two years later, the partnership was made coterminous with it.[114] The papers of John Wyatt are heavy with the twin anxieties of losing his inventions and of raising the money necessary to fund their development and implementation. The agreements he signed with successive creditors all provided for maintaining secrecy in one way or another. In 1733 Wyatt wrote to his partner, Lewis Paul, expressing his apprehension that, in the course of negotiations with potential investors, the secret (of his spinning machine) would escape: he was telling them everything about it 'except the means how'. He reluctantly concluded, 'I rather think we shall find it for our interest to be at the charge of a patent', but it was not until 1738, and with much outside assistance, that they finally afforded one.[115] Most of Wyatt's inventions were never patented, and he suffered the consequences.[116]

The sale of licences was an avenue open to inventors who lacked the will or the financial resources necessary to set up a full-scale commercial enterprise. It provided, in particular, a means of exploiting an invention of capital goods at a period when such equipment was rarely made by specialist firms. Others combined licensing with some productive enterprise. Wyatt and Paul, for instance, licensed their creditors and others to use a number of spindles, in tandem with their own efforts to establish a spinning factory.[117] Charles Tennant resorted to licensing when the problems of transporting his bleaching liquid made its centralized production unfeasible.[118] He offered to teach the process for a sum equal to half of what his client saved in a year by replacing the ashes normally used for bleaching.[119] Stanyforth and Foljambe were able to run a flourishing business based on the licensing of plough-wrights and farmers to make and use their patented plough. They employed a number of skilled craftsmen to travel the country promoting the implement and instructing ploughwrights in the niceties of its construction.[120] They were thus able to keep the profits of innovation in their own hands. In contrast, joiners and weavers of the Manchester area who mastered the construction and operation of the (unpatented) sprigg loom in the 1730s and 40s enjoyed among themselves the profits of instructing others – who were then in a position similarly to recoup their outlay.[121] In another instance, James Watt reported with alarm that a firm of London chemists had employed someone to travel the country teaching Berthollet's chlorine-bleaching process 'for ten guineas each bleachfield'. He reckoned that 'this will be ten times worse than the patent, as it will lay the matter entirely open as far as they know [the process] themselves'.[122]

Unlike a patentee who chose to monopolize manufacture, one who decided to sell licences could not bolster his patent rights with secrecy. Success hinged partly on his capacity to enforce the patent, partly on the need and financial resources of his potential licensees. The Steam Engine Proprietors were fortunate in both respects: the patent (for Savery's steam engine, under which they were exploiting Newcomen's atmospheric engine) was comprehensive and strengthened by parliamentary sanction, while the invention was highly distinctive and virtually impossible to conceal; their customers were wealthy mineowners, capable (if resentful) of paying high premiums and often desperate for some effective method of mines' drainage.[123] The Proprietors, John Meres and his partners in the City, carried out no manufacture. They acted as commissioning agents, and parts were supplied by subcontractors.[124] Over a hundred engines were erected by a small number of licensed engineers who competed among themselves for business and, as time went on, became restive under the London Proprietors' control. One of the earliest steam engineers, Stonier Parrott, joined two north-eastern coalowners, William Cotesworth and George Liddell, who had failed to reach agreement with the Proprietors. In 1725 Parrott proposed they should petition parliament for repeal of the Fire Engine Act (1699) on the grounds, first, that Savery's Act did not cover the Newcomen engines they were building ('as much a different engine as a distill is from a windmill'); and secondly, the Proprietors were inequitable in their administration of the patent. His allegations indicate how potentially lucrative this licensing business was:

in insisting on exorbitant rents of £400 per annum of some, . . . in letting some engines without rents at all . . . and in taking considerations from others to grant exclusive covenants not to suffer engines to be erected within certain districts of the kingdom and particularly not within the City or suburbs of London or Westminster except at York Buildings.[125]

In 1722 Marten Triewald, the Swedish engineer, had secured a patent for 'a certain machine or engine which by the power of the *atmosphere* will effectually draw water out of all the mines and collieries at a small charge', and entered an agreement to build the engines and take quarter shares in the profits with three engine-builders (although only one engine appears to have been built under this patent). These disagreements may have damaged the Proprietors' business, for their dividends after 1723 consistently fell below the £30 predicted in 1721, except in 1728 (£40) and 1730 (£30). But at least the company made a profit, albeit a small one, until 1738, five years after the patent's expiry.[126]

Patentees licensing less distinctive, and perhaps less essential inventions to poorer clients, especially in a decentralized industry, had far greater problems to contend with. John Kay experienced great difficulty in exacting licence fees for the use of his flying shuttle from weavers in remote Pennine valleys. In court he was unable to prove that the subtle alterations to the shuttle's winding mechanism were his invention against their assertion that such designs were already common among them. This was a standard defence, and in such arcane matters a fairly unassailable one.[127] Richard Brooks, a Wiltshire clothier who invented a device for inserting the warp evenly into the loom, had to recognize that its potential users were too poor to pay him a viable royalty. He obtained the signatures of 148 Wiltshire masters and journeymen weavers to a proposal, printed in the *Gloucester Journal*, that people concerned for the good of the woollen industry might 'consider' how he could be reimbursed for making it generally available.[128] John Geddes and his partners in a bee-hive patent suffered similar problems. A Bridgwater barber–surgeon, John Howe, was recommended to them as a local agent, but Howe was unwilling to lay out ready cash 'because he is not sure the invention will take in the country'. The great market for the hives, he thought, was among the 'middle and meaner sort', who would probably be unwilling to pay ten shillings (50p) for a licensed bee colony, but might just afford 2s 6d (12.5p) for a licence and a leaflet describing how to implement the principle in their own hives. Otherwise, he thought, the patentee 'might serve the public and his own profit more' by selling high-quality hives to the rich.[129]

Licensing on reasonable terms might help defuse opposition to a patent. Sir James Lowther advised, when one of his mining engineers attempted to secure one, that they should try 'to bring in the other coal owners not to oppose it upon settling licences on moderate terms, without which it will be in vain to solicit a patent'.[130] But it was not easy to judge what the market would bear. It was Matthew Boulton's opinion that Arkwright had lost his patent by overreaching himself: the high cost of his licences had made the risks of clandestine use, and the expense of litigation and of 'by-pass' patents all worthwhile.[131]

In some cases inventors sold their patent rights to manufacturers for a lump sum and withdrew entirely from the risks of commercial production. This was the rational strategy of the professional inventor.[132] It was often perhaps the only course open to necessitous inventors in need of a quick return. Jabez Stephenson, a Bethnal Green weaver, sold his method of weaving patterned silks to his co-patentee, John Batchelor, who can probably be identified as the senior partner in the firm of Batchelor, Ham and Peregal.[133] The patent also served as a (limited) insurance for the manufacturer against his purchase being pirated. Many other buyers of inventions chose not to take out this insurance, seeking their protection in strict security measures instead. Chapman suggests this was the common course of early-eighteenth-century Nottinghamshire hosiers who built 'safe-box' factories.[134]

A patent was a wise precaution even when there was no transaction with partners, licensing or sale of the invention, if large capital costs were involved. Otherwise, competitors could reap the benefits while the inventor struggled to recoup his investment in experiment and development. William Champion of Bristol related how in 1738, after six years, 'having overcome the principal difficulties', he obtained a patent and proceeded to build the necessary plant to make spelter (metallic zinc). Champion invested £7,000 in plant and development; the patent was, by comparison, a small cost. He was ruined in the event, not by rival manufacturers, but by the importers whose trade he had taken: they dropped their prices and traded at a loss to undercut him.[135] Thomas Lombe was in a similar position. Parliament was told in 1732 of his problems in starting production, including 'that it was three years after he obtained the patent, before he could possibly finish the engine'.[136]

5.5 THE MANUFACTURING INVENTOR

Least likely, before the mid-century, to regard a patent as a good investment were those inventors who were already established manufacturers, whose invention related to their own manufacture, and who were able to implement it without external assistance, especially if they believed their chance of keeping it secret to be good. The case of John Wayt of Worcester illustrates the differing strategies of the manufacturer who could improve his product or cut his costs without the bother of a patent, and of the inventor who had to set up a manufacturing operation or to sell his invention in some way. Wayt had been making salt from brine for fourteen years, using a fuel-saving method he had discovered, when in 1726 the rising price of coal goaded local competitors into probing his secret. It was only at this juncture that Wayt sought a patent, being unwilling to share his discovery and thereby dissipate his commercial advantage without some compensation. 'Wayt refuses to communicate the secret to your petitioners by which they may receive great advantage' unless his rights in the invention were protected by patent: twelve local brine proprietors supported his application.[137] In similar vein, Samuel Crompton recorded how he had invented the spinning mule, 'being grieved at the bad yarn I had to weave', and when successful, 'I spun upon it for my own use both warp and weft'. Patenting seems never to have entered his head, until it was too late, when manufacturers had taken his idea without payment. James Watt first invented the copying press for his own use, but Boulton insisted on its commercial potential and prompted Watt to patent it. Josiah Wedgwood was offered a new method of decorating his pottery in 1771, but 'I find that Mr Burdett does not mean to discover his art to us nor therefore to be paid by way of premium . . . he means to make the most of his discovery by working at it himself'.[138] Henry Hindley, the York clockmaker, never sought a patent for his many inventions. He incorporated them in his clocks and instruments, taking credit for the superb workmanship they helped him to achieve. He delighted in idiosyncracy: no two of his clocks were the same.[139] It may be imagined that such instances represent just the tip of an iceberg of unpatented inventions made by manufacturers and tradesmen.

The 'foreman–inventor' was also a type that was unlikely to seek a patent. In 1750 William Branwell, the overseer of Viscount Lonsdale's linen 'factory', remedied its chronic shortage of yarn when he modified the spinning wheels, so that 'they draw two threads at once, and on it they can spin full as much more as on the common wheel'. Branwell had overcome a specific problem for his employer; his sights were set on making a particular enterprise profitable, not on developing an invention commercially.[140] Not far away, the productivity and safety of Sir James Lowther's collieries were being improved by his mine steward, Carlisle Spedding. He invented the best, if not completely successful, answer to underground explosions before the Davy lamp – the 'steel mill' or 'flint and steel', which produced a safer light than candles. It could have been an ideal subject for a patent: it was distinctively novel with a potentially large market. But Spedding's interest was firmly rooted in Lowther's collieries – and he may have been unwilling to profit personally by a safety device.[141] Neither man sought a patent. Similarly, the winnowing machine that by the 1790s was said to be used by every husbandman and made by every country carpenter had been introduced from Holland nearly a century before by James Meikle. He had been bound by his employer, 'not to profit any more by this mill, nor communicate the arts he had learned to any other'.[142]

The feasibility of maintaining secrecy and hence exclusivity was a major determinant in deciding whether to patent. The independent manufacturing inventor was often in a good position to keep his methods secret. This was the course of several famous inventors and, one supposes, of scores of lesser known ones who succeeded to varying degrees in concealing their secrets from industrial spies. The name of Benjamin Huntsman, for example, became almost a byword for it: according to Smiles, Huntsman pledged his workmen to 'inviolable secrecy', strangers were excluded from the works and steel was smelted by the new crucible process only at night.[143] His contemporary in Sheffield, Thomas Bolsover, concealed for about a decade after 1742 his unpatented method of making 'Sheffield plate', from which he produced buttons.[144] John Sadler, a Liverpool printer, kept his transfer printing for pottery secret rather than patent it.[145] One of the most systematically kept industrial secrets was Bessemer's for bronze powder, for thirty-five years in the early nineteenth century, after he had realized, 'it would be impossible for us to maintain this price if all the details of my system were shown and described in a patent blue-book, which anyone could buy for sixpence'.[146]

For most of the eighteenth century patents inhabited the frontier regions of the economy. They became desirable when an invention had to be sold, or when an entrepreneur was breaking into a new sphere of manufacture. Most early patentees were in some way outsiders. Thus William Champion and Thomas Lombe were both merchants. William Sherwin, whose calico-printing factory was employing at least 200 workers in 1696, was originally an engraver. Richard Newsham was a pearl-button maker when he first started producing fire engines, John Baskerville a writing master and monumental mason before he broke into the japanning trade.[147] The examples could be multiplied, not least by the numbers of courtiers and immigrants possessing patents in the seventeenth century. In a sense, the patent was the outsider's charter, the passport permitting entry and offering a modicum of protection, or the letter of introduction (from the crown) establishing the bearer's credentials. It offered most to the newcomer to manufacturing; to the speculator or gentleman with a good idea he wished to exploit; to the inventor who needed to attract partners and yet prevent them from stealing his invention, or to sell it to a manufacturer; to the guildsman whose novel technique was not appreciated by his peers; and to the established manufacturer who sought greater profit from extending his invention to others. These were the inventors for whom secrecy was impossible or insufficient. In contemporary terms they were mostly 'projectors'.[148]

As the century progressed, however, they were joined and overwhelmed by established artisans and manufacturers who felt under pressure to secure themselves against their competitors. Both the positive feedback of the patent system and the changing structure of industry, as it became more centralized and more hierarchic in organization, imposed this pressure. The ranks of insiders were also swollen by escalating numbers of engine-makers, mill-wrights and other specialist producers of capital goods.[149] The last three or four decades of the eighteenth century, before the professional inventor arrived in force, were an interval when the insider had more to gain from a patent than an outsider.

Yet a patent was a better investment in some enterprises than in others, and the advantages, rather than the problems of enforcement, danced before the eyes of many who consequently invested £70 or more unwisely. Patents were not open to accurate, counterfactual calculations; their benefits were not always those conventionally expected of them, nor even perhaps those their purchasers envisaged. Failure to stifle imitation might have been amply compensated by a gain in prestige or an edge in bargaining power with creditors, partners or clients. It is clear, however, that the pressure to patent was greater in some crafts and industries than in others, and indeed in some parts of the country more than in others. The development of the patent system cannot be adequately explained nor the growth in the number of registered patents understood without reference to those disparities.

6

INVENTION OUTSIDE THE PATENT SYSTEM

There is nothing novel in claiming that there was inventive activity outside the purview of the patent system. I shall argue here, however, that omission was not random: it was far more likely to occur in some industries than in others, and in certain sectors within an industry. There are major disparities between the economic importance of most industries and their level of representation in the patent records. Looking at the period from 1750 to 1800, one finds that only textiles (including hosiery and lace) and metalworking (including plating and gunmaking) – each with approximately 14 per cent of total patents – defy this pattern and indicate their prominent place in the economy.[1] Agriculture, still in 1800 the employer of over a third of the workforce, took under 4 per cent of patents. The three largest industrial employers after textiles (the leather, building, and food and drink trades) accounted for 4 per cent each; the heavy industries (mining and metallurgy) for less than 4 per cent together. Nine per cent of patents were in transport, but two-thirds of them related to road transport (overwhelmingly, carriages and coaches for passengers), only a third to the shipping and canal traffic whose carriage of freight was of greater industrial importance. Engine-making, which was crucial to industrialization, accounted for 11 per cent; this was disproportionately large, however, in regard to its direct economic importance as either an employer of labour or a generator of wealth.[2] Out of all proportion to their economic significance were proprietary medicines and 'surgical aids' (6 per cent), clocks, watches and scientific instruments (5 per cent), and musical instruments (2 per cent).

Arguably, the patent records might accurately reflect the extent of inventive activity within these different industries which, of course, bears no necessary connection to their size. There are a number of reasons to doubt this. The structure of some industries was incompatible with the effective exploitation of a patent. In some, the key to technical change lay less in patentable hardware than in the reallocation of resources, the more careful or systematic management of materials, the application of ingenuity and experience to novel problems, or the acquisition of a knack communicable only by direct demonstration. Such innovations were not easily packaged into patentable form, or presented unassailable problems of enforcement that made a patent a poor investment. A patent was generally easier to enforce and more lucrative in the more centralized, highly capitalized and geo-graphically concentrated sectors of industry. In some industries there was a hostile ethos, and in others government controls, that militated against patenting. These influences changed, in some cases considerably, over this period, a factor in the increasing propensity to patent that I shall return to in chapter 8.

6.1 THE PRIMARY SECTOR: AGRICULTURE AND MINING

The manifestation of agriculture in the patent records before 1780 was very far from commensurate with either its position as the largest sector of the pre-industrial economy, or the widespread innovations in farming that enabled England to feed its growing population and even to become a major exporter of grain during the first half of the eighteenth century. Joan Thirsk comments that 'the pace of . . . [innovation] was probably as rapid in the years 1640 to 1750 as at any time before or since'.[3] Innovation consisted chiefly in new rotations of crops, the management of pastures, selective breeding and the keeping of more livestock. It was rarely amenable to patenting. The cultivation of a few 'new' industrial crops was patented in the Restoration, but the patentees seem to have operated on a small scale, not enforcing their patents on others.[4] Three patents, all after 1721, were for fertilizers, and there was one for swine-feed. Again it is hard to envisage how the patentees expected to exploit them, at a time when such substances were produced on the farm, not commercially supplied. Indeed one patentee, Thomas Liveings, finding no profit in his patent, attempted to commute it for a parliamentary reward, dressing his offer in the guise of philanthropy.[5]

Jethro Tull, rather than attempt to patent his new farming methods, secured copyright in his exposition of them, *The horse-hoing husbandry*; this accorded him the sole printing and publishing rights to the tract for fourteen years.[6] Basic to Tull's system was his belief in the nutrient properties of the air, and the technique it required was hoeing, which necessitated the accurate sowing of seeds in rows (it also economized on seeds). The famous hardware – the seed drill and the horse-hoe – was subsidiary. As Tull explained, he invented the drill to overcome the obstinacy of labourers who did not appreciate the point of even sowing.[7] It was open to him to patent the implements, but there were alternative ones in existence that others could have used equally well. Charles Baker, a Bristol seedsman, used the device of copyright in a limited edition, which he sold at a guinea per copy, to market his 'method to prevent the smut in wheat' in 1797; he also offered a thirty guineas reward for information on anyone using it without prior purchase of the tract.[8]

Agricultural implements were generally more suitable for patenting than were farming techniques. Yet, very few were patented before the 1780s: two ploughs and three pieces of barn machinery (a threshing and winnowing machine, a machine to clean clover seed and a hop-bagging machine). The Rotherham plough was extensively imitated, and the patent eventually revoked on the grounds that it was only an improvement.[9] It had, however, proved quite lucrative. The seed-cleaning engine, a small symbol of the great innovations in crop rotations, nitrogen-fixing crops and sown pastures, caused local outrage. Its inventor, Richard Haines, probably tried to exploit the patent by licensing, but its use does not seem to have spread outside his part of Sussex.[10] Nor were the others any more successful or influential.[11] Meanwhile, there was almost a craze for devising new seed-drills, ploughs and other implements, with varying degrees of success, but they only began to appear in the patent rolls after 1780.[12] Many other inventors, from Worlidge in the 1670s to Small and Forbes in the 1780s, advertised their agricultural implements in books of husbandry advice, without benefit of either patent or copyright.[13]

To a certain extent the appearance of patents for agricultural implements represented a real upsurge in their invention. The recovery of grain prices after 1750 encouraged a new interest in traditional (corn and grass) farming, and enclosure together with the consolidation of farms in fewer hands made investment in capital equipment more cost-effective. Growing labour shortages in lowland Scotland and the north of England provided a further incentive.[14] Neither should the efforts of the Society of Arts and its counterparts in Scotland, Ireland, and the provinces be overlooked: the offer of premiums for improved ploughs, seed-drills and other devices stimulated invention.[15] And when the premium offered for a threshing machine failed to produce acceptable results, William Winlaw, a London engine-maker, was approached by 'several noblemen and gentlemen his employers' to construct one, which he subsequently patented.[16]

This new demand for improved and specialized implements promoted a fundamental change in their production that, in its turn, stimulated patenting. Agriculture was one of the earliest industries to develop a specialized capital-goods sector. Implements had been produced by the local blacksmith, wheelwright, or carpenter to the farmer's specifications. The design usually replicated that traditional in the region or it might incorporate some new feature of the farmer's or craftsman's own invention. Innovation would normally begin and end there; sometimes other local farmers might be persuaded to follow the pioneer's lead. The second half of the eighteenth century, however, saw the appearance of several specialist firms of agricultural implement-makers (often evolving from blacksmiths or ironfounders): James Small in Berwickshire in the 1760s, James Sharp in London in the 1770s, Garrett's and Ransome's in Suffolk in the 1770s and 80s respectively.[17] This gave innovation an institutionalized push: such firms expected to sell their wares on a regional, even national scale; they offered an ever-widening range of specialized implements (with standardized replacement parts); and they competed for customers not only by price but also by improved quality and technical novelty. For these specialists patents provided a protection, as well as an advertisement, of their competitive edge.[18] Their existence also offered independent inventors a production and marketing outlet on a scale that warranted a patent. Garrett's, for example, manufactured Ball's patented threshing machine and Joseph Cornforth, a Staffordshire machine-maker, the drills of a Yorkshire patentee.[19] When Robert Ransome, then a Norwich ironfounder, patented plough-shares in 1785, he advertised them as available at all ironmongers in Norwich and some fifty outlets throughout East Anglia. The Reverend James Cooke, whose drill was generally acknowledged the best in its time, seems to have moved from Lancashire to London, given up the cloth, and set up in business making and selling his three patented devices.[20]

Even in the late eighteenth century, however, patenting was by no means automatic. William Marshall told of an unpatented plough invented by a Warwickshire wheelwright, named Bush, around 1770: by 1786 it was immensely successful and Bush was still the leading maker, yet all the principal ploughwrights of the region were making it too.[21] Bush probably did no worse financially than Andrew Meikle who was unable to enforce his 1788 patent for the threshing machine.[22] Some, like James Small, who published the methods of plough construction which had cost him extensive experimentation, seem still to have been inspired by an ethic of open communication.[23] Henry Baldwin of Suffolk was dissuaded from patenting his improvements to Cooke's seed-drill by one of Arthur Young's correspondents, 'as he thought that any monopoly of useful machines must be of general disservice to the community, and that it might possibly turn the attention of a good farmer from a good farm'.[24] The Society of Arts was also still providing an alternative focus for amateurs.[25] Nonetheless, there were 51 patents for agricultural implements in the 1780s and 90s. The largest categories were for seed-drills (11), ploughs (11) and threshing machines (9). It shows a marked rise over the total of 13 such patents in the preceding three decades and 4 in the ninety years before 1750.

Mining, another primary industry, and one whose output was expanding rapidly, was even less well represented in the patent records. It was again too diffuse and too empirical an enterprise to offer much scope for patenting.

The arts necessary to mining are many, and every mine almost requires a peculiar management: mining therefore must be learned by practice, by experience, and masters; not from books, the rules of which, though ever so just, must be frequently suspended, altered, qualified, and superseded, according as the various circumstances require.[26]

The extraction of coal and ores received little mention: no patent was sought for rock-boring tools or blasting techniques before 1760, and there were only 3 before 1800. Ventilation and 'fire-damps', the explosions which claimed many miners' lives, were pressing problems, repeatedly investigated by the Royal Society.[27] Three patents and 2 failed applications over this whole period is a weak reflection of contemporary concern. Meanwhile, new techniques were allowing miners to work more efficiently, and deeper and further from the point of distribution. 'Longwall' working increased productivity; it spread through many of the Midland, Lancashire, and Scottish collieries in the course of the eighteenth century.[28] Gunpowder began to be used for sinking shafts, if not for extraction, and more effective means of lining the shaft were devised. Overground and underground wagonways were constructed to ease the problems of transportation.[29] Coalviewers (mining engineers) devised techniques to combat the ventilation problem: Carlisle Spedding, for example, as well as inventing his 'steel mill', sank shafts and introduced partitions to promote the flow of air and pipes to draw off the gases. These were adopted in the north-east coalfields by around 1760.[30]

Provision of machinery to raise coal and ores offered more promising material for patents, and indeed was the subject of 7 by 1750. Such inventions were strictly mechanical, visible above ground and auxiliary to the miner's craft. The winding engine invented by Michael Menzies, an Edinburgh lawyer, spread quickly through the coalfields.[31] A further 14 patents for winding followed between 1763 and 1799, and mines were also potential beneficiaries of patentees' attention to ropemaking in the 1790s (16 patents, including 6 from Northumberland and Durham). All but 2 of the post-1750 winding patentees lived in mining areas, and 9 of them were engine-makers, millwrights, or coalviewers. John Curr, while employed as viewer at the Duke of Norfolk's collieries near Sheffield, obtained 3 patents for winding and ropes, the royalties from which provided him with an independent income. Unlike Spedding, his horizons stretched beyond his employer's mines: he established a foundry to make the cast-iron rails and parts of his new winding engine.[32]

The main representation of both agriculture and mining in the patent records before the last quarter of the eighteenth century is by water-pumping devices. These shared the patentable characteristics of winding machinery. Adequate drainage, the most pressing obstacle to the expansion of mining, attracted many inventors. In the period 1660–1750, 118 patents and extant applications covered water-raising devices or power sources that claimed water-raising as their main function. Twenty-five of them cited mines-drainage as their exclusive or principal application and a further 40 mentioned it as one of several functions. The need for drainage engines in agriculture, though great, was less immediate: 5 applications cited land drainage exclusively, and a further 27 inclusively; 8 mentioned irrigation. Steam engines were developed with a particular view to mines drainage, and 5 out of the 7 patentees who succeeded Savery before 1750 cited it as a major application of their designs. There were a further 9 before 1800, plus 7 for specifically mining pumps and 2 for windmill-driven systems (from coal-impoverished Devon and Cornwall). This corroborates what is known of the actual installation of Newcomen and other engines, and is hardly surprising when one considers both their cost-effectiveness and the scale of operation in mines in relation to other pump-using operations. The Newcomen engine represented 'the nearest approach to a technical revolution in the coal industry'. The Watt engine spread slowly in the coalfields, however, its fuel economy being of small interest to coalowners.[33]

6.2 THE TEXTILE INDUSTRIES

Certain parallels can be found between these primary industries and the largest manufacturing industry, textiles. One was geographical diffusion: for so long as it was domestically organized, the textile industry produced few patents relative to its importance. A second was the late appearance of its hardware in the patent rolls, and a third, the stimulus given to its patenting by the growth of a specialized capital-goods industry making textile machinery. A fairly high number of patents suggests a picture of innovation more nearly commensurate with its size, but this conceals an imbalance. Before the second quarter of the eighteenth century, its patents were overwhelmingly concerned with the finishing, rather than the manufacturing processes, and with the newer sectors, silk and cotton; alternatively, they covered new mixtures of fibres and types of cloth (many of them issued to Dutch and Huguenot immigrants). Patents covering new machinery and implements for carding, spinning and weaving appeared more frequently after 1720, but were still sporadic and rarely successful before 1770.[34] The difficulties experienced by Kay, Brooks, and later Hargreaves in exploiting their patents are particularly pertinent.[35] For, the domestic organization of much of the textile industry was not conducive to innovation, far less to patenting. The system itself had been a major cost-reducing innovation, and there was no incentive for employers to invest in technical change so long as the supply of labour was sufficient and cheap.[36] Moreover, a patent was hard to enforce where manufacture was diffused over a wide area, often in isolated cottages.

Innovations were made in domestic manufacturing either wholesale, through the immigration of protestant refugees who imported new fabric mixtures or superior methods, or by small changes in technique or tools, cheap and simple enough for the workers themselves to implement. Illustrative of the former were the innovations of the Dutch who settled in north Wiltshire in the 1670s: they were credited with improving fine woollen-cloth production, mainly by using better cards and methods of dressing, which also reduced the cost by an estimated 40 per cent. John Aubrey, describing Wiltshire in 1685, reported that, 'the art of spinning is so much improved within these last forty years that one pound of wool makes twice as much cloth (as to extent) as it did before the civil wars'.[37] An example of the latter type, if we may believe the weavers who challenged Kay's patent, was the small improvements to the shuttle that facilitated winding.[38] Not all the inventions even in the finishing processes were patented. Wadsworth and Mann consider, for example, that the most important development in finishing was the hot calender. It was introduced before 1750, every type of woollen cloth underwent its own special process and the variations in the calender were 'numerous'. Only 3 were patented – between 1788 and 1790.[39]

Where a sector or a process was centralized, it tended to possess more patents. Thus the silk industry and the finishing processes in all sectors were well represented in the patent records before 1770. Not only were they more centralized, they were also more subject directly to the dictates of fashion, requiring new dyes, finishes and patterns.[40] Yet, the rapid growth in the patenting of textile machinery in the final quarter of the eighteenth century was not simply a reflection of increased inventive activity by manufacturers driving to profit from the massive new demand for cheap cloth. It was also a product of the increased centralization of textile production and the emergence of a specialized textile machine-making industry.[41] Arkwright's water-frame was developed to use a centralized power source in the context of factory production: distinctive and factory-based, it was an ideal subject for patenting. A workman's complaint 'that the jennys are in the hands of the poor, and the patent machines are generally in the hands of the rich'[42] goes a long way to explain the difference between the fortunes of Hargreaves and Arkwright, their contemporary patented inventions orientated to the domestic system and the factory respectively. The control that Arkwright attempted to exert over the spinning and preparatory-process sectors of the cotton industry through his two patents not only drove other manufacturers to challenge the patents at law but also prompted a burst of patenting by those who attempted to bypass them.[43] Inventors could approach a clientèle among cotton spinners and machine-makers that had been sensitized to the value of (and the risks of not) patenting by their experiences with Arkwright.

6.3 ENGINEERING AND MACHINE-TOOL MAKING

Another rapidly progressing sphere of technical achievement was civil engineering, but there is little trace of it in the patent rolls.[44] On the one hand, this should not be surprising since an accumulation of engineering knowledge is distinct from inventive activity, and is not patentable; on the other, it is worth remarking since so much of what we conceptualize as 'the industrial revolution', especially in the sphere of transport, was the product of advances in engineering. A hint of activity is given again by patented pumping devices, employed in schemes for urban water supplies and to drain lands, by dredging equipment for clearing rivers, harbours and later canals,[45] and by the spate of patents in the 1790s, at the height of the 'canal mania', which addressed the problems generated by the ambitious schemes of canal engineers.[46] But very few of these patents were obtained by civil engineers, nor do

they bear adequate testimony to the novel feats of engineering being performed by members of the emergent profession, in constructing docks,
bridges, and canal or river improvements. Fundamental to this latter success
was the body of knowledge about the behaviour of construction materials
and of water that was gradually accumulated through both on-the-job
experience, and the experimental and theoretical investigations of men like
John Smeaton and John Rennie.[47]

But there were further reasons for the lack of patents in this sphere. Even
when, in the course of their work, many engineers devised machinery to solve
particular problems, they generally chose not to patent it. Charles Labeyle,
for instance, did not patent the *caissons* he used in constructing the piers of
Westminster Bridge nor the machine he invented to cut off the wooden piles
underwater.[48] Yet a pile-driver employed in the same undertaking and
invented by James Valoué, was patented.[49] It is significant that the patentees, Valoué and Pantin, described themselves as watchmaker and goldsmith
respectively: they were outsiders, who needed to sell the machine in order to
benefit from it. Professional engineers tended to patent only their 'side-lines'.
George Sorocold patented a whip-twisting machine and mechanical saw, but
his achievements in constructing urban water supplies and his millwrighting
at Crotchet's and Lombe's mills in Derby left no trace in the patent rolls.[50]
This tendency continued throughout the eighteenth century and into the
nineteenth. Of the great canal, bridge and dock engineers, Brindley took one
patent, for a steam engine, in 1758, before his civil engineering career began;
Smeaton one, for an oil-extracting machine, in 1787, when his professional
career was closing, and Rennie none at all – not even for his celebrated
dredging machine – yet all were renowned for their inventions over a wide
range of mechanical fields.[51]

The reasons why these early engineers shunned the patent system can only
be a matter for speculation. Engineering reputations were made by the
successful solution of novel problems of construction, not by the monopolization of particular machines. The contrasting approaches of mechanical and
civil engineers to secrecy and patenting appear in the respective views of
James Watt and John Rennie. Watt was horrified by Rennie's openness when
constructing the Albion Mills, but Rennie was eager to show off his
millwrighting abilities, and the advertisement, far from ruining him as Watt
predicted, established his reputation and led to a flood of commissions.
Although he set up a machine-making establishment, Rennie operated
primarily as a consultant.[52] Again, J. T. Desaguliers had implied that skilled
and reputable engineers were known by their achievements, while anyone
employing a cut-price 'man of practice', a plumber or millwright 'set up for
engineers' (with or without a patent), was making a false economy: 'thus
many people employ the apothecary to save the charge of the physician'.[53]
Patenting was perhaps even ruled out by an embryonic professional ethos
which enjoined the sharing and publication of experience, such as that which

Nasmyth so much admired in the nineteenth century.[54] There are many indications of mutual respect and consultation between members of the first rank of civil engineers. According to John Phillips, Brindley 'having no sinister ends to gratify, no contractual notions or ideas, nor jealousy of rivals, he concealed not his methods of proceeding, nor asked or solicited patents for the sole use of machines which he invented and exposed to public view'.[55]

Another major 'blind spot' for patenting was machine-tool making. Certainly, as an industry, machine-tool making was very much in its infancy in the late eighteenth century, but its pioneers long ignored the patent system, even though they took out patents for inventions in other fields.[56] Joseph Bramah, for example, took out eighteen patents for mostly mechanical devices between 1778 and 1814. One of these, in 1784, was for his justly famous lock, but manufacture of the locks foundered until he and his then employee, Henry Maudslay, had devised tools for 'their more accurate and speedy manufacture', which were never patented.[57] The engineer John Farey recorded that,

the secret workshops . . . contained several curious machines for forming parts of the locks, with a systematic perfection of workmanship, which was at that time unknown in similar mechanical arts . . . Mr Bramah attributed the success of his locks to the use of these machines, the invention of which had cost him more study than that of the locks.[58]

As H. W. Dickinson comments, 'the importance of these tools in the history of repetition manufacture can hardly be overestimated. If we compare the drawing in the specification with the lock as actually marketed, we can see that it has been redesigned to suit methods of manufacture'.[59]

A handful of eighteenth-century patents covered machine tools, but focused on the end product made with them. In 1760 Job and William Wyatt patented 'a certain method of cutting screws of iron commonly called woodscrews in a better manner than has been hitherto practised'. The specification suggests they had 'two types of special purpose lathe of very advanced design' that produced finished screws from forged blades in three operations. But the Wyatts' concern was with manufacturing screws, not lathes.[60] Two years later, Elizabeth Taylor of Southampton, recently widowed, patented the 'set of engines, tools, instruments and other apparatus for the making of [ships'] blocks, sheavers and pins', invented by her son and late husband (both called Walter Taylor). It was the blocks in which the Navy was interested and for the supply of which the Taylors subsequently held the contract until the end of the century, when Marc Isambard Brunel's machinery eclipsed theirs.[61] John Wilkinson, the ironmaster, was in a similar position with the machine he invented to bore cannons.[62]

Samuel Bentham specifically patented a planing machine in 1791 and a variety of machine tools in 1793, but this was exceptional and is indicative of Bentham's position on the periphery of the trade.[63] Maudslay obtained six patents from 1805 to 1824, but none of these was for the machine tools that established his reputation for precision workmanship.[64] Even his contemporary, Matthew Murray of Leeds, who manufactured machine tools for sale, did not include any among his six patents. One of his old employees told of a planing machine that Murray invented to manufacture the D-slide valve introduced into his (patented) steam-engine designs:

The machine was not patented, and like many inventions in those days, it was kept as much a secret as possible, being locked up in a small room by itself, to which the ordinary workman could not obtain access.[65]

Joseph Clement, James Fox, James Nasmyth and Richard Roberts (until 1847) followed the same policy. Nasmyth listed over thirty 'more prominent' inventions he had made between 1825 and 1862: the unpatented ones stand out as being either inventions to improve workers' safety which, on principle, he communicated as widely as possible, or machine tools.[66] This pattern was broken only by Joseph Whitworth whose thirteen patents between 1834 and 1849 included six for screw-cutting, boring, and turning machines. The difference in patenting practice may well lie in the structural difference between Whitworth's and his predecessors' firms. While the latter had prided themselves on flexible, general engineering, Whitworth 'specialised in the production of engineering machine tools to an extent that was quite unprecedented'.[67]

The omission of machine tools demonstrates that patenting remained a highly selective activity, even in the nineteenth century. Why this technically vital area was largely absent from the patent rolls is nowhere stated. It may have been the patent system's institutionalized prejudice that favoured end products and periodically doubted the patentability of manufacturing methods;[68] or perhaps that to their makers these lathes, planes, cutting and boring machines of unprecedented sophistication and accuracy were just (in Rolt's phrase) 'tools for the job' – means of achieving precision and fine workmanship in the finished product.[69] Alternatively, secrecy may have been their goal. As Whitworth's example suggests, it was only when machine-tool making became a capital-goods sector in its own right that patents for machine tools began to appear in strength.

6.4 THE 'CHEMICAL' INDUSTRIES

In manufacturing industries it was rational for those in possession of mechanical and chemical inventions to adopt respectively different patenting strategies. It was even suggested, in 1829, that there should be different regulations for patenting in the two categories.[70] For, the chances of keeping a chemical process secret were high, and higher still where it consisted in a 'knack' or the addition of some concealable, rather than gross, ingredients; ancient, empirical processes, such as brewing, were more immune to espionage than new, 'science-based' ones, like synthetic-alkali production.[71] Analytical chemistry was a rudimentary science: a qualitative analysis might reveal the presence of several ingredients, but one could not be sure of knowing them all, and their proportions were unascertainable. Dr James's fever powder, patented in 1747, was still providing chemists with an analytical brain-teaser in the early nineteenth century. White-lead manufacturers were long baffled as to why, of two apparently identical pots in their 'stack', one might produce good flakes of white lead, the other poor flakes or none at all.[72] Chemical processes were usually secure without patent protection. It was comparatively easy, however, to discover the construction of a machine or tool: if a visual inspection proved insufficient, a rival might be able to obtain it and take it apart. The inventor who patented and clearly specified his machine thereby staked his claim to priority.[73]

This bias is reflected in the patent records. Approximately 20 per cent of patents between 1660 and 1800 related to the 'chemical' industries – dyeing, bleaching, brewing and distilling, metallurgy, for example – but at least half of these covered a mechanical aspect, such as grinding machinery, furnaces, vats, or stills. Recipes or processes were chiefly, though not exclusively, patented by those with a heterodox use for them: proprietary medicines and oil-cements, for example, where proportions could be varied and otiose ingredients added to evade previous patents.[74] Richard Champion's parliamentary extension of Cookworthy's china-clay patent in 1775 proved a pyrrhic victory. Josiah Wedgwood had secured an amendment that allowed anyone to use the Cornish materials except in the precise combination and proportions stipulated in the specification that Champion was required to lodge. This effectively threw open the field.[75] Novel raw materials, such as dye plants, 'cement-stone', or china clay, were distinctive enough to patent for orthodox ends. Until, however, chemical reactions involving a number of ingredients could be described accurately, the only orthodox purpose for a patent covering a chemical process was defensive, and such patents tended to appear in multiples – perhaps a panic reaction.

The empirical nature of many inventions in the chemical sphere made them unsuitable for patenting. Success might hinge on the chemical properties of particular raw materials – the sulphur content of the coal or the phosphorus of the iron used in smelting, or the darkness of the malt in brewing, for instance. The manufacturer, dependent on impure materials and often lacking accurate gauges of temperature or density, relied on skills acquired through years of experience to determine the proportions and timing of his processes; he advanced by cautious empiricism. In metallurgy, for instance, great improvements in productivity might be achieved simply by altering the burdening of the furnace, by increasing the supply of water to the blast furnace's bellows, by adjusting the design of the furnace, or by recognizing from the colour of the flame exactly when to run the molten iron from the puddling furnace.[76] And in the late-eighteenth-century dyeing industry, while there were no spectacular inventions, extensive analysis and experimentation had produced a greater understanding and thereby regularization of processes.[77] On such things might rest the financial viability of an enterprise or the reputation of a manufacturer's product. He might seek a patent if his purpose were to raise capital or impress and stave off creditors,[78] but it was hardly the sort of information that rivals would be prepared to buy. Where an improvement in technique was more of a 'knack' than an invention, it was not only cheaper but also more effective to steal a workman who understood it. This reduced correspondingly the potential value of a patent, except as a purely defensive measure.[79] Josiah Wedgwood, offered a new manner of engraving, finally decided against buying it from the inventor, since 'I apprehend it wo[ul]d be the same thing to our selling the secret of throwing, turning, or handling, which after all the instructions we could give the purchaser it wo[ul]d require several years actual practice before he could do anything to the purpose'.[80]

Brewing is the industry that perhaps best demonstrates how major technical advances were made outside the cognizance of the patent system. It was a large, if localized, industry with a steady market. Where marketing conditions were right, which was in large cities, particularly London, 'a brewery became potentially more suited for large-scale production than most other contemporary manufacturing concerns'.[81] The crucial event that allowed this potential to be realized was the invention of 'porter', a dark beer which came rapidly into favour with London drinkers. It differed from other beers in using malt dried more 'high', indeed slightly scorched on the kiln. Hertfordshire was already famous for its brown malts, and porter probably owed its origin to a Hertfordshire maltster's negligence. It was first brewed in 1722 by Ralph Harwood, a partner in the Bell Brewhouse at Shoreditch, but he was not among those who best exploited its possibilities. While the technique of brewing porter remained fundamentally the same as for other beers, adjustments were gradually made that both improved its quality and allowed a more economical production. Brewers discovered that porter improved markedly if matured for a year or more: its capacity for bulk storage led after 1740 to the replacement of casks by large underground vats, and later whole cellars, that proved additionally beneficial in reducing the threat of infection and aeration. Higher drying permitted the use of poorer quality, cheaper malted grains, and since porter could withstand higher temperatures in the brewing, it was both more susceptible to large-scale production and to a longer brewing season. Brewers with sufficient capital took their opportunities. While most competent porter brewers prospered, a small minority that included Ralph Thrale, Benjamin Truman and Samuel Whitbread made fortunes out of it. The adoption of thermometers and 'saccharometers' (one or two of which were patented), from the mid-eighteenth century, permitted greater regularity of production and considerable capital savings.

Patents addressed to brewing were certainly not lacking, but before the 1780s they were scarce in relation to the size of the industry, and were rarely sought either by members of the trade or for the actual brewing process itself. Centralization, concentration and capitalization were insufficient to promote patenting. Commercial brewing was a hard trade to enter: apprentice-ships were few and carried a high premium, a considerable capital was required. The trade regulated itself through these constraints and by the absence of price competition, branding or aggressive advertisement. Compe-tition lay in quality, and that rested on careful buying of ingredients and the minutiae of manufacturing, secrets of success which owners and manufactur-ers kept closely to themselves.[82] Patentees looked to the provision of capital equipment – boiling vats to brewers, kilns and malting floors to maltsters. They included a watchmaker, a chemist, a doctor and several 'esquires'. Licensing and freelance construction were their chosen methods of oper-ation.[83] It was to the new and rapidly growing manufacture of spirits that patentees more in the 'projecting' mould turned. French brandy was an import ripe for substitution, and several patents were issued for the produc-tion of spirits from various soft fruits. None of them, however, seems to have hit on gin before the late 1750s. Nor indeed did the number (6, 1660–1750) or type of these distilling patents reflect the growth of the malt-distilling trade. It was said in 1747 that 'the distillery has gained ground prodigiously within half a century . . . malt-distillery . . . vies with the brewery for return of money and profit, for most of them are very large concerns indeed'.[84]

There was, however, a marked surge in patents of direct relevance to brewing and distilling from the late 1780s; 25 patents were registered in the period 1787–98, 17 of them in the four years 1795–8. Patentees concentrated on two important, mechanical developments: 'attemperation' and the mechanization of mashing, both embodied in new capital equipment. The former, first patented in 1790 by John Long, consisted in the regulation of temperatures in the mashing and fermentation tuns by the circulation of water through copper coils. It permitted an extension of brewing through the summer months and promised to reduce losses from infection. Steeply rising barley prices and fuel costs probably made brewers and distillers more receptive to such novelties. The mashing machine, first patented in 1787 by John Walker, was a major labour-saving device. Its invention seems to have been a spin-off from the installation of rotary steam engines in the mid-1780s; brewers and distillers sought the widest possible, and thereby most economi-cal, employment of their new investment. Rising production costs in general, and labour costs in particular, also increased their attraction. Patentees were found in the ranks of the trade itself, as well as among producers of capital equipment such as millwrights, engine-makers and platers.[85] In this respect brewing caught up with the general trend.

In the salt and sugar industries, the patent records give a fuller picture of the course and extent of technical change. This was because innovation, throughout the period, consisted chiefly in the introduction of improved mechanical devices or equipment – for which a patent was more appropriate. In saltmaking the substitution of iron pans for lead ones and their steadily increased size helped boost productivity.[86] Patentees repeatedly promised to save fuel by new pans and novel ways of arranging them, although, according to William Brownrigg, 'several patents have been obtained . . . but the salt boilers have found their old methods the most convenient'.[87] It was also the case in the sugar industry, where rollers to crush the cane, and coppers and stoves to boil it were patented. There was a spate of patents for sugar mills in the early 1770s, and a trickle at other times. Five of the 6 patents for sugar mills between 1770 and 1776 were obtained by one-time residents of Jamaica, Tobago and Grenada. Their overriding interest, according to their petitions, was in increased reliability and speed of operation, both vital in the industry's peculiar circumstances. Indeed, these islands witnessed an unprecedented boom in their sugar output in 1774–5.[88] The patents may reflect a burst of interest in efficiency, consequent upon attempts to introduce steam power to cane crushing in the 1760s, or they may have been a defensive reaction to the Jamaican Assembly's grant to John Stewart, in 1770, of the sole right to erect steam-powered mills there.[89] Here, as in saltmaking, large capitals were involved and plants were centralized. In both industries, unlike brewing, however, the processes involved were not arcane, nor was competition defused by 'gentleman's agreements' among members of the trade.

The pottery industry, despite the evidence of very few patents, grew rapidly until about 1720 with considerable, if gradual, technical change. In the following two decades growth was confined to the new sector, stoneware (for which Dwight had secured patents in the late seventeenth century). The upturn of the industry in the 1740s was again owing to the rise of new sectors, fine earthenware and porcelain.[90] There were 'no fundamental discontinuities in the ways that pottery was made', yet in these new sectors technical change persisted, with the gradual introduction of improved tools and techniques that allowed refinement of the wares and differentiation into new designs.[91] Lorna Weatherill's research into the probate inventories of north Staffordshire potters has revealed that there was far more change in their equipment before 1760 than had previously been imagined.[92] Casting and pressing in moulds, also developed at this time, allowed a greater range of shapes. It was a major stride towards mass production, as was Sadler and Green's method of transfer printing, invented in the mid-1750s.[93] The industry's domestic organization and its empirical procedures both militated against patenting.[94] Even more important was the potter's dependence for success on artistic design and execution. The industry's products were heterogeneous and highly specialized. An American observer described this specialization in Staffordshire in the 1790s:

The number of houses now engaged in the manufacture are nearly 150, each house is generally confined to some particular kind [of ware] according to the line in which their business extends, as those who supply the home demand, those for [Europe and the colonies], they require such different wares for each market that no-one could engage to make them all.[95]

With such scope, a patent was of marginal utility.

Soft porcelain was made at a number of centres in Britain from the mid-eighteenth century. Only one of these manufactures – that at Bow – was covered by a patent.[96] It cemented a partnership, securing the capital of Alderman George Arnold, which was essential to what became a large enterprise. Bow, unlike its contemporary rival at Chelsea, was heavily capitalized. Frye's second patent at Bow, on the other hand, covered the incorporation of a new and important ingredient, bone ash.[97] Similarly, Cookworthy's patent covered the materials he had discovered for making hard-paste porcelain.[98] As for Josiah Wedgwood, his many advances in techniques and design were recognized by but a single patent. Disillusioned by his experience of its infringement and the alarming costs of prosecution, he seems to have decided that secrecy combined with continuous innovation was a better investment.[99] Late-eighteenth-century pottery patents covered a miscellaneous assortment of wares, including crucibles for industrial use, ceramic buttons and a water filter – products in which potters could not compete on the basis of artistic design. The industry flourished meanwhile under the aegis of Wedgwood and his contemporaries, such as Spode and Minton, achieving standards of skill and artistic decoration admired throughout Europe.

This pattern of patenting began to be altered by the appearance of two new chemical industries – chlorine bleaching and synthetic alkalis – at the end of the eighteenth century. Both marked the application of chemical discoveries to industry and offered scope for patenting in a way that the 'rule-of-thumb' process industries did not. Chemistry was not yet, however, a strict enough science to permit tight control based on the exact specification of a chemical procedure. Moreover, since Berthollet refused to patent his discovery of chlorine's bleaching powers, numerous ways of introducing it into manufacturing practice were left open – too many to permit a complete monopoly for so long as English manufacturers experimented with different substances and techniques. The hesitancy to patent processes for manufacturing synthetic alkalis is less easily explained, but may betray a residue of traditional ways of thinking about chemical patents.

In both cases, there seems to have been a general attempt to avoid patenting (with its expense and litigation), and then panic when someone broke ranks a decade or so after the process was first known. The papers of James Watt and his circle evince a nervousness about preemptive patents in these two areas but also a hesitancy to go to the expense of a patent that contrasts with their practice regarding mechanical inventions. Watt urged Berthollet to patent chlorine bleaching, but the French scientist was uninterested in its commercial exploitation and communicated his discoveries to all who would read or hear. In these circumstances Watt was seemingly torn between keeping the secret to himself and his father-in-law, a Glasgow bleacher, and its open dissemination as a safeguard against anyone else patenting it.[100] In the event, Boneuil's attempt to monopolize the process by Act of Parliament was defeated by the textile and bleaching trades, which were able to marshall evidence of prior use. And opposition to Boneuil's subsequent patent subsided when it was found to cover only the apparatus, which was unlike (but not superior to) that used by others – a typical eighteenth-century 'chemical' patent, in fact.[101] A decade later, Charles Tennant's attempt to enforce his patent for an improvement to the process met with resistance from the trade and defeat in the law courts. Most bleachers prepared chlorine bleach solely for their own use, and for them a patent would have had only defensive value. In contrast, Boneuil and Tennant both aimed at producing it for sale to bleachers, and a patent promised them a monopoly.[102]

The processes discovered in the 1770s for manufacturing soda from common salt each represented a potentially lucrative break with traditional alkali production. That they were not patented before the rush of 1781–3 may perhaps be explained by doubts about their technical and commercial viability before the price of organic alkalis rose dramatically during the American revolution. The situation changed, however, when Alexander Fordyce broke ranks, with his petition to parliament for a remission of the excise on salt and his subsequent patent. There is some indication that he intended setting up as an alkali supplier.[103] Several others established alkali works, but their patents did no more than protect the particular process they used to produce soda for their own soap or glass manufacture.[104] There was a clearer rationale behind Lord Dundonald's alkali patents in the mid-1790s, since the Tyneside company in which he was a partner proposed to supply alkalis wholesale to soap- and glassmakers.[105] The development of a producer-goods sector in the chemical industry, combined with advances in the science of chemistry that permitted accurate specification, were to make the patenting of processes a more viable option.

6.5 GILDATED AND EXCISED TRADES

In all industries any totally new product had the advantage over a variation in an old one, for the disallowance of mere 'improvements' before 1776 militated against established manufactures. There were further discouragements to patent in the latter. First, there was sometimes the constraint imposed by official disapproval or even disallowance. The political wisdom of the government and the residual influence of the guilds went against the issuing of patents that might interfere with the supply of necessities or the livelihoods of established craftsmen. It may be significant that most of the patents for food and drink covered luxuries and 'decencies' such as coffee, chocolate, sugar and even game, rather than necessities.[106] London guilds intervened on a number of occasions, particularly in the late seventeenth century, to obstruct patents relating to their trades. The Clockmakers were especially vigilant. They spent over £500 to defeat three patents and two Acts between 1688 and 1718.[107] The Joiners and Painter Stainers Companies set up a joint committee in 1687 to campaign against John Chater's recent patent for marble chimney-pieces.[108] The Perukemakers had a patent for hairbleach stopped in 1673, while Thomas Hale complained in 1691 of harassment from both the Shipwrights and the Plumbers.[109] John Thorpe was prevented from obtaining a patent for madder by the Dyers Company as late as 1741.[110] The declining authority of the guilds and the increasingly *laissez-faire* principles of ministers both relaxed this constraint during the second half of the eighteenth century. The period 1760–1800 witnessed the arrival in strength of craftsmen patenting their stock in trade.

The guilds, of course, had had a reputation for stifling innovation even among their members. How far it was well deserved is an open question. A Commons committee was told in 1751 that prosecutions under the Statute of Artificers were directed 'against such as have excelled in their own trades by virtue of their own genius and not against such as have been ignorant in their professions, which is a great obstruction to industry and improvements'.[111] Certainly there is little evidence for technical innovation, for instance, in the leather and building trades (two of England's largest industries at this period) where the guilds remained quite strong until the mid-eighteenth century.[112] Both these trades experienced an outburst of patenting after 1760.

The clockmaking, instrumentmaking and pewter trades provide impressive counter examples of inventiveness unregistered in the patent records before 1760. The Clockmakers and Spectacle Makers Companies retained an active control into at least the second quarter of the eighteenth century that included an inveterate opposition to patents.[113] Their members, meanwhile, were consistently improving the standards of their wares both through the steady accretion of skill and ingenuity, and in co-operation with scientific investigators who were also their most exacting customers. New types of microscope were invented, new standards of accuracy achieved in astronomical and surveying instruments, and a variety of scientific instruments developed, notably the thermometer and barometer. English clocks and watches were justly famous. This was one area in which Campbell had to acknowledge no Continental superiority nor contribution.[114] When their guilds' notoriously tight reins were loosened after the mid-century, makers of clocks, watches, and instruments made extensive use of the patent system.[115] The late-seventeenth-century success of the pewter trade was more anonymous. An immigrant Huguenot, James Taudin, is generally credited with producing a new alloy, 'hard metal' pewter, to the initial displeasure of the Pewterers Company. Output rose after the Restoration to a peak in the 1690s, accompanied by a fall of almost 30 per cent in price (which cannot, however, be attributed to technical change). It was also 'the finest period of English pewter in terms of both design and workmanship'.[116]

Another constraint on patenting was the excise. It is clear that a number of applications for patents were rejected because they appeared to threaten the income from particular duties.[117] This almost certainly happened on a larger scale than the records show, inventors being deterred from applying by the too likely prospect of refusal. Certainly the excised trades are conspicuous by their absence after the turn of the seventeenth century when new, heavy excises were imposed. Patents for tobacco products, alcoholic drinks, paper,[118] soap, candles, glass and pottery were sparse, especially in the first three-quarters of the eighteenth century. This cannot be blamed entirely on the exciseman. Other constraints on patenting in these industries have been explored above. However, it is worth noting Watt's claim in 1780 that the alkali process on which he, Black, Roebuck and Keir had been working was not patented because of the duties on a major raw material, salt, and '*the disagreeable circumstance of being attended by excise officers* together with the moderate price of alkaline salts arising from the importation of American potashes'.[119] Watt and Keir seem to have decided against implementing a glassmaking discovery for the same reason.[120] Pitt's economical reforms may have eased the situation after 1780, when patents for these industries reappeared in greater numbers.

While it has been shown that there was much innovation in English industries outside the purview of the patent system, it remains impossible to quantify the proportions of patented and unpatented. Yet, one can detect tendencies and trends in patenting practice and deduce the reasons that may have brought in more inventions from some industries than from others. The representation in the patent records of the staple industries was by no means commensurate with their size or importance. This is not to say that all patents related to new or small industries. Such was clearly not the case, but where they did relate to established industries it was often at a tangent, in the performance of some auxiliary operation or the supply of capital equipment or materials which had previously been made on site; or it was an outsider identifying an opportunity that the regular practitioners were not interested in pursuing. Scale by itself was not sufficient reason for patenting (as the brewing industry demonstrates). It was only one element in a complex matrix which may be loosely characterized as a function of intensity of competition, extent of centralization, financial risk, and capacity for secrecy. Thus, it can be said that a patent was more likely to be sought for an invention that was mechanical rather than chemical, which pertained to a centralized, highly capitalized field, and where competition was fiercer than usual. Before the mid-eighteenth century, it would normally be sought by someone outside the normal structure of manufacturing to which it related; between 1760 and 1800 by a member of the trade.

7

PATENTS IN A CAPITALIST ECONOMY

It should be evident now that patents for invention were not all they might seem. Their reliability as evidence of technical change has been questioned by the discovery of interference from crown patronage and revenue protection, the overall lack of scrutiny, the deterrence of high costs and the heterodox uses to which patents were put. Reasons have been advanced why both established manufacturers and independent inventors might neglect, or decide not, to patent their inventions and improvements, and why the nature of their invention and the type of industry to which it related were important factors in this decision. The implication of this is that we need to be aware not only of legislative changes, such as the 1852 Patents Amendment Act, and shifts in institutional policy,[1] but also of the far more subtle developments occasioned by the different uses discovered for patents by the system's clients. Such a loosely administered institution was vulnerable to the impact of external, economic influences.

Further evidence that patents should be collectively interpreted in an economic framework comes from an analysis of patentees by occupation, place of residence and type of invention. It reveals the emergence during the eighteenth century of two major patenting contexts. One was firmly based in the London mercantile and manufacturing community, chiefly among the higher status crafts; the other in the manufacturing districts of the West Midlands and North-west. What both contexts shared was a highly competitive environment and a degree of capitalization unusual for that period. They also had in common the appearance of engine-makers specializing in equipping and servicing workshops and factories. Between them they accounted for over three-quarters of all patents obtained between 1750 and 1800; the remainder were spread quite thinly over the rest of England and Wales, Scotland, and Ireland, with a few European and American contributions.

7.1 THE DATA

Before considering this picture more closely, it is necessary to issue a few caveats about the data. Restoration patentees were extremely reticent about themselves: only 27 per cent mentioned their occupation or place of residence. Most probably thought it otiose to supply such information, being sufficiently well known at Court. It has indeed proved possible to trace the majority of them through the *Dictionary of national biography*, confirming thereby their frequent self-description of 'gentleman' and their lack of other occupation. Eighteenth-century applicants were both far less likely to warrant an entry in the *D.N.B.* (indicative in itself of the waning of Court interest in patents), and much more forthcoming with their personal details. During the period 1700–49 the figure rose to 83 per cent and, in the next fifty years, to 99 per cent, with all but a tiny minority giving both pieces of information.

Other than this shortfall of information, there are three major uncertainties inherent in the data. First, it is rarely possible to know whether the named patentee was the *bona fide* inventor or merely the capital backer or purchaser of the invention, nor, when several names were given, which (if any) of them was the inventor's.[2] The following discussion rides roughshod over this problem, and addresses itself simply to the named patentees. For simplicity of analysis it has been necessary to ascribe each patent to but a single name. Since it was fairly arbitrary whether financial backers were named in the patent, this should not produce undue distortion; but one should bear in mind the financial partners hovering behind many patentees. Where joint patentees did not share occupation and place of residence, the decision regarding whom to credit with the patent has been made on the basis of occupation: one declaring a trade, in preference to one giving a status, profession or mercantile description; and one in a trade relevant to the invention, over one not so connected. In partnerships between London and provincial residents of similar occupations, the latter has been given the benefit of the doubt, on the assumption that a provincial inventor was more likely to seek a London partner than vice versa.

Secondly, the prevalence of London addresses raises the question of whether some patentees gave the address where they were temporarily resident while securing a patent, rather than their permanent provincial one. Directories are frustratingly incomplete for this period, especially its first half. The London directories before 1805 restrict themselves to the cities of London, Westminster and Southwark, and overwhelmingly to the financial and wholesaling sectors,[3] but it is reassuring that most patentees in those categories can indeed be found there. For the commercial classes in this period, it is probably fair to state that one's place of residence, especially when it entailed the freedom of a gildated town, was as serious a matter of self-definition as was one's occupation, and therefore unlikely to be subsumed under a temporary address. Moreover, patentees do sometimes state both a place of origin and a temporary London address, tempting one to the supposition that they are the rule-proving exceptions. If there is any overstatement, it is likely to be among gentlemen, giving their London address rather than their country seat. In mitigation, assuming such men had other reasons to be there (for example, attendance at parliament), then it could be surmised that their presence in London was material to their seeking a patent. Also, London's share of 'gentleman-patentees' was not disproportionate: 58 per cent of them stated London as their place of residence in the second half of the eighteenth century, as did 54 per cent of other patentees.[4]

Thirdly, there is the extent of misdescription under the titles of 'gentleman' and 'esquire'. While prevalent and usually accurate in the late-seventeenth-century records, approximately one-fifth of eighteenth-century patentees accorded themselves these titles with varying degrees of justification. A few of them, such as Isaac Wilkinson, 'the potfounder', and John Curr, the mining engineer, can be identified with the practice of a trade; they have been redescribed accordingly. The majority, however, for lack of other information, must remain categorized by their status rather than their occupation. This includes such genuine gentlemen as Lord Dundonald who subsequently got their hands dirty. That the courtesy titles of gentleman and esquire were spreading down the social scale throughout the century is well known and suggests that the apparently constant proportion of gentleman-patentees should ideally be deflated decade by decade.[5] It is left to the reader, however, to make this unquantifiable mental adjustment. When 'occupational groups' are referred to, it is intended to include all those stating an occupation as opposed to a status: that is, it excludes gentlemen, esquires and peers.

A further difficulty arises in the categorization of the data according to occupation, both in deciding the basis of categorization and in the correct allocation of occupations to those categories. Under a single description could fall a range of activities (wholesale, retail, production, sometimes in combination), as well as both employer and employee. The latter is the most invidious since there is no readily available means of checking, but the assumption is made that journeymen would normally be excluded from patenting by the cost. This seems to be confirmed by the appearance in (socially exclusive) London directories of, for example, several patentees describing themselves as 'weaver' and 'throwster'. Involvement in production provides the first basis for discrimination. Among 'occupational groups', the professions, overseas merchants and financiers, members of purely distributive trades and those engaged in transport are considered to be the non-producers. From these I have tried, following the guidance of eighteenth-century directories and advice books, to exclude occupations which usually entailed some direction of production, such as 'hosier', 'clothier' or 'ironmonger'. Apothecaries and surgeons are anomalous in whichever category they appear, and have been assigned – as quasi-physicians – to the professional group, despite their continued organization in guilds and greater participation in production (of drugs and instruments) than, say, lawyers or naval officers.[6]

Among those engaged in production to a greater or lesser extent, I have distinguished four major groups, based principally on the structure of their trade.[7] In this I am attempting to separate out those trades in which artisanal structures of employment had been eroded in favour of more capitalistic, hierarchical ones. Artisans who still produced their own goods for retail or as bespoken, with the assistance of apprentices and journeymen, or who were members of the construction trades, form one group: for example, tailors, smiths, plumbers and carpenters. Masters in these trades could set up with as little as £50–100, rarely needing more than £500 capital.[8] Constituting the second group are the engine-building trades – millwrights, engine-makers, framesmiths. Although similarly organized to the first group, they are considered separately because of their increasingly specialized function as capital-goods producers. I have tried to isolate in the third and fourth groups those manufacturers who were operating on a more capitalistic basis, either outworking or centralized. Among the outworking trades are included both the principally rural-based, such as the hosiers, clothiers, buckle- and buttonmakers, and the chiefly metropolitan trades, such as clock- and instrumentmakers, cabinetmakers and coachbuilders, in which there was increasingly extensive division of labour, directed by the master-craftsman who often did little more than put his name to the article and sell it to the customer.[9] They regularly, if not necessarily, required a large capital investment. Apart from the makers of buttons, buckles and needles, they were counselled to start with no less than £100 capital, usually £500–1,000, and sometimes as much as £5,000. The centralized trades, constituting the fourth group, were also distinguished by an unusually large investment, and increasingly by the employment of labourers in place of journeymen: brewing, distilling, soapboiling and tanning provide examples.

7.2 LONDON PATENTEES

The most striking feature of the geographical distribution of patents is the persistent predominance of the capital.[10] The domination of patents by the Court in the seventeenth century makes London's majority share of those patentees who gave their place of residence in the period 1660–99 unsurprising. It is probably understated since courtiers were notable for giving no personal details. More remarkable is its maintenance of approximately one-half of the total right through the period, as may be seen in Table 7.1. Clearly, London's tally of eighteenth-century patents far exceeded its 11 per cent share of total population and, although indicative of its position as the country's leading manufacturing centre, was twice as large as its estimated share of industrial production.[11] It was not significantly higher, however, than its portion of the national wealth, urban population, nor indeed bankruptcies, each of which merit attention. One obvious advantage that Londoners had over all others was their proximity to Whitehall. It was much simpler for them to negotiate the patentee's obstacle course and chase

Table 7.1. *Patenting in London, 1720–99*

Area of London		Number of patents							
		1720–9	1730–9	1740–9	1750–9	1760–9	1770–9	1780–9	1790–9
City		12	13	9	14	28	29	33	25
	%	38.7	54.2	22.0	26.9	25.0	18.0	13.5	8.1
City Without		3	0	2	5	8	15	19	21
the Walls	%	9.7	0	4.9	9.6	7.1	9.3	7.8	6.8
Middlesex		7	6	22	29	65	101	156	202
	%	22.6	25.0	53.7	55.8	58.0	62.8	63.9	65.8
Surrey		4	2	3	4	7	11	25	45
	%	12.9	8.3	7.3	7.7	6.3	6.8	10.2	14.6
Kent		0	1	2	0	2	2	1	8
	%	0	4.2	4.9	0	1.8	1.2	0.4	2.6
Essex		0	1	2	0	0	1	0	1
	%	0	4.2	4.9	0	0	0.6	0	1.3
unspecified		5	1	1	0	2	2	10	2
	%	16.1	4.2	2.4	0	1.8	1.2	4.1	0.7
Total		31	24	41	52	112	161	244	307
	%	100.0	100.0	100.0	100.0	100.0	100.0	100.0	100.0
London as % of national total (known places of residence)		55.4	48.0	50.0	59.8	60.0	58.7	54.5	51.2

Notes:

1 The large parish of St Andrew's Holborn, which was divided between Middlesex and the City without the Walls, has been included in Middlesex's total, in accordance with the addresses given by the vast majority of its patentees.

2 Only the metropolitan parts of Middlesex, Surrey, Kent and Essex (a radius of approximately 2–5 miles from Whitehall) are included here.

officials to sign the necessary documents, without the time and expense of a protracted sojourn away from home. They were also more likely to be aware of the patent system's existence.

In London, the area north of the River Thames was predominant in patents as well as population. Yet there were changes in distribution over the course of the eighteenth century (prior to its second decade patentees rarely mentioned which part of the capital they inhabited). Chief among these was an inexorable shift westwards, away from the City and those Middlesex parishes east of it to Westminster and its northern environs. This is visible in Tables 7.1 and 7.2. The balance tipped between the fourth and fifth decades of the century, and by its close the share of the City had fallen to only 8 per cent (15 per cent if the extra-mural parishes are included). From the 1770s Middlesex provided over 60 per cent of the capital's patents, and Westminster more than half of these until the 1790s, when a serious challenge to its

Table 7.2. *Middlesex patents, 1750–99*

Division of Middlesex		Number of patents					
		1750–9	1760–9	1770–9	1780–9	1790–9	**Total**
Westminster		10	37	58	90	73	268
	%	34.5	56.9	57.4	57.7	36.1	48.5
Holborn (north)		8	14	21	31	72	146
	%	27.6	21.5	20.8	19.9	35.7	26.4
Kensington (west)		1	2	3	2	13	21
	%	3.4	3.1	3.0	1.3	6.4	3.8
Finsbury (north-east)		6	5	9	18	29	67
	%	20.7	7.7	8.9	11.5	14.4	12.1
Tower (east)		4	7	7	13	12	43
	%	13.8	10.8	6.9	8.3	5.9	7.8
unspecified		0	0	3	2	3	8
	%	0	0	3.0	1.3	1.5	1.4
Total		29	65	101	156	202	553
	%	100.0	100.0	100.0	100.0	100.0	100.0

dominance was posed by a group of parishes to its north (chiefly St Mary le Bon, St Pancras, St Giles in the Fields and St Andrew's Holborn), as Table 7.2 shows. The 1780s and 90s also saw a new interest in patents south of the Thames, particularly in the rapidly growing parishes of Lambeth, South-wark and Bermondsey. To a certain extent these changes were a reflection simply of London's demographic expansion and the increasing density of settlement in areas outside the City walls. They were also indicative, how-ever, of other trends which closer scrutiny will illuminate. The economic geography of London is reflected in its patentees, particularly with regard to the distribution of wealth.

The absolute population of the City within and without the walls was in gradual decline from the mid-seventeenth century. Proportionately, its population fell faster than its patents: in 1680 it contained only 24 per cent of the capital's population, while its share of patents fell to that level only a century later.[12] Its patentees lived predominantly (73 per cent) in the central parishes, which tended to be small but wealthy in comparison to those along the river or the walls. Even when the large extra-mural parishes are included in the total, the representation of these central parishes was still 50 per cent.[13] Indeed there was a patenting axis in Hanoverian London, along the main thoroughfare that ran east to west through the City, from Aldgate via the Poultry and Cheapside to Ludgate Hill, then into Westminster along Fleet Street and the Strand to Charing Cross. Between 1750 and 1800, on average, 9 per cent of London patentees gave addresses along this route; they were most marked in the 1770s (14 per cent) and 1780s (11 per cent) – those decades that witnessed the peak of patents for luxuries and decencies.[14] This was, of course, a major and extensive shopping street. While there was a strong tendency for the better shops to move to the West End, Fleet Street was still described in the 1830s as suffering from the 'very great concourse of carriages' belonging to wealthy shoppers.[15] Until the 1780s the City's gentlemen, professional, and mercantile patentees regularly outnumbered those involved in production. Increasingly, however, such 'non-producing' patentees gave addresses in Middlesex, indicative perhaps of the gradual departure of the wealthy from City residences.[16]

Westminster provided an entirely different picture (one which dominated that of metropolitan Middlesex as a whole). As Table 7.3 shows, it had a preponderance of gentlemen patentees, but also of outworking and artisanal patentees. And when the area to its north emerged in the 1790s, it also was well represented in these categories, suggesting a diffusion of high-patenting groups, rather than any fundamental change. By 1700 Westminster had become the fashionable area, attracting not only the top five per cent of English society (many on a seasonal basis only) but also those trades and professions which catered for its needs and tastes: tailors, furniture-makers, musical- and scientific-instrumentmakers, coachbuilders, lawyers, apothecaries, physicians and chemists.[17] Two parishes predominated in patenting: St Martin's in the Fields (thanks in part to its containing the Strand and Charing Cross) and St James's Westminster. Together they accounted for 140 (16 per cent) of London's patents in the second half of the eighteenth century. By Westminster standards they had relatively few gentlemen patentees (16 per cent), but especially large numbers of craftsmen, whether artisans or outworkers (47 per cent St James's, 64 per cent St Martin's). As Liliane Perez has remarked, their patents were for personal and domestic wares – clothes, furniture, musical instruments, watches, medicines and medical gadgets, W.C.s – and particularly for coaches (the coachmakers of Long Acre, a single street in St Martin's, obtained 13 patents).[18] Over half (58 per cent) of these craftsmen belonged to trades which had already progressed far towards a capitalist organization. In Westminster as a whole patentees in centralized trades were relatively scarce, as were patents for industrial goods. Those few which London possessed were to be found mainly on the outskirts of the city and, increasingly, south of the river, in the arc between Vauxhall and Rotherhithe.[19]

'Transpontine' London was different again from the two main centres across the river. Its few patentees were drawn from across the occupational spectrum, but with a relatively high proportion in centralized manufacturing, as befitted the area's economic profile. Cheaper land and ample water had been steadily attracting tanneries, glassworks, breweries, distilleries, vinegar manufacturers, gluemakers and soapmakers (many of which, being 'noisome trades', had been evicted from the more densely populated parts), as well as the shipping and victualling trades, for which it was an obvious

Table 7.3. Occupations/status of London patentees, 1750–99

Area of London		gent.	prof.	merchants	artisans	eng. makers	outworkers	central. mfrs.	retail/service	rural occs.	unspec.	Total
							Number of patents obtained by					
City		13	12	34	18	2	33	10	1	0	6	129
	%	7.7	13.9	44.7	10.8	3.3	15.9	13.7	16.7	0	22.2	14.7
City Without the Walls		12	6	6	13	1	26	2	1	0	1	68
	%	7.1	7.0	7.9	7.7	1.7	12.6	2.7	16.7	0	3.7	7.8
Middlesex												
Westminster		61	25	12	65	14	78	4	3	0	6	268
	%	36.1	29.1	15.8	38.9	23.3	37.7	5.5	50.0	0	22.2	30.6
Holborn (north)		34	22	9	24	10	33	10	1	0	3	146
	%	20.2	25.6	11.9	14.4	16.7	15.9	13.7	16.7	0	11.1	16.7
Kensington (west)		6	3	0	2	0	5	5	0	0	0	21
	%	3.5	3.5	0	1.2	0	2.4	6.8	0	0	0	2.4
Finsbury (north east)		6	5	2	18	5	17	11	0	0	3	67
	%	3.5	5.8	2.6	10.8	8.3	8.2	15.1	0	0	11.1	7.6
Tower (east)		9	3	2	8	3	4	7	0	1	6	43
	%	5.3	3.5	2.6	4.8	5.0	2.0	9.6	0	20.0	22.2	4.9
unspecified		2	1	2	0	0	3	0	0	0	0	8
	%	1.2	1.2	2.6	0	0	1.4	0	0	0	0	0.9

Essex		2	1	0	0	0	0	2	0	0	0	5
	%	1.2	1.2	0	0	0	0	2.7	0	0	0	0.6
Kent		2	2	4	3	1	0	1	0	0	0	13
	%	1.2	2.3	5.3	1.8	1.7	0	1.4	0	0	0	1.5
Surrey												
S. London		15	4	3	15	20	5	20	0	4	1	87
	%	8.9	4.6	3.9	9.0	33.3	2.4	27.4	0	80.0	3.7	9.9
S-W. London		3	0	0	0	0	1	1	0	0	0	5
	%	1.8	0	0	0	0	0.5	1.4	0	0	0	0.6
unspecified		4	2	2	1	4	2	0	0	0	1	16
	%	2.3	2.3	2.6	0.6	6.7	1.0	0	0	0	3.7	1.8
Total		169	86	76	167	60	207	73	6	5	27	876
	%	100.0	100.0	100.0	100.0	100.0	100.0	100.0	100.0	100.0	100.0	100.0

site.[20] South London was equally well represented by its engine-makers and millwrights: in the 1790s it provided 14 such patentees, 10 of them from Southwark. This was 41 per cent of London's total, and it would have been proportionately even higher if the prolific Joseph Bramah had not alone contributed 5 patents to Westminster's total of 10. The types of invention these south Londoners patented were correspondingly quite different to those of Westminster and the City; the picture was similar, however, to that of north-east London (from Clerkenwell to Stepney). They had little connection with the consumer market across the Thames; their interests lay in supplying industry and trade with capital goods (pumps, steam engines, ropes, ships' blocks), semi-manufactured goods, such as leather and metals, or building materials.[21]

7.3 PROVINCIAL PATENTEES

Provincial addresses were rare and dispersed before 1720, as Table 7.4 indicates. But the pattern was set early: Lancashire, Yorkshire and Warwickshire were prominent in the first half of the eighteenth century, and remained so; Bristol, which had the highest concentration of patents outside London (15 between 1700 and 1749) continued prolific, its 33 patents being largely responsible for keeping Gloucestershire fourth in the provincial rankings during the period 1750–99. The older industrial counties in the south-west were well represented during 1660–1749, and continued to supply over a sixth of provincial patents in the remainder of the eighteenth century, although few related to the textile industry, its traditional staple. East Anglia's pattern, with no heed to the region's old industrial activity, is closer to that of the low-patenting arable counties of the East Midlands and South. The extreme North-west remained virtually absent from the patent records, but the more London-orientated North-east registered 6 per cent of provincial patents, 1750–99, with Northumberland taking over from Durham as the dominant partner. But it was the area bounded by Birmingham to the south, Doncaster to the north-east and Liverpool to the north-west (with a radius of about fifty miles centred in the Potteries), that came to dominate provincial patenting, rising from one-third of provincial patents in the 1750s to just over one-half by the 1770s. It encompassed the Birmingham, Staffordshire, and Sheffield metalwares manufactures, the Potteries, the Manchester cotton district, the Nottingham hosiery trade and the Shropshire iron industry.[22]

Whatever its positive effect within the capital, beyond the metropolitan parts of the Home Counties, proximity to London was not a factor. Westmorland and Cumberland together produced only 4 patents during the whole period, 1660–1799, but equally distant Northumberland secured 32 and Cornwall 24, and 60 Scotsmen thought an English patent worth an even longer journey. Meanwhile, the non-metropolitan parts of the four counties closest to London together registered only 47. Unless one were resident in the capital, the pursuit of a patent required a protracted or repeated absence from home and work, compared to which the journey to London, whatever its length, was probably but a slight deterrent.

Beyond London, patenting cannot be correlated with what we know of the geographical distribution of wealth. This is not surprising since wealth has been assessed largely on landed income. All the high-patenting counties, especially Lancashire, showed significant advances in wealth during the eighteenth century but so, for example, did Leicestershire and Worcestershire, which produced few. We are looking here at nothing more than the redistribution of wealth resulting from the regional impact of industrialization. That industrialization was a necessary but not a sufficient condition for high levels of patenting is indicated by the poor record of Cumberland and Leicestershire; yet both featured among those counties with fewer than 40 per cent of their working population employed in agriculture in 1811.[23]

Significantly, however, there is close correspondence between patenting and bankruptcies. London led both league tables by a wide margin, although in both its lead was marginally cut during the eighteenth century, its bankruptcies falling from 42 per cent of the total in 1740–60 to 37 per cent in 1780–1800. The capital and the top 4 patenting counties – Warwickshire, Yorkshire, Lancashire and Gloucestershire – were also the top 5 areas for bankruptcies, although not in the same order.[24] Also, there was a tendency for those counties with very few patents to experience very few bankruptcies. This correspondence is of particular interest in the light of Julian Hoppit's argument that a high incidence of bankruptcy was indicative more often of rapid growth than of decline.[25] For, the risk-taking behaviour that could propel a man into bankruptcy, by overcommitment of capital, was likely to go hand in hand with the competitiveness that drove others, in that same environment, to seek an edge by patenting some improvement in their product or process.

Most important in determining London's lead were its 'urbanity' and its large, increasingly capitalistic, manufacturing sector. In 1700, 59 per cent of England's urban population lived in London; in 1750, 49 per cent; and in 1800, the figure was still 35 per cent.[26] If London's share of patents fell by nearly 9 per cent between the 1750s and the 1790s (see Table 7.1), the figures are indicative principally of the huge growth of both urban populations and patents in the provinces. For London's population grew by a quarter of a million and its decennial total of patents by 600 per cent in the second half of the century. Provincial patenting was also largely an urban phenomenon. For Warwickshire, one should read Birmingham (84 per cent of the county's patents), for Nottinghamshire, Nottingham (57 per cent), for Gloucestershire, Bristol (67 per cent), for Northumberland, Newcastle upon Tyne (57 per cent), and to a lesser extent for Lancashire, Manchester and Liverpool (53 per cent), for Yorkshire, Sheffield (30 per cent), and even for Somerset,

Table 7.4. *The geographical distribution of patents, 1660–1799*

County/country	1660–99	% Eng. & Wales	1700–49	% Eng. & Wales	provincial	1750–99	% Eng. & Wales	% provincial
London	31	59.6	112	51.8	n/a	876	54.9	n/a
South-east								
Beds.	0	0	0	0	0	5	0.3	0.7
Berks.	0	0	3	1.4	2.9	6	0.4	0.8
Bucks.	0	0	2	0.9	1.9	4	0.2	0.6
Hants.	0	0	1	0.5	1.0	20	1.3	2.8
Herts.	0	0	2	0.9	1.9	1	0.1	0.1
Kent	0	0	5	2.3	4.8	18	1.1	2.5
Middlesex	1	1.9	4	1.8	3.8	7	0.4	1.0
Surrey	0	0	1	0.5	1.0	6	0.4	0.8
Sussex	3	5.8	0	0	0	8	0.5	1.1
East Anglia								
Cambs.	0	0	1	0.5	1.0	1	0.1	0.1
Essex	2	3.8	0	0	0	4	0.2	0.6
Hunts.	0	0	2	0.9	1.9	0	0	0
Norfolk	1	1.9	2	0.9	1.9	14	0.9	1.9
Suffolk	0	0	1	0.5	1.0	1	0.1	0.1
East Midlands								
Derbys.	0	0	1	0.5	1.0	26	1.6	3.6
Leics.	0	0	0	0	0	6	0.4	0.8
Lincs.	1	1.9	1	0.5	1.0	4	0.2	0.6
Northants.	0	0	0	0	0	4	0.2	0.6
Notts.	0	0	0	0	0	44	2.8	6.1
West Midlands								
Herefords.	0	0	1	0.5	1.0	4	0.2	0.6
Oxon.	1	1.9	0	0	0	10	0.6	1.4
Salop	0	0	2	0.9	1.9	26	1.6	3.6
Staffs.	0	0	3	1.4	2.9	32	2.0	4.4
Warks.	0	0	7	3.2	6.7	99	6.2	13.8
Worcs.	2	3.8	3	1.4	2.9	7	0.4	1.0

	No.	%	No.	%	%	%	No.	%
Wales and Monmouth	0	0	1	0.5	1.0	0.6	10	1.4
South-west								
Cornwall	1	1.9	2	0.9	1.9	1.3	21	2.9
Devon	3	5.8	4	1.8	3.8	1.2	19	2.6
Dorset	0	0	1	0.5	1.0	0.2	3	0.4
Glos.	0	0	18	8.3	17.3	3.1	49	6.8
Somerset	0	0	3	1.4	2.9	1.5	24	3.3
Wilts.	1	1.9	3	1.4	2.9	0.9	15	2.1
North-west								
Cheshire	2	3.8	2	0.9	1.9	0.8	13	1.8
Cumberland	0	0	0	0	0	0.1	2	0.3
Lancs.	1	1.9	11	5.1	10.5	4.6	74	10.3
Westmorland	0	0	0	0	0	0.1	2	0.3
North-east								
Durham	0	0	6	2.8	5.3	0.7	11	1.5
Northumberland	0	0	2	0.9	1.9	1.9	30	4.2
Yorks.	2	3.8	9	4.2	8.5	5.6	90	12.5
Total England & Wales	52	100.0	216	100.0	100.0	100.0	1596	100.0
Scotland	1		3				56	
Ireland	1		1				9	
America & W. Indies	0		4				18	
Europe	8		1				12	
unspecified	180		162				21	
Total	242		387				1712	

Note:
1 London includes the metropolitan areas of Essex, Kent, Middlesex and Surrey.

Bath (25 per cent).[27] Such predominant provincial centres aside, patentees were overwhelmingly urban: 83 per cent of West Riding patentees came from 7 towns (although even by 1811 only 25 per cent of its population was urban); 89 per cent of non-metropolitan Kent's from 8 towns. Half of Staffordshire's 32 patents originated in metalworking centres such as Walsall and Wolverhampton, a third in Newcastle, Burslem and other towns in the 'Potteries', the remainder in Lichfield and Burton-upon-Trent. Half of Shropshire's 26 sprang from the Shrewsbury–Bridgnorth–Coalbrookdale ironworking triangle, and half of Cornwall's 21 from 4 tinning towns. Again, it may be questioned how far urban addresses can be trusted. Directories are on the whole scarce and erratic for this period, but it has been possible to identify 16 of the 22 patentees who, between 1768 and 1780, gave Birmingham as their address in *The Birmingham directory* of 1777.[28]

Urbanization may be held partly responsible for the growing use of the patent system. Since the majority of patents were obtained by residents of towns and cities, it is not unreasonable to expect that, as the urban population rose both absolutely and relatively (from 19 per cent of total population in 1700 to 23 per cent in 1750, to 35 per cent in 1800), the practice of patenting would also grow faster than total population. In explanation of the influence of urbanization, one probable factor was the more regular contact of townsmen with London, even if only through the news-circulating medium of a coaching or coasting service. More important may have been the more intensive competitiveness of an urban environment. Of course, townsmen might simply have been more inventive than rustics. But one factor that is indicative of competitiveness is the striking consistency with which urban tradesmen obtained a higher percentage of trade-related patents than did their rural counterparts, with large towns registering more than small ones. For instance, 83 per cent of the patents taken out by Londoners who were engaged in some form of identifiable production, between 1750 and 1799, related to that industry, compared to 68 per cent in the non-metropolitan parts of the Home Counties; 85 per cent in Sheffield, 79 per cent in all other Yorkshire towns, 62 per cent in rural Yorkshire; 86 per cent in Plymouth and Exeter, 60 per cent in the rest of Devon.[29] (The exceptions to this are the major mining, metallurgical and metalworking counties, which had a large number of industrial centres – Staffordshire, Shropshire, Cornwall – where 85–90 per cent of all patents were trade-related.) Also the subject matter of these patents suggests ingenuity rather than technical breakthroughs: from London's clocks and instruments to Birmingham's buttons and buckles, to Sheffield's scythes, to Nottingham's frames, the patents are overwhelmingly for small shifts in design or technique, signs of ingenuity that assisted in commercial success, but not giant leaps for technology.

Rural areas in counties containing high-patenting towns tended to be more prolific in patents than rural areas elsewhere. In this we are essentially comparing the proto-industrialized country of the North and West with the mainly agrarian South and East, and cannot pretend to be surprised at the outcome. It would seem that manufacturing and mining provided a greater stimulus to the village craftsman, gentleman–inventor, or farmer than did the problems of the farming community; the connection of, say, Edgeworth with the Lunar Society of Black Country businessmen provides but an extreme example of this.[30] Even agricultural patents originated overwhelmingly in London and the proto-industrial regions of the North and West. Metalworkers were more likely than farmers to patent a farming implement. Yet caution should again be urged. We may simply be perceiving a keener awareness of the patent system in the more industrial counties, while the records of the Society of Arts and similar bodies would tell a different story.

An urban environment, however, was no more than, at most, a necessary condition. Why Nottingham rather than Leicester; why Sheffield or Manchester, not Leeds; Birmingham, not Coventry; or Bristol, but not Norwich; why indeed, so overwhelmingly, London? Differences in population size can provide only a small part of the answer. A number of more important factors may be suggested: the degree of competitiveness and of guild control, the structure of local industries, and the regularity of contact with London.

The provincial centres which led the patents table were chiefly towns dominated by either metalworking or textile industries, where control of manufacturing was largely in the hands of a capitalist class, whether the Birmingham 'toy' manufacturers, the Nottingham hosiers, or the Manchester factors and calico printers. Seventy-eight per cent of Birmingham's patents related to the 'Birmingham trades' (metalworking, plating, gilding, japanning, button- and bucklemaking) and to metallurgy and enginemaking; 63 per cent of Sheffield's to metalworking, plating and steelmaking, a further 11 per cent to mining; 71 per cent of Manchester's to textiles, predominantly dyeing and printing; and a remarkable 92 per cent of Nottingham's to hosiery and lace.

The exceptions were Bristol and Liverpool, both major ports with a variety of industries. Yet they were similar to each other, with patents clustering in three groups: for the centralized, processing industries (for instance, alkali or sugar making), for metallurgy, and for engine- and machine-making. Ports generally had shown a greater propensity to patent than their hinterlands since the Restoration, although rarely did the patent's subject have a direct connection with their maritime role. Bristol far outpatented Norwich, its inland equivalent in size. Hull accounted for 3 of Yorkshire's 13 patents before 1750 (though only 2 after it), while Southampton was responsible for 12 of Hampshire's 20 patents in the period 1750-99, and virtually all Kent's patents originated in its ports. It may simply have been relative ease of communication with London that was responsible for this bias, or perhaps the concentration of manufacturing in places where both risk capital and mercantile astuteness were also available.

The ingenuity of Birmingham in devising new items for the 'toy' trade and new machines or tools with which to produce them was legendary. William Hutton commented on the variety and often ephemeral nature of the 'Birmingham trades', that 'if some are lasting, like the sun, others seem to change with the moon. Invention is ever at work'.[31] By 1800 the inhabitants of Birmingham had secured 90 patents, a third of them during the 1780s (nearly half of these being for buttons and buckles). The judgement of Richard Prosser is apt: 'some of these inventions may appear to be in the last degree trivial. So they are. But some of these contrivances have been a source of wealth to their inventors'.[32] Rowlands regards 1710–30 as 'the decisive period for the introduction of the new trades', yet only one Birmingham resident obtained a patent. Patenting was a phenomenon, rather, of the period after 1760 when a small number of 'great manufacturers' emerged, who maintained personal and direct control over all stages of production and marketing and began to replace the traditional families of ironmongers.[33]

Buckles were all the rage in the 1780s but went out of fashion in 1791 and the trade was 'practically extinct' by 1800. From 1779 to 1790, 27 patents were obtained for buckles, 10 of them by Birmingham men. The 1770 directory names 58 bucklemakers in Birmingham, but 127 in Walsall and 283 in Wolverhampton, which two towns were responsible for not a single buckle patent at this time.[34] Why this discrepancy? We are probably witnessing the impact of business conducted on different planes. The relative paucity of Birmingham master bucklemakers bore testimony, not to the size of its buckle trade, but rather to the concentration of capital in fewer hands. Boulton & Fothergill, for example, in 1762 were employing 600 workers and had £4,000 invested in producing buckles, buttons, and steel jewellery; eight years later Boulton estimated his investment so far as over £10,000.[35] Polarization of wealth accompanied such a development in most Birmingham trades.[36] And so did fierce competition. Boulton & Fothergill were told by one London retailer that 'Taylor, Gimblett, Ward and Rathbone [Birmingham manufacturers] had been with him like so many wolves for orders, the former offered him any encouragement he would accept of for the sake of a little business.'[37] They were also faced with the London jewellers' tight grip on the fashion trades. Patents were a part of the Birmingham manufacturers' response, in which novelty and marketing techniques played major roles.[38] The most prolific Birmingham patentee was Henry Clay, his 7 patents between 1772 and 1798 including 3 for buttons and 2 for japanning, in which latter trade he made his fortune. Clay also obtained royal patronage, becoming 'Japanner in Ordinary to His Majesty', and in 1790 he turned a fortune from trade into conventional status with election as high sheriff of Warwickshire.[39]

Sheffield's patent record was similarly dominated by the metal trades: 17 out of 27 patents, between 1779 and 1799, were for stamping, silver-plating, scythes, saws and steelmaking, and were obtained by men in related occupations. Already by 1710, over 50 per cent of the town's workforce was in these trades.[40] But Sheffield did not share Birmingham's reputation as a 'free-enterprise zone'. Its metal trades had been controlled since the early seventeenth century by the Cutlers Company of Hallamshire. The late date of Sheffield's first patent – 1779 – and its inhabitants' extensive use of the system after 1785 (following recovery from the American war) may be linked with the Company's decline and the rise of capitalist merchant–manufacturers. The Sheffield cutlery trades had not been moribund before that time: the number of boys apprenticed quadrupled in the first half of the eighteenth century, and the trades' ingenuity was crowned by Thomas Bolsover's invention of silver-plating in the early 1740s. But no patent marks Bolsover's achievement, nor that of Joseph Hancock, who developed the technique (nor indeed Huntsman's crucible steel).[41] Sheffield metalworkers began turning to the patent system when the Company's control and protection weakened and the trades became more highly capitalized. There is considerable evidence that this development was already advanced by the fourth quarter of the eighteenth century: in 1769 Arthur Young found women and children employed, in contravention of the Company's bye-laws; its supervision of trade-marks was so inadequate that in 1791 a number of masters established an independent society to prosecute infringements; in the same year a new, liberalizing Act led to an influx of freemen and allowed 'that freemen might employ persons who were not freemen in new inventions'.[42] The structure of the trade was becoming more polarized.[43] Hunter dated to the 1760s,

very material changes. . . . Some of the persons whose fathers had been manufacturers, established themselves in the character of merchants, general dealers in the long list of articles made at Sheffield. They employed considerable capitals, and opened extensive correspondencies immediately with houses on the continent and in America. . . . A regular and quick communication with the metropolis was formed.[44]

Silver-plating was factory-based from its inception, and by 1765 there were six firms making plated goods. One of Sheffield's most prolific patentees, Samuel Roberts, was also the owner of one of its largest plating works.[45]

Nottingham and its framework-knitting industry provides an analogous case. Although the industry remained largely decentralized, both capital and labour were being concentrated in the town of Nottingham. It witnessed a spectacular burst of patenting between the mid-1760s and late 1780s, which lifted the county into third place in the provincial patent table. In this interlude, Nottinghamshire framesmiths, knitters and hosiers obtained 17 patents for attachments to the knitting frame that produced new meshes including lace. A further 7 covered the mechanical spinning of their chief raw material, cotton. They were following the lead of Jedediah Strutt of nearby Derby, who took out the industry's first patent in 1758. Why Strutt should have broken with tradition to patent his 'Derby-rib' machine is unclear, but it may have been when visiting London to show specimens of his ribbed stockings that he first learned of patents or was prompted by his dealings with hard-bargaining hosiers to secure one.[46] Strutt came from outside the trade; he was a wheelwright seeking to break into the hosiery business. His example was followed in neither the Derbyshire nor the Leicestershire hosiery trades. Why then was it in Nottinghamshire?

It may have owed something to different scales of business and competition. The demise of the Framework Knitters Company can be formally dated to 1753, but its control over the Midlands industry had been waning and contentious for several decades before. Nottinghamshire's hosiery patents came overwhelmingly (15 of 17) from the county town, not from the rural industry. Nottingham, much more than either Derby or Leicester, was a hive of 'merchant prince' hosiers, dependent for their success in a highly competitive trade on the production of novel designs for the London fashion market. Their numbers doubled, to around one hundred, between the 1740s and 70s, the trade became much more (socially) exclusive, and their connections with the capital developed rapidly. They had also taken major steps towards concentrating their frames, although unmechanized, in proto-factories.[47] Patents were bought by 'a small interconnected group' of hosiers from, or on behalf of, inventive framesmiths and framework knitters. The hosier–patentees then defended their monopoly production of a particular line, ruthlessly prosecuting imitators, while their competitors tried to invent, and sometimes patent, around them. This started with the first Nottingham patentees, Thomas and John Morris, notorious for their litigiousness and harassments, who doubtless established the climate.[48] Derby and Leicester, which made mainly silk and worsted items respectively, could stand aside from the (largely cotton) Nottingham industry.[49] It may also be significant that Nottingham had a burgeoning, specialized frame-building industry in the second half of the eighteenth century. Chapman refers to it as 'the vanguard of technical development . . . stimulated by the patronage the merchant hosiers offered to the most successful'.[50] A patent would give a framesmith as well as his hosier patron an edge over his competitors and (potentially) secure him a lucrative share in the hosier's manufacturing success.

Manchester's 18 textile-related patents in the eighteenth century were chiefly concerned with the finishing processes of printing and dyeing, as befitted its role in the textile industry until the introduction of steam-powered spinning. Berg describes the Manchester smallware and check weavers as 'already well organized in trade societies by the 1750s. They were weaver–artisans, self-employed and 'working by the piece for a choice of masters'.[51] These weavers had communicated the making and use of the sprigg looms among themselves in the 1730s and 40s, without any help or hindrance from a patent. And in 1739, despite the impression given by but a single patent to that date, Manchester's textile dealers were said to be always 'contriving and inventing some new thing to improve or sell off their goods'.[52] Predominant among the patentees of Manchester, who began to appear in greater numbers from the 1760s, were men who gave their occupations as merchant, chapman, manufacturer and calico printer. In this they differed little from other Lancashire textile patentees. Apart from the calico printers, who were involved from the beginning in centralized production, they were the capitalists of the putting-out system. While their business rested largely on domestic weavers, their patents covered the centralized finishing processes and, increasingly, spinning as it was concentrated into factories.[53]

The concentration of patents for textile machinery in Lancashire was not a simple reflection of cotton's position as the leading sector in invention. In the Yorkshire woollen and worsted industries such large and concentrated units of production as Gott's Bean Inge factory at Leeds were the exception; mechanization took place on a much smaller scale, and the leading merchants mostly kept out of manufacturing.[54] They were barely represented in the patent records; the Midlands hosiery region registered more worsted patents.[55] In the Lancashire cotton industry (and its Nottinghamshire acolyte) large units were far more common, and merchants (and hosiers) invested in manufacture.[56] The Lancashire industry was prominent with 17 patents for textile manufacturing processes – this in spite of the oft-proclaimed hostility to patents amongst the county's cotton manufacturers and merchants.[57] When Leeds finally appeared in the list of textile patents it was not for a woollen or worsted invention but for flax spinning and carding machinery, from the highly capitalized factory of John Marshall. Like the factory-based cotton spinners, Marshall had been made aware of the patent system by payment of royalties to use patented machinery.[58] Woollen and worsted manufacturers had not been sensitized by the experience of Arkwright's patents, the legal struggle being over by the time worsted was spun mechanically with success. Neither did they have such close links with London as did the cotton trade, which was more keenly attuned to the capital's fashions.[59]

The artisanal structure of the Yorkshire woollen industry was also to be found in the Coventry silk-weaving and Norwich worsted trades. Like Leeds, neither of these cities was well represented in the patent records. Coventry's manufacturing guilds had decayed in the second quarter of the eighteenth century, those of its building trades in the third.[60] While being outstripped by Birmingham's rapid population growth, Coventry was bracketed with it in 1794 as a manufacturing town with 'flourishing trade'. The strength of Coventry's silk-weavers lay in this restriction on the city's physical growth – by the ring of common land around it – and in the rights of pasture they had on that land.[61] Two Coventry weavers shared a patent for a new weave of silk cloth in 1768, but the city's only other textile patents were both obtained in 1799 – by a man describing himself, significantly, as a cotton manufacturer. One Norwich weaver secured a patent for a loom in 1687, but he had no successors, and the city's six late-eighteenth-century patents reveal no trace of its worsted industry in its final years.

Mercantile money was often needed to afford a patent, a large investment

in centralized (or closely controlled) production required to make it worthwhile. It is striking how the towns and cities whose inhabitants accumulated
the greatest numbers of patents in the eighteenth century were either large
ports, with their own complement of merchants, or those which Chapman
cites as early experiencing 'the process of evolution in which provincial
verlagers . . . began to assume the functions traditionally performed by
merchants in London and the main regional centres': Birmingham, Sheffield,
Manchester and Nottingham.[62] Mercantile financial support and regular
contact with London each played a part. But probably more important was
the more keenly attuned sense of commercial competition to be found in such
places and the attendant perception of an invention as a potentially valuable
piece of property to be secured to the individual. A distinction between the
inventive or entrepreneurial talents of 'go-ahead' free towns and moribund
incorporated ones cannot be sustained.[63] Nor was it simply the case that free
towns had a greater propensity to patent than incorporated ones. It was
rather the capitalistic structure of manufacturing, which was possible where
guild control was weak or absent, that was crucial for a town's patenting
record; guilds or no, an artisanal structure was less conducive to patenting, as
the cases of Leeds, Coventry, or Norwich demonstrate.

7.4 OCCUPATIONAL DISTRIBUTION OF PATENTEES

The chameleon nature of the patent system during the first hundred years
after the Restoration is borne out by the major shifts in patentees' occupational backgrounds, as different groups discovered and found a use for it.
Apart from the decline of courtier interest which has already been charted,[64]
the most striking change in personnel between the seventeenth and eighteenth centuries was the replacement of merchants and wholesalers by 'industrial producers' as the largest occupational group. As Table 7.5 shows, the
former fell from 58 per cent of those who stated an occupation (exclusive of
gentlemen, etc.) in the period 1660–99 to 19 per cent in the first half of the
eighteenth century; the latter rose from 29 per cent to 61 per cent. The
artisans made the biggest gains, to become the largest single category (from
14 per cent to 31 per cent of all occupational groups); two-thirds of them gave
London as their place of residence. Patentees in the professions became
slightly more prominent. This can be accounted for almost entirely by
apothecaries, surgeons and 'doctors' patenting proprietary medicines. Their
apogee came in the 1750s, when they obtained 25 per cent of *all* patents,
before settling down to 8 per cent for the remainder of the eighteenth century.

Between the two halves of the eighteenth century, these gross trends were
magnified. The proportion of merchants and wholesalers fell further, to 10
per cent of occupational groups,[65] and that of 'industrial producers' rose to 76
per cent. Over the long term we are witnessing the 'industrialization' of the
patent system, and its colonization by extant manufacturers at the expense of

Table 7.5. *Occupations of patentees in England and Wales, 1660–1799*

Occupation	1660–99		1700–49		1750–99	
	Nos.	%	Nos.	%	Nos.	%
professional	7	13.5	26	16.4	145	11.5
merchants/wholesalers	30	57.7	30	18.9	126	10.0
retailers/service occupations	0	0	1	0.6	12	0.9
rural occupations	0	0	5	3.1	19	1.5
Industrial producers						
artisans	7	13.5	49	30.8	271	21.4
engine-makers	3	5.7	13	8.2	132	10.4
outworking/assembly trades	4	7.7	18	11.3	340	26.9
centralized manufacturers	1	1.9	17	10.7	220	17.4
Total industrial producers	15	28.8	97	61.0	963	76.1
Total	52	100.0	159	100.0	1265	100.0
As % of total patents England and Wales (including gentlemen and unspecified occupation and/or place of residence)	22.4		57.2		78.2	

'outsiders' – a trend subsequently reversed by the emergence in strength of the 'quasi-professional inventor'.[66] For the last three decades of the eighteenth century the four industrial categories accounted for an average 63 per cent of *all* patentees – probably more, given the widespread misappropriation of the titles 'gentleman' and 'esquire' by manufacturers.

Among these four categories, however, there are some instructive shifts, which are visible in Tables 7.6 and 7.7, for the provinces and London respectively. Artisans continued to account for 21 per cent of occupational patents in the second half of the eighteenth century, remaining particularly important still in London, while their provincial share is probably overemphasized by the dubious inclusion of the Sheffield metal trades among them.[67] In the provinces, artisans were overtaken from the 1770s by both the outworking trades and manufacturers in centralized industries, and in the 1790s by the engine-makers. Nottingham hosiers, Birmingham 'toy' manufacturers, Manchester cotton manufacturers and calico printers, and the masters of the capital's assembly trades now occupy the centre stage. Whatever the influx of artisans into the early-eighteenth-century patent system may have signified – attempts to avoid guild control or to substitute patent protection for waning guild protection – their outnumbering by members of the more highly capitalized trades, later in the century, reinforces the impression given by patents' geographical distribution. Patents flourished in competitive and capitalized soil.

Table 7.6. *Occupations/status of provincial patentees, 1750–99*

Occupation or status	1750–9			1760–9			1770–9			1780–9			1790–9			Total		
	Nos.	%	%NG	Nos.	%	%NG	Nos.	%	%NG	Nos.	%	%NG	Nos.	%	%NG	Nos.	%	%NG
gentlemen	4	11.4	n/a	14	18.7	n/a	17	15.0	n/a	33	16.2	n/a	55	18.8	n/a	123	17.1	n/a
professional	7	20.0	22.6	9	12.0	15.3	6	5.3	6.4	17	8.3	10.3	20	6.8	8.5	59	8.2	10.1
merchants/wholesalers	4	11.4	12.9	7	9.3	11.9	5	4.4	5.4	14	6.9	8.4	20	6.8	8.5	50	6.9	8.6
retailers/service trades	0	0	0	2	2.7	3.4	1	0.9	1.1	1	0.5	0.6	2	0.7	0.8	6	0.8	1.0
rural occupations	1	2.9	3.2	0	0	0	0	0	0	6	2.9	3.6	7	2.4	3.0	14	1.9	2.4
Industrial producers																		
artisans	6	17.1	19.3	11	14.6	18.6	17	15.0	18.3	30	14.7	18.1	40	13.7	16.9	104	14.5	17.8
enginemakers	3	8.6	9.7	6	8.0	10.2	9	8.0	9.7	12	5.9	7.2	42	14.3	17.8	72	10.0	12.3
outworking/assembly trades	3	8.6	9.7	14	18.7	23.7	27	23.9	29.0	42	20.6	25.3	47	16.0	19.9	133	18.5	22.7
centralized manufacturers	7	20.0	22.6	10	13.3	16.9	28	24.8	30.1	44	21.6	26.5	58	19.8	24.6	147	20.4	25.1
unspecified	0	0	n/a	2	2.7	n/a	3	2.7	n/a	5	2.4	n/a	2	0.7	n/a	12	1.7	n/a
Total	35	100.0	100.0	75	100.0	100.0	113	100.0	100.0	204	100.0	100.0	293	100.0	100.0	720	100.0	100.0

Note:
1 %NG = % of the total minus gentlemen and unspecified

London itself (despite its slightly different pattern of patenting to most) serves to illustrate these factors. London was a competitive hot-house. It not only serviced its own population with their personal and household needs, it was also the source of goods sold nationally and internationally, and in 1790 still handled nearly two-thirds of England's overseas trade.[68] Increasingly and without major technical change, many of these industries were adopting a more capitalistic structure and division of labour. It was the industries leading the way down this road that dominated the patent system. In 1792 a London directory named 492 different trades in the capital.[69] Yet 20 per cent of the patents obtained by members of London's 'industrial' occupations between 1750 and 1799 were taken out by just 5 trades: clock and watch-makers (30), scientific-instrumentmakers (14), opticians (15), musical-instrumentmakers (26) and coachmakers (23).[70] Furthermore, these 5 plus 12 similarly organized trades were responsible for 207 patents in the period 1750–99, compared with the 167 obtained by members of 56 still largely artisanal trades.[71] All 5, in the course of the eighteenth century, had largely become assembly trades: a range of specialized journeymen was employed, each to produce just one type of part for the master craftsman, who at most assembled the whole and dealt with the customer. They dealt in luxury and mostly precision items, in a national, sometimes international, market, and were highly concentrated in small areas of the capital (Westminster and its northern environs), producing increasingly for stock rather than to order. They were London's equivalent of the single-industry town or area which, as we have seen, was so prominent in provincial patenting. London's reputation in these trades was international, and (excluding musical-instrumentmaking) by 1750 at least half a century old. It was based on steady technical improvements, but patents were scarce before 1760. That they became so common after mid-century may be attributed to the intensification of competition, as guild control decayed and these trades became both more highly capitalized and hierarchic. Patents protected small improvements but also promised an advertisement of skill to the customer. At such close quarters, one could also hope to extract a royalty from competitors if the improvement were sufficiently important and unavoidable.[72]

The fourth industrial category has its own tale to tell. In it there feature those who described themselves as, for example, 'engine-maker', 'mill-wright', 'framesmith' and, by the 1790s, 'machine-maker'; that is, the craftsmen who constructed the machines required by manufacturers, miners and farmers. Some of them were itinerant jacks of all trades, like the millwrights whose trade was long established; others were already highly specialized, like the framesmiths and shuttlemakers. Together they helped form the nascent capital-goods sector. The growing demand for machinery was permitting this specialization. Arguably, the category should include carpenters, joiners, turners, founders, blacksmiths, even (and especially) clockmakers, all of which trades had previously constructed tools and ma-

Table 7.7. *Occupations/status of London patentees, 1750–99*

Occupation or status	1750–9			1760–9			1770–9			1780–9			1790–9			Total		
	Nos.	%	%NG	Nos.	%	%NG	Nos.	%	%NG	Nos.	%	%NG	Nos.	%	%NG	Nos.	%	%NG
gentlemen	13	25.0	n/a	16	14.3	n/a	32	19.9	n/a	48	19.7	n/a	60	19.5	n/a	169	19.3	n/a
professional	15	28.8	39.5	12	10.7	13.5	16	9.9	13.0	10	4.1	5.3	33	10.8	13.7	86	9.8	12.6
merchants/wholesalers	3	5.8	7.9	21	18.8	23.6	20	12.4	16.2	15	6.1	7.9	17	5.5	7.1	76	8.7	11.1
retailers/service trades	0	0	0	0	0	0	2	1.2	1.6	3	1.2	1.6	1	0.3	0.4	6	0.7	0.9
rural occupations	0	0	0	1	0.9	1.1	0	0	0	3	1.2	1.6	1	0.3	0.4	5	0.6	0.7
Industrial producers																		
artisans	9	17.3	23.7	20	17.9	22.5	29	18.0	23.6	50	20.5	26.3	59	19.2	24.6	167	19.1	24.5
enginemakers	0	0	0	4	3.6	4.5	6	3.7	4.9	16	6.6	8.4	34	11.1	14.2	60	6.8	8.8
outworking/assembly trades	7	13.5	18.4	20	17.9	22.5	43	26.7	35.0	76	31.1	40.0	61	19.9	25.4	207	23.6	30.4
centralized manufacturers	4	7.7	10.5	11	9.8	12.3	7	4.4	5.7	17	7.0	8.9	34	11.1	14.2	73	8.3	10.7
unspecified	1	1.9	n/a	7	6.2	n/a	6	3.7	n/a	6	2.5	n/a	7	2.3	n/a	27	3.1	n/a
Total	52	100.0	100.0	112	100.0	100.0	161	100.0	100.0	244	100.0	100.0	307	100.0	100.0	876	100.0	100.0

Note:

1 %NG = % of the total minus gentlemen and unspecified

chinery as requested, and many of whose members were now specializing in making them.[73] Thirty patents for power sources, mining equipment and production machinery were obtained by members of these trades in the period 1750–99, and 4 clockmakers patented water engines before mid-century. But the picture is clear enough without their contributions. For, the specialized engineering trades, which obtained 6 per cent of occupational patents in the late seventeenth century, accounted for 8 per cent between 1700 and 1749, and 10 per cent from 1750 to 1799. The greatest change occurred between the 1780s and 90s – from 8 per cent to 16 per cent as a national average (see Tables 7.6 and 7.7). And they were specialists in their patenting: 88 per cent of their grants (1750–99) covered capital goods, whether prime-movers, production machinery, or mining equipment. Half of those describing themselves as 'engine-makers' in the second half of the eighteenth century gave a London address, but they were outnumbered in the 1790s by men from provincial manufacturing and mining regions, particularly Lancashire, Staffordshire, Shropshire, Yorkshire and Cornwall. In the capital, the growing share of south London engine-makers has been noted. This may have been linked to their greater capitalization. While the majority of London engineering firms had their works north of the Thames, there was an early tendency for the larger firms to prefer the south bank.[74]

What we can see here is the emergence of a major new stratum within the economy for whom a patent was potentially a valuable asset. If the working practices of the civil engineer provided few suitable subjects for patenting, the products of the mechanical engineer most certainly did.[75] Once the market was large enough to support a specialized and standardized product, increasingly produced entirely in the workshop rather than constructed *in situ*, the engine-maker and millwright who invented or improved a piece of capital machinery was much better placed to exploit it. And a patent was correspondingly more valuable to him.

7.5 THE 'QUASI-PROFESSIONAL' INVENTOR

I have so far emphasized the growing preponderance of the manufacturer–patentee. Two other types of patentee were identified: the amateur inventor and the professional inventor.[76] The latter was recently brought to our attention by Harry Dutton's delineation of an 'invention industry', in which the 'quasi-professional' inventor was accorded a major role. Dutton offered four criteria which, if satisfied, would show 'that a considerable number of inventors were indeed economic men operating in what might be termed an invention industry'. These were: that 'the bulk of inventors' should patent their inventions; that 'a considerable proportion of patented inventions should be taken out by quasi-professional inventors, that is, inventors holding several or numerous patents'; that 'quasi-professional inventors . . . should diversify their inventive portfolio by inventing in a number of differ-

Table 7.8. *The distribution of patents among patentees, 1750–99*

Number of patents	Number of patentees holding one or more patents, beginning in:											
	1750–9	%	1760–9	%	1770–9	%	1780–9	%	1790–9	%	Total	%
1	67	82.7	131	76.2	187	77.9	294	81.0	356	75.0	1035	77.8
2	10	12.4	28	16.2	34	14.2	51	14.0	73	15.4	196	14.7
3	1	1.2	6	3.5	8	3.4	2	0.6	16	3.4	33	2.5
4	2	2.5	4	2.3	2	0.8	8	2.2	11	2.3	27	2.0
5	0	0	1	0.6	2	0.8	1	0.3	7	1.5	11	0.8
6	1	1.2	2	1.2	3	1.3	1	0.3	4	0.8	11	0.8
7	0	0	0	0	1	0.4	0	0	1	0.2	2	0.2
8–12	0	0	0	0	1	0.4	6	1.6	5	1.0	12	0.9
13–18	0	0	0	0	2	0.8	0	0	2	0.4	4	0.3
Total of multiple patentees	14	17.3	41	23.8	53	22.1	69	19.0	119	25.0	296	22.2
Total	81	100.0	172	100.0	240	100.0	363	100.0	475	100.0	1331	100.0

ent areas or industries'; and that 'a vigorous trade in (patented) inventions should exist'.[77] I should not wish to disagree with the depiction of inventors – or patentees – as economic men. But I would suggest that the case for an 'invention industry' is much stronger for the first half of the nineteenth century than for the second half of the eighteenth, as indeed Dutton's own figures indicate. I have already argued that there was a large amount of inventive activity outside the purview of the patent system in the eighteenth century. This is compatible, however, with the case for the bulk of *patentable* inventions being patented: if we confined ourselves to, say, mechanical devices, then Dutton's first criterion would be, at least, hard to disprove. As for the fourth criterion, Dutton's own figures suggest it does not hold for the later eighteenth century: using contested patents as his sample, he found that only 7 per cent of them were sold between 1770 and 1799, compared with 18 per cent, 1800–29, and 22 per cent, 1830–9 and 1840–9.[78] It is the second and third criteria that I wish to concentrate on here.

By focusing on patents held by 'multiple' patentees as a proportion of all patents, rather than on 'multiple' patentees as a proportion of all patentees, Dutton overemphasized the importance of the professional inventor. While 38 per cent of patents in the period 1750–99 were held by 'multiple' patentees, only 22 per cent of patentees held more than one patent. Of these, as Table 7.8 shows, 15 per cent held 2 patents each, 2 per cent 3 patents, and 5 per cent 4 or more; only 16 of the latter (1 per cent of the total) were 'truly heroic', holding 8 or more. Dutton regarded 1781–1831 as the period when the 'truly heroic' were at their most important, 'when they consistently accounted for . . . one fifth of total patents sealed', but the 1780s saw only 6 'heroic' inventors obtaining their first patents and the 1790s only 7, accounting for less than 2 per cent of all patentees in their respective decades. While Dutton's figures help us to explain the rise in patenting in the later eighteenth century, they obscure the fact that the vast majority of patentees at this time held but a single patent.[79]

The importance of the 'quasi-professional' inventor diminishes further when one looks more closely at the types of invention that their patents were covering. Dutton's third criterion, which appears also to be part of the definition of a 'quasi-professional' inventor, was that he should diversify his portfolio and invent across several industries. In examining this criterion, I have recast the definition to discover what proportion of 'multiple' patentees were inventing within their own trade. To qualify as 'trade-related' a patentee must have taken at least 50 per cent of his patents for inventions within his own industry: I exclude such men from the category of 'quasi-professional' inventors. In one way this is a more stringent demand, since patentees who invented entirely or largely within a single industry which was not their own would not qualify as 'trade-related'; this would necessarily include all those who gave a status rather than occupational description. On the other hand, it includes as 'trade-related' those (with 4 or more patents) who satisfied the basic criterion (of 50 per cent) but diversified outside it. In another way, I have also relaxed the criterion by assuming that those who gave the occupations of 'millwright' or 'engine-maker' had a very wide sphere of action while remaining within a single industry – provided there is no evidence that they sold the rights to their patents, rather than the goods produced under it. What emerges is contrary to expectations of the 'quasi-professional' inventor. Those who obtained between 2 and 7 patents showed consistently greater trade-relatedness than did those who obtained but a single one (65 per cent compared with 55 per cent). Even those with 8 or 9 patents were predominantly 'trade-related'. But taking those with 8 or more patents, only 7 out of 16 (44 per cent) were 'trade-related'.

To flesh out these bare statistics with some examples, I shall look first at those few who do fulfil the criteria for 'quasi-professional' inventors. Four of them, Marc Isambard Brunel, Robert Salmon, William Bundy and the Marquis de Chabannes, obtained only one patent in the late 1790s, the overwhelming balance in the next century, and therefore may be discounted here. This leaves us with 14 fairly clear examples of 'quasi-professional' inventors – men with 4 or more patents, the majority of which related to industries other than their own. Nine of them, in fact, gave a status or professional description. Four of the 14 held 8 or more patents. The most prolific was A. G. Eckhardt, F.R.S., with 15 patents between 1771 and 1809, in most of which he described himself as 'gentleman, of London', except for a short time in the 1790s when he became a 'manufacturer'; his patents covered pumps, textile printing, a table, a chair-cover, a grate, and a metronome. The second most prolific, and most famous, was Edmund Cartwright, whose transition from a country parson to the inventor of the power loom is well-known. His first 4 patents, in the years 1785–8, covered prototypes of the power loom, his next 3, in the years 1789–90, woolcombing machinery; during the 1790s, he launched out into fire-preventive bricks and steam engines. Originally, Cartwright attempted to use the power loom in a spinning and weaving factory he established at Doncaster. But, by the late 1790s, he was being advised to adopt behaviour characteristic of the professional inventor, and to sell the rights to his inventions. Robert Fulton, the American famous for his role in steam navigation, counselled Cartwright in 1797,

if you could sell the invention [fire-proof tiles] for a reasonable sum, I should think it advisable. My idea of many of those things, which may be considered as only the *overflowings of your mind*, is to convert them into cash, and adhere firmly, even without partners, to some of your more important objects, such as the steam engine, boat moving by steam, or cordelier.[80]

Two other inventors with 8 or more patents beginning substantially in this period were perhaps borderline cases. Archibald Cochrane, the Earl of Dundonald, obtained patents for various chemical processes relating to the distillation of coke. He has not been deemed a 'quasi-professional' inventor because he attempted to work most of them himself. The other, James Tate, a London ironmonger, held patents across several industries but they were all for metalwares and related therefore to his trade. The remainder, like John Wilkinson of Bersham and John Curr, the mining engineer, confined themselves to their own industry. This was also true of the majority of patentees holding more than 4 patents. Eight of them were engine-makers: 7 held between 4 and 6 patents each, while Joseph Bramah was way ahead, with 18 patents between 1778 and 1814. Bramah's patents were diverse, but they covered items that he manufactured for sale, whether locks, water-closets, fire-engines, or hydraulic presses.[81] Multiple, trade-related patentees clustered in several other, less obvious industries: 4 of them in coachmaking, 4 in metalworking and plating, 3 in hosiery, 3 in ropemaking, 2 in each of scientific- and musical-instrumentmaking.

The quasi-professional inventor had appeared on the scene, but as yet his was only a walk-on part. Manufacturers held the centre stage in the second half of the eighteenth century. That some of them had multiple holdings of patents is indicative principally of the defensive attitude to patenting that grew up as awareness of the system spread. They calculated that the risk involved in not patenting successive improvements to their product or process outweighed the financial costs of repeated patents. Patents were most valued in those areas of the country and sectors of the economy which had moved furthest towards a hierarchical, competitive and capital-intensive structure. London was still the country's major manufacturing centre. Its share of patents was, however, double that of its share of production. Not only did its residents have the advantage of proximity to the bureaucracy that issued patents; they were also in a highly competitive environment, with a dense concentration of trades whose artisanal structures were collapsing. Within a radius of one or two miles of Whitehall, London contained twice as many patentees as did the next 'centre' of patenting in a radius of fifty miles. Here, in the Midlands, pockets of capitalist enterprise were spread out between a number of urban and proto-industrial centres, from the metal-workers of Birmingham to the cotton merchants of Manchester and the hosiers of Nottingham. Yet in each of these towns there were economic pressures, similar to those in the capital, that were driving manufacturers in increasing numbers to purchase a patent – to secure their property in techniques and designs as well as in plant and equipment.

8

THE LONG-TERM RISE IN PATENTS

When John Davies, who combined employment at the Rolls Chapel Office with a patent agent's practice, published his treatise on patent law in 1816, he commented on the spectacular growth of business he had witnessed over the preceding thirty years.

Whether the great increase in the number of patents in the present age has arisen from the increased ingenuity, or from the greater spirit of speculation of our contemporaries, or from what other cause, is not for us to inquire.[1]

Davies's example notwithstanding, I shall now draw together points made in the previous three chapters in an attempt to explain the late-eighteenth-century rise in the patent totals. Fifty years before Davies wrote, the annual figures had started their exponential climb: in 1766 the unprecedented total of 31 had been reached; in 1816 Davies and his colleagues dealt with 118 patents.

It can never be disproved that the positivist explanation of the rise in patents – an upsurge in inventive activity or of new found technical talent – is incorrect. The list of well-known inventions that date from the later eighteenth century suggests that it certainly contains some degree of truth (though partly at the expense of the Saverys, Newcomens, Wyatts and Pauls of the century's first half). But to ask why it should have occurred then and in England is to enter anything but a positivist realm: from the impact of the scientific revolution to explanations couched in terms of socio-psychology, historians continue to speculate, while some take refuge in the 'randomness' of invention's timing.[2] It is therefore worth considering whether the rise in patent totals may bear witness less to an upsurge in inventive activity than to developments both in the patent system and in the economy at large that increased the propensity to patent. Already the positivist case has been shaken by Crafts's new estimates of productivity change. These 'indicate that the first part of the eighteenth century matched the 1760–1800 period in productivity growth'.[3] The agricultural sector was responsible for much of that in the early part of the century. The implication remains, however, that productivity growth between 1760 and 1800, at 0.2 per cent a year, was slow. Perhaps as much as half of it was accounted for by the cotton industry.[4]

144

Although textiles as a whole featured prominently in the patent records, they did not exceed 11 per cent of patents over that period.[5] Iron, the other major 'revolutionized' industry, accounted for less than a further 2 per cent. Nine out of ten patents, therefore, arose in industries which, on these estimates, saw little technical innovation.

The late eighteenth century was keenly aware of the economic potentialities of technical change in a way that was unknown to earlier generations, and invention was encouraged by the offer of premiums and prizes.[6] The outcome, perhaps, was not only a greater readiness to experiment and develop new processes and products but also a heightened self-consciousness and conceptualization of one's activities as 'invention'. Thus, on a personal level, people were more likely than before to categorize their activity as inventing. And, I shall suggest, they were readier to patent its results. This was the product not only of a spreading awareness of the patent system's existence and of the concomitant dangers of preemption if one tried to ignore it, but also of structural changes in the economy. Not least among these were the growth of a national market, the increasing differentiation of the capital-goods sector, and perhaps the development of a 'consumer society'. These were the factors which exerted long-term pressures to seek a patent on inventors, manufacturers and craftsmen. It is also necessary to consider the fluctuations which the patent statistics exhibit in the short term. For, as the graph in Figure 8.1 shows, they rose by fits and starts, not in a smooth crescendo.

8.1 NEW PRESSURES TO PATENT

No legislative changes affected the patent system between 1624 and 1835. Although the same was true for judicial precedents between 1660 and 1766, we should enquire what effect the renewed attentions of common-law judges after the mid-eighteenth century had on patenting practice. If anything, the reported hostility of judges and juries to patents, combined with the new judicial emphasis on the specification and readiness to set it aside on a technicality, should have put a brake on patenting just at the time when the numbers surged upwards in the last quarter of the century; it may indeed have restrained them.[7] Gravenor Henson, in 1831, thought that one decision in particular had had a more positive effect – Lord Mansfield's in *Morris* v. *Branson* in 1776. 'By this celebrated decision, the maxim of the law was revised, by which patents, from this period, were held to be valid for additions and improvements', with the result, he believed, that 'the applications for grants, since that time, have more than trebled'.[8] It is difficult to believe, however, that this decision was anything more than enabling in its effect. If it had gone the other way, then reinforcement of the decision in Bircot's case, particularly by an authority so weighty as Mansfield's, would probably have reduced the subsequent number of patents. There is little sign, however, in

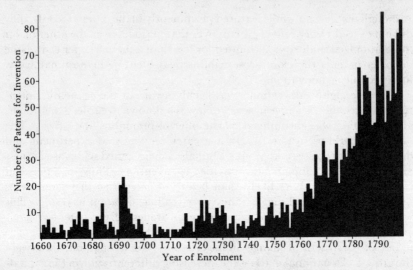

Figure 8.1 *Annual totals of patents enrolled, 1660–1799*
Source Bennet Woodcroft (ed.), *Chronological index of patents of inventions* (1854),
corrected and amended (see p. 224, n.31); see also Table 8.2.

the patent records themselves that prior to this judgement patentees had
refrained from protecting improvements. Stanyforth had lost her Exchequer
case in 1741 on the ground that her patent covered a mere improvement, but
the decision had not entered the ranks of precedents consulted in subsequent
cases.[9] Nonetheless, Henson may have had a point, in so far as Mansfield's
decision made the system appear a little more 'user-friendly'.

Of rather more importance was the growing accessibility of the patent
system – in several ways. First, although a patent remained an expensive
item, its cost was relatively lower at the end of the eighteenth century than at
its beginning, thanks to inflation, and there were also more people in the
wealth brackets able to afford it.[10] Secondly, with road transport becoming
quicker and more regular, it grew easier to travel to London to solicit a
patent. This also assisted the third factor, the spread of knowledge about the
patent system's existence. This was chiefly promoted by the publicity given to
patents in journals and newspapers (whether announcements of patents
granted or reports of legal cases), and in the advertising broadsheets and
books of patentees themselves. More specialized journals appeared at the end
of the period (too late to have prompted the upsurge in patenting, but not too
late to sustain it). The *Repertory of Arts and Manufactures*, launched in 1794,
aimed 'to establish a vehicle, by means of which new discoveries and
improvements, in any of the useful arts and manufactures, may be transmitted to the public', and used a large part of its space to reprint patent
specifications. It gave a complete list of new patents from 1797, 'conceiving

that it would be interesting to our readers to be informed what patents are taken out',[11] as did the *Annual Register*. It was followed into print by *The Philosophical Magazine* in 1798, which offered short critiques of recently patented inventions. Lambasting, in the first volume, Samuel Bentham's 1795 patent for performing various industrial operations in a vacuum, the editor considered that 'the duty we owe to the public calls upon us to point out the faults as well as the merits of patent inventions'[12] – a warning indicative in itself of the more central role of patents. Extending awareness of the system is evinced by the much wider geographical distribution of patents as the eighteenth century progressed: from 19 counties represented in the 1750s to 38 in the 1790s.

Accessibility, knowledge, and at times painful experience established a positive feedback mechanism in the patent system: the more it was used, the more it was likely to be used, since people calculated that they could not afford not to seek a patent for their invention, design, or, simply, product. The patent system generated its own logic, and encouraged a 'first-strike' mentality. Just when it reached 'critical mass' is impossible to say, but traces of this type of reaction are evinced in the fears of preemptive patenting expressed, for instance, by James Watt in 1782 when he urged Boulton:

[to] spur on Mr Hadley with the patent and at the same time cause to enquire what new patents are now going through the office, for I do not think that we are safe a day to an end in this enterprising age. One's thoughts seem to be stolen before one speaks.[13]

With piracy of inventions so rife, Lord Eldon counselled inventors not even to trust their own brothers with their secrets until their 'right was secured by the great seal'.[14] Those with less money, fear, or confidence in the feasibility of their invention could obtain a caveat, as James Keir did in 1771, to prevent others securing a patent that might forestall him and his associates.[15]

There was greater competitiveness among inventors and patentees, such as there was in most spheres of English commercial life at this period. The growth of a national market, and the disintegration of the guilds together with the residual controls they had exercised over relations between their members, all helped promote the use of patents. Whether a patent was designed to protect an important invention, a small shift in design, or a well-established, staple item of trade, it assumed greater commercial value as the market expanded and became more impersonal. Not only were potential sales greater, but so were potential losses if the invention, design, or product were pirated; it was harder to keep a check on competitors, and customers were more dependent on reputation and advertisement than on the knowledge gained through personal contact.

It has been shown why some industries, previously barely represented, began to register patents in the later eighteenth century.[16] This may be considered a once-for-all change that permanently increased their propensity to patent. Higher expenditures on capital equipment and the central-

Table 8.1. *Patents for capital goods, 1750–99*

	Number of patents					
Type of invention	1750–9	1760–9	1770–9	1780–9	1790–9	**Total**
power sources/pumps	10	21	17	47	74	169
textile machinery	5	6	19	23	53	106
agricultural machinery	1	3	5	22	27	58
brewing/distilling equipment	0	1	2	4	17	24
Subtotal	*16*	*31*	*43*	*96*	*171*	*357*
machine tools	1	4	1	2	3	11
saltmaking equipment	2	3	2	1	2	10
sugarmaking equipment	0	1	7	1	1	10
general chemical equipment	0	3	2	9	9	23
building tools and machinery	1	2	4	2	5	14
mining machinery	1	5	3	7	5	21
metallurgical equipment	6	9	11	18	19	63
shipbuilding/docking/ropemaking	4	14	7	17	37	79
canal and road building	2	1	1	2	24	30
other industrial machinery	1	5	11	13	18	48
Total	34	78	92	168	294	666
% of all patents	37.0	38.0	31.3	35.2	45.2	38.3

ization of production were particularly influential. In this regard, the emergence of a specialist capital-goods sector needs further attention. As may be seen in Table 8.1, the number of patents for capital goods rose throughout the period but surged forward in the 1790s. Of course 'capital goods' is a wide category, ranging from ships to pig iron, and in this formulation there was little change over the period (patents for metallurgical, mining and building equipment, and for shipbuilding showing a relative decline in the second half of the eighteenth century). Where there was growth was, more specifically, in patents for production machinery and equipment, especially in textile and agricultural machinery and engine-making (prime-movers and pumps) from the early 1780s, and in brewing and distilling apparatus from the late 1780s. Together these four types of capital equipment accounted for a fifth of all patents granted in the 1780s and over a quarter in the 1790s.

A variety of factors were at work stimulating inventive activity in this sector where inventions were of a type well suited to patenting. An obvious one was the expansion of industries that used such equipment, and one might see this increase in numbers merely as further testimony to the burgeoning consumer goods industries and requirements of a growing population. But that was not all. For, during the period 1790–1830, if not earlier, the balance of investment shifted towards higher fixed-capital ratios. Cotton led the way (and was the only industry in which fixed capital represented over half the investment); the other textile industries followed.[17] Whatever the proportions of fixed to working capital, rising (if fluctuating) amounts of the former were embodied in production machinery and equipment during the second half of the eighteenth century. Potentially this increased the opportunities for innovation and, in particular, for patentable inventions. To take one crucial invention, the introduction of Watt's steam engine was common to a number of industries. It gave a double impetus to both inventive activity and patenting: by attempts, first, to patent round Watt's Act and to effect rotary motion; secondly, to invent and patent new machines either made feasible by the new power source or requiring adjustment to it.[18]

With the growing investment in capital equipment there emerged a separate, specialist capital-goods sector. Many early textile mills hired their own labour force of joiners, carpenters, smiths, clockmakers, and so forth, to produce and maintain machinery, and brewers usually employed their own coppersmiths and millwrights, but there was still massive scope for independent contractors.[19] The value of patent protection to these specialists grew as they began to produce machinery in larger quantities and to meet new requirements, and as they themselves invested in fixed plant. The mounting participation in the patent system by such men, describing themselves as engine-makers, millwrights, or machine-makers, has already been noted: it rose from 3 per cent of all patents in the 1750s to 6 per cent in the 1780s, and 13 per cent in the 1790s. That metallurgists and mine-owners tended more to use their own workers to produce equipment (except steam engines) may have been significant in the failure of their industries to keep pace with the patenting of capital equipment.[20]

Another economic factor worth consideration, especially in the light of the 'consumer' patents discussed in the next section, is the increase in disposable incomes. The consumer society's exact date of birth is the subject of some considerable debate: claims have been made for the mid-sixteenth century, early eighteenth century, and the period 1750–80, respectively. It would therefore be unwise to assert here that the upsurge in patents of the second half of the eighteenth century was in any way representative of 'the birth of a consumer society' at this particular time. What all of these hypotheses allow, however, is that a consumer society had been born by the third quarter of the eighteenth century, while the third emphasizes its buoyancy and growth during that time. Although per capita consumption may have fallen in the 1770s and 80s, gross private consumption levels appear to have continued growing.[21] More crucially, whatever may have happened to real wages in general, provided the sector of society able regularly to afford 'decencies' (even occasionally luxuries) grew at least as fast as population in general, an expanding home market was assured to the patentee whose goods were aimed at the 'middling sort'. Eversley's estimates suggest it was growing even faster. He points to rising domestic production accelerating in the 1770s. Crafts's figures also indicate rising domestic expenditure in the same decade (concentrated among capitalists, landowners and rentiers), while McKendrick notes

Table 8.2. *Annual totals of patents enrolled, 1660–1799*

1660	2	1710	0	1760	14
1661	5	1711	3	1761	9
1662	4	1712	3	1762	17
1663	7	1713	2	1763	20
1664	2	1714	3	1764	18
1665	4	1715	4	1765	14
1666	2	1716	9	1766	31
1667	2	1717	6	1767	23
1668	5	1718	6	1768	23
1669	3	1719	2	1769	36
	36		38		205
1670	0	1720	7	1770	30
1671	3	1721	8	1771	22
1672	4	1722	14	1772	29
1673	7	1723	6	1773	29
1674	5	1724	14	1774	35
1675	10	1725	9	1775	20
1676	4	1726	5	1776	29
1677	7	1727	7	1777	33
1678	7	1728	11	1778	30
1679	3	1729	8	1779	37
	50		89		294
1680	0	1730	12	1780	33
1681	6	1731	9	1781	34
1682	8	1732	3	1782	39
1683	7	1733	5	1783	64
1684	13	1734	8	1784	46
1685	5	1735	1	1785	61
1686	3	1736	5	1786	60
1687	6	1737	4	1787	55
1688	4	1738	6	1788	42
1689	1	1739	3	1789	43
	53		56		477
1690	3	1740	4	1790	68
1691	20	1741	8	1791	57
1692	23	1742	6	1792	85
1693	19	1743	7	1793	43
1694	11	1744	17	1794	55
1695	9	1745	4	1795	51
1696	5	1746	4	1796	75
1697	3	1747	8	1797	54
1698	7	1748	11	1798	77
1699	5	1749	13	1799	82
	105		82		647
1700	2	1750	7		
1701	1	1751	8		
1702	1	1752	7		
1703	0	1753	13		
1704	5	1754	9		
1705	1	1755	12		
1706	4	1756	3		
1707	3	1757	9		
1708	2	1758	14		
1709	3	1759	10		
	22		92		

Source: Bennet Woodcroft (ed.), *Chronological index of patents of inventions (1854)*, corrected and amended (see p. 224, n.31).

the continued conspicuous consumption of the last twenty years of the century.[22]

8.2 SHORT-TERM FACTORS

There were new, constant and general pressures to patent, but there were also short-term, overlapping and coincidental phenomena which prompted members of first one trade or industry and then another to seek patents. During the first half of the eighteenth century it was unusual for the annual total of patents to reach double figures. In 1766 it rose suddenly to 31, an unprecedented figure, but the annual average for the 1770s was to be scarcely less; in 1783 it leapt to 64, which was to be the annual average in the 1790s. Whenever the annual total slumped it fell no further than the preceding plateau, from which it proceeded to climb higher still. The relationship between the long-term and short-term movements that produced this ratchet-like trend is not easy to decipher. It is possible that the short-term rises merely mark the opportunistic patents, the froth brought in on a tide of financial optimism; yet they may also have played a causal role in the long-term growth, by increasing public awareness of the system and concomitant defensiveness among inventors and manufacturers. T. S. Ashton remarked 'the fact that so many patents were taken out in years of prosperity, and so few in years of depression', and Dutton has since shown the close correlation after 1788 between 'general fluctuations in the major [trade] cycles' and those in the numbers of patents registered.[23] Not surprisingly, before the appearance of a regular trade cycle, the eighteenth-century pattern does not fit so neatly. As with patents, so with crises, there was no single type: markets rose and fell for diverse reasons, and one might reasonably expect the decisions of different categories of patentees to be affected variously.[24] Some people had both eyes focused on the stock market; others kept at least one on their competitors. It is necessary to disaggregate the figures to identify the stimuli to which different groups of patentees responded.

The first great surge in the annual patent figures occurred in the early 1690s. It was the product of a bullish stock market, which also sparked off a wave of joint-stock company formation. At its root were William III's wars in Ireland and France, stimulating certain industries directly, and others indirectly by imposing constraints on international trade and financial markets.[25] The climax in patents collapsed early in 1694: the boom in stocks was foundering, and patents were too closely entangled not to go down with it. Repeated disappointments, only modest successes, and revelations of fraud, mismanagement and 'pernicious' stock-jobbery had burst the bubble and revived suspicions of projectors. Patents not only lost their propaganda value but, worse, were tarred with the brush of stock-jobbing and projecting. Both inside and outside the new joint-stock companies, patentees were implicated, some of them deservedly. The stigma lingered: patentees protested for the next twenty years that theirs was 'no new project' and merited exemption from the general opprobrium.[26] In addition, the investing public, wearied of 'wild projectors', was presented in the spring of 1694 with a major new outlet for its capital that promised a safer return – the National Debt. At first the Bank of England and the Million Lottery, later the New East India and South Sea Companies, long-term annuities and further lotteries drew off capital, a squeeze felt even by the overseas trading companies.[27]

Patents continued to demonstrate sensitivity to the financial climate. Following the crisis that hit the London money markets in late 1704, nobody applied for a patent in 1705, and none were issued for more than two years subsequent to August 1709, a time of 'acute financial panic', harvest failure and political crisis.[28] Annual totals of patents edged slowly upwards in the company of financial confidence during the last three years of Anne's reign, rose to 9 in 1716 as interest rates dropped, then steadied, and fell again with stocks in 1719. There were sufficient unwary speculators in England to fuel the stock-jobbing boom that climaxed in the South Sea Bubble and carried a number of patents with it, although probably not so many as there would have been without the Lord Justices' prompt, if heavy-handed, action.[29] Most, but not all, eighteenth-century crises in public finance were registered by a fall in the annual patent figures. The last crisis in purely public finance, according to Hoppit, occurred in 1761, before the patent figures began to 'take off'. Neither of the crises in the private sector that occurred in 1772 and 1788 resulted in a patenting slump, nor did those affecting both sectors together in 1763 (a relatively minor affair) and 1778; those in 1793 and 1797, however, did.[30] Patents totals also reflect surges of speculation in 1769, 1774, and 1783. Eighteenth-century patentees, however, showed themselves to be responsive also to particular stimuli, irrespective of the general health of the financial markets, and during the three decades after 1760 they registered a few independent peaks, most notably in 1766, 1779, and 1787.

Four examples will indicate how some patentees reacted to the opportunities offered by the price movements of particular commodities. All these cases involved a mixture of types of patentee: some with an extant interest in the particular industry and some with apparently none, the latter being in a small majority, especially where the technology involved was relatively simple. The clutch of patentees who suggested a series of different seeds from which to extract oil, in the nine years 1713–21, probably had their eyes on the boom in the woollen-cloth industry that peaked in 1717.[31] One of their number, Aaron Hill, having despatched agents to discover the demand for oil in the woollen districts, told prospective investors he had received enthusiastic reports of its buoyancy. His Cornish agent claimed to have met 'a whole knot of woolcombers, and I find they are overjoyed at so good an oil; the want of sweet oil having always been a great damage to their business'.[32] Renewed interest was shown in seed oils between 1742 and 1751 when there were four patents: war with Spain was reducing the supply of olive oil and, as its price rose from £26 to £60 per gallon, there was widespread protest from the West Country in 1743.[33]

Despite, or perhaps because of, the new prohibition on dividing patents into more than five shares, the 1720s saw a renewed interest, with 94 patents issued between 1721 and 1730. They caught some of the optimism current in the more speculative parts of the economy, notably the construction industry and transport.[34] Eight of 1724's 14 patents and 3 of 1725's 9 covered pumps – 4 of them with particular application to urban water supplies, 3 (including Newsham's) for fire engines – and there were also 2 patents for water pipes, and one for a chemical fire-extinguisher. This coincided with a period of intense building activity, particularly in London. The rise in iron prices, resulting from wartime interruption of Swedish iron imports between 1716 and 1720, produced a rash of applications to patent processes for smelting pig iron with mineral fuels, which continued through the 1720s.[35] Seeking a patent in 1721, Jonathan Brown and William Wright confessed that their invention was not new: they had first smelted iron with coal twenty years before, but had not thought it worth applying for a patent 'by reason of the cheapness of wood and the plenty of foreign iron which was then sold at a low price'.[36]

When, in 1751, the price of pearlash (a finer derivative of potash, used by several industries) had risen by 50 per cent over a decade, parliament thought the situation sufficiently severe to warrant the removal of duty from ashes imported from the American colonies.[37] There had been no patents in this field since 1718; now there were three in two years, one specifically for the American product. Unfortunately for the patentees, these favourable conditions did not last long. The price, which had risen still further – to £34 per ton in 1753 (double its 1740 level) – dropped back to £28 two years later, and the 'American' patentees, based in Derbyshire, found they could not compete with the finer Mediterranean product.[38] With a similar regard to the cost of ashes, the various methods discovered to derive alkalis from common salt were not patented for over a decade.[39]

To focus now on the two largest late-eighteenth-century peaks in patenting, 1783 and 1792, the most salient point to remark is that they differed in intensity but not in kind from the 'landscape' surrounding them. They differed slightly from each other, but only in a way characteristic of their respective decades: in the former, consumer goods predominated; in the latter there were rather more capital goods. But both were composed of the steady contribution of manufacturers *plus* the patents of 'projectors' who were responding to particular stimuli. It was the former element that was responsible for maintaining the underlying upward trend, which distinguished the late-eighteenth-century picture from the pre-1760 oscillation of the decennial totals around an average of approximately 60. But the upward trend was largely of a serial and spasmodic nature; against a background of widening markets and crumbling controls, manufacturers and craftsmen kept one eye on their commercial opportunities, the other on their competitors. They responded in waves, whose occasional coincidence produced peaks in the patent totals. This happened in 1783 and 1792.

The eighteenth-century patent system was buffeted by successive concentrations of patents for a fairly small group of consumer goods, most of them intended for a middle-class market. The first invasion of the system was by proprietors of medicinal nostrums, who obtained 22 per cent of all patents granted between 1740 and 1760. The numerical contribution of medicinal patents stayed steady for the rest of the century while their relative share waned. No other industry ever dominated the system to such an extent. The 1770s saw the arrival *en masse* of Nottinghamshire hosiers and lacemakers, and their baton was taken up in the 1780s by button- and bucklemakers from Birmingham and London. Together these industries accounted for 26 patents (9 per cent) in the 1770s, 48 (10 per cent) in the 80s, falling back to 19 (3 per cent) in the 90s.[40]

There was also a miscellaneous undercurrent of patents for middle-class consumer goods, most of them obtained by members of the relevant trades. Personal items appeared most markedly in the 1780s: shoes, clogs, pattens, skates, gloves, coats, breeches, braces, umbrellas, wigs, shaving materials, trusses, spectacles and false teeth provided 6 patents (2 per cent) in the 1770s, 25 (5 per cent) in the 80s, and 17 (3 per cent) in the 90s. Household items – from fire-grates to fire-alarms, washing machines to water-closets, candlesticks to cooking utensils – also featured in large numbers.[41] They accounted for 35 patents (12 per cent) in the 1770s, 76 (16 per cent) in the 80s, and 77 (12 per cent) in the 90s.[42] Less utilitarian items of furniture demonstrate similar patterns: musical instruments with 9 (3 per cent), 13 (3 per cent), and 14 (2 per cent) patents over the three decades in question; clocks, watches and scientific instruments with 16 (5 per cent), 18 (4 per cent) and 22 (3 per cent).[43] In total, items of domestic and personal consumption (excluding medicines, foodstuffs and buildings) represented 92 patents (31 per cent) in the 1770s, 176 (37 per cent) in the 80s, and 140 (22 per cent) in the 1790s. This compares with 7 (8 per cent) and 48 (18 per cent) in the 1750s and 60s respectively. The picture of a crescendo of 'consumer' patents in the 1770s and 80s that this presents is reinforced by figures which show that the 1780s was the peak decade for patents that may be classed under the heading of 'design': 50 (10 per cent) of its patents revealed no element of invention beyond a variation in design or appearance, while 61 per cent of all patents of this type in the 1750–99 period were issued in the 1780s.

Patents for proprietary medicines were obtained overwhelmingly by people inside the medical trades and professions. They were sought with an eye to competition between vendors, rather than in response to external stimuli. Neither epidemics nor wars prompted their appearance; they tended to arrive, rather, in the wake of epidemics (as, for instance, that of 1740–1). The kudos lent by a patent offered a competitive edge at a time when an epidemic retreated, leaving an oversupply of quacks and nostrums. It was time to compete for the steadier business in chronic aches and minor pains that had assumed less importance when sufferers were living in terror of fatal infectious disease. Proprietary medicines were perhaps the first articles for which a sustained demand was created by concerted advertising. Their star rose with the popular press. Provincial newspapers began to appear in the first years of the eighteenth century: by 1740 there were 31, peaking at 41 in late 1745.[44]

Most other patents for these consumer goods were also taken out by members of the relevant trades: where once a 'seed' of patenting had been planted, it was unusual for it not to proliferate among close rivals.[45] The London coachmakers, resident chiefly in Long Acre, provide a good example. Doubtless, the increase in coaching services and purchase of carriages for private use created a generally optimistic climate. They showed no particular response, however, to the rage for turnpike Acts in the early 1750s, while the start of their prolific patenting during the 1760s anticipated the General Turnpike Act of 1765 and continued beyond it. Instead, they concentrated on particular problems: during the years 1750–72 the emphasis was on springs – 13 of the 22 patents connected with coaches. In the same period only 4 covered axles, but in the 1780s there were 12 for axles and none for springs. Both sets of patents were obtained overwhelmingly by men in the trade – coachmakers and springmakers – and by a few other, related craftsmen, such as smiths, turners, and cabinetmakers; three-quarters of them were resident in London. This is typical of most late-eighteenth-century patents: the identification by craftsmen of potential improvements that might influence customers' choice among rival suppliers. The value of a patent lay in kudos and, potentially, in the collection of royalties; the inventions were very similar, but did not prompt law suits.

The clearest example of an exception to this trade-relatedness concerned a relatively new household gadget, the washing machine, which 'belonged' to no trade. There were 13 patents for washing machines in the period, all concentrated between 1780 and 1793: 10 were obtained in the five years 1789–93, the height of the building boom – by a carpenter, a scientific-instrumentmaker, a goldsmith, a victualler, a printer, a gentleman, a builder, a clockmaker and a dyer, all but the last three being Londoners.[46] There were similar rashes of patents, at the same time, for oil-lamps and water-closets and, in the early 1770s and again in the mid-1780s, for fire-escapes and alarms. These were household luxuries that the gentry and middling sort might be persuaded to buy on a scale profitable to their patentees, new goods that could be invented without the specialist knowledge and skills needed to invent, say, an improved piano or telescope. It might attract the gentleman–inventor and the tradesman with a view to extending his product range. One particular concern that they identified and attempted to profit by was urban crime, theft and burglary in particular. The last quarter of the century saw 28 patents obtained for anti-crime devices, principally locks, burglar alarms and devices to outwit pick-pockets; another patentee, in 1796, designed a coffin to combat body-stealing.[47] In Prosser's words, 'panics, fashions, and popular crazes generally leave their mark upon the patent records'.[48]

The patents peak that occurred in 1792 was in large part the product of the general rise in business confidence consequent upon low interest rates, which had fallen steadily since the mid-1780s. It contained a large number of patents for production and agricultural machinery and engines, and for canal construction – all of which related to parts of the economy that were benefiting from the availability of relatively cheap capital. The first category has already been examined as part of a long-term shift towards higher rates of fixed-capital investment. Undoubtedly, it was also sensitive to short-term movements in the interest rate. Capital-goods producers are notorious observers of the trade cycle; carrying this observance over into their patenting practice, they helped promote both the depressions and the peaks in patent totals. Their long-term rise to prominence probably had some responsibility for the close correspondence between patent totals and the trade cycle after 1788. The typical 'projector's patent' of the early 1790s covered canal locks or alternatives to locks, dredging apparatus and barges: 12 such patents appeared at the height of the canal mania between 1791 and 1796. The speculative nature of this cluster of patents is further indicated by the high proportion (50 per cent) of patentees describing themselves as 'gentleman' or 'esquire', in contrast to approximately 18 per cent normally. Patents also had a speculative connection with building cycles until the 1790s, when the depression starting in 1794 was largely ignored. Twenty-three patents for building materials, tools, and designs were registered in the 10 years of prosperity from 1785 to 1794, and 18 in the succeeding 5 years. Approximately half of these were obtained by members of the building trades.

Behind the seemingly straightforward statistics of eighteenth-century patents there lurked a heterogeneous collection of industries, types of patentee, and indeed motivations. If major manufacturing sectors, such as textiles and metalworking were well represented, so was the quackery of patent medicines and their promoters. Some patents covered major inventions, most a small improvement, a gadget, or a minor shift in design. Few, however, were obtained without some immediate financial end in view, whether it was to exact royalty payments, to give one's product some prestige, or fearfully to preempt other potential patentees. They had a little to do with inventiveness, a lot to do with emergent capitalism. Their short-term fluctuations, often in tune with those of interest rates, cannot be used to establish anything about the timing of invention – whether, for instance, it occurred most often during booms or slumps – since the decision to patent frequently was quite independent of the decision to invent and separated from it by a varying number of months or years. Superficially the dramatic growth in patents of the eighteenth century's last quarter appears to support the 'cataclysmic' account of the industrial revolution, as a sudden and fundamental discontinuity that occurred or 'took off' around 1780. However, this particular prop gives way when it is recognized that the patents of the period were related to technological change in an erratic and tangential manner. They were linked more assuredly to the restructuring of the English economy that had been occurring since at least the late seventeenth century. If they can be taken as a gauge of anything, then it is primarily of the increasing awareness of the patent system's existence and a defensive – or opportunist – reaction to it. This was itself symptomatic of improved communications, particularly between London and the provinces, and the consolidation of a national market. Secondarily, when disaggregated, they provide a rough index to the centres of competition in an increasingly capitalist economy and reveal the emergence of a new sector within the economy, the specialist capital-goods industries. Furthermore, it is only after disaggregation that one can begin to discover what some of the technological preoccupations of eighteenth-century Englishmen may have been.

9

THE GOALS OF INVENTION

The conclusion of the preceding three chapters, that the patent rolls have little value as an accurate reflection of the directions of technical change or of the timing and pace of invention, is not a sufficient reason for dismissing them as merely a record of patenting *per se*. While certainly not inclusive of all inventions and deficient in some areas more than in others, patents do have something to say about inventive activity. The prevalence of certain types of invention is indicative of stresses and opportunities at those points in the economy to which they are addressed, and with caution they can be tentatively interpreted. What should be avoided is the assumption that they represent the *total* picture. Up to this point I have looked beyond the gross statistics to investigate what types of invention were patented, in which industries and by whom. This information by itself is insufficient to discover the technological problems and possibilities that exercised the brains of inventors. These may be approached, however, by examining the explanation of the invention which the patentee himself gives. By this means something may also be discovered about more general, underlying assumptions concerning the economic functions of technology in England at this period and changes in those assumptions over time. Which was more important: saving labour or saving capital? Did the notorious leisure-preference of the workforce inspire technical innovation, or was the burden of unemployment on the parish rates a weightier consideration? Were there chronic shortages which demanded a shift in the resource base?

Conclusive answers to these questions are too much to expect from this single, imperfect source. Such an inquiry neither begins nor ends with the patentee's self-explanation. On the one hand, I have supplemented this source with comparative, literary evidence; on the other, there are major methodological difficulties with its use. First, preceding chapters lead to the obvious objection that patents were not synonymous with inventions. Secondly, the majority of patentees offered no self-explanation. Thirdly, one cannot be sure that those who did announced their true purpose: they may have said what they thought would carry most weight with the government; or they may have failed to state 'the obvious' and given a second-level explanation. It must be stressed, therefore, that the findings in this chapter are offered as merely suggestive, in no way definitive, evidence of the technical problems and opportunities that concerned inventors and manu-facturers. Since, however, there were few other occasions on which inventors provided any rationale for their activities, it does allow a rare, direct access to their intentions. It gives an alternative perspective to that derived from deducing their motivation from the types of invention being patented or from the imbalance of resources believed to exist in the economy (for example, a 'timber famine' or a disproportion of spinning and weaving capacities).

9.1 LABOUR-SAVING INVENTIONS

Although economists have been prepared to admit, for half a century or so, that technical progress has not always been dominated by labour-saving inventions,[1] this does not appear to have become a popularly accepted view. It is a common assumption that the major goal of technical change is to save labour. That it was not always so is worth stressing. Samuel Smiles recog-nized a change within his own century. Speaking of the period around 1800, he commented that 'labour-saving processes were not then valued as they now are'.[2] It was a rare patentee or commentator before 1720 who cited saving labour as a personal or national objective, but their numbers and their confidence in the validity of attempts to increase the productivity of labour grew with the eighteenth century.

For, *pace* the anonymous correspondent of the Society of Arts in 1760 who thought that 'the great object of all improvements in arts and manufactures is to find out such methods as will enable us in any given time to do the most work with the fewest hands',[3] patentees throughout the period showed a consistently greater interest in improving the quality of products and in saving capital. As Table 9.1 demonstrates, even if one includes 'saving time' (as an undifferentiated or coded way of expressing economies in labour), there is still an overwhelming capital-saving bias in the goals evinced by patentees throughout the period.[4] Of course, one must be careful not to put too much faith in their professed motives. In particular, the labour-saving potential of new technology was – and is – highly controversial. Patentees may have thought it unwise to attract unnecessary attention to the likely impact of their invention on local employment, at a time when only an optimistic minority were confident of the compatibility of labour-saving technology with expanding employment opportunities. Lurking, never far in the background, was the Poor Law and the responsibility it placed on each parish to maintain its own unemployed. As the *Irish Farmer's Journal* con-cluded in 1814, 'What is gained in money is often lost in sustaining those who are thrown into distress from poverty, the result of inoccupation.'[5] The direct and immediate burden of relief had a capacity to concentrate the attention of all inhabitants on the state of employment in local industry in a way

Table 9.1. Patentees' stated aims of invention, 1660–1799

Aim		Number of patents									
		1660–1719	1720–9	1730–9	1740–9	1750–9	1760–9	1770–9	1780–9	1790–9	Total
create employment		22	8	4	4	3	1	1	0	0	43
	%	*7.3*	*9.1*	*7.1*	*5.0*	*3.3*	*0.5*	*0.3*	*0*	*0*	*1.9*
improve working conditions		5	3	1	0	1	4	5	3	9	31
	%	*1.7*	*3.4*	*1.8*	*0*	*1.1*	*2.0*	*1.7*	*0.6*	*1.4*	*1.4*
save labour		3	3	2	2	4	9	10	13	47	93
	%	*1.0*	*3.4*	*3.6*	*2.5*	*4.3*	*4.4*	*3.4*	*2.7*	*7.2*	*4.2*
save time		11	4	2	2	7	7	21	24	43	116
	%	*3.6*	*4.5*	*3.6*	*2.5*	*2.2*	*3.5*	*7.1*	*5.1*	*6.6*	*5.2*
save capital		89	51	23	26	36	51	65	135	214	690
	%	*29.5*	*57.9*	*41.1*	*32.5*	*39.1*	*25.1*	*22.0*	*28.3*	*33.1*	*30.8*
reduce price to consumer		22	5	4	4	7	7	15	7	15	82
	%	*7.3*	*5.7*	*7.1*	*5.0*	*3.3*	*3.5*	*5.1*	*1.5*	*2.3*	*3.7*
improve quality		43	17	13	16	20	63	114	170	201	657
	%	*14.2*	*19.3*	*23.2*	*20.0*	*21.7*	*31.0*	*38.7*	*35.6*	*31.1*	*29.3*
import substitution		38	4	5	10	6	9	3	4	2	81
	%	*12.6*	*4.5*	*8.9*	*12.5*	*6.5*	*4.4*	*1.0*	*0.8*	*0.3*	*3.6*
government revenue		7	3	2	5	5	1	0	2	0	22
	%	*2.3*	*3.4*	*3.6*	*6.3*	*2.2*	*0.5*	*0*	*0.4*	*0*	*1.0*
other govt benefits		25	11	2	4	0	0	2	2	1	47
	%	*8.3*	*12.5*	*3.6*	*5.0*	*0*	*0*	*0.7*	*0.4*	*0.2*	*2.1*
unspecified		339	67	54	87	107	254	354	594	762	2618
	%	*112.2*	*76.1*	*96.4*	*108.7*	*116.3*	*125.1*	*120.7*	*124.6*	*117.8*	*116.8*
Total cases		604	176	112	160	184	406	590	954	1294	4480
(% ÷ 2)	%	*100.0*	*100.0*	*100.0*	*100.0*	*100.0*	*100.0*	*100.0*	*100.0*	*100.0*	*100.0*

Notes:

1 Up to two aims have been counted for each patent. The total number of cases is therefore twice that of patents issued. Percentages, however, reveal the proportion of *patents* that cited a particular aim. 'Save Capital' is slightly overestimated on this basis, since a single patent has been counted twice when a patentee gave two motives that both involved saving capital, e.g. economizing on fuel and on fixed capital.

2 Where a patentee offered one aim, 'unspecified' has been registered once. Where he offered no aim, 'unspecified' has been registered twice.

inconceivable now that it is lost in a national taxation budget. Ratepayers and workers shared a common anxiety in treating new technology warily. However, although the inclusion of those patents which were likely to be labour-saving in effect (whatever their *stated* purpose) produces a more balanced picture of factor substitution, the capital-saving bias remains (see Table 9.2).

In his commentary on the Statute of Monopolies, Coke had judged that a patent for invention fell under the disqualification of 'inconvenient' if its implementation would result in the displacement of workers.[6] The employment of 'many thousands of poor' and similar promises remained a common consideration offered to the government by applicants for patents: 38 patentees (and a further 7 extant petitions) between 1660 and 1750 said explicitly that their inventions would create employment. The converse boast was rare: only 7 applicants announced emphatically that their invention would save labour, while a further 6 mentioned 'less labour and charge', or similar, as a subsidiary benefit. The first 3 offers of the former type, between 1698 and 1721, proceeded – perhaps significantly – no further than the petition.[7] George Capstack, a London glover, was granted a patent in 1696 for oil-grinding rollers, with which 'greater quantities of those seeds may be ground and beaten in less time and greater quantities of oil produced with more advantage and less labour and charge than by any mill or engine which is now used in England'.[8] Since Capstack was merely replacing one set of rollers by another, more efficient set, his invention did not present a major threat of technological displacement. Hostility was generally reserved for those inventions that mechanized a manual or semi-manual operation. Several patentees gave specific reassurances that their ostensibly labour-saving devices would in fact create employment. John Watlington, for example, stressed that his new, fur-cutting engines would employ the same number of people as before in preparing and cleaning the skins.[9]

Yet there is no evidence that any patent was refused or voided, in this period, on the ground of technological displacement of workers, and only the most conscientious of law officers, John Somers, went so far as to investigate a patent application which appeared to threaten unemployment.[10] Some interested parties clearly thought more control should be exercised. The weavers and woolbeaters of Colchester expressed their surprise in 1733 that John Kay had been allowed a patent for his wool-dressing engine and shuttle which, he claimed, could do the work of four and two men respectively.[11] This more casual attitude, contrasting markedly with Coke's strictures, may well reflect changes in governmental perception of England's economic circumstances and needs during the course of the seventeenth century: population pressure had eased, markets had widened, and the economy had shown itself resilient in the face of disaster in 1665–7. As Joan Thirsk has said: 'fear that a million mouths could not be fed no longer haunted men like a spectre. They saw rather a million pairs of productive, busy hands'.[12] It was, however, well into the eighteenth century before more than a tiny minority would draw the conclusion that the addition of mechanical 'hands' to the workforce would be beneficial.

The balance between creating employment and saving labour, in patentees' considerations, began to shift perceptibly around the mid-eighteenth century. The last patent to mention the former was William Betts's, for an attachment to the stocking frame, in 1777. Were it not for Betts, the last such patent would ironically have been Richard Arkwright's, for the water frame, eight years before. It is a tribute to the persistence of the employment ethic that Arkwright chose to recommend his archetypal labour-saving machine as 'employing a great number of poor people in working' it. He was, of course, correct in his prognosis; there was no necessary contradiction, but there were several painful decades of dislocation and adjustment to factory conditions before cotton (and woollen) spinners were convinced.[13] Concern for creating and maintaining employment did not disappear, but obeisance to it ceased to be required. When employment returned to centre stage, in the 1790s, the emphasis was entirely on saving labour: 47 patentees cited it, more than in all the preceding decades of the century together. This upsurge of interest merits exploration. But, to keep it in perspective, so does the fact that this represented only 7 per cent of patents: 93 per cent were not recommended for their labour-saving potential.

There was a deeply rooted prejudice against labour-saving technology, as both wasteful of human resources and socially dislocating in its effects. Those who tried to dispel it knew they were swimming against a strong tide. Yet exceptions were made. There could be little objection to the replacement of human labour in those cases where economy and humanity coincided. Woollen workers, opposing the introduction of new machinery into their own trade, were willing to concede that,

machinery may be called in as an auxiliary to human labour where mechanical contrivance will release [people] from occupations too servile or degrading for rational beings, or too slavish and harassing to their strength, or abridge, facilitate or expedite man's labour, still keeping him employed. [However] . . . too much machinery may be applied to wool, and there is a point . . . where it begins to defeat the very end for which it was adopted.[14]

The most clear-cut exceptions were made for ships' pumps, where the need for fewer hands might make the difference between a ship's sinking and its survival, and for mines drainage, where hundreds of men and women had often to be employed continuously in conditions akin to the galleys.[15] Dean Tucker contrasted the resistance to introduction of machinery in the textile industry with its welcomed and extensive use in mines and metal working.[16] Thomas Savery promoted his steam engine as a remedy for two major mining problems – fatal damps, and water that made it 'not worth the expense of draining them by the great charge of horses, or hand labour'. Use of the engine would allow the output of mines to double or even treble within a few years.[17] Case Billingsley (of York Buildings notoriety) took this argument a step further in 1732: his water engine would clear mines which had defeated other pumping engines, and would thereby keep in work many thousands of miners who had always looked to the parish in wet seasons wherever engines were insufficient to the task.[18] It was a neat (and justifiable) transmutation of labour-saving into work-creation. Many mines would have become idle without the invention of the steam engine and more effective pumping mechanisms.

Concern for the ratepayer was also evinced by those who presented labour-saving inventions in a charitable guise. By replacing skills or effort machinery would offer employment to those otherwise too infirm, too young, or too old to work. A pamphlet by Richard Haines, published in 1677, provides a good example, and reveals the thinking behind the spinning engine which he patented the following year.[19] Haines proposed that an almshouse should be erected in every county, where the poor would be employed in producing linen cloth, thereby reducing poor rates and imports of linen in a single blow.[20] The biggest obstacle he could foresee was that potential employees might be too weak to make linen of sufficient quantity and quality. So, he had invented an engine with which,

one man may turn fifty spinning wheels, which shall serve an hundred persons to spin with at once, so that the spinners shall have nothing to do but to employ both hands to draw tire [i.e. flax] from the distaff . . . As also an engine by which fifty men may, without striking a stroke, beat as much hemp in a day as an hundred shall do in two days.[21]

Haines's vision of the potential economic benefit of new technology was, by this account, well intentioned but very restricted. He was treating symptoms, not causes, and failed to analyse the economic ramifications of his scheme except in terms of objectives that had become clichés. Naïvely, he intended to restrict the use of these engines to charitable institutions, 'so that the same may be improved only for their benefit, and private persons not take advantage thereof, to the prejudice of this our pious and necessary design'[22] – perhaps this was the purpose of the patent. The myopia of such workhouse projects was the butt of Defoe's scathing attack in 1704. Unless additional markets were found, said Defoe, setting the poor to work on established manufactures would be 'taking the bread out of the mouths of the poor of Essex, to put it into the mouths of the poor of Middlesex'.[23] The justification reappears, however, in at least three other patents for labour-saving textile machines.[24] One of the most fiercely resisted innovations in England was the mechanically driven saw. John Booth, a merchant, had the bright idea in 1683 of claiming that his would enable military veterans 'to earn an honest competency for the maintenance of them and their families'.[25]

It is, in fact, not always easy to discover whether patentees are using the term 'saving labour' to mean increasing labour productivity or to mean easing the burden of, or sparing, the labourer. A tiny, but steady, minority of patentees recommended their case in these ambiguous terms. Doubtless, some were motivated by horror at the drudgery or danger of the labourer's work, but paternalism is always tempered with a degree of economic necessity. Samuel Taylor, for example, said in 1723 that his thread engine performed 'with much more expedition and safety to the worker, whereby much cost and labour is spared'.[26] While Taylor clothed the application in humanitarian concern, beneath it was the harsh economic fact that, as the demand for textiles grew, clothiers were having to pay higher wages to their workers.[27] Such concern was even more pertinent in those industries where the danger to the workers' health was so obvious that it acted as a serious deterrent to employment. In the pottery industry, Thomas Benson's invention of a device to grind flints underwater, which reduced the risk of contracting lung disease from the dust, was a response to the difficulty of attracting workers to perform this task.[28] William Collins, a Birmingham button maker, promoted his new method of gilding as a means of reducing the exposure of workers to mercury.[29] The 1790s witnessed a revival of interest in these problems: three patentees attempted to minimize the risk of lead poisoning among pottery, glass, and white-lead workers respectively; one to preserve the health of seamen; another of maltsters; while a surveyor, Daniel Davis, had invented an apparatus that swept and extinguished fire in chimneys 'which entirely prevents the necessity of sending any person up the chimney for either of the above purposes'.[30]

The second quarter of the eighteenth century saw patentees more prepared to take the mechanical bull by the horns. In 1727 Peter and Isaac Blanchard unashamedly claimed that their machine to make silk-lacing would allow one man to produce as much in a day as twenty did without it, and in 1730 Kay announced his twisting engine would do three days' work in one.[31] 'The grand objection to our project that we are apprehensive of is the diminution of the labour of a certain set or class of our people', wrote John Wyatt in 1736, preparing to defend the spinning engine that he and Lewis Paul wished to patent.[32] He drew up a lengthy, careful argument involving intricate calculations of how much labour was likely to be displaced and the rate at which it could be absorbed into other employments. A clothier employing a hundred workers might turn off thirty 'of the best of them', but take in ten children or disabled persons, whereby the clothier would gain 35 per cent, the parish £5 (in saved poor relief), and 'the kingdom thirty able people'. Wyatt did not retreat into a hackneyed 'charity to the parish' defence at this point, but took up the challenge. 'It now remains to find employment for these thirty, and [I] must own could these machines be dispersed all over the kingdom at once we might have many to keep which we should not employ', but with gradual introduction of the machines, these workers (mainly young women) would have no trouble finding agricultural employment. Yet the adoption of machinery would also have a dynamic effect: the clothiers' profits would incite them to expand their trade, generating employment, not least in the mechanized spinning section, which would.

take back some of those who had been dismissed. Wyatt, recognizing that workers might not appreciate these 'self-evident' arguments, counselled clothiers not to rely on economic reasoning, but to give spinners some material incentive to accept the machinery.[33] The Attorney General, Dudley Ryder, was satisfied with Wyatt's argument. He reported that, although at first sight it might appear that fewer people would be employed in spinning, 'upon consideration it will not be liable to this objection or at least that if it be that this inconvenience will be greatly overbalanced by the advantage that will accrue thereby to our woollen manufacture'. There was, he thought, a good chance that English clothiers would be able to undersell the French, and 'persons who are now of no use at all will thereby be rendered useful to the public'.[34] The report contained a significant shift in priorities: with a backward glance at the livelihoods of thousands of workers, the Attorney General identified the interest of the woollen manufacture with that of the employing clothiers and the parish ratepayers.

In doing so, Ryder was swimming with the turning tide. It was not a new outlook by any means, but it was becoming more confident, less abashed, and could be openly admitted without the same risk of opprobrium that attended it in the previous century. Seventeenth-century proponents of labour-saving devices had argued that they were unavoidable, if unpleasant, necessities to meet foreign competition, and that it was myopia bordering on the insane to choose to do things the hard way (why write when one could print? why dig when one could plough?).[35] By the turn of the century, however, a minority began to argue that there was nothing to lose (and much to gain) by using labour-saving machinery, since the expansion of supply contingent on its introduction would maintain full employment.[36] This optimistic view was dependent on a new-found faith in the elasticity of markets. Although not generally reflected in the economic literature for another half century, it remained current in the stock of arguments of interested parties – visibly in Wyatt's apology. There remained some hesitancy, in part no doubt because workers resisted every innovation which threatened to reduce their skills to a mindless minding of machinery, to regulate and discipline their patterns of work, and (if they did not take the leap of faith in expansion) to throw them onto the charity of the parish.[37] Their collective case was forcefully put by the *Birmingham Gazette* in December 1780:

An invention having taken place of casting nails, it is well worth the consideration of the public, how far that important branch of manufacture may be effected [*sic*] thereby . . . Shall so great a branch of our manufacture be subverted by so partial an innovation? Shall the welfare of 40,000 useful subjects be put in competition with forty?[38]

It was a view that continued to hold sway among British workers, not without some justification.[39]

Yet the 1730s seem to have marked a stage in the acceptance of labour-saving machinery by the governing classes. Wyatt was not a solitary advocate. Marten Triewald wrote to the Royal Society in 1736 to encourage them 'to invent engines to do those services that by mere labour have been effected'.[40] Another correspondent in 1737, an optician, proposed a lens-grinding engine which, he was confident, would be taken up by the grinders because 'a labouring man whom they hire for less wages being by the help of this machine able to do more work in a day than a skilful artificer without it in two days'.[41] Later editions of Defoe's *Tour* show a remarkable lack of embarrassment in canvassing the labour-saving potential of Lombe's silk-throwing mill,[42] and John Smith, a lawyer, described a linen loom that economized on labour approvingly, if somewhat incredulously, in 1747.[43] Ten years later, Dyer lauded Wyatt and Paul's spinning machine for its labour-saving capacity:

> it draws and spins a thread
> Without the tedious toil of needless hands.[44]

There was vacillation in high places but the trend was definitely towards acceptance. Dean Tucker thought that 'the majority of mankind, and *even some persons of great name and character*' regarded it 'a monstrous paradox' that 'the abridgement of labour' would lead to 'a much greater number of hands' being employed.[45] There is perhaps a parallel to be drawn here with the contemporary shift from paternalistic upholding of local marketing of grain towards advocacy of the untrammelled, national market as the safeguard of food supplies.[46] Both required a leap of faith in the self-regulating efficiencies of the market. Increasingly, members of the political nation were prepared to take that leap. Lombe's silk engines were praised in parliament in 1732 for spinning greater quantities of silk and more finely 'by much fewer hands, than can possibly be done by any engine that was ever yet invented'.[47] The Silk Throwers Company recognized its employment-creation potentialities: ten times the number of Lombe's employees could be taken on 'if they were at liberty to make and use the said engines'.[48] In 1738 the Commons debated a bill proposed by handworkers of silk and mohair buttons to confirm an Act of 1722, against the intrusion of those who wove the bindings on a loom. It was said in the handworkers' defence that:

the late practice of weaving silk and mohair in looms, for the making of buttons and button-holes, is but in a very few hands, when compared with the numbers who get their bread by the needle-work manufacture.[49]

Henry Archer, M.P. for Warwick and a practising lawyer, retorted that this was indeed a good reason for opposing the bill:

because as the manufacture may be carried on by a much fewer number of hands, with equal advantage to our trade in general, those who are employed in the needle-work way, are so many hands taken from other arts and other manufactures, in which they might be better employed to much better purpose.[50]

He proceeded to argue for their redistribution to those manufactures where wages were kept high by the scarcity of labour, and then launched into a paean to labour-saving inventions, ridiculing those who opposed them. He advanced, as a general proposition, that:

it is undeniable that every improvement, which, by diminishing the number of hands required in a manufacture, reduces the price of the commodity, ought to meet with encouragement from this House.[51]

Finally and conclusively, having shown that the cheaper, loom-made bindings were the object of a much greater trade, Archer reminded the House that, if it should pass the bill, 'we shall do a thing which I am sure every gentleman in this House would willingly avoid', that is:

we make an encroachment, Sir, upon the private property of our fellow subjects. We deprive them of the natural right which every man in a land of liberty ought to enjoy, of gaining bread in an honest and lawful way. Nay more, Sir, we give a total discouragement to any future improvement of arts and manufactures.[52]

Archer's appeal to the liberty of the manufacturer won the day: the bill was rejected by 85 votes to 111.

According to the 1772 edition of Jacob's *New law dictionary*, patents were still liable to be voided as 'inconvenient' if they resulted in technological displacement of labour. Significantly, it discussed patents under the heading of 'Monopoly', which itself is indicative of how far the law was trailing behind patenting practice. Thirty years later, the first treatise specifically on patent law swept past this obstacle: displacement of labour no longer provided a ground for voiding a patent.

It has been discovered that the protection and improvement of the trade of this country has, in an eminent degree, depended upon the application of machinery to save human labour, and the principal objects to which patents have been directed, are for this express purpose.[53]

The judicial bench was less sure of this principle, however, than Collier liked to think. It was remarked in 1855 that prejudice against labour-saving machinery had, until recently, 'found its firmest stronghold on the Bench'.[54] If the judiciary retained some misgivings, parliament apparently did not. Edmund Cartwright recounted how, in response to the alarm occasioned by his invention of woolcombing machines, more than forty petitions had been presented to parliament and a bill for their suppression introduced in the Commons; 'it was, however, rejected by a great majority'.[55]

The 1790s had indeed seen patentees finally lose their inhibitions about proclaiming the labour-saving potential of their inventions. Not only was there an upsurge in their numbers to 47, as has already been remarked, but there was a newly professed interest in labour *productivity*. Between 1750 and 1770 the emphasis had been almost entirely on accomplishing by machines tasks that were barely feasible by hand – in mines and ships and on the docks. Speed, not reducing labour costs, was of the essence. James Story, a Tyneside shipwright, suggested that by using his invention one man could 'pump as much or more water out of any ship, mine, or pit, as could be done . . . before by thirty men, by which means various misfortunes might be effectually prevented'.[56] Interest in labour productivity emerged slowly during the 1770s and 80s, featuring in 14 out of the 23 patents that cited reducing labour. The metalworking trades led the way with 5 such claims, followed by agriculture and textiles (2 each). A London goldsmith with the unlikely name of Dru Drury was explicit: by his method hafts for cutlery would be 'finished in a quarter of the time, and the price so reduced by the great labour saved as to be afforded in some cases for a quarter of the price'.[57] Such declarations were commonplace in the 1790s, when all but one of the 47 patents in this category were concerned with labour productivity. The textile, metal, and leather trades were all prominent, with agriculture, ropemaking, docking and brewing also making a show. Three nail-making machines were patented between 1790 and 1796. William Finch, a Staffordshire ironmaster, envisaged a plethora of good reasons for adopting his: he would save coal and iron as well as labour; because the machine required little strength, he could employ children; he could concentrate his workforce under one roof, 'whereas by the old method, the workmen lived many miles asunder, and cannot be overlooked'; as an added bonus, the workmen would no longer be lamed within seven to ten years 'and obliged to be maintained by the parish'.[58] Another 3 patentees, in 1798–9, claimed the replacement of adult male workers by women or children as an advantage of their machines. Since this was at the heart of much resistance to new technology, it was a bold step indeed to voice it.[59] Two other patentees strode into the sensitive area of substitution of unskilled for skilled labour. Samuel Bentham's wood-planing tool achieved 'superior accuracy' and saved labour: 'the essence . . . consists in having divested that operation of the quantity of skill and attention at present necessary, in such sort that brute force may be employed in it'.[60] And 'the real intention' of Samuel Miller's invention of a machine to prepare cork was 'to prevent that perpetual loss of time in cases where the hand must have a constant reference to the mind before it can execute its will'.[61]

It is worth considering how far this new profession of interest in labour productivity among patentees was a direct reflection of conditions in the labour market. Labour shortages were not a new phenomenon in English industry – the Lancashire textile industries, in particular, had suffered a chronic shortage of hand-spinners and latterly of spinners willing to work in its mills – but they became both more intense and more generalized in the 1790s. The rapidly expanding cotton, iron, and coal industries were all intensifying their demands for labour, especially in the north of the country, while new skills were required to provide them with machinery, made as far away as London.[62] Already under pressure, the labour supply in some parts of the country was stretched to the limit by the massive use of labour in the 'canal mania', succeeded by mobilization to fight the French revolutionary wars.[63] Joseph Lowe, in 1822, reckoned that one-tenth of the adult male workforce was under arms by the late 1790s, while a recent estimate suggests it may have been as high as one-eighth.[64] In advertising his invention of a machine to make hay, John Middleton of Lambeth explained that 'at a time when the price of labour is high, and hands not always to be procured, I was induced . . . to turn my thoughts to the subject'.[65] Robert Owen attributed new labour-saving inventions directly to this loss of labour:

> the want of hands and materials, with this lavish expenditure [on the army and navy], created a demand for and gave encouragement to new mechanical inventions and chemical discoveries, to supersede manual labour in supplying the materials required for warlike purposes.[66]

It might be unwise to follow Owen too far down this train of thought. Yet, if contemporary awareness of a squeeze on the labour supply did not directly induce technical change embodying a particular factor-saving bias, then at least it promoted a greater acceptability of labour-saving inventions.[67]

Attention to what patentees did *not* say about their inventions adds a further facet. It is usually possible to judge from a patent specification whether an invention would be labour-saving in effect, whether or not the patentee chose to mention this aspect. Obviously this is a subjective exercise but, by using the same criteria throughout, it is at least possible to make fairly accurate comparisons between decades.[68] It emerges that not only did the total number of labour-saving patents increase in the 1790s, both absolutely and as a proportion of all patents, but so apparently did the willingness of patentees to state the labour-saving effect of their invention. As Table 9.2 shows, the ratio between the unstated and the stated fell to only 2:1 in the 1790s. (It may have been unusually high in the preceding two decades because of extensive anti-machinery riots in the textile areas during the late 1770s.) Breaking these figures down by industry, there appears a particular reticence among patentees of textile inventions and threshing and corn-cutting machines. Not surprisingly these were some of the most controversial. (The few patentees of sawing machines *never* admitted to their labour-saving potential.) This contrasts with the relative willingness to admit to labour-saving among those with metalworking inventions; it gains in interest in the light of Dean Tucker's remarks on these respective industries.[69] Again, both textile- and agricultural-machinery patentees were more forthright in the 1790s than they had previously been. A perceptibly tightening labour market may have been reducing some of the threat posed by labour-saving inventions (and concurrently to the inventors of unpopular machines). Alternatively, one must consider whether the labour-saving potential of spinning machines, power looms and threshing machines may not have been just too obvious to deserve mention.

William Toplis, a Nottinghamshire worsted manufacturer, provides a clear example of 'understatement'. The labour-saving potential of 'his new invented machinery for combing and preparing of wool' is not referred to in the patent he obtained in June 1793.[70] But the petition he submitted to

Table 9.2. *Patents for inventions intended to save labour, 1660–1799*

Aim	Number of patents								
	1660–1719	1720–9	1730–9	1740–9	1750–9	1760–9	1770–9	1780–9	1790–9
(a) labour-saving stated	3	3	2	2	4	9	10	13	47
(b) effectively labour-saving	19	7	7	7	10	22	41	63	93
Total labour-saving	22	10	9	9	14	31	51	76	140
Total labour-saving as % of all patents	7.3	11.4	16.1	11.3	15.2	15.3	17.3	15.9	21.6
Ratio of (b) to (a)	6.3	2.3	3.5	3.5	2.5	2.4	4.1	4.8	2.0

parliament nine months later, in response to the woolcombers' campaign for
the suppression of such machines, shows that it was at the front of his mind:

experiencing great inconveniences from the inadequate number of woolcombers for
the purposes of trade, when the same is extensive and flourishing, and from their
irregular and improper conduct in forming themselves into societies and combinations, . . . [he] invented a machine for combing wool, to be worked by water. . . . the
use of machines for combing wool will reduce the quantity of manual labour
consumed in the fabrication of worsted goods, and consequently enable the manufacturer to bring them to market at a lower price, and to undersell the manufacturers of
other countries.[71]

Not only was Toplis explicit about his interest in increasing productivity, he
also evinced an equal concern for undermining the attempts of employees to
keep control over their working conditions and maintain bargaining powers,
which provided the motive for many nineteenth-century innovations.[72] He
also gave vent to a common complaint among proto-industrial employers –
leisure preference. When trade flourished, woolcombers would combine into
clubs and restrict the intake of apprentices; they could earn 28 shillings per
week 'when they choose to work every day', but wages averaged only 10
shillings because of 'their refusing to do more work'.[73]

It remains the case, nonetheless, that even in the 1790s only one in 5
patentees (including those who did not actually state this aim) were concerned with saving or controlling labour. This is explicable to some extent by
the high proportion of patents that covered product inventions, but even
when confined to process inventions, the saving of capital predominates over
the saving of labour. By the 1790s capital-saving and labour-saving inventions were patented in an approximate ratio of 3 to 2. Recent studies suggest
that this is a more accurate reflection of the factor bias prevailing in the late-
eighteenth-century economy than the traditional view of the industrial
revolution would have led us to suppose. Charles Feinstein has calculated
that 'from 1760 to 1830 the growth of capital and of labour kept broadly in
step, meaning that there was effectively no change in capital per worker'.[74]
This is corroborated by Crafts, who considers that the rise in home investment before 1820 was only just sufficient to maintain the capital-to-labour
ratio.[75] In these circumstances, manufacturers would be just as keen to
economize on capital as on labour. With capital and labour costs in equilib-
rium, there was no incentive on a national scale to economize on one at the
expense of the other, although on a local, disaggregated basis there may have
been. The diversion of labour supplies to military ends was a much easier
phenomenon for contemporaries to observe than were such matters as these.
So visible a problem may have promoted a search for labour-saving inventions that outran the requirements of manufacturers. Then again, not only
labour but also capital was liable to become more expensive as it too was
diverted from productive to military investment: the manufacturer would
feel this pinch even if the disinterested observer failed to remark on it.[76]

Table 9.3. *Patents for capital-saving inventions, 1660–1799*

Aim		1660–1719	1720–9	1730–9	1740–9	1750–9	1760–9	1770–9	1780–9	1790–9	Total
						Number of patents					
save time		7	2	1	4	3	8	5	9	26	65
	%	7.9	3.9	4.4	15.4	8.3	15.7	7.7	6.6	12.1	9.4
save fuel		10	6	2	7	5	9	8	20	35	102
	%	11.2	11.8	8.7	27.0	13.9	17.6	12.3	14.8	16.4	14.8
save raw materials		3	1	0	2	5	5	6	12	9	43
	%	3.4	1.9	0	7.7	13.9	9.8	9.2	8.9	4.2	6.2
increase output		12	6	4	1	3	3	8	16	15	68
	%	13.5	11.8	17.4	3.8	8.3	5.9	12.3	11.9	7.0	9.8
increase power		12	5	3	5	1	4	9	15	26	80
	%	13.5	9.8	13.0	19.2	2.8	7.8	13.8	11.1	12.2	11.6
reliability of equipment		7	3	0	2	4	6	10	16	18	66
	%	7.9	5.9	0	7.7	11.1	11.8	15.4	11.9	8.4	9.6
regularity of product		1	6	3	2	4	8	4	16	22	66
	%	1.1	11.8	13.0	7.7	11.1	15.7	6.2	11.9	10.3	9.6
save running costs in general		28	16	7	2	6	8	11	28	43	149
	%	31.4	31.3	30.5	7.7	16.7	15.7	16.9	20.7	20.1	21.6
Total: save working capital		80	45	20	25	31	51	61	132	194	639
	%	89.9	88.2	87.0	96.2	86.1	100.0	93.8	97.8	90.7	92.6
save fixed capital		9	6	3	1	5	0	4	3	20	51
	%	10.1	11.8	13.0	3.8	13.9	0	6.2	2.2	9.3	7.4
Total: capital saving cases		89	51	23	26	36	51	65	135	214	690
	%	100.0	100.0	100.0	100.0	100.0	100.0	100.0	100.0	100.0	100.0

A reduction in labour costs was but one economy the capitalist could expect from accomplishing a process in a shorter time: his circulating capital requirement as a whole would be lessened.[77] The value of saving working capital was, for example, a major element of John Cary's famous passage on contemporary increases in productivity, which has often been mistaken for an account of purely labour-saving innovation. Several of his examples were of new, faster processes, in sugar refining, distilling, or glassmaking, where labour was only a small part of the expense.[78] A century later, Joseph Watts recommended his new method of dressing leather in a similarly even-handed way:

Skins are dressed, this new way, in less than one-fifth part of the time they are in the old method; consequently, a much less capital is required by the manufacturer. Also, more than 5 shillings on every 100 of skins is saved in workmen's wages, and in the materials of lime, bran, salt and coal; besides the saving of several hundred pounds in building lime pits, constructing drench-troughs, and erecting drying-stoves.[79]

In a number of industries, it was probably thought more important to save on draught animals, which often cost considerable sums to replace as well as to keep, than on human labour. Weishammer, patenting sugar mills in 1709, was concerned to save on the 20 to 30 oxen required by each mill each year, while Eugene in 1740 claimed that with his machine one horse could do the work of 20.[80] There were only 3 patents designed to economize on animal power between 1750 and 1790. The demands of war, however, soon created a shortage of horses and escalating prices for fodder,[81] and in the 4 years from 1796 to 1799 there were 5 such patents.[82]

9.2 CAPITAL-SAVING INVENTIONS

There were numerous ways of saving capital. Table 9.3 offers a breakdown of those reasons stated by patentees that in one way or another would economize on capital requirements or increase output from a given amount of capital investment. Some are more clear-cut than others: 'saving fuel', for example, is a well-defined category; 'reducing running costs' is a catch-all category, used when it was unclear which of the specific means of economizing on circulating capital the patentee had in mind. Most striking, however, is the relative indifference to economizing on fixed capital investment. Even in the 1790s (with their relatively high interest rates),[83] when 20 patentees cited it, they represented less than one-tenth of all those with stated capital-saving motives. Four of these offered to reduce the construction costs of canals, 4 the costs of building steam engines and other prime movers, and 3 the expense of making and accommodating textile machinery.[84] Investment in industrial machinery, equipment and buildings may have trebled or quadrupled between the periods 1760–80 and 1780–1800, but it still accounted for only a small proportion of national income.[85]

Economies in working capital were likely to attract greater attention. There was much to be gained from a quick turnover, not least a reduction of interest payments to creditors who were most often the suppliers of a manufacturer's raw materials.[86] The figures for 'saving time' offered in Table 9.3 are for those cases in which there was little or no likelihood that labour would also be saved; a more accurate picture of patentees' concern to economize on running costs by working 'more expeditiously' can be gained by adding the more ambiguous cases included under 'saving time' in Table 9.1.[87] The prime example in this period of an innovation that reduced the time of a process expensive in capital was chlorine bleaching. The lengthy procedures of exposing cloths to sunlight, interspersed with soakings in acidic and alkaline solutions had already been shortened in the mid-eighteenth century by the substitution of sulphuric acid for buttermilk.[88] But the time was reduced far more drastically – from months to hours – by the introduction of chlorine in the 1780s. Not only did the bleacher achieve a much faster turnround of stock, he was also relieved of the expense of renting bleachfields, and he could work throughout the year, not merely in the summer months. Seven patentees, between 1789 and 1799, recommended their inventions in bleachmaking in such terms. The most explicit was Charles Tennant, who took the further step of providing the bleach in powder form for ease of transportation.[89] A marked interest in the acceleration of time-consuming operations was also evinced in the brewing and distilling industries,[90] and amongst tanners. The rising demand for leather in the 1790s, stimulated by the French wars, made the tedious soakings of hides a major frustration for those who wished to cash in on it. Of 10 patents for tanning leather in the 1790s, 8 were obtained between 1794 and 1799 and all of these addressed this problem. It also arose in the pages of the *Repertory of Arts*, where an advantage of speeding up the process was reported: 'the returns being so slow, the trade can never be carried on to advantage but by persons possessed of a large capital'.[91]

A specific means of speeding up industrial processes was to curtail the delays caused by unreliable machinery and equipment. Machinery which broke down, which was not easily maintained and repaired, or which depended on an erratic power source could result in expensive delays. Raw materials might rot or the market be missed before all returned to working order. This is nicely encapsulated in William Harding's patent for sugar mills in 1720, although probably exaggerated by reason of the more extreme conditions of Jamaica. Harding substituted cast iron rollers for wooden ones,

which rollers must be made of a particular sort of timber and by such experienced artificers as are difficult to be found in many parts of our said island, by reason whereof sometimes the whole works are stopped many days, while the sugar canes being ripe are spoiling.

The iron rollers could be repaired by workmen at the mill within four or five hours, and at an eighth of the cost.[92] Isaac Wilkinson made similar claims for his iron cylindrical bellows in 1738. They would 'in all probability last an hundred years, with little or scarce any repair, and any labourer who is employed about the work may repair them in a quarter of an hour'.[93] One advantage that was canvassed for John Passman's new drive mechanism for spinning machines was its

not [being] liable to be out of order, which is of great moment to all mills, as well as getting rid of the evil and expense of straps, lifts, etc., which are continually out of order, and renders every calculation upon the produce of a mill, both as to quantity and twist in the thread, uncertain.[94]

Various pumps were also recommended for their reliability and easy maintenance.[95] Greater durability promised some savings in fixed capital, but it was the running costs that appear to have been uppermost in patentees' minds.

It was, above all, in the generation of power that the greatest drive for reliability was in progress. Attempts to escape the constraints of natural power sources were by no means new. The long fascination with 'perpetual motion' bears ample witness to this. Several such chimeras were patented, chiefly in the first half of this period, as were a few mysterious engines that gave no indication of their power source except that it was *not* wind, water, fire or animals.[96] There was a strongly contested invention of a corn, sugar, and pumping mill to work with springs in 1660–3.[97] Weights and counterpoises were mentioned in corn mills and bellows; there were 2 'moveable engines', and 2 others for ironmaking.[98] But it was the invention of the atmospheric engine that offered for the first time a significant degree of control over the timing, strength and direction of the force applied. Savery patented his pump in 1698 and confirmed it by Act of Parliament a year later; Newcomen's engine was worked under this Act, and Triewald patented a version of the atmospheric engine in 1722.[99] There were 3 improved steam boilers between 1729 and 1736.[100] These and 3 designs to save fuel in steam boilers bear witness to the expense of fuel which helped delay the diffusion of Newcomen engines, particularly in Cornwall.[101] A mechanism to transmit rotary motion from the engine was patented in 1740, while in 1736 Jonathan Hulls patented a steam-driven boat.[102] The latter marked the culmination before 1750 of many attempts to discover a way to by-pass the wind, whose unreliability could be a strategic disaster in sea battles and a commercial hindrance for merchantmen.[103] Seven years previously, John Allen had patented a gunpowder engine for the same purpose, and Samuel Morland in the seventeenth century had envisaged the deployment of gunpowder engines in mines and for land drainage.[104] Air pressure created by heat was used in a small way for turning roasting spits, and applied on an ambitious scale to operate corn mills and hammers, and to raise water.[105]

The chief problems besetting water mills were the shortage of water in summer, ice in winter and, less predictably, flooding; access to running water also restricted the location of dependent industries.[106] Four late-seventeenth-century patents directly addressed the problem of fluctuating water supplies, principally by recycling or reversing the water-flow or altering the height of the wheel,[107] while 2 later ones anticipated Smeaton's work in calculating the effort and resistance in order to produce more efficient overshot wheels.[108] Three patentees took up the challenge again between 1787 and 1794. One of them made an instructive comparison: by his method watermills could be built for £3,000 – the annual cost of coals needed to power the Albion (steam) Mills, which had cost £70,000 to construct.[109] Wind power retained its popularity. Indeed a new surge of interest is evident in the wake of Newcomen's effective but expensive atmospheric engine: in the second quarter of the eighteenth century there were 7 patents and one application, 4 of them for horizontal-sailed mills.[110] The invention that gave wind power a new lease of life was Edward Lee's self-regulator, the 'fan-tail', patented in 1745. As with water so with wind, there were inconveniences, even dangers, in too little or too much of it. By constantly keeping the sails into the wind and regulating them according to its strength, the fan-tail was designed to utilize weaker breezes and to prevent the damage incurred from sudden shifts of direction and gusts of speed.[111] There were 13 patents for wind power in the second half of the eighteenth century: 5 made claims for increased reliability and a further 2 for greater regularity of motion. Two covered more efficient designs for sails – building on the advantage, offered by the fan-tail, of working in uncertain weather conditions – although Meikle's important spring-sails were not patented.[112] Wind power was far from obsolete. The number of windmills in Britain probably doubled between 1760 and the 1820s, although the proportion of the national horsepower that they provided was halved, over the same period, to approximately 6 per cent.[113]

Avoidance of such difficulties altogether was, perhaps, the greatest attraction of steam power. It liberated humanity, for the first time, from the vagaries of nature. It also offered a much greater flexibility of location. Ironically, these were largely unspoken goals so far as patentees were concerned. They were too fundamental, too obvious to be normally stated. They were, however, encapsulated in a paper by John Cooke to the Royal Irish Academy in 1795:

Water is seldom convenient; wind is a feeble and precarious agent; and muscular force is very expensive and very limited; but steam is free from each of these imperfections, and is superior to all in strength and duration.[114]

Patentees of steam engines concentrated instead on the major drawback of steam power – its expense. Nature provided wind and water irregularly but freely; cost-conscious manufacturers were often prepared to ignore the irregularity in order to benefit from the minimal running costs.[115] And so patentees of steam engines feature largely among those who cited the saving of fuel as a goal of their invention; Watt's separate condenser was but the most successful among many, prior to the compounding of steam engines (pioneered by Jonathan Hornblower and successfully resumed by Arthur Woolf early in the nineteenth century).[116] Not that steam engines did not have reliability problems of their own: Edmund Cartwright promoted his chiefly for its fuel-saving potential, but also reckoned to have overcome a defect of other steam engines, their propensity 'without great care and attention, to be frequently out of order'.[117] A water wheel might run foul of the weather, but it was mechanically far more dependable and quicker to repair than were early steam engines.[118] Reducing fuel consumption was mentioned by 7 of the 8 patentees of steam engines in the 1750s and 60s, and by 13 out of 30 in the remaining three decades of the century. A major, unstated goal of those 30 was the evasion of Watt's patents and Act of 1775, chiefly in the area of fuel economy. Watt also led the field in extending the application of steam engines to textile manufacturing and other industrial processes that required a rotary motion.[119] There were 13 patents, including Watt's, for rotative motion between 1779 and 1799. Here again the unspoken goal was to compete with the smoothness of motion so valued by corn millers and cotton spinners in their water wheels. A common compromise reached by textile manufacturers, in particular, was to keep their steam engines in reserve for those times of year when water power was unavailable.[120]

Another advantage offered by mechanization was the elimination of variability in products; this was an unavoidable feature of those made by hand or with elementary tools or machines. Beyond the simple improvement of quality, increasing the regularity of products promised to save capital in several ways. Its major benefit was recognized by the Attorney General when recommending Wyatt and Paul's spinning machine for a patent in 1738. By all existing methods, he reported, 'it is extremely difficult to spin yarns . . . to such a degree of size or twist as may be wanted for any particular work', so that a clothier, to get a particular type or size of yarn, must have larger quantities spun than he needed; the remainder was dead stock on his hands for a long time, and weavers could be left without work while the clothier waited to accumulate the right yarns. The spinning machine, however 'is capable of being set so as instantaneously to spin wool, cotton . . . to any degree of size or twist with the greatest easiness'.[121] In quite a different industry Thomas Miller, a Fulham brickmaker, believed the quality of English bricks left much to be desired: with his new clamp 'he can burn them all hard and therefore (there being little or no waste) produce good bricks, as cheap or cheaper than bad ones are now sold for'.[122] The advantage of drawing iron into bolts by a machine was, for Andrew Yarranton, the consistency and standardization in size thereby achieved: hand-hammered bolts, in contrast, were uneven in thickness and thus less strong for fastening planks.[123] His concern was echoed by two patentees of bolt-making machines a century later.[124] This search for regularity was also explicit or implicit in patents for lens-grinding, rope- or whip-twisting engines, thimble-making, and sword-blade engines. It was fundamental to the patents for machine tools that began to appear in the second half of the eighteenth century. One motivation, as we have seen, was to reduce the need for skilled wood- and metalworkers; another, of equal importance, was to achieve a more regular and accurate product. The prime example of the latter in this period must be John Wilkinson's boring machine, which allowed Watt to reach the new standards of accuracy needed for his design of the steam engine to be successfully implemented.[125]

The drive for accuracy and regularity was not confined to the engineering industries. Patents for hydrometers and pyrometers held out the prospect of a closer control of chemical and metallurgical operations.[126] And many patentees offered improved equipment to regulate such processes, particularly those which involved the application of heat. Their primary concern had often been to save fuel. Ways were devised to transmit heat from a single source to a number of furnaces, pans or rooms.[127] This was discovered to have the additional, potential advantage of improving the product through gentler, steadier heating, out of the smoke's contaminating range; and indeed greater safety where the materials were combustible or explosive. The second half of the eighteenth century witnessed an upsurge of interest in steam-heating. As Sutton Thomas Wood, an Oxford brewer with four patents to his name, explained, it would reduce the losses occasioned when substances were 'scorched, burnt, and materially injured, and sometimes rendered totally useless'.[128]

The patent records reveal throughout the period an overwhelming concern with efficient energy production. This is visible in the many patents for prime-movers and in several for anti-friction devices, also in the industry-wide attention to saving fuel by improved furnace, kiln, and still construction. The use of coal was now taken for granted in many industries (and in patents pertinent to them). But its application to those processes, chiefly metallurgical, in which the fuel had normally come into contact with the raw material was still experimental before the mid-eighteenth century; and refinements of technique were being made in those industries where it had been introduced earlier.[129] The price of coal was probably stable or falling in real terms during most of the eighteenth century, although temporary or local shortages may have forced manufacturers in some parts of the country to thriftier utilization.[130] Reducing fuel costs was a long-running interest of patentees that gained new momentum from the adoption of steam engines by manufacturers.

In 1728 John Payne of Bridgwater accompanied his petition with a lengthier than usual description and justification, which asserted that in all works using heat fuel was a major expense, but few, if any, had made any considerable improvements in furnaces or other heating vessels. His way of extending the heat to twice the number of salt pans would, he said, save five shillings (or 25 per cent) per ton of coal.[131] Saltmaking was indeed a fuel-intensive industry, particularly in the coastal, sea-water section.[132] The imposition of excise made saltmakers, competing with European importers, even more conscious of fuel costs.[133] Of 25 patents and petitions for saltmaking before 1750, 12 cited saving fuel as their goal. A further 12 either claimed they had a cheaper, more efficient method of producing salt or had a new way of applying heat, without explicitly mentioning the cost advantages. Four of these also aimed at a better quality salt (larger grain, better tasting) – the goal specified by the sole remaining patentee. There were only 10 patents for saltmaking in the second half of the century, but 6 of them explicitly offered to save fuel.

Conservation of timber stocks remained important. At a time when charcoal was still a major ingredient of iron, it is hard to see there would have been much saving of timber in substituting iron corf bows (coal containers) for wooden ones, as Hodson's patent proposed, but it may well have been his intention to use imported Swedish iron.[134] A second County Durham man, Elias Thornhill, evinced a comparable concern when patenting iron wheel rims for coal waggons; this was intended to extend the waggons' service beyond the current one or two years.[135] A similar idea for ordinary carts had been patented by a Birmingham ironmonger, Richard Baddeley, in 1722, but he had claimed to be interested in preserving the public roads.[136] Abraham Darby's use of coke had been largely confined to the relatively small casting sector of the industry.[137] The sharply rising costs of charcoal after 1750 prompted renewed interest in smelting with mineral fuels among ironmasters producing pig for the wrought-iron branch. Their gradual shift to coal was based on extant technology, assisted by the adoption of steam engines for operating the blowing mechanisms.[138] The increase in charcoal prices also hit the refining sector. There were 9 patents between 1761 and 1784 that aimed at using coal throughout the forge, and 3 others burned coke instead of raw coal. The most important before 1790 were those of John and Charles Wood for 'potting and stamping' (breaking the pig iron into small pieces, then heating it in pots with lime in an air furnace to remove carbon and sulphur). Hyde attributes the 70 per cent rise in wrought iron output between 1750 and 1788 almost entirely to potting.[139] Much more important in the long term was 'puddling', where pig iron was refined in a coal-fired air (or reverberatory) furnace without either pots or fluxes. There were several unsuccessful anticipations of either or both parts of Henry Cort's puddling and rolling process (the air furnace and the grooved rollers). But Cort's patents of 1783–4 marked only the beginning of a long development process in which success was finally achieved by one of his licensees, Richard Crawshay of Cyfarthfa, after he had altered the construction materials of the furnace in 1791. His success was well timed: wartime demand, combined with the cost-reduction offered by puddling, led to its rapid diffusion.[140] British ironmasters were now in a position to recapture the home market.

Yet, despite industry's decreasing dependence on wood as a fuel, the costs and the conservation of timber remained a problem. The pressure on British stocks consequent upon the expansion of overseas trade and shipping had been eased during the eighteenth century by the growth of the American shipbuilding industry. But this recourse was not open to the Royal Navy. The problem of timber supplies features in the patent records chiefly in an indirect manner: there was a regular stream of patents to preserve ships' timbers, either by the application of worm-pitch or by sheathing. The demands of the Royal Navy in wartime led to renewed interest in the 1790s, which made its main appearance in the pages of the *Repertory of Arts*. William Randall of Maidstone was planning for the long term when he proposed a method of training young trees so that they grew into appropriate shapes. His thoughts had been prompted by 'the scarcity and very high value of compass-shape timbers, the enormous waste in his majesty's yards, as well as loss of time in cutting them out from large trees'.[141] To economize on timber was the object of two inventors of new constructions for barn floors in 1797. John Upton, of Petworth (Sussex), considered that 'the barn-floors now in common use consume the large and valuable oak timber, often such as might be converted into two-and-a-half-inch ship-plank; and which is, at this time, very difficult to be procured at any price'.[142] Their anxieties found only one explicit echo in the patent records, again for a pitch composition with which ships could be caulked:

the rapid decay of ships, and their perpetual repairs, are attended with an enormous expense . . . and claim the most serious attention, particularly as the oak of this country cannot much longer supply the increasing occasion for it.[143]

In summary then, there was a growing interest throughout the eighteenth century, if not before, in labour-saving technology. Even accounting, however, for unwillingness among patentees to state intentions that appeared to threaten employment, it was always subordinate to the desire to save capital. Not surprisingly in an economy whose fixed assets were still simple and cheap, the focus was almost entirely on working capital. To speed up a mechanical, chemical, or metallurgical process promised reductions in the cost of trade credit; it might also cut fuel costs, overheads (and even wage payments). These ends were also sought in the drive for greater regularity of products and reliability of processes and machinery. In the nineteenth century many 'labour-saving' inventions were prompted not by a desire to economize on the costs of labour, but to circumvent the power of organized labour and the fallibility of workers. The search for regularity and reliability, which in the eighteenth century had focused on the vagaries of nature and the fragility of machinery, came increasingly to centre on the substitution of reliable and regular machines for unreliable and irregular humans. The new attitude is encapsulated in the famous words of James Nasmyth, the engineer:

the irregularity and carelessness of the workmen . . . gave an increased stimulus to the demand for self-acting machine tools, by which the untrustworthy efforts of hand labour might be avoided. The machines never got drunk; their hands never shook from excess; they were never absent from work; they did not strike for wages; they were unfailing in their accuracy and regularity, while producing the most delicate or ponderous portions of mechanical structures.[144]

This was a far cry indeed from John Wyatt's apprehensive petition in 1735 which had expressed fears that 'the grand objection to our patent' would be 'the diminution of the labour of a certain set or class of our people'. There may have been little factor bias in the economy, but goals such as Nasmyth's were increasingly drawing capitalists' thoughts towards concentration on inventions that disciplined or displaced labour.

IO

PATENTS: CRITICISMS AND ALTERNATIVES

Before the mid-eighteenth century the question of how best to promote invention was rarely discussed with reference to the patent system. Likewise, on those few occasions when any writer thought fit to mention the patent system it was unusual for it to be in the context of stimulating inventive activity. Patents were still regarded, first and foremost, as monopolies. The close association of letters patent with Court patronage until the end of the seventeenth century (and the range of grants for which they were used) defined them principally as instruments of the royal prerogative; the stigma lingered. When the patent 'system' was discussed it was usually as an established institution: given its existence, was it either ethical or cost-effective to use it? There were few proposals for its reform before the 1780s, and explicit calls for its abolition were a rarity before the mid-nineteenth century (when free-traders launched a noisy attack).[1] Among those who sought a means of stimulating technological development it was largely ignored. Since in the seventeenth century such concerns were confined principally to members of the Hartlib circle, who were politically at variance with the Stuart Court, it is unsurprising that they looked beyond patents. When interest was revived a century later, there was as much desire to promote the diffusion of extant best practices as to prompt inventive activity. The patent system, which at that time made virtually no demand on the inventor to reveal his secrets, tended to be dismissed without a second thought; other means of rewarding innovation were proposed. In the eighteenth century's last quarter, however, the growing competitiveness of patenting and its exposure to the often hostile environment of the law courts generated a new concern for reform among patentees themselves. And the patent system began to elicit theoretical defences amongst those who regarded the market for inventions – not parliament or other 'visible hand' – as the fairest arbiter of reward.

10.1 THE ACCEPTABLE FACE OF MONOPOLY?

The theory that monopoly privilege was a just reward for services rendered to the commonwealth was well established by the late sixteenth century.

Francis Bacon made the classic statement of it in 1601.[2] In the ensuing furore, the patent baby was carefully saved from being thrown out with the monopoly bathwater. While a monopoly was conceived as consisting 'in restraining the common right', there was no unjust encroachment in the case of invention since nothing had existed previously.[3] Exclusive control for a limited time continued to be thought an appropriate reward for the effort and expense incurred in invention. When Sir Thomas Lombe's patent was debated by parliament in 1732, the sole reported challenge to its extension opened with the claim:

that patents had always been looked upon as prejudicial to the trade and manufactures of this kingdom, more especially when continued for any long term of years: for which reason their ancestors had been so wise as to make a law against granting of any patent for a longer term than fourteen years.[4]

This ambiguous appeal to the old bogey, monopolies, was not concerned, however, with the threat to established livelihoods. New anxieties, about hindering the diffusion of a valuable invention, were uppermost; that the patent's prolongation might act as a 'great discouragement to all new improvements or manufactures, and consequently of dangerous consequence to the trade of this nation'.[5] The patent was not extended, but Lombe was given a monetary reward (with which he was probably better pleased). Opposition to particular patents came increasingly to focus on attempted extensions beyond fourteen years: only a temporary monopoly was deemed legitimate.[6]

Neither the economic function of patents, nor their form had been given serious consideration since Lord Burghley's heyday. Burghley had experimented with various clauses and conditions to achieve what must always be the aim of any patent system – a nice balance between protecting the inventor and securing the public interest in discovering and disseminating inventions.[7] Often mentioned with the 'reward-by-monopoly' justification were two related theses, which emerged in their own right as justifications for the patent system in the late eighteenth century: that the granting of patent monopolies would act as an incentive to invent; and that they were the quid pro quo for the disclosure of the inventor's secret to the public.[8] That patenting was economically beneficial was not systematically examined and rarely even doubted. A happy coincidence between rewarding individual effort and furthering the national interest was assumed rather than analysed. Petitioners for a patent increasingly based their claim on 'the hazard and expense' or 'labour and costs' they had personally suffered to bring their idea to fruition; advantages to the commonwealth were assumed to follow.[9]

Most opposition was of an ethical rather than an overtly economic nature, but it was often informed by a concern that the benefits of a discovery should be widely disseminated. Sir William Petty, although sceptical of the benefits a patent gave the inventor,[10] cited recompense for effort and expense as their justification. 'A monopoly may be of real use for a time', he added, 'at the first introducing of a new manufacture, wherein is much nicety to make it well, and which the generality of men cannot judge of the performance'; it protected the public from shoddy imitations until other manufacturers learned the correct methods of production.[11] Petty's treatment of the subject was off-hand, conventional and unenthusiastic. One of the period's most original economic thinkers and a patentee himself, Petty apparently considered patents unworthy of detailed analysis. This is less surprising when one remembers that invention and innovation rarely featured among the topics discussed in seventeenth-century economic treatises.[12] Yet, this is not the whole explanation. Carew Reynell, who was unusual for his time in emphasizing the importance both of manufacture and of innovation as its complement, totally ignored the patent system. Although most of the inventions he thought particularly praiseworthy had been patented, Reynell pronounced that 'many such useful inventions and discoveries would daily be produced, if rewards and encouragements, or pensions were appointed for the inventors', without so much as a nod in the direction of the patent system.[13] Similarly, at the start of Anne's reign, there was an anonymous proposal for an Act to protect and encourage inventors, which seems to regard the Statute of Monopolies as a stillborn piece of legislation and the patents it permitted as inadequate to stimulate invention:

That the first inventor of all new arts . . . shall (upon his entering such his invention at a proper office, or otherwise) have to himself such advantages thereby, as the laws of this land have already in that behalf provided, and further as to your great wisdom shall seem meet.[14]

Restoration patents were seen as minor courtly perquisites, not as instruments of economic policy.

A rare piece of sustained prose suggestive of original thought on the subject was written by Andrew Yarranton, the engineer and projector of several social and economic schemes.[15] It was a damning indictment of the Restoration patent system, firmly within the context of patents as monopolies. Yarranton's view was instructed by his own experience, of finding his tin-plating business ruinously impeded by a patentee whom he considered incapable of working the patent.[16] Inadequate administration permitted abuse, he believed, with the result that patents 'commonly drive trade out of the kingdom'.[17] It was right that people who invented things that genuinely benefited the public should be rewarded,

but I am against all such persons in their practices, that get patents upon pretension of benefiting the public, and so creep into some great men to favour their business; and next, to gather up some young cullies, and squeeze them till their purses are as dry as their brains; . . . the things made under the patent must be dear, because some great men have shares therein . . . Then commonly it falls out, that some . . . beat their brains, and are turning every stone to find where these commodities may be made cheaper than by the patentee, though out of England; and at last they fix to set it on foot either in New England, Virginia or Ireland, and then they comply with a workman or two of the patentee's, . . . and so carry that art quite away into another nation, where the materials are cheaper, and things better fitted for the purpose.[18]

Yarranton's solution was not reform but abolition. The Statute of Monopolies should be interpreted much more tightly, so that every part of an invention must be new. This would disallow, for example, new types of pump since pumps were already in use, or new methods of whitening hemp and flax, since women since Eve had been improving the art. One suspects that this proposal is a *reductio ad absurdum*, patentable inventions by his criteria becoming so rare as to make the system virtually inoperable.[19]

Indeed Yarranton had already expressed ethical misgivings about craft and guild secrecy, which could be extended, by implication, to patents. A clothier in an imaginary dialogue who opposed the description of a new fulling mill, in order to 'have all the benefit of these mills to ourselves at Salisbury', was reprimanded as 'not a good commonwealthsman, if you do not give me leave to print this; for it will be of general good to the clothing-trade'. The fictional clothier was stung into conceding his companion's point, even offering 'five pounds towards the charge, and send the printed papers all over Wiltshire, Dorsetshire and Somersetshire'.[20] Such 'commonwealth' thinking was not new; nor was tension between open communication and the restriction of information to a privileged one or few. Ideally the inventor should not have to be rewarded by the state nor 'bribed' to reveal his invention, but should be glad to communicate it freely to the community. In 1596 John Harrington, remembered for his invention of the water-closet, bemoaned the difficulties of securing a patent, but counselled:

let us then make a virtue of necessity, and since we cannot get these monopolies, let us say we care not for them, and a vengeance on them that beg them . . . And if Mr [Hugh] Plat will follow my advice he shall impart his rare designs gratis, as I do this, and so we may one day be put into the chronicles as good members of our country.[21]

A century and a half later, the Quaker ironmaster, Abraham Darby II, lived up to his philanthropic reputation by not seeking a patent, allegedly saying, 'he would not deprive the public of such an acquisition'.[22] From an extreme religious position, the Baptist, Matthew Caffyn, had attacked Richard Haines's patent in 1675: patents might be lawful by the law of God or men, but a Christian (especially a 'separate' or 'professor') should abstain from them 'when any thereby was grieved or offended'.[23]

10.2 THE BACONIAN CRITIQUE

Implicitly at odds with the patent system was the prospectus for scientific discovery advanced by Francis Bacon (although personally, as Lord Chancellor, he seems to have had no scruples about administering the patent system, and that with no great degree of probity).[24] The Baconian programme of extensive, inductive research and its application inspired the numerous schemes of Samuel Hartlib and his circle for the wholesale reform of society during the Commonwealth and Protectorate and, at the least, provided a coherent philosophy to which the early Royal Society could appeal in justification of its activities.[25] Essential to it were collaboration and the unhindered diffusion of information among natural philosophers.[26] It was a tenet of Renaissance humanism that knowledge was cumulative.[27] Bacon, for one, believed that it was only in the mechanical arts that any progress had been made; the philosophical and intellectual sciences had stagnated. The significant difference, he conceived, was collaboration. His goals became to free the liberal arts and sciences from the tyranny of authority by remodelling their methodology on that of the (idealized) mechanical arts, and to reinforce the latter with a new, scientific rigour, through which discovery would be less at the mercy of chance. The natural philosopher's aim should be to improve the lives of humanity as a whole.[28] Implicit was disapproval of the patent system, which rewarded the individual at the expense of the community and took little trouble to ensure dissemination.

Bacon became the posthumous ideologue of much seventeenth-century English science, and the Royal Society's espousal of his philosophy may partly explain why so few of its fellows sought patents for their inventions.[29] Although the Society made no explicit criticism, it had both ideological and pragmatic reasons for disapproving of fellows seeking patents. Unlike the French Académie des Sciences and the Florentine Academia del Cimento, there was no pretension to communal responsibility and prestige for discoveries.[30] The solitary exception was a curious multiple patent to Abraham Hill on behalf of the Society in 1665.[31] It appears to have covered the inventions and researches of several fellows, and may have marked an early attempt to deal with the problem of priority disputes. The honour of discovery, not the profit, lay at the root of many internecine struggles in the scientific community, and prompted natural philosophers to devise schemes that employed anagrams, cyphers, or sealed envelopes to establish priority.[32] Disputes were sufficiently vitriolic without exacerbation by the prospect of exclusive commercial gain.[33] The bitterness engendered between Robert Hooke and Henry Oldenburg by the latter's attempt to patent Christian Huygens's spring-balance watch in 1675 offered the Society a sharp lesson. Hooke queried Huygens's claim to the first invention, and looked on Oldenburg's attempt to profit by it as 'treachery'.[34] It was settled, in the event, by the refusal of a patent to either party, but the Royal Society suffered since Hooke set up a splinter group of disaffected fellows.[35] In May 1681 Hooke was again in dispute with a colleague, this time Nicholas Mercator, over a map-making technique. According to the Society's journal book:

Mr Hooke dissuaded Mr Mercator from taking out a patent for the said invention; . . . he himself was making maps by another way, the properties of which far exceeded those of the planisphere; for which nevertheless he would not take the benefit of a patent, but desired that the use and benefit thereof might be free.[36]

Denis Papin expressed similar self-abnegation in print that same year. He did not think it 'right, in a thing of so general use, that a man by virtue of a patent should hinder other people from working that may perhaps have more skill in doing things good and cheap'.[37] Nehemiah Grew seems to have resisted patenting his own invention for as long as possible and, after much difficulty enforcing it, sold the rights.[38] Colleagues suggested that the best way to suppress dangerous counterfeits of his salts was to reveal the correct method of making them; also that secrecy was consistent with his membership of neither the Royal Society nor the College of Physicians.[39]

Hooke was certainly alive to the possibilities of financial gain from invention. There is a draft in his hand, entitled 'Proposals for the good of the Royal Society', which may be tentatively dated to 1673, when concerted efforts were being made to revive fellows' interest in scientific matters and to put the Society on a firmer financial footing.[40] Among various administrative proposals is the suggestion:

That any person that has found out any new and useful invention, . . . shall receive from the Society a public attestation thereof under their common seal and be further gratified by a medal, picture or some mark of honour and respect suitable to his invention. . . . That a certain number of the Society be appointed to manage the prosecution of any new invention so as to bring it into use and make it profitable for the Society and the inventor.

He proposed that any profits should be divided equally between the Society and the inventor. The desirability of patents to protect these joint rights over an invention is not intimated, and the scheme has the ring of an alternative to the patent system, along the lines depicted more grandly in the *New Atlantis* (1660), which was probably also written by Hooke.[41]

The Royal Society provided throughout this period an alternative forum for invention, both for its more practically minded fellows and for others who sought its approval, occasionally in support of their patent applications, generally with no intention of patenting.[42] Many of the inventions communicated to it were of improved scientific and navigational instruments, while their inventors tended to be professional men with no commercial goals.[43] Some received a public airing in the *Philosophical Transactions*, and it was to the Royal Society that early schemes for promoting inventions were addressed.[44] The Royal Society had no corporate attitude to patenting. It was not a homogeneous body, certainly not one given to issuing definitive judgements on politically sensitive matters. Neither was patenting an issue of moment, even for a body so vitally interested in discovery and invention. Nor was a vote for open communication necessarily a vote against the patent system. Part of the complaint of fellows such as Papin and Hooke was that many inventors would rather see their discoveries lost for ever than share them with others.[45] Although not ideal, a patent system could lure such secrets into the open. But, it must be remembered, the English system was in limbo at this period. A patent had once been, and was again to be, specifically intended as a reward for making an invention available to the public; but this rationale had presently lapsed.[46] To that extent, patent versus open communication, while valid for this particular period, is generally a false contrast. Judicial insistence on full and accurate specification was to remove a major source of criticism and provide a much-needed safety valve in the patent system.

From the other side of the fence, open communication of technical knowledge was the shibboleth appealed to by guildsmen, who usually regarded patents as an unfair obstruction to the course of their business. The Clockmakers, for example, bolstered their successful resistance to various patents and private Acts with the argument that they restricted the free exercise of a skill whose development had always depended on small improvements, freely exchanged among craftsmen.[47] Improvements were communicated, however, in very uncertain ways – by the bartering of 'secrets' or by espionage and theft – and the Clockmakers' petition gave an idealized picture of guild fellowship. (The clockmakers probably came closer than most to living up to the ideal.)[48] This pragmatic objection to patents, as obstructive of improvement, was frequently employed to support the case against particular grants. It neatly linked the private to the public interest. The London pump-makers invoked it against Samuel Morland's bill in 1675: 'he would endeavour to exclude the invention of others', and thereby hinder improvements.[49] A major strand in the City of London's case against the Convex Lights bill in 1692 was that it tended 'to discourage ingenuity and invention for the public good'.[50] The Jewellers, opposing Facio's bill in 1704, stated as a general proposition that, 'all mechanic operations improve by being open and free' – open and free, that was, within the guild.[51] There are echoes here of Yarranton's strict interpretation of the Statute of Monopolies, to exclude all except totally new inventions, and of the judgement in Bircot's case over a century before.[52]

10.3 CRITICISMS OF THE ENGLISH PATENT SYSTEM

Until personally affected, either as an inventor, investor, or victim of a patentee's monopoly, few gave the patent system much thought or formed an opinion of it. There appears to have been little objection to the byzantine administrative structure, so offensive in its inefficiency to nineteenth- and twentieth-century eyes. Not even the cost of patenting incited much comment. The fee-gathering obstacles seem to have been accepted as part of legitimate government fund-raising, to which petitioners were resigned. Such murmurings as there were among disgruntled patentees were directed against the insecurity of patents, particularly the problems of enforcement and prosecution.[53] Individual patentees complained in print and sought to rectify their particular situation by obtaining stronger powers from parliament, but until the last quarter of the eighteenth century they generally did not demand changes in the patent system. In 1785 a group of patentees met in a London tavern to form a defence association against the twin, perceived threats of Pitt's proposed Irish Commercial Treaty and the cancellation of Arkwright's patent, which some, including James Watt, regarded as the product of sectional lobbying by Manchester merchants. The association appears to have been small and short-lived.[54] Watt, however, who kept his distance from this group, went on to draft detailed proposals for reform, which were circulated to judges, lawyers and M.P.s, and may have informed a bill presented to parliament, unsuccessfully, in 1793. In keeping with the law courts' (and therefore his own) preoccupation with the specification, Watt's thoughts were directed principally to reducing the patentee's vulnerability on this point.[55]

It was an old complaint of the mercantile community that government officials and judges were incompetent to determine matters that related to trade. But it marked a new departure when in 1690 Dalby Thomas, a substantial West India merchant, projector and plantation owner, included patents for invention among the commercial affairs which he thought should be considered by specialists. He was extremely critical of official methods, and recommended the setting up of a 'professional' committee to review and report on issues concerning 'the plantations, foreign negotiations, manufactures, trade or patents for new inventions'. Such a committee 'would be an infallible touchstone to try the intrinsic value of all notions, and projects, that mankind can invent, either for the general good or particular advantage'.[56] Some twenty years later, the government proposed to the Royal Society that it might screen applications for patents, in imitation of the French Académie des Sciences, but nothing came of it.[57]

The speculative disasters of the 1690s and 1720–1 prompted further suggestions that the government should protect the public by a more thorough scrutiny of patents. Marten Triewald, F.R.S., the Swedish mining engineer and patentee, considered the diving suits and bells that had been projected in profusion. He concluded,

that for contriving and improving such an invention a solid knowledge of natural philosophy is required, not only in those who set up for inventors, but also in those who are to be judges, when projects are to be examined into for the sake of the public good.[58]

The question was largely subsumed each time in that of joint-stock regulation. As we have seen, there was a tightening of the administrative reins but no substantial reform of the patent system.[59] Yet, the stock-jobbing of indiscriminately granted patents remained the anxiety uppermost in J. T. Desaguliers's mind. Without, he instanced, the intervention of a mechanically astute peer, a defective new water-engine would have received parliamentary sanction, and 'a great many persons were ready to subscribe considerable sums to the project; which money of course would all have been lost, and perhaps some families ruined'.[60] By the mid-century, concern had shifted from the investor's pocket to the consumer's health, since the system came to be dominated by 'patent' medicines. The *Gentleman's Magazine* published a cautionary tale of one who believed that 'King George the Second . . . was too good a prince to give authority for poisoning his subjects' and suffered accordingly. It continued:

> Perhaps, nothing reflects so much upon the integrity or the understanding of those in power, as this prostitution of patency. . . . The establishment of patents was undoubtedly good; but the present use of them is intolerable. . . . it was supposed that enquiry would be made, whether they were deserved, before they were granted . . . Little was it imagined that the whole ceremony would be the paying the fees, and taking the seal.[61]

David D'Escherny echoed these sentiments. He attacked the patent system as a good piece of legislation in intent, but open to abuse, particularly through the lack of scrutiny. He was among the first to propose that it should be reformed by the legislature.[62]

10.4 THE PROMOTION OF INVENTION

Commentators such as Desaguliers, D'Escherny, and Watt began with the query, 'what should be done about the patent system?' – to make it a more efficient or equitable instrument. More numerous were those who asked themselves a rather different question: 'how can we best promote invention?'. It was a question that surfaced frequently in the Hartlib circle in the mid-seventeenth century and again, more generally, a century later. Significantly, the solutions offered did not usually include the patent system, either extant or reformed. The demand was rather for direct and immediate, financial or honorary reward. The inventor would benefit from, and be encouraged by, a reward that was independent of the hazards of commercial exploitation, and the public would gain from a swifter, more widespread diffusion of inventions. This (usually implicit) attack on the patent system called forth an unprecedented defence of it, from economists and patentees, in the eighteenth century's last quarter.

Purchase of an invention by the public for its immediate use and improvement appealed strongly to those who preferred the moral economy to the rules of the market place. Francis Bacon, in his philosophic guise, was prepared to accord fame and some tangible reward, if not monopolistic rights, to those individuals who made public their inventions.[63] Similarly, the Hartlib group, while espousing the ideal of free communication of knowledge, appreciated the need in a less than perfect world for incentives to invention and its publication. Attempts to formulate schemes that would 'ensure efficiency and guarantee adequate rewards, but prevent degeneration into uncontrolled monopolies' mostly involved the state purchasing the inventor's rights over the invention.[64] They found it was no easy task to devise an appropriate system that was also acceptable to inventors.[65] 'Examining and rewarding of ingenuities and purchasing them for public use' was a major function assigned to the Office of Address, which Hartlib and his associates urged on parliament in the late 1640s. The Office was intended to pursue Bacon's goal of disseminating information, both to assist people in their daily lives and 'for the advancement of universal learning, and all manner of arts and ingenuities'.[66] To it Gerrard Winstanley, the Digger, may have owed the idea for his parish postmasters who would publicize inventions and other useful information. As for the inventors, 'let everyone who finds out a new invention have a deserved honour given him; . . . for fear of want, and care to pay rent to taskmasters, hath hindered many rare inventions'.[67]

The restoration of Charles II terminated much radical planning, but programmes for economic development and social change were still hopefully produced, often with an eye to the stronger executive powers available to a benevolent despot. One of these was the curious, self-professed continuation of Bacon's utopian tract, *New Atlantis*, bearing the same title and dedicated to the king in 1660. The author, 'R.H.', was familiar both with the ideas of contemporary 'improvers' and recent scientific researches; his concern with proper recognition for inventors and ingenious scientists makes it tempting to follow the usual identification with Robert Hooke, although there is no definitive evidence.[68] Among proposals for social and legal reforms, there are seventeen pages devoted to the wonders of scientific discovery on 'Salomon's Island'; thirteen of them describe how 'the ingenious Verdugo' was rewarded with great pomp and circumstance.[69] The author would use the stick as well as the carrot to elicit new ideas and inventions.

We have great encouragement for all ingenious persons, and give great honour and reverence as well as large rewards to the authors . . . of all artificial inventions, . . . either at home by rewarding them with great pensions, or from abroad by erecting their statues . . . We study the public good so much, that whereas we reward those that discover, so he is in some measure punished that conceals and hides a benefit which may pleasure his country.[70]

The reward was 'always made proportionable to the worth of the invention and the merits of the person'.[71] There followed a description of an elaborate celebration to reward inventors with all the honour and tribute normally reserved for military conquerors.[72] Recording the invention and 'the true manner of effecting it' constituted a major part of the ceremony. The reasoning behind this contained several barely hidden barbs for the concept of patenting:

[it] was not so much to prevent monopolizing or ingrossing that beneficial commodity to himself, whereby he only might vend his bad wares (which would be but the enriching of one man to beggar many) but chiefly to instruct others also in it, that the invention should not perish with the author; and be rather meliorated and augmented by the emulous wits of ingenious imitators.[73]

Nothing came of such grand proposals; even the Royal Society, founded in 1662, received royal good wishes but no financial assistance.

Despite this, Andrew Yarranton, who had suffered at the hands of a patentee, entertained hopes of 'a society of persons incorporate, that might inspect, advise, travel and present to authority the best means . . . of improving the manufacture and minerals of England, that the benefit thereof might be rightly applied'; perhaps a college at both the universities might be turned over to this work.[74] Personal experience also prompted William Petty to consider alternative ways of rewarding inventors. Disenchanted by lack of commercial success with his patented 'double-writing machine' and sugar-boiling pans, Petty grumbled in 1662 that 'few new inventions were ever rewarded by a monopoly'. Invention was, he thought, too important a matter to be left to the whims of the market place, where the inventor was at the mercy of financial backers who wanted to 'improve' the invention and quibbled over their shares in it, and of conservative consumers, unwilling to try anything new.[75] In 1648 he had proposed a state-funded research institution, which would draw on the skills and knowledge of practising craftsmen: 'all trades will miraculously prosper, and new inventions will be more frequent, than new fashions of clothes and household stuff'.[76] It was an artificial environment, immune from any economic stimulus to invention and from any economic reward. The conservative climate of 1662 did not lead him to renew such radical proposals, and his comments on patents have an edge of despair.

Such proposals, calling on the state to give a strong lead, began to be heard more often, and be taken more seriously, in the early eighteenth century. Grew, like Petty a fellow of the Royal Society and a disappointed patentee, admired the French example: 'for promoting the invention of any manufacture, if proof be first made of its being beneficial to the public, to encourage the author as is done in France would be great use'.[77] In outlining a plan for the improvement of hospitals and medical care John Bellers, the Quaker philanthropist, proposed that new medicines should be tested in controlled conditions and, if they succeeded repeatedly, 'a gratuity should be given by the government, to the owner of such medicines, to make a public discovery of them'; the inventor should be further rewarded with the offer of a post as physician in a hospital 'where his medicine is proper'.[78] Bellers also contended that the Royal Society should be endowed by the state, to enable it to continue improving natural knowledge, and to offer annually 'a prize to every mechanic that shall produce the best piece of work, or anything new'.[79] Not only new inventions but also their diffusion and the improvement of skills were to be rewarded. Bishop Berkeley considered there was 'still room for invention and improvement in most trades and manufactures', which could be elicited by 'premiums given . . . to ingenious artists'.[80] Malachy Postlethwayt again looked to France, listing the material rewards and assistance that were there employed 'to purchase at the *public expense* the particular secrets . . . and to grant rewards proportional to the importance of such new undertakings'. He had just discussed English patents in the context of monopolies and their hindrance to the spread of industry: grudgingly he conceded 'a kind of mitigated patent . . . limited to a small number of years, or to one, or at the most two counties, or provinces'. At a time when specification was not enforced, Postlethwayt looked back to an older expedient for disseminating the patentee's secret – to 'take a certain number of national apprentices'.[81]

Occasionally, the state had made deals with individual inventors, buying their rights in the invention where it was of direct use to the government in its administrative or military roles.[82] An important precedent was set, however, when financial rewards were ordained by the Longitude Act of 1713 – up to £20,000 for a method of determining the longitude accurately to within thirty miles after a voyage to the West Indies.[83] Justification was offered in the preamble:

but besides the great difficulty of the thing itself, partly for want of some public reward to be settled as an encouragement for so useful and beneficial a work, and partly for want of money for trials and experiments necessary thereto, no such inventions or proposals, hitherto made, have been brought to perfection.[84]

It was 1737 before the Longitude Commissioners first met, to examine the claims of John Harrison, whose first chronometer had been tested by the Royal Society and had proved its worth on a voyage to Lisbon. It took Harrison a further thirty-three years, four more chronometers, a great deal of negotiation, and finally the intervention of George III and Lord North to exact most of the £20,000 to which he was entitled. However, without the grants made him by the Board, totalling £3,000 between 1741 and 1761, it is most unlikely that Harrison could have perfected his chronometer.[85]

In 1732 parliament awarded Thomas Lombe £14,000, partly in recognition of the utility of his 'invention', partly in compensation for his failure to profit from the patent.[86] Eight years later, it again made an award, this time to Joanna Stephens for her medicine to dissolve kidney stones, on condition that she reveal the recipe. This followed a campaign in the *Gentleman's Magazine* to raise the sum Stephens demanded, which had fallen short by over £3,500.[87] For many M.P.s the stone was probably a problem more pressing than the longitude and just as intractable. In the midst of this excitement, Thomas Liveings offered to renounce his four-year-old patent 'for the national advantage, upon having such reasonable allowance as the House shall think fit'.[88] Lewis Paul and John Kay, also finding little commercial benefit in their respective textile inventions, unsuccessfully solicited parliamentary rewards.[89] At least eight Acts were passed between 1750 and 1825 to authorize the offer of awards for specific inventions, and additionally parliament granted substantial sums to specific inventors, which amounted to over £77,000 by 1815, including £30,000 to Edward Jenner for his vaccine.[90] Such intervention was itself indicative of the need for reform in the patent system.

It was largely left to public-spirited individuals, however, to finance a system of premium awards for invention and innovation. Two early eighteenth-century proposals envisaged schemes which would run in harness with the existing patent system: no inventor would fail and no invention be lost for lack of financial backing to procure and exploit a patent. An anonymous writer in 1722 proposed a society, financed by public subscription, that would sponsor experiments in inventions and new manufactures, and reward inventions 'by which trade or occupation is benefited, and where the property cannot be secured to the inventor by a patent'. Where an invention proved profitable, the society might expect to 'have a certain share in the patent, or other advantage arising from it'.[91] Similarly, Philip Peck proposed to the Royal Society in 1738 that it raise a £1,000 fund among the fellows: to assist deserving inventors 'with money to procure a patent, reserving a share or yearly sum out of the produce to be added to the capital fund'.[92]

Positive steps were already being taken in Ireland and Scotland to encourage agricultural and industrial development with premiums and sponsorship of research. In Scotland a fund, financed out of the malt excise, was established at the Union, to be administered by a Board of Trustees for the Improvement of Manufactures in Scotland.[93] The linen industry in particular benefited from this Malt Fund, since the Board supported and rewarded research into better methods and machinery. Prizes of £100 or more were paid to inventors out of the Model Fund, established in 1727. But the Board was also concerned to disseminate the improvements throughout Scotland, paying inventors to teach their new methods, and there was a two-way flow of information with its Irish counterpart.[94] The Dublin Society was founded in 1731 among landowners to finance new manufactures and agricultural experiments.[95] In 1740, disillusioned by the ineffectiveness of 'merely printing instructions and distributing a few premiums for inventions', it adopted Samuel Madden's plan for awards to be offered in annual competitions of skill – for the best woven piece of linen, for example.[96] Between 1761 and 1767 alone it distributed £42,000 of government money in the promotion of agriculture and manufactures.[97]

When William Shipley, an artist and member of the Northampton Philosophical Society, proposed a similar society for England in 1753, he found a ready, if initially small, audience.[98] Nearly half the founder members of the Society of Arts, which emerged from Shipley's proposals, were fellows of the Royal Society. Influenced as they were by a revival of interest in Bacon's philosophy, their priorities bore his hallmark of collaborative research and diffusion of useful knowledge.[99] By 1761 the Society had a membership of nearly 2,000 and an income from subscriptions of £3,656.[100] As far as one can tell, the patent system was totally ignored by the early Society. Shipley may have disapproved of it, since he never attempted to patent any of his own inventions.[101] The Society's position was clarified, however, in the Rules and Orders for 1765, which laid down that 'no person will be admitted a candidate for any premium offered by the Society who has obtained a patent for the exclusive right of making or performing anything for which such premium is offered'.[102] A later attempt to require prizewinners not to obtain a subsequent patent was not, however, accepted by the Society.[103] There was little overlap between the Society's awards and the patent system. No more than twenty patentees have been identified among those receiving premiums or medals during the Society's first thirty-five years – a small minority of both patentees and awardees.[104]

The premium system operated by the Society demanded a commitment to communication on the part of inventors which the patent system only began to approach in 1778 and has never fully enshrined. Once submitted to the Society, an invention became *de facto* public property. Models and examples of mechanical devices that received premiums were placed in the Society's Repository of Inventions, which amassed an excellent collection of agricultural and industrial machinery, open to public inspection.[105] The Dublin Society, similarly, had imported machinery from England and Holland, keeping it all together for Irish farmers and manufacturers to examine, imitate and, they hoped, improve upon.[106] They were implementing an idea mooted originally by Francis Bacon: Salomon's House was to contain a gallery of inventions, and the idea was repeated by Baconians like Petty throughout the seventeenth century.[107] Nehemiah Grew had suggested in 1707, as part of his ambitious improvement scheme presented to Queen Anne, that there should be 'a repository in every county' to contain examples or models of all tools, machines and materials, with the aim of prompting invention and improvement.[108] Because it was not operating a 'first past the post' system, the Society was in a position to reward effort towards, and improvement on, inventions. Shipley proposed to give 'the greatest [premiums] of all to those who shall most amply execute or cause to be executed, the said inventions or improvements'.[109] He was echoed by a Dorset subscriber, who thought 'the great point to be laboured at is to stir up an universal spirit of all attempting improvements', and by Lord Folkestone, who was 'persuaded we must not only invent, but find a way to put in practice too, before we can make things answer our wishes'.[110] Similar goals informed the activities of other societies founded at this period, such as the Bath and West Society or the Royal Institution.[111] Their emphasis on improvement and diffusion was alien to the patent system.

Less altruistic motives prompted groups of manufacturers to establish subscriptions that might forestall an inventor's plan to patent. In 1765, Derbyshire hosiers proposed to raise £400 to reward a local man who had invented a simpler and cheaper stocking frame, 'rather than they should be deprived of the benefit by the obtaining a patent'.[112] The Manchester Committee for the Protection of Trade was systematic in its opposition to patents:

Caveats have been entered . . . against the obtention of any patents that are likely to affect the trade or manufacture of this country, by which means the Committee . . . will have early notice of every application for patents of that sort, and will thereby have an opportunity of opposing them and of . . . recommending some other mode of reward for ingenuity so as to prevent the pernicious effects of patents.[113]

Inventors, like Samuel Crompton, were often deceived in their expectations of the manufacturers' show of gratitude under these alternative arrangements.

10.5 PATENTS DEFENDED

Patents and premiums, exclusive in operation, were complementary in some ways, and judgements of their respective value tended to vary according to the particular industry concerned. The Society of Arts was important, for instance, in stimulating the invention and improvement of farming implements, promoting increased accuracy of mapping, and fostering inventive activity in small-scale, often craft-oriented manufactures.[114] On the other hand, it was criticized for neglecting more radical inventions and proposals. Thus Thomas Bentley complained of the Society's indifference towards the Grand Trunk Canal scheme in 1765: 'but they have been too immersed in the little scheme of bringing fish to London!'[115] Its scope was also restricted by modest financial resources. Lack of response to a premium for ironmaking prompted the Society's secretary, Robert Dossie, to comment: 'none but the proprietors of considerable works could possibly perform what was required to be done and they have infinitely greater inducements than the sum offered'.[116]

Critics of the Society usually preferred to put their faith in the market's hidden hand to reward inventors according to merit. But out and out free traders in invention were rare before 1850: the patent system was deemed to provide a suitable, temporary protection and framework for an invention's implementation and its inventor's reward by monopoly. In a considered treatise, published in 1774, W. Kenrick, Doctor of Laws, thought parliamentary premiums 'will always run the risk of being inadequate' to the invention's utility or the inventor's effort, while the examples he gave suggested, rather, that he considered parliament had been too generous in its awards.[117] 'Of the petty premiums presented by the Societies for the Encouragement of Arts and Manufactures . . . I shall say little, as indeed but little is to be said', he continued; candidates complained of injustice and cabals, and the Societies' 'laudable purposes . . . have been seldom attained'.[118] Patents, argued Kenrick, were 'the most plausible and politic method of bestowing that encouragement . . . by which the eventual utility of such inventions is made the measure of reward'.[119] In a letter to the *Gentleman's Magazine*, Edward Goodwin, of Sheffield, claimed patents were preferable because, unlike premiums, they did not waste public money on 'visionary schemes, idle projects, or trivial attainments'; if an invention was of real utility, then 'society and the inventor are mutually benefited'.[120] A similar judgement was offered anonymously in 1791, with a forecast that, if patents were replaced by an alternative system of rewards, then 'the stimulative of exclusive right no longer operating, there would be an end to invention'.[121]

The patent system won the support of the classical economists, usually as a corollary to their opposition to state interference in the economy. In 1776 Adam Smith justified patents for new machinery and copyright over books in terms that would have been familiar to Coke: they were 'the easiest and most natural way the state can recompense them for hazarding a dangerous and expensive experiment, of which the public is afterwards to reap the benefit'.[122] More than ten years before, Smith had cited patents for invention as a rare example of a harmless, exclusive privilege: it was probably the fairest reward for ingenuity that could be devised, since it was unlikely that the legislature could give 'pecuniary rewards . . . so precisely proportioned to the merit as this is. For here, if the invention be good and such as is profitable to mankind, he will probably make a fortune by it; but if it be of no value he will also reap no benefit.'[123] These arguments continued to appear in the writings of economists through the first half of the nineteenth century.[124]

Contemporary with, and often informing, this new concern for invention and its appropriate reward, was a novel conceptualization of it as 'intellectual property'. This offered a new justification for patents, independent of the 'monopoly' arguments. However, this rationale did not become popular in England. Even in that heyday of natural rights, the late eighteenth century, it made little progress against the appeal to precedent and statute law.

If the concept of intellectual property was current in the seventeenth century, it was rarely articulated. It arose first in respect of copyright in literary works. When petitioning parliament in 1643 that copyright should be secured to individual printers, the Stationers Company advanced the argument that:

there is no reason apparent why the productions of the brain should not be assignable, and their interest and possession (being of more rare, sublime, and public use, meriting the highest encouragement) being held as tender in law, as the right of any goods or chattels whatsoever.[125]

Similarly, but more colourfully, John Dunton in 1705 told of his resolve to crush the competition of Brown and Pate's *Lacedemonian Mercury* to his own, original publication, the *Athenian Mercury*:

upon this, I was resolved one way or another to blow 'em up, in regard, 'twas both ungenerous and unjust, to interlope upon a man, where he has the sole right and property, for the children of the brain are as much ours, as those we beget in lawful wedlock.[126]

Copyright, which involved more clear-cut 'inventions' in the texts of the book-selling and publishing trades, than did patents in the sphere of technical invention, was a more immediate and controversial issue in the seventeenth century. Printing patents were disputed in the law courts far more frequently than patents for invention. Fourteen years after the lapsing, in 1695, of licences for publication the need for some enforceable guidelines was recognized in the first Copyright Act.[127] The notion of property in literary inventions continued to exercise both English and Scottish judges during the eighteenth century.[128]

The first mention of intellectual property that I have found in regard of a technical invention is in the title of a pamphlet published in 1712, *Reasons for the bill entituled, A bill for securing to Mr John Hutchinson the property of a movement invented by him for the more exact measuring of time.* By the proposal, made in 1722, for a subscription society to sponsor inventors, it was intended to give monetary rewards 'where the property cannot be secured to the inventor by a patent',[129] and, in 1724, Robert Pantoune requested a patent 'for securing to him the property in the practice of the said method'.[130] The concept reappears sporadically in patent applications later in the century, and is enshrined in the Act extending James Watt's patent in 1775 ('his property in the said invention secured'). In the technological sphere, ideas of providential invention had perhaps militated against notions of intellectual property.[131] If the inventor was no more than God's instrument in bringing His gifts to the community, then he could at most claim user's rights over them. A more secular understanding of the inventive process, however, prompted a growing regard for the individual inventor and an anxiety that he should be rewarded and encouraged. The shift from use rights to absolute property in land had been in progress for at least two centuries, if not longer.[132] It is indicative of the slight regard paid to technical change before the mid-eighteenth century that the concept of property in invention was so late on the scene. Adam Smith contended, in 1762, that 'the property one has in a book he has written or a machine he has invented, which continues by patent in this country for fourteen years, is actually a real right'.[133] But it remained unclear what this might mean, since the inventor's property was unprotected in law until he bought its certification from the crown in a patent. This was not directly tested in the courts. Before anyone took the opportunity to argue a natural right to his unpatented invention, matters were brought to a head on copyright.

In a legal dispute over the nature of literary property which reached the House of Lords on appeal in 1774, the *lack* of a natural right in mechanical inventions provided a fixed pole of the debate.[134] Those who argued for an author's natural right to his printed copy in perpetuity felt obliged to distinguish between literary and mechanical inventions; those who denied it, and contended that the Copyright Act created a protection that had previously not existed, drew analogies between them. Two law lords were prepared to speculate that, perhaps, 'previous to the monopoly statute, there existed a common law right, equally to an inventor of a machine and an author of a book'.[135] But the opinion which prevailed was that the author's natural right in his literary property ceased on publication of his manuscript, in the same way that an inventor's did when he revealed his secret. Their only subsequent property was the temporary one secured to the author under the

Copyright Act and to the inventor by a patent granted under the Statute of Monopolies.[136] With no custom to guide him, Lord Mansfield had turned to natural law and ruled that 'it is *just* that an author should reap the pecuniary profits of his own ingenuity and labour; it is *just* that another should not use his name without his consent'.[137] The law lords, upholding the appeal against Mansfield's ruling, had taken issues of principle into account, but their judgements had been couched largely in terms of precedent: they debated whether a common-law right existed, not whether a natural right ought to prevail.

Ironically in the light of the Lords' ruling, Kenrick proceeded to argue for a liberalization of the patent system by analogy with copyright. Inventors he considered to possess an 'equal claim to the natural rights of genius' with authors and a 'superior right to public encouragement on principles of political expediency'.[138] He protested that the state was failing to erect this natural right into a property right by charging large sums for patent protection and by limiting it, indiscriminately, to fourteen years. Authors might have failed in the House of Lords to secure a perpetual copyright, but they were still accorded an automatic and free protection of their printed copy for a minimum of fourteen years by the 1709 Act; inventors had to buy protection of their rights, and often could not afford to.[139] A patent was defined in 1791 as 'a grant of the crown substantiating private property' (a property which the House of Lords had considered not to exist).[140] And six years later, Joseph Bramah distinguished between 'natural principles', which were 'the common property of all men' and could not be patented, and 'invention . . . those efforts of the mind and understanding', which 'may justly be denominated the right of every individual, . . . unconnected with any political regulation' and could be.[141]

The concept of a natural right in intellectual property was the basis of patent and copyright laws passed in France and some of the American states in the late eighteenth century. The National Assembly, in 1790, declared that 'it would be a violation of the Rights of Man . . . not to regard an industrial discovery as the property of its author'.[142] In England the common-law tradition, with its appeal to custom and precedent, militated against natural-rights theories. Patentees and their supporters felt themselves on surer ground with the older, utilitarian rationales: the crown, with the express sanction of parliament, granted a temporary monopoly as reward, incentive, or exchange for secrets (this latter increasingly emphasized by the courts' insistence on full and accurate specification).[143] Justification of patents by a natural-rights argument was never common in England, and fell into disuse in the early nineteenth century.[144] It was subject, in common with natural-rights theories as a whole, to a battery of criticism.

The foundation of the Society of Arts and the large public interest and support that it excited was indicative of the mounting concern for invention and innovation in mid-eighteenth-century England. The patent system, however, was largely ignored as at best ineffective, or at worst a brake on invention and its dissemination. It was left to inventors and innovating manufacturers themselves to 'rediscover' the patent system after 1760 and employ it to their best abilities, despite the huge financial costs and inconvenience of the unreformed system and the frequent hostility of judges and juries. It was also they who began to propose reforms to deal with such problems. Debate was prompted by several well-publicized legal cases and, on the other hand, by sometimes controversial, parliamentary rewards to inventors. It was largely conducted in terms of the rival merits of patents and premiums, but this prompted some scrutiny of the patent system. Outside the circle of patentees themselves, however, the debate was muted. The rights of authors, publishers and printers were hard fought in the law courts and attracted considerable attention, some of which was reflected onto mechanical invention. There was relatively little public controversy about patents, since the promotion of invention and technical change was only just beginning to assume a national importance. England's heroes were still Shakespeare, Milton and Locke; few had heard of Arkwright and Watt, let alone of Kay or Newcomen.

II

A NEW CONCEPT OF INVENTION

The focus of this final chapter is not the patent system but invention itself and the ways in which it was conceptualized in the seventeenth and eighteenth centuries. This period witnessed not only a gradual reawakening of interest in technology, but also the birth of a new concept of invention. Seventeenth-century discussions of invention were rare and couched largely in metaphysical terms; eighteenth-century ones were comparatively numerous, and their context increasingly economic. Also, while the metaphysical balance shifted from divine to human agency, the economic one moved from the preservation of employment to the benefits of labour-saving inventions.

Lynn Thorndike has remarked on 'a lack of widespread interest in mechanical invention' in the seventeenth century, in contrast with the high middle ages and the late eighteenth century and thereafter.[1] This may seem a strange judgement on the century that saw the foundation of the Royal Society in England and of similar societies elsewhere in Europe. But, if one excepts these groups with their passionate interest in all things scientific and technological, then Thorndike's opinion is just. Technical change there was; but manufacturing innovations attracted little notice and scant debate about their role, source, or effect. There persisted a fascination with mechanical *wonders*, which the seventeenth century had inherited from the middle ages. It was evinced by the 'virtuosi', those leisured gentlemen who found recreation in 'learned pleasure and delight' and collected 'mechanical toys, wooden birds and iron flies, and parlour tricks'.[2] The Royal Society was ambivalent towards this stance and on the whole discouraged it. In Bishop Sprat's words, the Royal Society 'endeavours rather to know, than to admire: and looks upon admiration not as the end but as the imperfection of our knowledge'.[3] This was an interest in technology completely divorced from economic concerns. Yet the alternative, utilitarian attitude which the Royal Society promoted was barely more economically informed. Its fellows took pride in being able to substitute reason for necessity as 'the mother of invention', believing that disinterested, scientific enquiry would produce a wealth of technical benefits. The first two sections of the present chapter explore their approach.

Outside the Royal Society's idealist orbit, contemplation of invention exercised few minds. Technical change, as the third and fourth sections demonstrate, was apparently deemed either unlikely or unnecessary; in fact it was something best left to foreigners – for Englishmen to copy and improve upon. It also carried the threat of unemployment and unrest. As we have seen in chapter 9, seventeenth-century patentees stressed the creation of employment rather than the saving of labour. Economic writers were no keener to explore labour-saving possibilities: section 5 examines the reasons for this and why they began, in the next century, to give it a hesitant, then an enthusiastic, welcome.[4]

The revival of interest in invention that one finds in print in the second half of the eighteenth century is the subject of section 6. It stemmed in part from a resurgence of Francis Bacon's utilitarian influence, but it was chiefly stimulated by recognition of actual developments in manufacturing technologies and their potential economic importance. Excitement at inventive achievements and fear at their impact on employment both had a part to play. Economic writers increasingly found a place for technical change in their analyses and prescriptions. A reawakened popular admiration was extended from automata and clever illusions to the power of the steam engine and the productive capacities of silk- and cotton-spinning machinery. Although lacking in immediate economic value, the 'conquest' of the air, so long dreamt of and at last achieved in 1783 in hot-air and hydrogen balloons, must have added to the sense that humanity's technical powers were limitless.[5] Despite this latter French achievement, the British were boosting their collective ego. They ceased, during the eighteenth century, to look to continental Europe for a technological lead and began to pride themselves on being in the vanguard of invention.

The metaphysic of invention was reshaped independently of its economic aspect, by those more interested in the source than the application of ideas. By limiting divine intervention to an initial 'winding of the clock', the Newtonian world view promoted humanity from the mere agent of God's providence to a rational manipulator of nature. A fatalistic view, in which inventions were released as God saw fit, was gradually replaced during the eighteenth century by one in which an infinitude of inventions could be produced solely by human effort and ingenuity. This shift in conceptualization of invention, and its relationship to new ideas about intellectual property and the patent system are examined in the final section.

11.1 THE ROLE OF PROVIDENCE

Concepts of technical progress prevailing among intellectuals in the late seventeenth century were fatalistic. Improved methods of discovery gave every confidence of a wealth of new inventions to come, but progress could only be as fast as Providence allowed or dictated. The received notion was

Platonic, which is unsurprising when one considers the influence of neo-platonism among Renaissance natural philosophers: Providence kept a stock of useful inventions, to be released and materialized at appropriate times, provided humankind made an effort to discover them – implying both need and desert. Symptomatic, perhaps, of this is the frequent use – noticeable in patent applications – of the words 'discover' or 'find out', where we would now write 'invent'. 'Invention' was also used in a way closer to its classical root, in the sense of uncovering something that had been there all the time – on a par with new lands, planets, or laws of nature.[6] In contrast, our present-day understanding of technical 'invention' assumes a creative act or an imaginative leap, synthesis rather than analysis.[7] Such a usage, in the seventeenth and eighteenth centuries, was reserved primarily for literary creativity.[8]

Emphasis on the role of Providence above human efforts is strongest in the more conservative writers, like Meric Casaubon and Jonathan Edwardes.[9] Since innovation was, in general, something to be wary of, a providential account helped accommodate it. In his Boyle lecture of 1712, William Derham depicted the inventor as subject 'to the agency or influence of the spirit of God', acting as God's agent 'to employ the several creatures; to make use of the various materials; to manage the grand business'. He believed that some things, flight for example, had remained undiscovered, not through lack of human industry nor because of technical impossibility. It was rather,

because the infinitely wise Creator and Ruler of the World has been pleased to lock up these things from man's understanding and invention, for some reason best known to himself, or because they might be of ill consequence, and dangerous amongst men.[10]

Protestant divines liked to regard the invention of printing as part of God's preparations for the Reformation,[11] and James Tennant of Norfolk engagingly recommended his military invention to Bishop Gilbert Burnet, in 1689, as having been revealed at that particular time by 'the wisdom of Providence . . . to change the poise and balance of the European world'.[12]

Proponents of the new philosophy put greater stress on human wit in its meeting with Providence. Robert Boyle noted how many phenomena were discovered only when a problem was considered from a new angle, or when two things were unusually brought together and considered in relation to one another.[13] Basic to this idea was a conception of nature as one grand, interrelated design, comprehensible by rational investigation.[14] Joseph Glanvill was explicit: the Royal Society believed that,

there is an inexhaustible variety of treasure which Providence has lodged in things, that to the world's end will afford fresh discoveries; and suffice to reward the ingenious industry and researches of those that look into the works of God, and go down to see his wonders in the deep.[15]

The balance between individual effort and the workings of Providence shifted increasingly in the former's favour. By the mid-eighteenth century, the Anglican churchman, prolific inventor and founder-member of the Society of Arts, Stephen Hales, contended that not to consider new remedies for old inconveniences was to renounce human reason. His account was unselfconsciously secular.

It is to be remembered that new and useful discoveries are . . . the reward of careful and diligent researches. For the power of a proper series of experiments for making new discoveries is very great.[16]

Underneath the metaphysical explanation for that intractable puzzle, the source of invention, practical men had not been blind to the fact that technical advances sprang from their own activities. Aaron Hill's urbane formula of 'downright industry, and thinking a little out of the beaten road' was not uncommon.[17] And one person's Providence was another's 'luck'. Stories of invention by chance seem to have been part of popular folk-lore then as now.[18]

11.2 FRANCIS BACON AND THE NATURAL PHILOSOPHERS

Demand for recognition of the dignity of the mechanical arts, not only of their intrinsic value as funds of information, but also of their methods as models for procedure in the investigation of nature, was a major element in the transformation of scientific enquiry in the seventeenth century.[19] Adoption of the artisan tradition, in Rossi's words, 'implied the rejection of a certain conception of science, . . . as a disinterested contemplation of truth [and] as an investigation that comes into being and is pursued only *after* the things necessary to life have been attended to'.[20] Francis Bacon was its most famous polemicist in England, but its roots went much wider geographically and deeper chronologically. From the early fifteenth century, treatises had been written by craftsmen, engineers and artists to communicate the elements of their trades, both practical and theoretical.[21] A prime example was George Agricola's treatise on mining and metallurgy, *De re metallica* (1536), where current practice as he had witnessed it was described and illustrated.[22]

Many of the most scientifically active and thoughtful fellows of the early Royal Society drew strength from the confidence of Bacon and his artisan predecessors and from their own awareness of recent scientific and technical triumphs. The abundance of new discoveries, uncontemplated by the Ancients, was frequently used as an argument that nature's riches were still waiting to be tapped.[23] Geographical discoveries and the 'new worlds' opened up by optical instruments were particularly influential in this respect.[24] The conventional, sixteenth-century tryptich of inventions – printing, the compass and gunpowder – gradually shed its embarrassing third element during the seventeenth century; it was replaced by recent discoveries, particularly the telescope, microscope and circulatory system.[25] Optimism was further engendered by the belief that even the most complex structure could be reduced to a few simple principles. In 1654 Christopher Wren stressed the multiplicity of possible solutions to a single problem: they could be reached 'by an easy manduction [sic] and method . . . not only in this but any other mechanical invention'; then one determined the simplest and most effective solution among them by a process of experimentation and elimination.[26]

The period's most cogent and far-seeing exposition of the faith founded on Bacon's philosophy was written by Robert Boyle. *Some considerations touching the usefulness of experimental philosophy* was a work of major significance. With the advantage of greater, personal experimental practice and another half-century's scientific developments behind him, Boyle refashioned Bacon's programme.[27] The first part, published in 1663, was intended to assuage fears that the new philosophy would lead to atheism, and to give a reasoned assessment of the contribution experimental philosophy could make to medicine.[28] In the second part, which appeared in 1671 ('it could scarce come forth more seasonably to recommend the whole design of the Royal Society'),[29] Boyle treated extensively and systematically the reciprocal benefits that might be expected from co-operation between experimental philosophy and workshop practice, and of the ultimate practical value of even pure mathematics.[30] He dispensed with Bacon's distinction between 'fructiferous' and 'luciferous' experiments, on the grounds that all investigations had both theoretical and practical implications and were mutually contributory. Many benefits would depend on *future* scientific achievements.

And perhaps I should not hyperbolize, if I should venture to say that there is scarce any considerable physical truth, which is not, as it were, teeming with profitable inventions, and may not by human skill and industry, be made the fruitful mother of divers things useful.[31]

In mechanics the benefits were often immediately obvious; in chemistry and the life and earth sciences much more work had to be done before they could be usefully applied.[32] Boyle's hope was that, in investigating the artisan's practice, the philosopher would both be able to suggest improved methods of working and gain insights into the operations of nature.[33] Even greater advantage was to be expected from a comparative survey of trades. Boyle here propounded the rationale behind the Royal Society's cherished History of Trades project, which had been pursued energetically by several leading fellows in the 1660s.[34]

Natural philosophers, such as Boyle, looked forward in the long term to a land of better food supplies, improved communications, longer and healthier lives, greater leisure, and a deeper understanding of nature and thereby of God. Economic appraisals of the mechanisms by which this nirvana would be effected went no deeper than an appeal to the state to finance research and information services.[35] New inventions and discoveries were still viewed outside any economic context and, except in promotional literature and scientific descriptions, were mentioned most frequently as trophies – evidence of the superiority of the new philosophy over the Aristotelian.[36] Reason was to govern the realm of invention: it would produce far greater effect than leaving invention to mere chance, and guide invention in more profitable directions than did the patronage of the rich demanding luxury items.[37] But it was a reason largely uninformed by economic desiderata. There existed a curious hiatus between perceptions of actual (economic) stimuli to invention, on which natural philosophers themselves often operated, and the isolated, reason-dominated utopias they presented.[38] Demand functions were barely considered beyond casual repetition of the commonplace that 'necessity is the mother of invention'.[39]

Both Boyle and Sprat defended the Royal Society's mechanical pursuits against the accusation that they would injure craftsmen with the argument that philosophers would supply them with new, better methods. 'For these inventions of ingenious heads', thought Boyle, '. . . set many mechanical hands a work, and supply tradesmen with new means of getting a livelihood, or even enriching themselves.'[40] He conceded, however, that necessity had called forth ingenuity to happy effect.

As it is proverbially said, that necessity is the mother of invention, so experience daily shows, that the want of subsistence, or of tools and accommodation, makes craftsmen very industrious and inventive, and puts them upon employing such things to serve their present turns, as nothing but necessity would have made even a knowing man to have thought on. By which means, they discover new uses and applications for things, and consequently new attributes of things.[41]

Boyle was here edging towards recognition of an economic dynamic to invention, but he mentioned it merely as one of the ways in which tradesmen might be able to assist scholarly research, of no more than subsidiary relevance to his overall scheme. Sprat, however, explicitly removed invention from the tradesman's court, denying that the promptings of necessity could be fruitful: 'invention is an heroic thing, and placed above the reach of a low and vulgar genius'.[42] The only necessity he envisaged as a spur to invention was near-starvation, but it was unproductive:

[Necessity] often indeed engages men to brave attempts, but seldom carries them on to finish what they began. It labours at first for want of bread; and that being obtained it commonly gives over: it rather sharpens than enlarges men's wits. It sooner puts them upon small shifts, than great designs: it seldom runs to high, or magnanimous things. For the same necessity which makes men inventive, does commonly depress and fetter their inventions.[43]

'Non-artificers' possessed several advantages: they brought a fresh mind, neither stultified by routine nor 'subdued and clogged' by constant toil; they could afford mistakes (which might ultimately be fruitful); while those who laboured for their livelihoods 'cannot defer their expectations so long, as is commonly requisite for the ripening of any new contrivance'.[44] In this assessment Sprat was echoing the master, Bacon.[45]

11.3 AN ECONOMIC PERSPECTIVE ON INVENTION

If authors in the Baconian tradition looked at technical change chiefly in terms of the supply of inventions, even those in the mainstream of economic writing recognized the stimulus of demand only in the most general terms. Writers on economic subjects might have been expected to consider two types of technical change. One would be to effect a shift in the resource base consequent upon intolerable strains placed on existing resources, typically by a surge in population. This may be termed fundamental change, since it was likely to involve the whole society in altering its mode of production to a greater or lesser degree.[46] The other type is less urgent and is endemic to a competitive, capitalistic market, where the consumer's surplus income is the target in view – to be secured by the provision of greater variety and choice, cutting costs, or improving quality. The former received little attention, the latter became comparatively an obsession, but for most of this period implied improvement and variation in design, rather than technical invention.

Neither natural philosophers nor economic writers advocated any fundamental change, any shift in the resource base (although many of the former were preoccupied with the conservation of timber stocks). The most radical insight into the powers of technology to overcome resource bottlenecks predates this period. In 1639, after a century in which England's population had doubled in size, Gabriel Plattes, a member of the Hartlib circle, offered a remarkably sanguine account of how technology had always met the challenge of population pressure. Plattes trusted to God's revelation of improvements as required. This optimism was partly grounded on his having to hand new farming methods to forestall the imminent crisis. Application of these techniques would, he believed, provide for human sustenance 'for many ages, though wars should cease and people increase marvellously', but eventually the ceiling would again be reached.[47] Plattes was writing after a run of bad harvests and consequent rural destitution. As a result of the adoption of such farming techniques, combined with the stabilization of population totals, the 'Malthusian' spectre was laid to rest for a century after 1660.[48] Harvest crises did not disappear, but they were interspersed with long periods when the overriding problem was extremely low grain prices. 'Populousness', a call for increase, became the cry: the ravages of disease, not the uncontrolled increase of numbers, appeared as the threat to national wealth and welfare.[49] Population expansion began to receive more cautious consideration again from the mid-eighteenth century, as numbers started to rise more steadily. It became the received orthodoxy to assert that population will always advance to the limit set by availability of resources – with more, or less, alarm depending on the author's confidence in humankind's capacity to push forward its technological horizon.[50] Notoriously, it culminated in the disconcerting thesis of Thomas Malthus's first edition of *Essay on the principles of population*, published in 1798, which took no account of the potentialities of technical change.

Englishmen betrayed a sense of complacency, tinged with envy, when they contemplated Dutch achievements. The Dutch appeared to provide the paradigm of necessity being the mother of invention; it was a necessity that was thought not to press on England. Most attributed Holland's 'eminence of manufacture, industry and arts' to the stimulus of land shortage.[51] John Houghton fastened rather on their shortage of labour: the Dutch had been forced 'to supply hands, invent all the engines for quick dispatch imaginable', but, he added, 'I will not wish such necessity upon ourselves to the like improvement'.[52] A fellow of the Royal Society, Houghton was looking to disinterested reason and scientific investigation to promote invention.

Even where necessity did seem to impinge, invention was not their regular recourse. The danger of overexploiting timber stocks, whose regrowth (for construction purposes) took a man's lifetime, was being impressed on seventeenth-century Englishmen, anxious for the royal and merchant fleets and fearful of dependence on Baltic timber imports.[53] The number of industries in competition for wood was being reduced by the changeover to mineral fuels that is visible in the patent records throughout the century. However, during the century's middle decades, when the problem of timber supply was most acute, neither ferrous nor non-ferrous metal refiners had any alternative to charcoal, whose price, like that of timber, was rising steeply. Iron works, in particular, were commonly regarded as a villain, not just another victim, of the timber shortage.[54] It is indicative of the lack of expectation of technical solutions to problems of supply that there was no call for research into the substitution of mineral for wood fuel in these industries. The Navy Commissioners enlisted the help of John Evelyn and the Royal Society, but his *Sylva* was concerned with planting and conservation.[55] There was no obvious, or specialized source from which inventions might spring – in the guise of institutionalized, heavily capitalized, scientific research. Moreover, the discovery of the New World and optimism about future discoveries of territory promised fresh supplies of foodstuffs and raw materials within the existing resource base. Tomorrow seemed well catered for. Again, seventeenth-century Englishmen did not regard themselves as an inventive race; they received the benefits of necessity at second hand. There existed, it was generally thought, a sufficiently large pool of technical know-how and machinery on the continent of Europe to be drawn upon; the sole requirement was for Continental processes to be imitated and, wherever possible, improved upon. Faith was put in the skill and ingenuity of the English artisan to effect this. Defoe voiced a common sentiment when he wrote:

it is a kind of proverb attending the character of Englishmen, that they are better to improve than to invent, better to advance upon the designs and plans which other people have laid down, than to form schemes and designs of their own and which is still more, the thing seems to be really true in fact, and the observation very just.[56]

When a new item of technology was needed, it was assumed that foreign artisans would be imported to demonstrate it or build machinery.[57]

If technical innovation under the stimulus of resource limitation was not a feature of economic writing between 1660 and 1750, neither did it often appear in any other guise. Before the late eighteenth century there was little expectation of continuous invention – at least in the sense of 'invention' as something that would be 'not obvious to one skilled in the art'.[58] A ceiling even to improvement, both technical and economic (independent of population growth), was the assumption revealed by various writers outside 'scientific' circles. David Hume expressed his conviction that economic growth had natural limits: 'the growth of everything, both in arts and nature, at last checks itself'.[59] This was a much debated proposition and some of Hume's contemporary critics, notably Tucker, regarded technical innovation as a source of continuing growth.[60] And Hume was criticized specifically on this argument in 1804 by Lauderdale, for not considering 'the unlimited resources that are to be found in the ingenuity of man in inventing means of supplanting labour by capital'.[61] But the classical economists as a whole were in sympathy with Hume, not the optimistic Lauderdale. It was not a failure in the supply of labour, but in that of raw materials, which informed the pessimism of Smith, Malthus, Ricardo (and even J. S. Mill in the mid-nineteenth century). They warned that the land's capacity to produce both food and industrial raw materials was finite, and growth therefore limited. At best one could hope for stabilization at a relatively high level of real wages; if, however, population increase was unconstrained, immiseration was the long-term prospect.[62]

11.4 INVENTION AND THE ARTISANS

Gradual, even steady, improvement in existing techniques, within the existing resource base, was the general expectation. Here Providence was quiescent: its major role was in the release of new inventions of major significance; improvement was the affair of artisans, beneath the notice of philosophers. 'Industry' and 'application' were called on far more frequently than was 'invention' to increase productivity. Indeed, while 'invention' retained many pejorative aspects – Johnson's *Dictionary* gave 'forgery' as one of its meanings – 'ingenuity' and 'improvement' had only positive connotations. Above all, progress was located in the improvement by working men of their own skills. Grew, for example, reckoned that 'more skill and more hands will infallibly make cheap', and Davenant regarded 'skill and neatness' as the key to success of English watches.[63] Mandeville stressed repeatedly that 'skill and industry' were at the root of improvement. His praise for the empiricism and industriousness of working men as the source of all improvements (and inventions) belies disillusionment with the potentiality of science to effect technical development.[64]

Concern for high quality was persistent. Some thought it offered a safer alternative to cutting labour costs. Defoe in 1728, for example, rejected the claim that low wages were a precondition of commercial success: England's high standard of living was her pride and the basic ingredient of high-quality workmanship.[65] He had earlier insisted that the quality of English cloth (which sold on its reputation) would fall with wages.[66] But there was a further requirement, at least for luxury goods, and that was fashion. Snobbery, 'good taste', demanded French or East Indian wares.[67] Barbon acutely based his opposition to import bans on this perception: fashion, the desire for novelties and rarities, not necessity, was the chief spring of trade.[68] Most writers called for the Court to lead the way in making English wares fashionable at home.[69] The other solution proposed was to produce English goods that would actually *set* the fashion. In this the role of the practising artisan was again emphasized. He was urged to utilize his 'invention' (mental capacity) to produce fashionable commodities. 'Inventor' came to be almost synonymous with 'designer' in this usage.[70]

Similarly, the magic ingredient which seventeenth-century 'improvement' writers expected to effect agricultural development was not any major invention but 'ingenuity' – know-how or informed commonsense, especially in the efficient use of resources. This intangible resource appeared vital, but it was a difficult thing to teach in a handbook.[71] Walter Blith, in 1652, stressed its importance in his programme:

study improvements, which though they may not be said to be either father or mother of plenty, yet it is the midwife that facilitates the birth . . . . This very nation may be made the paradise of the world, if we can but bring ingenuity into fashion.[72]

11.5 THE THREAT OF LABOUR-SAVING INVENTION

Technical progress became controversial when it seemed directly to jeopardize employment. The introduction of machinery threatened to cause sudden, dramatic dislocation. The inference from the generally accepted, labour theory of value – that greater wealth could be produced by adding mechanical 'hands' to the labour force – was rarely drawn. Instead, the labour theory of value was employed to imbue the call for 'populousness' with greater theoretical cogency.[73] The simplest and least risky means to increase national wealth was to multiply the units of production, the labourer – by encouraging natural increase and immigration.[74] A second expedient was to intensify the labour input of the existing population: either by reducing that sector of the workforce which produced nothing for immediate consumption (the professions and 'service industries');[75] or by providing employment for the able poor and curing the 'work-shy' attitude which writers almost unanimously deplored.[76] This latter problem was not sufficiently acute, however, to turn employers' thoughts towards replacing recalcitrant labour with machinery.[77] Specializing the tasks of labour offered a third means; it was increasingly remarked upon from the early eighteenth century. Unlike mechanization, the division of labour was not perceived to pose a threat to employment, although having the same intended effect – higher productivity. Perhaps because the change would be more gradual, less dramatic, and easier to adapt to, it was harder to identify and conceptualize the threat.[78]

A bigger population was desired for economic and military reasons but, unless it was gainfully employed, it would be a liability, not a benefit. Carew Reynell put the problem in a nutshell: 'we want people, and yet as the case stands we want means to sustain them'.[79] The establishment of new manufacturing industries and the expansion of old ones was called for; by implication new skills and techniques and, perhaps, new machinery would be required.[80] In a period of endemic underemployment (with its impact on parish rates), it was immaterial, even preferable, if such manufactures were labour-intensive. Blith dismissed worries about the costs of labour-intensive (agricultural) improvements with the argument:

And what parts he with? or at what rate purchases it he at? Even only with the wages of the labouring man, whom he is bound both by the law of God, nature and the land, to maintain, who may be were he not maintained in work would cost as much to be maintained idly.[81]

A minority of seventeenth-century writers praised particular new, labour-saving items, but were generally wary of pressing the opportunity they offered to cut labour costs; the saving was to be taken up in greater ease or leisure. 'Improvers' welcomed technical devices which might ease the labourer's burden – a commendable concern for welfare.[82] 'I conceive', wrote Gabriel Plattes, in 1639, against a background of rapid population increase:

that in the new inventions, it is for the general good to save men's work by engines; for if one workman can do as much with his engine, as ten men can do without it, here is nine men's maintenance saved to the commonwealth; whereby plenty is increased to everyone.[83]

Plattes did not face squarely the problem of technological unemployment. His overriding concern was to feed the incessantly growing population. Moreover, he assumed that, in his idealized society, the benefits of mechanization would be distributed equally, not retained by a capitalist to the detriment of nine-tenths of his employees.[84] Christopher Wren thought it 'the same thing, to add more hands, or by the assistance of art to facilitate labour'.[85] Bishop Sprat, writing in the same 'Baconian' tradition, considered that:

The hands of men employed are true riches: the saving of those hands by inventions of art, and applying them to other works, will increase those riches.[86]

Petty went further in integrating this concept into his economic theorizing. With the Dutch in mind, he remarked that a small country could rival a far larger one by the *quality* of its labour inputs:

one man by art may do as much work, as many without it; viz. one man with a mill can grind as much corn, as twenty can pound in a mortar; one printer can make as many copies, as an hundred men can write by hand.[87]

He even raised 'art' (skill or ingenuity) into a factor of production, along with 'lands, . . . labour, and stock', and attempted to calculate its contribution to production, using an example of labour saved to agriculture by 'studying a more compendious way, and . . . contriving tools for the same purpose'.[88]

These comments were exceptional. Neither contemporary concerns nor the nature of economic discourse promoted discussion of technical change. Technological displacement was only rarely a live issue before the mid-eighteenth century: workers organized in guilds usually had government support in opposing the introduction of new labour-saving machinery.[89] Before labour-saving devices could be viewed as economically cost-effective and beneficial, two perceptions were required: the necessity for economies of labour, and the difference between the productivity and the money costs of labour. Both rested on faith in the elasticity of demand. The increasing competitiveness of international trade and, in particular, the battle waged between the East India Company and English cloth producers breathed new life into the subject.[90] Three ways of reducing English labour costs were suggested: first, to cut wage rates, either directly or by reducing the price of provisions; secondly, to compete only in those spheres where England was economically strongest; thirdly, and often as a corollary to the second option, to decrease the labour component by mechanization.

William Petty, in a treatise published in 1691 but written as early, perhaps, as 1665, had offered two of these options, both with a technical bias. Labour costs could be cut indirectly by improving agriculture and thereby reducing the price of food, or directly by using the 'fewest hands' in making the cloth.[91] But Petty left this insight high and dry, isolated – a good idea which he did not pursue. One of the few, rare apologists for the first solution in the early eighteenth century was Jacob Vanderlint, a merchant. By no means, however, a subsistence-wage theorist, he also gave agrarian improvement a more integrated role in the economy. His programme was to bring waste lands into cultivation by the application of new agricultural techniques, in order to outstrip the demands of a growing population.[92] But his faith in the powers of technology was limited:

for the land in use does certainly, generally, produce as much as it can well be made to bear; . . . to double the produce, there must be double the number of people employed in cultivation of land.[93]

The second option, concentration on those areas of trade where England had a natural advantage, began to be advanced by economic thinkers around 1700. The case for opportunity costs ran quite contrary to the established orthodoxy of manufacturing (and growing) everything possible at home. Charles Davenant in 1697 boldly asserted that England should not be diverted from profitable enterprises by futile attempts at self-sufficiency. It was wiser to wear Indian silks and stuffs, whose prime cost in India was but a quarter that of English woollens, and thereby to release more of the latter for export. Despite this controversial recommendation, Davenant's proposals for improving and increasing exports were conservative: to discourage 'sloth' through compulsory workhouses, 'for we want hands, not manufactures'. Probably reacting against the recent projecting mania, and aware of the burden of war, he cautioned that England's 'stock' should be carefully husbanded:

and therefore should not be diverted upon uncertain objects, and turned upon new inventions, in which it cannot be determined in many years, whether we get or lose, and how the balance stands; and of this kind are the silk and linen manufacture in England.[94]

No such caution informed the writing of John Houghton, possibly impressed, from the vantage point of his apothecary's shop near the Exchange, by the floods of City cash and credit to be spent or speculated. Like Davenant, he advanced a theory of opportunity costs, but proceeded to draw unorthodox conclusions about the value of labour-saving machinery. In 1677 he had proclaimed the benefits of 'high-living' as a stimulus to enterprise and improvement.[95] In later works Houghton developed this radical alternative to the common current of thought that demanded frugality at home in order to capture a greater share of the limited cake of world trade.[96] Others took up the theme.[97]

As a corollary to this trading policy, Houghton also adopted the third option and sought increased competitiveness and higher productivity by economies of labour. Not only would he import Norwegian timber to free English land for more profitable uses, he would process it with 'a thousand saw-mills, [since] . . . they might do us as much kindness as the engine-loom, and for all the talk of the short-sighted rabble, employ twice the people too'.[98] Houghton strongly denied the charge of technological displacement. He was convinced that the demand for cheaper commodities, produced with less labour, would be insatiable: 'if we can sell cheapest we shall do so, and our excessive quantities will make us more than amends'. Furthermore, he looked to the manufacturing of capital goods and to various auxiliary industries to take up any spare labour.

These complainants see no further than just the weaving; they never consider the increase of labour in making these looms, and all other trades and employments in other matters relating to these manufactures.[99]

The most cogent exposition of comparative costs and its implications for labour-saving technology at this time was by Henry Martin, a lawyer and whig apologist. In *Considerations upon the East India trade* (1701), Martin brought together and developed ideas similar to those that Houghton had scattered through his news-sheets.[100] Inspired to defend the East India trade against its critics, Martin displayed total confidence in the economy's capacity for domestic expansion and full employment, quite at odds with customary fears of overproduction and large-scale unemployment. On this basis he even reversed the orthodoxy that only raw materials should be imported, insisting their working-up often consumed labour which could be better employed elsewhere. Under pressure from East Indian competition, labour would be deployed more efficiently.[101] Wages, Martin insisted, would not fall: goods could be produced with less labour and sold more cheaply, for 'arts, and mills, and engines which save the labour of hands, are ways of doing things with less labour, and consequently with labour of less price, though the wages of men employed to do them should not be abated'.[102] Martin's most striking perception is of the internal dynamic of technical innovation in a capitalist economy. He apparently entertained no doubts that whatever innovation was needed could be produced.

Such things are *successively* invented to do a great deal of work with little labour of hands; they are the effects of necessity and emulation; every man must be *still inventing* himself, or be *still advancing to farther perfection* upon the invention of other men; if my neighbour by doing much with little labour can sell cheap, I must contrive to sell as cheap as he.[103]

'Necessity' had been integrated into an economic framework. It was an idea that found few echoes, however, in the ensuing decades.[104] And, despite his faith in the economic potential of invention, Martin expressed no opinion about the sources of technical change – nor indeed about patents as a means of stimulating it.

John Cary, the Bristol merchant, had reached a position favouring mechanization by a different route, whose goal was protection of the woollen industry. That wages could be kept high without entailing unemployment was the cornerstone of Cary's argument for stimulating the domestic market:

new projections are every day set on foot to render the making our manufactures easy, which are made cheap by the heads of the manufacturers, not by falling the price of poor people's labour; cheapness created expense, and expense gives fresh employment, so the poor need not stand idle if they could be persuaded to work.[105]

Cary had witnessed the successful introduction of new capital- and labour-saving techniques, and had been led to make the novel distinction between labour productivity and labour costs. Defoe was able to propound a programme similar to Cary's, however, without calling in the assistance of machinery. He trusted rather in effecting higher productivity by the incentive of higher wages and the availability of goods to spend them on.[106] Unconvinced of the economy's capacity to absorb redundant labour, he was wary of the dangers of technological displacement. He was more typical of his time.

Perhaps most influential in sustaining fears of labour-saving technology was the widespread socio-religious concern to provide employment or sustenance for a chronically underemployed population: the Poor Law made seventeenth-century Englishmen particularly concerned for full employment. Labour-saving innovations in a period of increasingly competitive foreign trade, combined with assumptions about the inelasticity of markets, seemed a priori a recipe for disaster. Neither did there seem any great need to make drastic changes: it was a period of relatively high real wages and of improving standards of living for many. In addition, attitudes to wealth remained ambiguous: sumptuary laws were repeatedly suggested, many tracts represented trade in luxury goods as a perverse and wasteful drain on national resources, and usury was defended as, at best, a necessary evil.[107] Moreover, there was no obvious, ready supply of machinery. Machines and tools were made to order by the local smith or carpenter. Houghton, Petty, Sprat and Wren, who have been noticed as advocates to some degree of higher productivity through mechanization, were all fellows of the Royal Society, infused with the optimism of Baconian idealism. They, with Cary and Martin, argued largely on the basis of what had been achieved already in particular industries, often by only a small minority within them. Without a specialist machine-making industry, the impetus for mechanization lacked a major, self-interested sponsor.[108]

Contemporaries probably paid Houghton, Martin and Cary no more and no less attention than the general run of projectors and special-pleaders. Martin prefaced his tract with the significant observation that 'most of the things in these papers are directly contrary to the received opinions'.[109] They seem to have attracted no explicit denunciation in print. Over the next half century, labour-saving technology continued to be a minority interest among economic writers. That it was an embattled one is perhaps suggested by the frequent anonymity of those tracts recommending it. The tone is apologetic; the treatment cautious and hedged with reservations. The danger of unemployment is regularly met with the reassurance that cheaper production would entail greater demand in overseas markets and, thereby, an expansion of employment.[110] The author of *Reflections on various subjects relating to arts and commerce* (1752) was more hesitant still. Success in overseas trade depended on 'cheapness of labour at home', and only a non-trading state could safely reject labour-saving machinery. Under certain conditions a commercial state should reject them too, principally when they would 'lessen our home markets, more than increase our foreign ones'; indeed most recent inventions 'tend only to take the trade out of the hands of thousands, and by a shameful monopoly to enrich one or two'. Although his conclusion was that if they had not already been admitted, 'I should not wish to see them in use here', he had previously reached the position that cheaper labour would result in expanded employment.[111] Five years later Malachy Postlethwayt made a similar distinction between trading and non-trading states, but came down more firmly in favour of labour-saving devices: 'in short, the prejudice we are speaking of is incompatible with the preservation of the foreign trade of a state'. Expansion of employment, however, would not be immediate, and the government ought to take care that alternative work or at least 'a subsistence' was ready for those displaced. Nor should this policy be extended to agriculture, where 'every machine tending to diminish their employment would really be destructive of the strength of society, the mass of men, and home consumption'.[112]

11.6 THE ACCEPTANCE OF MECHANIZATION

From the mid-eighteenth century mechanization received greater notice and, with it, a more balanced, considered treatment by economic writers. They began to assert without hesitation that higher output, as such, was the end in view, and that a bigger workforce or, preferably, its mechanical equivalent was the means to this end. This was a significant reversal of priorities. Josiah Tucker, like his turn of the century predecessors, argued on the basis of experience. He enumerated the many labour-saving machines already at work in England, attributing to them both 'prodigiously lowered' prices and expansion of employment.[113] James Steuart stated unapologetically in 1767 'as for the advantages of . . . [machines], they are so palpable that I need not insist upon them'. His logic was clear: machines provided 'a method of augmenting (virtually) the number of the industrious, without the expense of feeding an additional number'.[114] The sole hypothetical case he could imagine where mechanical innovation might be inadvisable begged the question of more conservative writers; namely, where there was 'no possibility of increasing either circulation, industry, or consumption'.[115] Steuart, like Houghton and Tucker, insisted on the paradox that mechanization would require a higher input of human labour, through not only the expansion of production but also the creation of new tasks – making and servicing machinery, and meeting the new administrative and distributive demands of large-scale production.[116] In the short term, dislocation to some degree was unavoidable, and it was the government's duty to cushion workers against these 'inconveniences'.[117] With no foreboding of the dramatic upheaval that mechanization on a large scale was to entail in the next century, Tucker and Steuart both ridiculed the cautious for failing to see how their present civilization rested on earlier inventions, as ancient and basic as the plough and as recent as the printing press.[118] Arthur Young also pointed to 'our present machines' as creators of employment, citing 'silk-mills, stocking-frames, water-mills, wind-mills, iron and copper works'. Their introduction was, he thought in 1772, a controversial question, but the need to undersell foreign competitors and the availability of employment on 'waste and uncultivated lands' decided him in their favour.[119]

Adam Smith's lack of interest in technical change has often been cause for remark.[120] *Pace* Young, however, the controversy was still a minority skirmish at the time that Smith wrote. A quarter of a century later, he was taken to task for his omission by both Dugald Stewart and Lord Lauderdale: the division of labour, on which Smith placed so much emphasis, was but a poor relation of machinery in speeding up and cheapening production, and it did not itself promote mechanization.[121] Lauderdale's work, published in 1804, opened a new chapter in conceptualization of the economic role of technical change. For him it consisted, purely and simply, in the substitution of capital for labour. It was inevitable, rational and entirely beneficial. Taking an example from the hosiery industry, Lauderdale explained:

a part of the capital of the country becomes vested in a stocking-loom; and the profit of the stock so employed, is derived from the stocking-loom's supplanting the labour of a number of knitters.[122]

Similarly, the capital invested in a plough replaced the labour of 5 men with spades or 299 men digging a field with their nails.[123] Lauderdale integrated the concept of technical change into his demand-led account of economic growth. The nature of demand determined not only the rate but also the direction of technical change. Basic to his thesis was the distribution of wealth: the concentration of wealth in the hands of a few, to the impoverishment of the many, was the chief obstacle to economic growth ('the increase of public wealth'). He made the usual contrast between the luxury products of France and the coarser, mass-produced English manufactures, but this provided no cause for complaint. To his mind the advantages all lay with England, since the satisfaction of an elite few provided no basis for growth:

their habits cannot possibly suggest expenditure, for the purpose of supplanting labour they are never called on to perform. . . . [In contrast] a proper distribution of wealth ensures the increase of opulence, by sustaining a regular progressive demand in the home market, and still more effectually, by affording to those whose habits are likely to create a desire of supplanting labour, the power of executing it.[124]

This represented the culmination of more than a century's debate on high versus low wages, home demand versus exports and frugality, and the pros and cons of labour-saving machinery. If discussion of the last element had been relatively muted until recently, Lauderdale now thrust it to the very heart of his thesis. Labour-saving machinery was not, for him, a necessary evil in the fight against foreign competition but the very source of wealth. It was, moreover, inevitable in its progress and the defining characteristic and prerequisite of human civilization.[125]

So what was at the root of the change expressed in economic writings from the third quarter of the eighteenth century? First, it should be remarked that, although there was a perceptible change, it was not overwhelming. Lauderdale, echoing Henry Martin a century earlier, prefaced his book with the admission that many of his views were 'not only new, but even repugnant to received opinions'.[126] The 'machinery question' had emerged, but it was still a minority interest among those not immediately affected by it. It did not yet attract the degree of attention that was to make it the focus of political economy and indeed 'a truly national issue of debate' in the first half of the nineteenth century.[127] Part of the explanation is internal to the discipline. Pioneered by the Scottish universities, economic analysis began to achieve an academic status. There was no shortage of tracts still designed to further a particular case, drawing on stock, unanalytical propositions, but alongside them the more rigorous treatise, with aspirations to offer a 'science' of political economy, was gaining ground. The adoption of political economy as an academic subject both recognized and advanced the trend towards a more analytical, conceptual approach. The new breed of writers was concerned to discover general laws, to determine what held good for an idealized situation. Consequently, the logic of mechanization could be followed through relentlessly, with little regard to the 'unfortunate' distress of workers who lost their traditional livelihoods and lifestyles or of small masters who lacked the resources to keep pace with their larger competitors.

There was no sudden change of direction, but rather a slowly turning tide. Where once those who advocated technical change had been an isolated few, they increasingly found themselves in the company of others; their voices became more confident, their treatment of the subject more elaborate. Economic theorisers did not, however, lead the way. They lent greater cogency to the argument, but they followed in the wake of capitalists, inventors, and their supporters whose self-interest had prompted them to discover a viable case to legitimize their activities, in the face of opposition from displaced workers and parsimonious payers of the poor rate. The second half of the eighteenth century witnessed a new urgency infused into this question by mechanical threats to employment on an unprecedented scale. Nearly every process in textile manufacturing was subject to attempts (not always successful) at mechanization; nailmaking, filemaking and a host of other trades received similar treatment. Anxieties were running high, and there were repeated outbreaks of machine-breaking on the part of workers. It became an issue of social and political stability as well as of poor relief.[128] The gravity of events promoted pamphlet debates, particularly following the machine-breaking riots in Lancashire in the late 1770s.

On the other hand, there was growing excitement about technological developments and their role in stimulating lucrative new industries. British manufacturing industry had been advancing in technical competence to the point where, in many cases, it outstripped its European rivals: further innovation had to be home produced, not merely imitated from Continental practice. Repeated attempts since the early eighteenth century to prevent by statute the emigration of English artisans and the export of machinery reflect the recognition of Britain's steadily mounting technical ability. With the exception of Smith, major economic writers showed themselves to be aware of, and impressed by, recent technical change. From Cary to Tucker to Lauderdale and Stewart, they list a range of innovations that goes beyond the obvious.[129]

Two early-eighteenth-century inventions were particularly influential: Newcomen's engine and Lombe's silk-throwing machinery (its Italian origins quickly forgotten). Both had symbolic appeal, being highly visible, distinctly novel, and technically if not always financially successful. English tourists as well as foreign travellers went out of their way to see such marvels. Moreover, the atmospheric engine, which offered for the first time a power source immune from the vagaries of wind and water, was clearly a fit subject for the poetic and artistic imagination, steeped in the ancient mythologies of Vulcan, Prometheus, and their ilk; poets, such as John Dalton, Anna Seward and Erasmus Darwin, and painters, like Joseph Wright of Derby, took up the challenge.[130] In 1787 the *European Magazine* seized the opportunity presented by the completion of the Albion Mills to print a four-page potted history of steam power from the Marquis of Worcester to Boulton and Watt. Of the mills themselves, it considered, 'every lover of science, and every friend to mankind, will receive pleasure from the inspection of this immense machine'.[131] But it was Lombe's silk machinery that attracted the most consistent attention among economic writers. Its size and complexity excited admiration. It demonstrated that mechanization on a large scale and integration of production within a single factory were viable. And it offered a straightforward and acceptable example of labour-saving machinery, since it made possible a process that had been barely feasible by hand: no workers had been displaced by it, and it could be seen to have created employment.[132]

Inventiveness was also becoming a source of national pride. Confidence in England's technical superiority informed the optimism of Josiah Tucker, particularly in regard to the production of capital goods: 'few countries are equal, perhaps none excel the English in the numbers and contrivance of their machines to abridge labour'.[133] The anonymous author who defended the introduction of labour-saving machinery so vehemently in 1780 contradicted 'the common but erroneous remark, that the French excelled most in invention, and the English in making improvements', with the statement that 'perhaps no nation has produced more original geniuses than this'; there was no other area in Europe of the same size which 'had brought forth an equal number of important discoveries and original inventions'.[134] William Hutton, of Birmingham, with even less hesitation, claimed that 'it is an *old* remark, that no country abounds with genius so much as this island', when discussing the printer and inventor, John Baskerville, in 1782.[135] It has remained part of our national mythology for two centuries.[136]

11.7 THE DEMISE OF PROVIDENCE

A new metaphysic of invention also emerged. Providential explanations of events had been in retreat since early in the eighteenth century; human agency was brought centre-stage by the thinkers of the Enlightenment. 'Providence' was at hand to sugar any bitter pills (the displacement of labour consequent upon new textile machinery proceeded from 'the general order of Providence'),[137] but clever new pieces of technology could usually be celebrated as the product of human, especially English, genius. The neo-platonic concept of discovering preexisting forms completely disappeared and, with it, the idea of a finite (if large) stock of inventions. The roles of God and humanity were now strictly demarcated: He supplied the raw materials, which included laws of nature; humanity utilized them, combining and recombining them in an infinity of useful discoveries and inventions. An early example can be found in a philosophical piece by John Locke, whose deism and empiricism may explain why he did not share the prevailing neo-platonic concept of invention. Locke wrote, in 1677, that 'Nature furnishes us only with the material, for the most part rough, and unfitted for our use; it requires labour, art, and thought, to suit them to our occasions'.[138] A century later, Joseph Bramah, contesting Watt's patent for the steam engine, elaborated this view. 'Invention', he defined as 'those efforts of the mind and understanding which are calculated to produce new effects from the varied applications of the same cause, and the endless changes producible by different combinations and proportions.' 'At what point of creation do the works of men begin?', asked Bramah. He answered his own question:

just where the independent works of God end, who by his own secret *principles* and *methods* . . . established the elements and their properties, and stocked the universal storehouse already mentioned; out of which the same creating will directs every man to go and take materials, fit in kind and quality, for the execution of his design.[139]

At some time in the eighteenth century this view had become the orthodox one: too few authors between Locke and Bramah addressed the subject of invention for it to be possible to specify a watershed. All one can say is that by the century's end it was commonly expressed. Invention was regarded as a matter of synthesis, rather than analysis. This was the model underlying Adam Smith's discussion of inventions: he conceded that really novel inventions could be expected only from 'philosophers', outsiders who could stand back, observe, and 'apply things *together* to produce effects to which they seem no way adapted.'[140]

This conceptualization generated a new optimism. 'Few are the mechanical powers, but infinite are their combinations'.[141] The expectation of continuous invention arose, and speculations that, for example, '"the most extensive operations may" hereafter "be within the reach of *one* man"' were seriously debated.[142] In the view of Dugald Stewart there was an '*inexhaustible fund* of mechanical inventions, in which we have now left all our competitors far behind'. Foreign competition provided the spur of necessity; Stewart had no doubt that 'the invention would be forthcoming' in response.[143] Here was a major new resource, to which the British in particular seemed to have found the key.

This new understanding of invention had ramifications for the patent system and the wider question of how best to encourage invention and innovation. Emphasis on the efforts and 'genius' of the individual fostered an 'heroic' explanation of invention, which was to come to fruition in the nineteenth century when inventors and engineers were indeed lauded as national heroes. For the present, invention was still a largely anonymous achievement: Newcomen's engine was 'the fire engine' and Cartwright's power loom was known as 'the Doncaster loom';[144] the *Gentleman's Magazine*'s list of deceased 'English worthies of the eighteenth century', published in 1803, found no place for inventors. Arkwright, Watt and Wedgwood, as successful businessmen, received attention that was denied to most inventors.[145] When the fourth edition of the *Encyclopaedia Britannica*, published in 1810, defined 'invention' it gave the technical meaning first, the literary one last, but its choice of examples – gunpowder and printing – was extremely conservative. Yet invention was now recognized as the achievement of individuals; they were more than the agents of Providence, and without their efforts there was no God-given guarantee that an invention would be made by someone else. The fatalism of the providentialist argument became submerged beneath an heroic ideology. It was thought vital, therefore, that the individual should be encouraged. Some regarded direct, monetary rewards as the most efficient method. But, for many, faith in the justice distributed by a free market dictated that a temporary monopoly, awarded by patent, would produce the fairest results and potentially a much greater reward.

New ways of conceptualizing invention were also enmeshed with new concepts of property.[146] When Lord Camden, in 1774, inveighed against the proposition that there was a common-law right to property in an invention, either mechanical or literary, he protested that those who thought otherwise 'forget their Creator, as well as their fellow creatures' by trying to monopolize 'his noblest gifts and greatest benefits'. To deny the very concept of intellectual property, Camden enunciated a providentialist (although not neo-platonic) view of invention, which by then had an old-fashioned ring.

Those great men, those favoured mortals, those sublime spirits, who share that ray of divinity which we call genius, are entrusted by Providence with the delegated power of imparting to their fellow creatures that instruction which heaven meant for universal benefit.[147]

Camden's argument verged on begrudging even a patent to inventors. In contrast, espousal of the concept of intellectual property usually entailed a more secular understanding of invention.

'Use rights' might be appropriate where the inventor was no more than God's agent, but when God had been reduced to the supplier of raw materials and the inventor elevated to a creative 'genius', then he was entitled to claim a property in the produce of his own brain – in something which had not previously existed and which might never have existed without him. The least the state could do was award a patent; pressure began to be exerted to award it freely or, at least, much more cheaply. For, the state was conceived by many to be either confirming an extant natural right in the inventor's intellectual property, or to be entering a contractual relationship with the inventor whereby a temporary monopoly was exchanged for disclosure of his secret.

Late-eighteenth-century Englishmen believed themselves to be living in an 'inventive age', a 'scientific age', or a 'century . . . remarkable for an accumulation of ingenuity'.[148] They were proud of their country's technical achievements and a few recognized their potentiality for economic growth. They discovered there already existed, in the patent system, an institution intended to protect and promote invention. Some doubted its merits, but the wisdom of the political economists supported those who considered, in typical English fashion, that it could be adapted to suit present needs. While the French and the Americans took the opportunity of political revolutions to pass new patent laws, the English, confident that they had already succeeded under the auspices of the Statute of Monopolies, persisted with this relic of the *ancien régime*.

Notes

Introduction

1 Phyllis Deane, *The first industrial revolution* (Cambridge, 1965), p. 128; B. R. Mitchell and Phyllis Deane, *Abstract of British historical statistics*, 2nd edn (Cambridge, 1971), p. 244; D. C. Coleman, *The economy of England, 1450–1750* (Oxford, 1977), pp. 153–5.

2 Jacob Schmookler, *Invention and economic growth* (Cambridge, Mass. 1966), p. 56.

3 The indexes are respectively chronological, by name of patentee, and by subject of patent. For Woodcroft's methods of working and the size of his task, see Bennet Woodcroft (ed.), *Alphabetical index of patentees of inventions* (repr. 1969), pp. v–vii; and for his biography, John Hewish, *The indefatigable Mr Woodcroft* (1982). The patent rolls are in the Public Record Office, class C66.

4 Examination to determine whether the invention was accurately described was introduced by the 1883 Patents Act (46 & 47 Vict.c.57).

5 Liliane Perez, 'Le "Privilège", source d'histoire économique et révélateur d'une politique au XVIIIe siècle' in F. Caron (ed.), *Les Brevets: leur utilisation en histoire des techniques et de l'économie* (Table Ronde, C.N.R.S. 1984, Paris, 1985), pp. 71–9; Harold T. Parker, *The Bureau of Commerce in 1781 and its policies with respect to French industry* (Durham, N. Carolina, 1979), pp. 47–68.

6 William Cobbett (ed.), *The parliamentary history of England* (36 vols., 1806–20).

7 *Report from the select committee appointed to inquire into the present state of the law and practice relative to the granting of patents for invention*, P.P. 1829, III.

8 Thomas Savery, *The miner's friend, or an engine to raise water by fire* (1702).

9 J. W. Gordon, *Monopolies by patents, and the suitable remedies available to the public* (1897), p. 1; H. G. Fox, *Monopolies and patents: a study of the history and future of the patent monopoly* (Toronto, 1947), p. 6; William Hyde Price, *The English patents of monopoly*, Harvard Economic Studies, vol. 1 (1906), pp. 130–2.

10 A. A. Gomme, *Patents of invention: origin and growth of the patent system in Britain* (1946). See also H. Harding, *Patent Office centenary* (H.M.S.O., 1952).

11 E. Wyndham Hulme, 'The history of the patent system under the prerogative and at common law', *L.Q.R.*, 12 (1896), 141–54; *idem*, 'On the consideration of the patent grant, past and present', *L.Q.R.*, 13 (1897), 313–18; *idem*, 'The history of the patent system under the prerogative and at common law: a sequel', *L.Q.R.* 16 (1900), 44–56; *idem*, 'On the history of patent law in the seventeenth and eighteenth centuries', *L.Q.R.*, 18 (1902), 280–8; *idem*, 'Privy Council law and practice of letters patent for invention from the Restoration to 1794', *L.Q.R.*, 33 (1917), 63–75, 181–95; D. Seaborne Davies, 'The early history of the patent specification', *L.Q.R.*, 50 (1934), 86–109, 260–74.

12 Klaus Boehm and Aubrey Silberston, *The British patent system: i, administration* (Cambridge, 1967), preface.

13 Surveyed in H. I. Dutton, *The patent system and inventive activity during the industrial revolution* (Manchester, 1984), pp. 1–3.

14 Ibid., p. 10.

15 Ibid., pp. 108–15, 202–5.

16 Nathan Rosenberg, *Inside the black box: technology and economics* (Cambridge, 1982), pp. 48–9.

17 Yet see N. F. R. Crafts, 'The eighteenth century: a survey' in Roderick Floud and Donald McCloskey (eds.), *The economic history of Britain since 1700: volume 1, 1700–1860* (Cambridge, 1981), p. 5.

18 N. F. R. Crafts, *British economic growth during the industrial revolution* (Oxford, 1985), pp. 71–2, 81–2.

19 Ibid., p. 80.

20 Rosenberg, *Inside the black box*, pp. 23–7.

21 T. S. Ashton, *The industrial revolution, 1760–1830* (Oxford, 1948), p. 58.

22 Akos Paulinyi, 'Revolution and technology' in Roy Porter and Mikulas Teich (eds.), *Revolution in history* (Cambridge, 1986), pp. 272–84. See also David S. Landes, *The unbound Prometheus: technological change and industrial developments in western Europe from 1750 to the present* (Cambridge, 1969), pp. 1–3; W. W. Rostow, *How it all began: origins of the modern economy* (1975), pp. 180–4.

23 D. N. McCloskey, 'The industrial revolution 1780–1860: a survey' in Floud and McCloskey, *Economic history*, pp. 108–17; G. N. Von Tunzelmann, 'Technical progress during the industrial revolution' in ibid., pp. 143, 158–63.

24 R. Samuel, 'The workshop of the world: steam power and hand technology in mid-Victorian Britain', *History Workshop*, 3 (1977), 6–72; also A. E. Musson, *The growth of British industry* (1978), pp. 139–42, 149–51.

25 J. U. Nef, 'The progress of technology and the growth of large-scale industry in Great Britain, 1540–1640', *Ec.H.R.*, 1st ser. 5 (1934), 3–24; Lewis Mumford, *Technics and civilization* (1934), pp. 156–67; E. A. Wrigley, 'The supply of raw materials in the industrial revolution', *Ec.H.R.*, 2nd ser. 15 (1962), 1–16; J. R. Harris, *Industry and technology in the eighteenth century: Britain and France* (Birmingham, 1972).

26 Crafts, *British economic growth*, pp. 17–34, 84–6. See also Deane, *First industrial revolution*.

27 E. A. Wrigley, 'Continuity, chance and change: the character of the industrial revolution in England', the Ellen McArthur Lectures, University of Cambridge, 1987.

28 Ibid.; N. F. R. Crafts, 'The industrial revolution in England and France: some thoughts on the question "Why was England first?"', *Ec.H.R.*, 2nd ser. 30 (1977), 429–41.

29 Crafts, *British economic growth*, pp. 46–7; C. K. Harley, 'British industrialization before 1841: evidence of slower growth during the industrial revolution', *Jnl Econ. Hist.*, 42 (1982), 267–89; P. H. Lindert, 'English occupations, 1670–1811', *Jnl Econ. Hist.*, 40 (1980), 707. This gradualism is, of course, evocative of J. H. Clapham, *The economic history of modern Britain* (3 vols., Cambridge, 1926–38) and E. Lipson, *The economic history of England* (3 vols., 1934).

30 R. Baker, *New and improved . . . inventors and inventions that have changed the modern world* (1976), pp. 14–16, 154–162.

31 Christine MacLeod, 'Patents for invention and technical change in England, 1660–1753' (unpubl. Ph.D. thesis, University of Cambridge, 1983), pp. 206–12;

A. A. Gomme, 'Date corrections of English patents, 1617–1752', *T.N.S.*, 13 (1932–3), 159–60.
32 Simon Kuznets, 'Inventive activity: problems of definition and measurement' in Richard R. Nelson (ed.), *The rate and direction of inventive activity* (Princeton, 1962), pp. 19–43.
33 Schmookler, *Invention and economic growth*, esp. pp. 1–11; Dutton, *Patent system*, pp. 103–8; A. E. Musson (ed.), *Science, technology, and economic growth in the eighteenth century* (1972), pp. 49–56.
34 Thomas Webster, *Reports and notes of cases on letters patent for inventions* (1844), pp. 435–54.
35 Archibald Clow and Nan L. Clow, *The chemical revolution: a contribution to social technology* (1952), pp. 5–6.
36 S.R.O. 'Calendar of Scottish patents and specifications, 1712–1812'.
37 Christine MacLeod, 'The 1690s patents boom: invention or stock-jobbing?', *Ec.H.R.*, 2nd ser. 39 (1986), 560–1.
38 Robertson Buchanan to Alexander Mundell, 13 Apr. 1813, and 22 May 1813, Edinburgh University Library, MS La.II.311.
39 See Ashton, *Industrial revolution*, p. 19.
40 D. Griffiths, 'The exclusion of women from technology' in Wendy Faulkner and Erik Arnold (eds.), *Smothered by invention: technology in women's lives* (London and Sydney, 1985), pp. 51–8, provides a starting point for considering why this was the case.

1 Patents 1550–1660: law, policy and controversy

1 William Blackstone, *Commentaries on the laws of England* (4 vols., Oxford, 1765–9), vol. 2, p. 346; see also Edward Chamberlayne, *Angliae notitiae; or the present state of England*, 18th edn (1694), p. 81; Ephraim Chambers, *Cyclopaedia: or, an universal dictionary of arts and sciences*, 5th edn (2 vols., 1741), sub 'Letters Patent', 'Patent'.
2 William Holdsworth, *A history of English law* (17 vols., 1922–72), vol. 4, pp. 343–5; Hulme, 'History of the patent system', pp. 142–4; Fox, *Monopolies and patents*, pp. 39–43.
3 This and the following paragraph are based on Maximilian Frumkin, 'Early history of patents for invention', *T.N.S.*, 26 (1947), 47–55, where further details and references may be found. See also Frank D. Prager, 'A history of intellectual property from 1545 to 1787', *Jnl of the Patent Office Society*, 26 (1944), 714–19.
4 Frumkin, 'Early history', p. 52.
5 Ibid., p. 51.
6 Mary Dewar (ed.), *A discourse on the commonweal of this realm of England, attributed to Sir Thomas Smith* (Charlottesville, 1969), p. 88.
7 W. Cunningham, *The growth of English industry and commerce*, 3rd edn (3 vols., Cambridge, 1896–1903), vol. 2, pp. 57–61, 79–84. Cunningham stresses Burghley's interest – sometimes financial – in these ventures.
8 Hulme, 'History of the patent system', p. 152. The same conclusion is reached in the most recent research on the subject: G. D. Duncan, 'Monopolies under Elizabeth I' (unpubl. Ph.D. thesis, University of Cambridge, 1976), pp. 40–8; and Joan Thirsk, *Economic policy and projects: the development of a consumer society in early modern England* (Oxford, 1978), pp. 33–4, 47–9.
9 Davies, 'Patent specification', pp. 98–105.
10 Duncan, 'Monopolies under Elizabeth I', pp. 36–8.

11 John Stow, *The survey of London* (1598), bk 5, p. 244, quoted in Cunningham, *Growth of English industry*, vol. 2, pp. 76–7.

12 Of the 31 patents for the introduction of new arts issued between 1558 and 1585 only 11 were for native inventions.

13 Fox, *Monopolies and patents*, p. 233.

14 See below, p. 18.

15 Stephen D. White, *Sir Edward Coke and 'The grievances of the commonwealth', 1621–1628* (Chapel Hill, 1979), p. 134.

16 Duncan, 'Monopolies under Elizabeth I', p. 22. The most familiar 'evidence' for this point lacks substance, for the story of William Lee's being refused a patent for the stocking knitting frame seems to be of nineteenth-century invention, first appearing in Gravenor Henson's account in 1831: *Felkin's history of the machine-wrought hosiery and lace manufactures*, ed. S. D. Chapman (Newton Abbot, 1967), pp. 26–38, 51.

17 Hulme, 'History of the patent system', p. 152.

18 See below, pp. 67–8.

19 Edward Coke, *The third part of the institutes of the laws of England*, 4th edn (1669), p. 184. See also the decision of King's Bench in *Clothworkers of Ipswich* (1614), quoted in L. Getz, 'History of the patentee's obligation in Great Britain', *Jnl of the Patent Office Society*, 46 (1964), 68.

20 P.R.O. SP44.338, pp. 6–8; SP44.336, p. 296.

21 See below, p. 49.

22 The justification for patents remained a matter for learned debate into the nineteenth century: Dutton, *Patent system*, pp. 17–22.

23 Duncan, 'Monopolies under Elizabeth I', p. 99; see also Thirsk, *Economic policy and projects*, pp. 86–7.

24 Duncan, 'Monopolies under Elizabeth I', pp. 116–31, 172–3; export licences were also sold to the highest bidders, ibid., pp. 147–70; see Thirsk, *Economic policy and projects*, pp. 95–9, 101, and chs. 3 and 4, *passim*.

25 Fox, *Monopolies and patents*, pp. 74–9; Price, *English patents of monopoly*, pp. 20–2, 31–3.

26 Fox, *Monopolies and patents*, p. 217. A facsimile of the *Book of bounty* is printed in Gordon, *Monopolies by patents*, pp. 161–92.

27 John Chamberlain to Sir Dudley Carleton, 8 July 1620, in N. E. McClure (ed.), *The letters of John Chamberlain*, (2 vols., Philadelphia, 1939), vol. 2, p. 311. See Fox, *Monopolies and patents*, p. 102.

28 For a more specialized treatment of events, see Price, *English patents of monopoly*, pp. 20–5; Fox, *Monopolies and patents*, pp. 100–15; Holdsworth, *History of English law*, vol. 4, pp. 343–53; Elizabeth Reed Foster, 'The procedure of the House of Commons against patents and monopolies, 1621–1624' in W. A. Aiken and B. D. Henning (eds.), *Conflict in Stuart England: essays in honour of Wallace Notestein* (1960), pp. 59–85.

29 Gordon, *Monopolies by patents*, p. 9.

30 Fox, *Monopolies and patents*, pp. 214–20; White, *Sir Edward Coke*, pp. 130, 134.

31 William R. Scott, *The constitution and finance of English, Scottish and Irish joint-stock companies to 1720* (3 vols., Cambridge, 1912), vol. 1, pp. 167–78.

32 Quoted in Eleanor S. Godfrey, *The development of English glassmaking, 1560–1640* (Oxford, 1975), pp. 112–13. Godfrey argues that Mansell's patent was beneficial to the development of an English glass industry. See also White, *Sir Edward Coke*, pp. 125–6.

33 Edward Hyde, 1st Earl of Clarendon, *The history of the rebellion and civil wars in*

England (3 vols., Oxford, 1702–4), vol. 1, p. 53; see Scott, *Joint-stock companies*, vol. 1, pp. 220–3.

34 Gordon, *Monopolies by patents*, p. 10.

35 Scott, *Joint-stock companies*, vol. 1, pp. 208–18; Fox, *Monopolies and patents*, pp. 127–39; Price, *English patents of monopoly*, pp. 35–46.

36 Fox, *Monopolies and patents*, pp. 140–50; Scott, *Joint-stock companies*, vol. 1, pp. 221–3; and see, Lewes Roberts, *The treasure of traffike, or a discourse of forraigne trade* (1641), p. 47.

37 Rhys Jenkins, 'The protection of inventions during the Commonwealth and Protectorate', *Notes & Queries*, 11th ser. 7 (1913), 162–3.

38 Fox, *Monopolies and patents*, p. 155n.

39 — to Sir Edward Cartwright, 2 June 1664, enclosing letter to the king: P.R.O. SP29.99, no. 12.

40 P.R.O. SP29.103, nos. 60, 61. For Garill's application, see below, pp. 32, 42–3.

41 *Vox et lacrimae anglorum; or, the true Englishmen's complaints to their representatives in parliament*, in P.R.O. SP29.234, no. 85, p. 10.

42 Price, *English patents of monopoly*, p. 45.

43 *East India Company* v. *Sandys*, quoted in Fox, *Monopolies and patents*, p. 354.

44 Henry Horwitz (ed.), *The parliamentary diary of Narcissus Luttrell, 1691–93* (Oxford, 1972), pp. 248–9, 340, 355, 401, 453.

45 Aaron Hill, *Proposals for raising a stock of one hundred thousand pounds* (1714), pp. 12, 13.

46 Cobbett, *Parliamentary history* vol. 10, cols. 927–8.

47 Josiah Tucker, *The elements of commerce and the theory of taxes* (1755), p. 120. See also, John Dyer Collier, *An essay on the law of patents for new inventions* (1803), p. 19; and Fox, *Monopolies and patents*, p. 153n.

48 Holdsworth, *History of English law*, vol. 4, p. 353; Hulme, 'History of the patent system . . . a sequel', p. 55; Boehm and Silberston, *British patent system*, p. 17; Fox, *Monopolies and patents*, pp. 124–5.

49 Boehm and Silberston, *British patent system*, pp. 17–18. For Coke as representative of the emergent economic liberalism of the common law, see Donald O. Wagner, 'Coke and the rise of economic liberalism', *Ec.H.R.*, 1st ser. 6 (1935–6), 30–44. This is contested by Barbara Malament, 'The "economic liberalism" of Sir Edward Coke', *Yale Law Jnl*, 76 (1967), 1321–58; and modified by White, *Sir Edward Coke*, pp. 115–41, esp. pp. 136–41.

50 Coke, *Institutes*, p. 184. See Gordon, *Monopolies by patents*, pp. 21–70.

51 Fox, *Monopolies and patents*, pp. 220–31.

52 For elaboration of Coke's views on this point, see White, *Sir Edward Coke*, pp. 124–5.

53 Coke, *Institutes*, p. 184. See below, pp. 59, 161.

2 The later-Stuart patent grant – an instrument of policy?

1 Jenkins, 'Protection of inventions', pp. 162–3.

2 See below, pp. 40–1, 76.

3 P.R.O. SP29.44, no. 70.

4 Patents 159–162, 164–168.

5 P.R.O. SP29.45, no. 47; SP29.90, no. 47.

6 See, for example, R. Latham and W. Matthews (eds.), *The diary of Samuel Pepys* (11 vols., 1970–83), vol. 4, p. 415; vol. 5, pp. 5–6.

7 P.R.O. SP35.30, no. 24.

8 P.R.O. SP44.61, p. 4; SP44.71, p. 265; patent 253 (1687).

9 J. R. Jones, *The revolution of 1688 in England* (1972), p. 145.

10 P.R.O. SP44.236, pp. 65–6; C66.3325(1).

11 Gomme, *Patents of invention*, p. 16; my emphasis. Overseas trading companies continued to enjoy monopoly privileges over specific regions. For the rents exacted under Elizabeth I, see Hulme, 'History of the patent system . . . a sequel', pp. 45–51.

12 Rents were sometimes demanded in Elizabethan patents specifically as compensation for the crown's loss of customs revenue: Davies, 'Patent specification', p. 108.

13 P.R.O. SP44.71, pp. 394, 402; PC2.72, pp. 622, 631; patent 261 (1688).

14 P. G. M. Dickson, *The financial revolution in England: a study in the development of public credit, 1688–1756* (1967), pp. 342, 415–16.

15 Edward Hughes, *Studies in administration and finance, 1558–1825* (Manchester, 1934), pp. 179–80.

16 Hughes, *Studies*, p. 427; *Calendar of Treasury Books*, vol. 23, pt 2 (1709), p. 230. Hughes was mistaken in his belief that the patent had not been granted: patent 384 (1709).

17 Hughes, *Studies*, p. 428; *Calendar of Treasury Books*, vol. 27, pt 2 (1713), p. 394.

18 Hughes, *Studies*, p. 428.

19 P.R.O. SP35.30, no. 30.

20 P.R.O. SP35.12, no. 123; see L. Gittens, 'Soapmaking and the excise laws, 1711–1853', *Industrial Archaeology Review*, 1 (1976–7), 365.

21 P.R.O. SP36.8, fol. 118.

22 P.R.O. SP44.255, pp. 325–7.

23 P.R.O. SP36.47, fols. 264, 271, 309; SP36.50, fol. 283; SP36.51, fols. 215, 217, 219; SP44.258, pp. 522–4; SO3.25.

24 See below, pp. 113–14.

25 See, for example, *H. of C. Jnl*, vol. 37 (1780), p. 896. But see also Hughes, *Studies*, pp. 431–2.

26 E.g. P.R.O. SP29.20, nos. 8, 22. *C.S.P.D.*, November 1660, offers a good sample of the various types of demand which were made on the restored monarchy.

27 R. W. K. Hinton, 'The decline of parliamentary government under Elizabeth I and the early Stuarts', *Cambridge Historical Jnl*, 13 (1957), 116–32.

28 P.R.O. SP29.20, no. 82.

29 See above, pp. 16–17.

30 Buckingham was described in 1668 as the king's 'chief minister of state instead of the Chancellor [Clarendon]': Matthew Sylvester (ed.), *Reliquiae Baxterianae* (1696), pt iii, pp. 21–2. I am grateful to Mark Goldie for this reference.

31 P.R.O. SP44.13, pp. 312, 334; SP29.75, p. 153.

32 Patents 134 (1662), 140 (1663); *D.N.B.*, sub 'Martin Clifford (d.1677)', and 'Thomas Paulden (1626–1710?)'. For Tilson's involvement, see Victoria and Albert Museum, MS 86.JJ.8, fols. 1–3.

33 Guildhall, MS 5554, fol. 7.

34 Charles II, *By the king, a proclamation for the prohibiting the importation of glass plates*, (1664).

35 P.R.O. PC2.57, p. 135; PC2.60, p. 424; see B.L. MS Sloane 857, fol. 44.

36 P.R.O. PC2.60, pp. 44, 59, 63, 70. The Venetian ambassador, Alberti, made frequent references to the duke's capacity to manipulate the glass trade through his influence at Court: *C.S.P.V.* vol. 37, pp. 299–300; vol. 38, p. 7.

37 Patent 176 (1674), to George Ravenscroft.

38 Dept. Medieval and Later Antiquities, British Museum, MS, 'Articles of agreement made concluded and agreed upon 18 August 12 Charles II, 1660'.

39 Victoria and Albert Museum, MS 86.JJ.8, fol. 1.

40 B.L. MS Sloane 857, fols. 18, 20, 24; E. S. de Beer (ed.), *The diary of John Evelyn* (6 vols., Oxford, 1955), vol. 4, pp. 13, 98–9; *C.S.P.V.* vol. 37, p. 300; vol. 38, p. 2.

41 P.R.O. SP44.235, p. 57; SP44.339, p. 160; C66.2982(8) (1661); patent 303 (1692); H.M.C. 7th Report, *House of Lords MSS*, p. 164.

42 P.R.O. PC2.55, pp. 614–15.

43 Patent 148 (1666); P.R.O. PC2.59, p. 310; SP29.195, no. 88; SP29.198, no. 117; *D.N.B.*, sub 'Sir John Reresby (1634–89)'. The grant of this patent is indicative of how perfunctory was the scrutiny of applications: see below, pp. 41–8.

44 P.R.O. SP29.370, no. 220; PC2.64, pp. 485, 506–7; patent 181 (1675).

45 Basil Duke Henning (ed.), *The parliamentary diary of Sir Edward Dering, 1670–1673* (New Haven, 1940), p. 13.

46 P.R.O. SP44.8, p. 8, patent 133 (1662); also, for example, patent 155 (1668).

47 Patent 356 (1698).

48 Patent 141 (1664); *D.N.B.*, sub 'Lawrence Hyde, Earl of Rochester (1641–1711)', and 'Francis Willoughby, fifth Baron Willoughby of Parham (1613?–66)'.

49 Patent 255 (1687). For Albemarle's appointment to Jamaica, see Peter Earle, *The wreck of the Almiranta: Sir William Phips and the search for the Hispaniola treasure* (1979), p. 163.

50 See below, p. 82.

51 P.R.O. SP29.33, no. 30; SP29.34, no. 9; patent 129 (1661); my emphasis.

52 P.R.O. SP29.22, nos. 102, 102(1); C66.2943, no. 37 (1660).

53 Samuel Smiles, *Industrial biography: iron workers and tool makers*, ed. L. T. C. Rolt (Newton Abbot, 1967), pp. 52–8; P.R.O. SP29.37, no. 49. See also Scott, *Joint-stock companies*, vol. 2, pp. 465–6.

54 See above, p. 21.

55 *D.N.B.*, sub 'Richard Coote, first Earl of Bellamont (1637–1701)'.

56 P.R.O. SP44.235, p. 43; patent 237 (1684).

57 P.R.O. PC2.73, p. 368; SP44.339, p. 182.

58 P.R.O. PC2.72, p. 411; PC2.74, p. 134.

59 Patent 171 (1673); P.R.O. SP29.335, no. 84. Hulme suggested that Chamberlain's interest in a patent was to prevent the growth of a native manufacture in order to reap the profits of imported tin plates: comment on T. S. Ashton, 'The discoveries of the Darbys of Coalbrookdale', *T.N.S.*, 5 (1924–5), 13.

60 Andrew Yarranton, *England's improvement by sea and land . . . the second part* (1681), pp. 150–1. For Yarranton's thoughts on the patent system resulting from this experience, see below, pp. 184–5.

61 Smiles, *Industrial biography*, pp. 61, 66–9.

62 Yarranton's accusation that Chamberlain was ignorant of tin-platemaking was, perhaps, not entirely justified: W. E. Minchinton, *The British tinplate industry, a history* (Oxford, 1957), pp. 4, 7.

63 Patent 190 (1676); H.M.C. New Series, vol. 2, *House of Lords MSS*, p. 242; Muriel Clayton and Alma Oakes, 'Early calico printers around London', *Burlington Magazine*, 96 (1954), 136–9.

64 Patents 274 (1691), 335 (1694); *D.N.B.*, sub 'Thomas Phillips (1635?–93)', 'Jacob Richards (1660?–1701)'.

65 See below, pp. 186–7.

66 Bodl., MS Rawlinson A. 180, fols. 254–5. For an appreciation of Bayly's engines

– 'an incomparable invention likely to be lost for lack of patronage' – see T[homas] H[ale], *An account of several new inventions and improvements now necessary for England* (1691), pp. 53–60.

67 Bodl., MS Rawlinson A. 180, fol. 266; patent 196 (1676).

68 P.R.O. SP29.281A, no. 6; PC2.66, p. 388; patent 150 (1667).

69 J. H. Thomas, 'Thomas Neale, a seventeenth-century projector' (unpubl. Ph.D. thesis, University of Southampton, 1979), pp. 110–76, 268–315.

70 MacLeod, 'The 1690s patents boom', pp. 567–9.

71 J. V. Beckett, *Coal and tobacco: the Lowthers and the economic development of west Cumberland, 1660–1760* (Cambridge, 1981), pp. 121–4.

72 Ibid., pp. 212, 217. See also J. V. Beckett, 'The eighteenth-century origins of the factory system: a case study from the 1740s', *Business History*, 19 (1977), 64.

73 Patent 431 (1720); P.R.O. SP35.29, no. 48; SP35.30, no. 24. See also P.R.O. SP35.25, no. 3.

74 P.R.O. SP36.7, fols. 84, 86; patent 505 (1728).

75 P.R.O. SP36.31, fol. 56; patent 546 (1734).

76 *Calendar of Treasury Books*, vol. 8, pt 2 (1685–9), pp. 602, 670.

77 Guildhall, MS 3952, fol. 40.

78 See below, p. 38.

79 Dutton, *Patent system*, pp. 79–80. For the concept of intellectual property in this period, see below pp. 197–9.

80 See below, pp. 41–8.

81 P.R.O. PC2.73, p. 421.

82 P.R.O. SP29.414, nos. 27(1), 27(2); SP44.51, p. 398; SP44.55, p. 125; patent 211 (1680).

83 See below, pp. 42–3. Where the advantages seemed so obvious and it was itself a major beneficiary, the government was willing, it seems, to establish a monopoly. It may partly have been its experience of the hostility this patent aroused (see above, p. 16) that made it more cautious in granting monopoly powers: P.R.O. SP29.82, no. 32; SP29.83, no. 109; SP29.85, nos. 19, 20; SP44.15, pp. 265–7; SO3.15, p. 208.

84 P.R.O. SP29.93, nos. 60, 61; PC2.57, pp. 204–13. Garill sought his revenge on the wiredrawers by harassment in law suits and by 'informing' on them to the government: P.R.O. PC2.58, pp. 152, 159; SP44.18, p. 327.

85 Sir John Craig, *The Mint: a history of the London Mint from A.D. 287 to 1948* (Cambridge, 1953), pp. 184–97.

86 P.R.O. PC2.59, pp. 4, 84; patent 147 (1666); Charles II, *By the king, a proclamation prohibiting the importation of blue paper*. The Stationers' estimate seems to have been fairly accurate: D. C. Coleman, *The British paper industry, 1495–1860: a study in industrial growth* (Oxford, 1958), pp. 13, 58–9.

87 6 & 7 Gul III, c.18, appended to patent 261*. See Scott, *Joint-stock companies*, vol. 3, p. 84.

88 P.R.O. PC2.72, pp. 338, 411, 433, 444, 449, 470.

89 E.g. P.R.O. SP29.378, nos. 26, 26(1); PC2.65, pp. 91–2.

90 Patent 459 (1723); P.R.O. PC2.88, p. 510.

91 For a concise summary of the legislation by which successive governments attempted to prevent the exportation of machinery and skills in the eighteenth century, see Holdsworth, *History of English law*, vol. 11, pp. 432–4.

92 Ralph Davis, 'The rise of protection in England, 1689–1786', *Ec.H.R.*, 2nd ser. 19 (1966), 308–13.

93 See also below, pp. 81–4.

94 In this they were approximating the French practice, in which new inventions were regularly rewarded with a variety of concessions: Parker, *Bureau of Commerce*, pp. 58–9.

95 P.R.O. SP29.49, no.32; SP44.5, p. 116; SP44.235, p. 57; SP44.339, p. 162; SP36.55, fol. 54.

96 Charles Webster, *The great instauration: science, medicine and reform, 1626–1660* (1975), pp. 404–11. See also Pepys, *Diary*, vol. 3, p. 265; vol. 4, pp. 70, 144–8; Craig, *The Mint*, pp. 158–67.

97 P.R.O. SP44.7, pp. 60–1, 67–8; SP29.60, nos. 10, 10(1). The patent was not included in Woodcroft's lists.

98 Patents 128 (1661), 137 (1663); P.R.O. PC2.55, p. 240; SP29.91, no. 93.

99 Pepys often commented with pleasure on the royal interest, e.g. J. R. Tanner (ed.), *Samuel Pepys' naval minutes*, Navy Records Society (1926), p. 115.

100 Daniel Baugh, *British naval administration in the age of Walpole* (Princeton, 1965), p. 19; Pepys, *Diary*, vol. 3, p. 528.

101 John Ehrman, *The navy in the war of William III, 1689–1697* (Cambridge, 1953), pp. 19–20.

102 See P.R.O. ADM. 1.3527, fols. 113–14; PC2.77, pp. 343, 431; PC2.79, pp. 99, 124; PC2.81, p. 202, for Charles Ardesoif's repeated attempts to secure a contract for the use of his composition (patent 341) by the Navy.

103 These are detailed in T[homas] H[ale], *The new invention of mill'd lead, for sheathing of ships against the worm* (1691). Thomas Hale and partners had taken over the patent (254) in 1687; it had been extended by a private Act in 1669 (23 Car. II, c.15), printed as patent 158.

104 Ibid., pp. 114–15.

105 See, for example, the report of the Office of Ordnance to the Duke of Marlborough, 29 May 1705, about Mr Ramondon's invention of 'shooting by night': B.L. MS Add. 61,165, fols. 115, 117.

106 Thomas Savery, *Navigation improv'd, or the art of rowing ships of all rates in calms* (1698), pp. 8–9, 18–19.

107 P.R.O. SP44.237, p. 74; ADM. 1.3577, fol. 113; patent 335 (1694). See also John Streater's plea in 1667, P.R.O. SP29.229, no. 183; and William Presgrave's in 1687, SP44.71, pp. 331, 362.

108 Pepys's papers are full of correspondence with patentees and other inventors regarding negotiations for contracts and seeking payment. See, for example, the case of Captain Von Helmskirke: Pepys, *Diary*, vol. 9, pp. 171, 198; P.R.O. PC2.60, pp. 300–1.

109 See, for example, B.L. MS Add. 61,308, fols. 23–5.

110 P.R.O. PC2.95, pp. 48, 304, 341.

111 A. E. Clark-Kennedy, *Stephen Hales D.D., F.R.S., an eighteenth-century biography* (Cambridge, 1929), pp. 152–69, 207.

112 Stephen Hales, *A treatise on ventilators* (1758), pp. 96–7.

113 The relationship of government to inventors of military devices only began to be regulated with the passing of an Act in 1859, which gave such inventors the power to assign patents to the Secretary of State for War. This revised the judgement in an earlier test case, when the government was allowed to invade patent rights: Holdsworth, *History of English law*, vol. 14, p. 94.

114 2 Gul & Mar, sess.2, c.9.

115 P.R.O. SP29.372, no. 165; patent 184 (1675).

116 R. E. W. Maddison, 'Studies in the life of Robert Boyle, F.R.S.: part ii, salt water freshened', *Notes and Records of the Royal Society of London*, 9 (1952), 196–213;

patent 226 (1683); P.R.O. PC2.70, p. 56. In 1695 Walcot regained control, when he was allowed protection of his invention for thirty-one years by private Act of Parliament.

117 Patents concerning gunpowder and ordnance had been specifically exempted from the provisions of the Statute of Monopolies: see above, p. 17.

118 P.R.O. SP44.235, p. 109; SP44.341, p. 22; patent 266 (1691).

119 P.R.O. SP44.235, pp. 241, 254; SP44.341, pp. 308–12.

120 P.R.O. SP44.235, p. 289; SP44.341, pp. 374–7; PC2.74, pp. 401, 412, 429.

121 See below, pp. 47–8.

122 Patent 1063 (1774); P.R.O. PC1.10.75; PC1.11.150; L. T. C. Rolt, *Tools for the job: a short history of machine tools* (1965), pp. 45–7, 53.

123 Berks. C.R.O. Hartley-Russell MS 07/4; patent 1037 (1773).

124 Patents 2068 (1795); 2086, 2097, 2099 (all 1796); P.P. 1829, III, p. 438.

125 See, for example, the cases of John Cumberland, patent 427 (1720), in P.R.O. SP35.19, nos. 33, 33(1); SP35.20, nos. 84, 84(1); and William Crispe, patent 572 (1740), in P.R.O. SP44.259, pp. 32–5.

126 See below, p. 193.

127 Boehm and Silberston, *British patent system*, pp. 25–6.

128 Humphrey Quill, *John Harrison, the man who found longitude* (New York, 1966), pp. 203–5. Harrison had reached the standard required by the Act in 1761, but it took the next twelve years to wrest the reward from the government: ibid., pp. 100–15.

129 12 Anne, c.15.

130 P.R.O. SP35.5, nos. 68, 68(2). For French, see E. G. R. Taylor, *The mathematical practitioners of Hanoverian England, 1714–1840* (Cambridge, 1966), pp. 118–19; she considers 'his method was worthless'.

131 Such delays were a common complaint made to the 1829 select committee: P.P. 1829, III, pp. 432, 465, 519, 530.

3 The development of the patent system, 1660–1800

1 27 Hen VIII, c.11, sec.8. The alternative was a private Act of Parliament, but they were normally sought only to extend or strengthen existing patents: see below, pp. 72–3.

2 Dutton, *Patent system*, pp. 86–7.

3 Gomme, *Patents of invention*, pp. 16–18. For the costs involved in patenting, see below, pp. 76–7. An early-eighteenth-century resumé of the procedure and official fees payable can be found in P.R.O. SP36.30, fols. 374, 376.

4 G. Doorman, *Patents for invention in the Netherlands*, trans. Joh. Meijer (The Hague, 1942), pp. 21–7.

5 Frank D. Prager, 'Examination of inventions from the middle ages to 1836', *Jnl of the Patent Office Society*, 46 (1964), 287–9; Harold T. Parker, 'French administration and French scientists during the Old Regime and the early years of the Revolution' in Richard Herr and Harold T. Parker (eds.), *Ideas in history, essays presented to Louis Gottschalk* (Durham, N.C., 1965), pp. 91–3; Roger Hahn, *The anatomy of a scientific institution, the Paris Academy of Sciences, 1666–1803* (1971), pp. 10–30.

6 For the priority of revenue conservation, see above, pp. 22–4.

7 *Report of the Deputy Keeper of the Public Records*, vol. 2 (1841), pp. 27–8.

8 See below, p. 76.

9 Giles Jacob, *A new law dictionary*, 9th edn (1772), sub 'Non Obstante'.

10 P.R.O. SP44.55, p. 131; patent 219 (1682).

11 P.P. 1829, III, p. 437. See also the criticisms made by Jeremy Bentham, in John Bowring (ed.), *The works of Jeremy Bentham* (11 vols., Edinburgh, 1843), vol. 3, p. 72; vol. 5, p. 373; and by Charles Dickens, 'A poor man's tale of a patent' in *Household words* vol. 2 (19 Oct. 1850), p. 70, repr. in *Reprinted pieces* (1925), and recast as part of a wider assault on bureaucracy in *Little Dorrit* (1855–7), ch. 10.

12 *The patent: a poem by the author of The graces* (1776), p. 4.

13 P.R.O. SP29.104, no. 76; see above, p. 32.

14 P.R.O. PC2.57, p. 213.

15 See above, p. 32.

16 P.R.O. PC2.57, p. 213; SP29.83, fol. 109.

17 E.g. P.R.O. SP29.371, no. 80; SP44.235, pp. 205, 210.

18 P.R.O. SP29.318, no. 158; patent 165 (1672).

19 P.R.O. SP29.374, no. 234; J. R. Tanner (ed.), *A descriptive catalogue of the naval manuscripts in the library at Magdalene College, Cambridge*, 4 vols., Navy Records Society (1903–23), vol. 4, p. 465; D. McKie, 'James, Duke of York, F.R.S.', *Notes and Records of the Royal Society of London*, 13 (1958), 6–18; see above, pp. 35–6.

20 See below, pp. 112–13.

21 See below, p. 186.

22 P. P. 1829, III, p. 435.

23 P.R.O. SP29.378, no.137. For Fox, see Christopher Clay, *Public finance and private wealth: the career of Sir Stephen Fox, 1627–1716* (Oxford, 1978), esp. pp. 163–4.

24 Bentham, *Works*, vol. 10, pp. 168–9.

25 John Davies, *A collection of the most important cases respecting patents of invention and the rights of patentees* (1816), pp. 447–9; Dutton, *Patent system*, p. 183.

26 MacLeod, 'Patents for invention', pp. 206–7.

27 Gomme, 'Date corrections', pp. 159–60.

28 Dutton, *Patent system*, p. 198, n. 58.

29 P.R.O. SP44.99, p. 102; patent 310 (1692).

30 See above, pp. 12–13.

31 P.R.O. SP44.235, pp. 281, 294. A caveat was subsequently entered against incorporation by the Silk Throwers Company and the proceedings were stopped at the great seal, without any indication of the reason: SP44.73, p. 14; PC2.75, p. 347.

32 E.g. P.R.O. PC2,74, pp. 228, 232; PC2.75, p. 179; PC2.75, p. 301.

33 Robert M. Adams, 'In search of Baron Somers' in Perez Zagorin (ed.), *Culture and politics from Puritanism to the Enlightenment* (Los Angeles and London, 1980), pp. 167–72; also William L. Sachse, *Lord Somers: a political portrait* (Manchester, 1975), pp. 41, 57. For Yarranton's views, see below, pp. 184–5.

34 For Buckingham's glassmaking interests, see above pp. 25–6.

35 P.R.O. SP29.360, p. 223. Ravenscroft had been at pains to point out that he was not encroaching on established interests: see my 'Accident or design? George Ravenscroft's patent and the invention of lead-crystal glass', *Technology and Culture*, 28 (1987), 789–90.

36 P.R.O. SP29.414, nos. 102, 128, 132, 147. The patent was successfully challenged even before its enrolment, by one Richard Clark, who made a claim to priority of invention: P.R.O. PC2.69, pp. 163, 175.

37 P.R.O. SP44.343, p. 234; patent 307 (1692). For the Company of White Paper Makers' Act, see Joan Thirsk and J. P. Cooper (eds.), *Seventeenth century economic documents* (Oxford, 1972), pp. 314–18.

38 P.R.O. SP35.75, no. 36; patent 458 (1723). See Ambrose Godfrey, *An account of the new method of extinguishing fires by explosion and suffocation* (1724).

39 P.R.O. SP35.21, nos. 9, 64; SP35.25, no. 61; SP35.65, no. 90. Yorke had reported that making iron in some degree malleable with coal was not new, but making it sufficiently malleable to produce bar iron serviceable for most manufactures was: B.L. MS Add. 36,140, fol. 12.

40 See below, p. 55.

41 Charles M. Andrews, *British committees, commissions, and councils of trade and plantations, 1622–1675* (Baltimore, 1908), pp. 106–8, 127.

42 Ibid., pp. 88–94.

43 P.R.O. SP44.33, p. 2; SP29.263, no. 62; SP29.265, no. 166A; the patent was apparently never enrolled.

44 For the Cockayne project, see B. E. Supple, *Commercial crisis and change in England, 1600–1642* (Cambridge, 1959), pp. 33–51.

45 Thomas Birch, *The history of the Royal Society of London* (4 vols., 1756), vol. 1, pp. 391, 397. This was possibly a scheme to raise revenue for the Society: ibid., p. 379. B.L. MS Sloane 4026, fol. 240. See also below, p. 189.

46 Sir George Clark, *A history of the Royal College of Physicians of London* (3 vols., Oxford, 1966), vol. 2, pp. 456, 524.

47 Ibid., vol. 1, pp. 235, 335, 336.

48 E.g. P.R.O. PC2.56, pp. 200, 220.

49 P.R.O. SP29.82, fol. 32.

50 P.R.O. SP29.414, no. 27(2); patent 211 (1680).

51 P.R.O. SP29.335, no. 84; patent 171 (1673).

52 P.R.O. SP35.29, no. 18; patent 439 (1721).

53 P.R.O. SP35.32, no. 15; patents 448 (1722), 452 (1722).

54 P.R.O. SP34.16, no. 59(1); patent 388 (1711).

55 David Lieberman, 'The province of legislation determined: legal theory in eighteenth-century Britain' (unpubl. Ph.D. thesis, University of London, 1980), esp. pp. 141–82. For the role of the law courts in the patent system, see below, ch. 4.

56 Gomme, *Patents of invention*, pp. 26–35.

57 15 Car II, c.12; 22 & 23 Car II, c.15; patent 261 (1688). For earlier seventeenth-century examples, see Davies, 'Patent specification', pp. 271–2.

58 E.g. patent 542 to John Kay (1733); patent 613 to Roger Plenius (1745). This point is well illustrated by Isaac Wilkinson's patent, no. 565 in 1738: MacLeod, 'Patents for invention', appendix 2.

59 Patent 454 (1723).

60 P.R.O. SP36.7, fol. 274. The second offer was made in a petition to parliament, ostensibly by 'several gentlemen, farmers, gardeners, and others', with regard to Liveings's Irish patent, granted in 1729: *H. of C. Jnl*, vol. 22 (1733), p. 121.

61 5 Geo III, c.8; reprinted in Webster, *Reports*, pp. 38–9.

62 Dutton, *Patent system*, pp. 75–6, and see below, p. 187. The award of the prize for determining the longitude had recently been withheld from John Harrison according to the Act of 3 Geo III, c.14, 'until he shall have made a full and clear discovery of the said principles (of the mechanism) and method (of construction) and the same shall have been found practicable and useful to their satisfaction': Quill, *John Harrison*, p. 139; see also, ibid., p. 122.

63 Ken Baynes and Francis Pugh, *The art of the engineer* (Guildford, 1981), chs. 1, 2, *passim*; Peter J. Booker, *A history of engineering drawing* (1963), pp. 68–72, 114–16, 120–1.

64 J. R. Harris, 'Skills, coal and British industry in the eighteenth century', *History*, 61 (1976), 167–82; Peter Mathias, 'Skills and the diffusion of innovation from Britain in the eighteenth century', *T.R.H.S.*, 5th ser. 25 (1977), 90–113.

65 Patent 517 (1730); P.R.O. PC2.91, pp. 631–3. For another example of inaccurate specification, see J. Allen Ransome, *The implements of agriculture* (1843), p. 212.

66 Woodcroft's index contains a number of patents for which no specification was apparently enrolled; and see W. Carpmael, *The law of patents* (1832), p. 113; Davies, *Collection*, p. 157.

67 See Dutton, *Patent system*, p. 198, n. 58 and p. 199, n. 67.

68 See the reproof in *Repertory of Arts*, 3 (1795), p. 146, and below, pp. 62–4.

69 Patents 722 (1758), 734 (1759).

70 For specification strategies, see also below, pp. 106–8.

71 Patent 1977 (1794).

72 P.P. 1829, III, p. 454.

73 Patents 673 (1752), 764 (1753).

74 He was the proprietor of Joanna Stephens's unpatented cure for the stone, his trade under pressure from Walter Baker's patented 'Liquid Shell' remedy: David D'Escherny, *A treatise of the causes and symptoms of the stone* (1755), title page, preface, pp. 24, 65–6, 72.

75 [David D'Escherny], *Short reflections upon patents* (1760), pp. 4–7.

76 Davies, 'Patent specification', p. 90; Hulme, 'Consideration of the patent grant', p. 317.

77 This was the belief of James Watt: Eric Robinson, 'James Watt and the law of patents', *Technology and Culture*, 13 (1972), 125.

78 Dering, *Diary*, p. 13.

79 Harold W. Brace, *History of seed crushing in Great Britain* (1960), p. 29.

80 P.R.O. SP36.2, nos. 41, 41(1); patent 495 (1728); B.L. MS Add. 36,136, fols. 331–45.

81 'The Attorney or Solicitor General always hears each party separately, they are never confronted': Gravenor Henson, *The civil, political and mechanical history of the framework knitters* (Nottingham, 1831), ed. S. D. Chapman (Newton Abbot, 1970), p. 269.

82 P.R.O. SP34.15, no. 161(1); SP34.16, no. 88; patent 387 (1711).

83 P.R.O. SP44.259, pp. 112–13; patent 401 (1715).

84 P.R.O. SP36.42, fols. 5, 7, 9, 11–12; patent 559 (1737). More elaborate means were devised to keep secret Joseph Booth's specification for making woollen cloth in 1792: P.P. 1829, III, p. 589.

85 See below, pp. 88–93.

86 See above, pp. 46, 48.

87 B.L. MS Add. 36,157, fol. 90.

88 Patent 505 (1728); P.R.O. SP36.7, fols. 78–86, 93–5. Payne was being harassed by would-be partners and spies, see below, p. 88.

89 See below, pp. 66–8, 92.

90 P.R.O. SP36.22, fol. 95; patent 526 (1731).

91 P.P. 1829, III, p. 420.

92 Ibid., pp. 19, 436–8.

93 P.R.O. SP44.237, pp. 250–1; SP44.241, pp. 329–30.

94 Henry Trueman Wood, 'The inventions of John Kay (1704–70)', *Jnl of the Royal Society of Arts*, 60 (1911), 81–2.

95 See above, p. 47.

96 MacLeod, 'The 1690s patents boom', pp. 559–68.

97 J. G. A. Pocock, 'Early modern capitalism: the Augustan perception' in E. Kamenka and R. Neale (eds.), *Feudalism, capitalism and beyond* (1975), pp. 62–8.

98 Daniel Defoe, *The Review*, ed. A. W. Secord (22 vols., New York, 1938), vol. 7, p. 463.

99 Described as 'a whig who would often vote tory', Northey was first removed by the whig Junto, reinstated by the tories, and survived the triumphant whig return to office in 1714: Romney Sedgwick (ed.), *The House of Commons, 1715–1754* (2 vols., 1970), vol. 1, p. 300.

100 Armand Budington Dubois, *The English business company after the Bubble Act, 1720–1800* (New York, 1938), pp. 2–21; 6 Geo I, c.18.

101 Curious though this seems, the Statute of Praemunire had come by the mid-seventeenth century to be used quite frequently in statutes to encompass a variety of acts deemed prejudicial to the state's interests: see, for instance the 1661 Treason Act (13 Car II, c.1). I owe this reference to Mark Goldie.

102 P.R.O. SP35.22, no. 78. See Scott, *Joint-stock companies*, vol. 1, p. 417; T. S. Ashton, *Economic fluctuations in England, 1700–1800* (Oxford, 1959), p. 121.

103 P.R.O. PC1.3.103, fol. 2.

104 P.R.O. PC2.86, p. 438. See John Carswell, *The South Sea Bubble* (1960), p. 15.

105 The Bubble Act itself was rigorously enforced: Scott, *Joint-stock companies*, vol. 1, pp. 437–8.

106 P.R.O. SP35.57, no. 101; B.L. MS Add. 36,136, fol. 223; patent 492 (1727); *H. of C. Jnl*, vol. 22 (1733), p. 259.

107 P.R.O. SP36.19, fols. 63–76; patent 502 (1728). For a summary of Wood's project, see Beckett, *Coal and tobacco*, pp. 127–30.

108 P.R.O. SP36.16, fols. 130–41, patent 518 (1730). Foljambe seems to have had considerable success despite this early set-back: see below p. 67. For a similar case, see P.R.O. SP44.251, pp. 543–4.

109 P.R.O. PC1.5, p. 3.

110 Dutton, *Patent system*, pp. 34–56.

4 The judiciary and the enforcement of patent rights

1 Dutton, *Patent system*, chs. 4 and 9.

2 *Mechanics Magazine*, 24 (1836), p. 460, quoted in Dutton, *Patent system*, p. 79.

3 P.R.O. PC2.61, pp. 244, 269, 313; patent 154 (1668).

4 P.R.O. PC2.55, p. 240; patents 128 (1661), 137 (1663).

5 Hulme, 'Privy Council law', pp. 69, 72, 73, 180. Patentees appear to have preferred equity to common-law jurisdiction: MacLeod, 'Patents for invention', pp. 114–15.

6 Holdsworth, *History of English law*, vol. 6, p. 331. Hulme, 'Privy Council law', pp. 63–75, 181–95, summarizes the cases recorded in the registers of the Privy Council (P.R.O. PC2 series).

7 P.R.O. PC2.71, pp. 481, 489, 494; patent 251 (1686).

8 P.R.O. PC2.99, pp. 101–2, 326–8, 358–9; patent 587 (1742).

9 For example, B.L. MS Add. 36,140, fols. 45–8; patent 396 (1714); P.R.O. SP44.259, pp. 300–2; patent 647 (1749).

10 This paragraph is based on Hulme, 'Privy Council law', pp. 189–91, 193–4.

11 W. H. Bryson, *The equity side of the Exchequer* (Cambridge, 1975), p. 3; J. Coryton, *A treatise on the law of letters patent* (1855), pp. 319–20.

12 Dutton, *Patent system*, p. 181.
13 Hulme, 'Privy Council law', pp. 191, 193–4.
14 Henson, *Framework knitters*, p. 274; see also Davies, *Collection*, pp. 432–3.
15 P.P. 1829, III, p. 448.
16 See Joseph Parkes, *A history of the court of Chancery* (1828), pp. 230–1.
17 Roger North, *Lives of the Norths*, ed. Augustus Jessop (3 vols., 1870), vol. 1, pp. 257–9; see also ibid., vol. 1, pp. 259–68 *passim*; John Oldmixon, *The history of England* (1735) p. 784.
18 Wood, 'Inventions of John Kay', pp. 73–4; my emphasis. For private Acts of Parliament, see below pp. 72–3.
19 John Crosbie to John Palmer, 12 Sept. 1753, S.C.L. MS Bagshawe C. 493. See also Dutton, *Patent system*, pp. 181–2.
20 Henson, *Framework knitters*, pp. 309, 327, 351, 366.
21 R. S. Fitton and A. P. Wadsworth, *The Strutts and the Arkwrights, 1758–1890* (Manchester, 1958), p. 35.
22 *Felkin's history of the machine-wrought hosiery and lace manufactures*, ed. S. D. Chapman (Newton Abbot, 1967), pp. 93–4.
23 Eric Robinson and Douglas McKie (eds.), *Partners in science: letters of James Watt and Joseph Black* (1970), p. 150.
24 John Farey, in 1829, believed patentees were 'very often' deterred from prosecution by both the cost and the uncertainty of the law: P.P. 1829, III, p. 565.
25 Richard Francis, *Maxims of equity* (1727), 'To the Reader', p. 1; Francis, however, contended that courts of equity were no more uncertain in fact than common-law courts. See also, Lord John Campbell, *The lives of the Lord Chancellors* (8 vols., 1845–69), vol. 6, p. 97; and Lieberman, 'The province of legislation determined', p. 87.
26 Hulme, 'Patent law', p. 283.
27 Quoted in Robinson, 'James Watt', p. 116.
28 Holdsworth, *History of English law*, vol. 11, p. 425.
29 Dutton, *Patent system*, pp. 72–5. This continued to be a point of judicial uncertainty and debate. One witness in 1829 thought that half the patents overturned in the courts were lost on the judge's adverse definition of 'manufacture': P.P. 1829, III, pp. 521–2, 530.
30 P.P. 1829, III, pp. 454, 486.
31 Collier, *Law of patents*. It 'met with a very rapid sale': Davies, *Collection*. p. vii.
32 Watt's attempts to grapple with the conceptual and pragmatic difficulties involved are elucidated in Robinson, 'James Watt', *passim*.
33 Holdsworth, *History of English law*, vol. 11, p. 428; Hulme, 'Patent law', pp. 284–7; Dutton, *Patent system*, pp. 75–6.
34 W. Carpmael, *Law reports of patent cases* (3 vols., 1843–52), vol. 1, p. 145.
35 P.P. 1829, III, p. 437.
36 P.R.O. SP29.366, p. 125; patent 152 (1667).
37 Wellcome Institute, MS 3013 III, pp. 6–7; patent 626 (1748).
38 P.R.O. E134. 14 Geo II, Easter no. 7, Yorks, fol. 10; C11.2456.21.
39 Josiah Peter, *Truth in opposition to ignorant and malicious falsehood* (1701), pp. 31–3; see below, p. 69.
40 P.R.O. E134. 15 Geo II, Mich. no. 15, Notts & Yorks, fol. ii.
41 See Hutchinson's complaint, below p. 73.
42 Patent 653; see also David Stephenson's careful application in P.R.O. SP44.258, pp. 198–202, and specification of patent 558 (1737); and the threats contained in the specifications of patents 2042 (1795) and 2103 (1796).

43 See below, pp. 106–8.

44 B.R.L. MS Wyatt I, fol. 45. John Batchelor issued a similar 'cri de coeur' in his specification to patent 652 (1750).

45 Richard L. Hills, *Power in the industrial revolution* (Manchester, 1970), pp. 34–5.

46 P.R.O. SP44.251, pp. 429–30. The warrant was not acted upon because Haskins died shortly afterwards: SP44.253, pp. 7–8. For Desaguliers's involvement, see R.S.L. MS RBC XI, pp. 5–16.

47 Dutton, *Patent system*, p. 73. See, for example, patent specifications 1144 (1777) and 1169 (1777).

48 Rhoda Edwards, 'London potters, *circa* 1570–1710', *Jnl of Ceramic History*, 6 (1974), 56; Lorna Weatherill and Rhoda Edwards, 'Pottery making in London and Whitehaven in the late-seventeenth century', *Post Medieval Archaeology*, 5 (1971), 163.

49 Patent 164 (1672).

50 Mavis Bimson, 'References to John Dwight in a seventeenth-century manuscript', *Trans. English Ceramic Circle*, 4 (1959), pt 5, 10–12; Henry W. Robinson and Walter Adams (eds.), *The diary of Robert Hooke, M.A., M.D., F.R.S., 1672–1680* (1935), p. 89; Robert Plot, *The natural history of Oxfordshire* (Oxford, 1676), pp. 250–1; Weatherill and Edwards, 'Pottery making', pp. 163, 165.

51 Guildhall, MS 5556; Edwards, 'London potters', p. 57.

52 Patent 234; see Edwards, 'London potters', p. 58.

53 P.R.O. C24.1188(50), printed in Edwards, 'London potters', p. 105.

54 Lorna M. Weatherill, 'The growth of the pottery industry in England, 1660–1815' (unpubl. Ph.D. thesis, University of London, 1981), p. 454; P.R.O. C8.538.23; C5.107.13; C5.108.15.

55 Dwight claimed that the 'confederates conduct their business so secretly that he cannot make full discovery and proof thereof as may be sufficient to maintain an action at law', but this may have been a conventional formula: P.R.O. C8.538.23.

56 Edwards, 'London potters', p. 59; Llewellyn Jewitt, *The ceramic art of Great Britain* (2 vols., 1878), vol. 1, pp. 124–7. Matthew Garner testified that after twelve years' production of white stoneware (i.e. *ca*. 1692), 'then the business of his trade [was] declining': P.R.O. C5.156.9.

57 Edwards, 'London potters', p. 59.

58 Weatherill and Edwards, 'Pottery making', pp. 162–3.

59 P.R.O. C5.107.13, printed in Edwards, 'London potters', p. 61.

60 P.R.O. C7.333.13; Edwards, 'London potters', pp. 89, 107–8.

61 Several factories producing soft-paste porcelain were opened in England in the mid-eighteenth century, and imitation of Chinese wares in design and attempts to discover the 'true' porcelain were common from the seventeenth century.

62 I am grateful to Jill Denton for discussions which have helped elucidate some finer technical points of pottery making.

63 P.R.O. C8.535.23; C5.107.13; C24.1188(50); F. H. Garner, 'John Dwight, some contemporary references', *Trans. English Ceramic Circle*, 1 (1937), pt 5, 30–1.

64 P.R.O. C8.538.23.

65 Ibid. Although Talbot won this case, he was fined £66 8s (£66 40) for selling stoneware pots in 1696: Edwards, 'London potters', p. 107.

66 P.R.O. C8.538.23; Edwards, 'London potters', pp. 78–9.

67 P.R.O. PC2.76, p. 49. See also the statement contained in P.R.O. C6.404.24.

68 P.R.O. C11.699.10, fol. 3.

69 P.R.O. C11.2456.21; see also C11.2452.15.

70 White, *Sir Edward Coke*, p. 127; Malament, 'The "economic liberalism" of Sir Edward Coke', p. 133; see above, pp. 12–13.

71 P.R.O. C12.379.15, evidence of Arthur Else.

72 For Shaw, see below, p. 71.

73 See above, p. 48.

74 Richard T. Godfrey, *Printmaking in Britain* (Oxford, 1978), p. 32; Holdsworth, *History of English law*, vol. 15, p. 40.

75 W. Kenrick, Ll.D., *An address to the artists and manufacturers of Great Britain* (1774), p. 26.

76 Patent 518 (1730); P.R.O. E134. 14 Geo II, Easter no. 7, Yorks.

77 P.R.O. E134. 15 Geo II, Mich. no. 15, Notts & Yorks.

78 P.R.O. E126.27 Mich. 1743, no. 6.

79 P.R.O. E134. 14 Geo II, Easter no. 7, Yorks, fol. 6, evidence of John Mathias.

80 Ibid., fols. 5, 6; E134. 15 Geo II, Mich. no. 15, Notts & Yorks, fol. ii.

81 Ibid., fol. ii; E126.27, Mich. 1743, no. 6.

82 P.R.O. E134. 14 Geo II, Easter no. 7, Yorks, fols. 8–9.

83 P.R.O. E126.27 Mich. 1743, no. 6.

84 James Watt to J. McGrigor, 30 Oct. 1784, in S.R.O. GD1.500.72.

85 Robinson and McKie, *Partners in science*, p. 229. For further details of Boulton and Watt's prosecutions, see Jennifer Tann, 'Mr Hornblower and his crew: Watt engine pirates at the end of the 18th century', *T.N.S.*, 51 (1979–80), 96–101.

86 Davies, *Collection*, p. 13; Webster, *Reports*, p. 35; Hulme, 'Privy Council law', pp. 71–2.

87 *East India Company* v. *Sandys* (1684), quoted in Fox, *Monopolies and patents*, p. 123n.

88 Dutton, *Patent system*, pp. 71, 81, n. 9.

89 R.S.L. Jnl Book, 5 June 1679; Peter, *Truth in opposition*, pp. 27, 32.

90 B.L. Add. MS 4037, fol. 77.

91 P.R.O. SP44.238, p. 236; SP44.347, p. 212; patent 354. See also Grew's threat to prosecute counterfeits in his announcement of the patent: *London Gazette*, 3414 (27 July–1 Aug. 1698).

92 The following account is based on Peter, *Truth in opposition*, pp. 58–9. Moult published his translation as *A treatise of the nature and use of the bitter purging salt contain'd in Epsom, and such other waters* (1697). It contained an advertisement for Moult's business, including the salts. Moult was something of an entrepreneur, financing Robert Eaton's patenting and production of styptick balsam in 1722: [Robert Eaton], *An account of Dr Eaton's styptick balsam* (1723), p. 56; taking shares in Robert Lydall's tin-plating project around 1700: P.R.O. PC2.81, pp. 180–1, 227, and patent 374 (1705); while in 1716 a Francis Moult 'of London, esq.', took out a patent for refining tin (406), where he said he had 'for several years dealt in smelting and refining of tin'.

93 Peter, *Truth in opposition*, pp. 21, 53.

94 See below, p. 187.

95 Peter, *Truth in opposition*, p. 54; R.S.L. MS RBC xi, p. 65.

96 P.R.O. C11.699.10, fol. 3. Ffowke openly competed with Newsham: see, for instance, his advertising broadsheet, *John Fowke [sic] of Nightingale Lane, Wapping, London, Engineer . . .* [1726], B.L. 816 m.10(96). J. T. Desaguliers firmly believed that Newsham's claim to the invention was indisputable: *A course of experimental philosophy* (2 vols., London, 1734–44), vol. 2, pp. 516–18; similarly, Stephen Switzer, *An universal system of water and water works, philosophical and practical* (1734), pp. 351–2.

97 *A general description of all trades* (1747), p. 84.

98 The case was referred to the court of Common Pleas: Hulme, 'Privy Council law', pp. 191–2.

99 Henry C. King, *The history of the telescope* (1955), pp. 144–54.

100 It is also possible the elder Dollond, originally a silk weaver by trade, regarded the patent as simply enabling: see below, pp. 82–4.

101 Katherine Farrar (ed.), *Letters of Josiah Wedgwood* (3 vols., repr. Manchester, 1973), vol. 2, pp. 22, 31–2; patent 939 (1769). .

102 Kenneth G. Ponting (ed.), *A memoir of Edmund Cartwright* (Bath, 1971), p. 191. See also Dutton, *Patent system*, pp. 193–4.

103 See above, p. 64.

104 See above, p. 29.

105 Leonard Jay (ed.), *Letters of the famous eighteenth-century printer John Baskerville of Birmingham* (Birmingham, 1932), p. 9. Baskerville himself obtained a patent (no. 582) for japanning, in 1742.

106 Dutton, *Patent system*, p. 194.

107 Tann, 'Mr Hornblower and his crew', p. 101.

108 Patent 541 (1733).

109 Simeon Shaw, *History of the Staffordshire potteries* (1829, repr. Newton Abbot & Wakefield, 1970), p. 147. This is thought to be the first instance of the revocation of a patent by an assize court: Hulme, 'Privy Council law', p. 189.

110 Shaw, *Staffordshire potteries*, p. 148; *D.N.B.* sub 'John Astbury (1668?–1743)'.

111 A. P. Wadsworth and J. de L. Mann, *The cotton trade and industrial Lancashire, 1600–1870* (repr. Manchester, 1965), p. 490.

112 H. W. Dickinson, *Matthew Boulton* (Cambridge, 1937), p. 128.

113 Dutton, *Patent system*, pp. 77–8.

114 Geoffrey W. Tookey, 'Patents and public policy under the British common law' in Association Internationale pour la Protection de la Propriété Industrielle (ed.), *Venetian patent law* (Milan, 1974), p. 304.

115 Richard Holt, *A short treatise of artificial stone* (1730), p. 43. See also evidence to this effect in P.P. 1829, III, pp. 428, 434.

116 *Angliae tutamen; or, the safety of England* (1695), p. 23.

117 *London Gazette*, 2867 (1–4 May, 1693); John Houghton, *A collection for improvement of husbandry and trade* (12 vols., 1692–8), vol. 3, no. 67; patent 322 (1693). See also the threat of John Tatham, in *London Gazette*, 2835 (9–12 Jan. 1693), again indicative of the problems of enforcement.

118 R.S.A. Guard Book III, p. 66; patent 552 (1736), to Joshua Coles for 'liquid blue' had expired six years before, in 1750.

119 H[umphry] Walcot, *Sea water made fresh and wholesome* (1702), pp. 8–13, reprints the Act of 6&7 Gul. III and relates the troubled history of the invention.

120 P.P. 1829, III, p. 583.

121 Guildhall, MS 3952, no. 4.

122 P.P. 1829, III, p. 446.

123 Dutton, *Patent system*, p. 179.

5 The decision to patent

1 This is considered more fully in chapter 6 below.

2 Gomme, *Patents of invention*, pp. 16–18. See the estimates offered in: D'Escherny, *Short reflections*, p. 6; Desaguliers, *Experimental philosophy*, vol. 1, p. 133; Kenrick, *Address*, p. 29.

3 P.P. 1829, III, p. 431.

4 A. A. Gomme, 'Patent practice in the eighteenth century: the diary of Samuel Taylor, threadmaker and inventor, 1722–3', *T.N.S.*, 15 (1734–5), 210–16; P.R.O. SP35.33, no. 170b.

5 Davies, *Collection*, p. 11.

6 Gomme, 'Patent practice', p. 210.

7 See above, p. 45.

8 P.R.O. SO35.45, no. 11; patent 463 (1723).

9 D. G. C. Allan, *William Shipley, founder of the Royal Society of Arts* (1968), p. 14; see below, p. 194.

10 R.S.A. Guard Book, III, no. 57; see also ibid., III, nos. 70, 71, 101; IV, nos. 23, 49.

11 P.R.O. SP44.352, pp. 37–9; patent 436 (1721).

12 B.L. MS Add. 61,686, fols. 95–6; patent 419 (1718).

13 In 1801 only 5 per cent of the population had annual incomes over £60: W. D. Rubinstein, *Men of property: the very wealthy in Britain since the industrial revolution* (1981), p. 44.

14 B.L. MS Sloane 3646, fol. 88.

15 Percy C. Rushen, *The history and antiquities of Chipping Camden, in the county of Gloucester* (Woodbridge, 1899), p. 64; patent 556 (1736).

16 Eliza Meteyard, *The life of Josiah Wedgwood*, ed. R. W. Lightbourn (2 vols., 1970), vol. 1, p. 153; patents 487 (1726) and 536 (1732).

17 Sir Henry Bessemer, *An autobiography* (1905), p. 25.

18 Patents 642 (1749), 663 (1751), 664 (1751).

19 S.C.L. MS Bagshawe C 493, *passim*.

20 Patent 647; P.R.O. SP44.259, pp. 300–2.

21 See below, pp. 124–5.

22 Clow and Clow, *Chemical revolution*, p. 428.

23 Dutton, *Patent system*, p. 178.

24 P.P. 1829, III, p. 554.

25 Dutton, *Patent system*, pp. 77–9.

26 Patents 1662 (1788), 1732 (1790). For Ducrest, see R. B. Prosser, *Birmingham inventors and inventions* (Birmingham, 1881), p. 41; *D.N.B.*, sub 'Charles, 3rd Earl of Stanhope (1753–1816)'.

27 Desmond Clarke, *The ingenious Mr Edgeworth* (1965), pp. 28–34, 44, 50; Desmond Clarke (ed.), *Memoirs of Richard Lovell Edgeworth* (2 vols., Shannon, 1969), vol. 1, pp. 148–53, 172–6; Robert E. Schofield, *The Lunar Society of Birmingham* (Oxford, 1963), pp. 46–59, 129.

28 Clarke, *Memoirs*, pp. 170–1.

29 Schofield, *Lunar Society*, p. 108; my emphasis. For another example, James Hall, see William Pole (ed.), *The life of Sir William Fairbairn, Bart.* (1877, repr. Newton Abbot, 1970), pp. 94, 97.

30 Clow and Clow, *Chemical revolution*, pp. 396–423.

31 See below, pp. 139–43.

32 F. W. Gibbs, 'Bryan Higgins and his circle' in Musson, *Science, technology, and economic growth*, pp. 195–202.

33 This category is further divided below, pp. 117–18.

34 See above, p. 30.

35 Carlo Cipolla, *Clocks and culture* (1967), p. 103.

36 See above, pp. 34–8.

37 Patents 186 (1675), 353 (1698); Thomas, 'Thomas Neale', pp. 123–5; P.R.O. SP44.238, p. 180; SP29.263, no. 116; SP29.266, no. 185.

38 P.R.O. SP44.18, p. 51; PC2.64, pp. 314–15; PC2.70, pp. 208, 215; patent 135 (1663).

39 In a subsequent grant this exception was removed in his favour: P.R.O. PC2.73, p. 237; SO3.19; patent 262 (1689).

40 P.R.O. SP44.246, pp. 353–4, 496–7; patent 398 (1714).

41 P.R.O. PC2.71, p. 397; patents 227 (1683), 232 (1684).

42 Scott, *Joint-stock companies*, vol. 1, pp. 54–8; P.R.O. SP44.235, pp. 297, 321; SP44.236, p. 268; patents 372 (1704) and 382 (1708).

43 E.g. P.R.O. SP29.153, no. 76; SP44.245, pp. 168–70; SP44.250, pp. 292–3. There was an isolated one for life insurance in 1778 (patent 1197).

44 Thirsk and Cooper, *Economic documents*, pp. 313–14.

45 Patent 130 (1661); L. A. Clarkson, 'English economic policy in the sixteenth and seventeenth centuries: the case of the leather industries', *B.I.H.R.*, 38 (1965), 150–9.

46 Fox, *Monopolies and patents*, p. 157.

47 34 Geo. III, c.63; summarized in P.P. 1829, III, p. 590.

48 See above, pp. 29–30.

49 Warren C. Scoville, 'The Huguenots and the diffusion of technology', *Jnl of Political Economy*, 60 (1952), 294–311.

50 Identified in W. A. Shaw, *Letters of denization and acts of naturalization for aliens in England and Ireland*, The Publications of the Huguenot Society of London, vols. 18 (1911), 27 (1923).

51 P.R.O. SP36.18, fols. 146–7.

52 Michael J. Walker, 'The extent of guild control of trades in England, *c.*1660–1820: a study based on a sample of provincial towns and London companies' (unpubl. Ph.D. thesis, University of Cambridge, 1986), pp. 69–102, 119–22, 249.

53 P.R.O. SP29.287, no. 73; see also John Hatcher and T. C. Barker, *A history of British pewter* (1974), p. 226.

54 Guildhall, MS 5667 II, p. 106; *A true state of the case between Francis Watson and the painters of London*, in P.R.O. SP29.230, no. 115; patent 158 (1669).

55 Patents 267 (1691), 269 (1691); *London Gazette*, 2749 (14–17 March, 1692); Harold Nockolds, *The Coachmakers: a history of the Worshipful Company of Coachmakers and Coach Harness Makers, 1677–1977* (1977), p. 27.

56 See below, p. 188.

57 Guildhall, MS 4655 IX, 14 Jan. 1683–4, 28 July 1684; Alfred Plummer, *The London Weavers Company, 1600–1970* (1972), pp. 137–8.

58 Guildhall, MS 4646, fols. 122–3.

59 P.R.O. PC2.72, pp. 622, 706, 717; patent 261 (1688).

60 Patents 207 (1679), 530 (1731); P.R.O. C66.3379(22) (1694); SP44.16 p. 125 (1661).

61 Nicholas Goodison, *English barometers, 1680–1860* (1969), p. 33.

62 Ibid., p. 27.

63 J. R. Kellett, 'The breakdown of guild and corporation control', *Ec.H.R.*, 2nd ser. 10 (1957–8), 388; P.R.O. SP35.8, no. 21; SP44.360, pp. 14–17; SP35.74, no. 57; patent 433.

64 Walker, 'The extent of guild control', pp. 126, 188–214, 225–6.

65 Patent 183 (1675); Bodl., MS Rawlinson A 180, fols. 1–8.

66 Patent 517 (1730).

67 MacLeod, 'Patents for invention', pp. 137–8.

68 T. Girtin, *The mark of the sword: a narrative history of the Cutlers Company, 1689–1975*

(1975), pp. 277, 293–4; Hatcher and Barker, *British pewter*, pp. 170–1; F. I. Schechter, *The historical foundation of the law relating to trade-marks*, Columbia Legal Studies, vol. 1 (New York, 1925), pp. 94n, 122. Trade-marks as signs of authenticity were advertised, e.g. *London Gazette*, 2355 (11–14 June 1688).

69 P.R.O. SP44.241, pp. 444–5; patent 322 (1693). See also the patentees' handbills reproduced in E. A. Entwistle, 'The Blew Paper Warehouse in Aldermanbury, London', *Connoisseur*, 125 (1950), 94.

70 *Gentleman's Magazine*, 18 (1748), p. 347; Wellcome Institute, MS 3013 1, fol. 4.

71 J. H. Young, 'Proprietors of other days', *Chemist and Druggist*, 106 (1927), 833–4.

72 P.R.O. C11.46.38.

73 See above, p. 67.

74 Timothy Byfield, *A short but full account of the rise, nature and management of the small-pox* (1711). On Byfield's death in 1723 his widow assured patrons they could still purchase 'the sal volatile, which she always prepared with her own hands, *near 30 years*' (i.e. approximately eighteen years before the patent): Timothy Byfield *The artificial spaw, or mineral waters to drink* (1684), B.L. copy, extract from unidentified London newspaper on inside cover; my emphasis.

75 Young, 'Proprietors of other days', p. 833; Clark, *Royal College of Physicians*, vol. 1, p. 363; *London Gazette*, 2507 (18–20 Nov. 1689); Leslie G. Matthews, *History of pharmacy in Britain* (Edinburgh and London, 1962), p. 283.

76 G. A. Cranfield, *The development of the provincial newspaper* (Oxford, 1962), pp. 12–22, 208–9, 221–2.

77 P. S. Brown, 'Medicines advertised in eighteenth-century Bath newspapers', *Medical History*, 20 (1976), 152–7.

78 *Daily Courant*, 6 July 1732. See also George Griffenhagen, *Medicine tax stamps worldwide* (Milwaukee, 1971), pp. 6–8.

79 D'Escherny, *Short reflections*, p. 7.

80 D'Escherny, *Treatise*, p. 65; patent 674 (1753).

81 Wellcome Institute, MS 3013 1, fols. 3, 5.

82 Kenneth Dewhurst, *The quicksilver doctor: the life and times of Thomas Dover, physician and adventurer* (Bristol, 1957), *passim*; A. J. Viseltear, 'The last illness of Sir Robert Walpole', *Bulletin of the History of Medicine*, 41 (1967), 200–4; S. Stander, 'Eighteenth-century patent medicines', *History of Medicine*, 7 (1976), 69; Charles Welsh, *A bookseller of the last century* (1885), pp. 22–5.

83 *London Gazette*, 3025 (5–8 Nov. 1694); patent 313 (1693). See also, for example, *London Gazette*, 2351, 2365, 2379, 3445.

84 *London Gazette*, 3086 (6–10 June, 1695); patent in P.R.O. C66.3379(22). See *A general description of all trades*, p. 100, which refers to fullers, better known as 'scourers', 'whose chief business is cleaning of men's clothes, sometimes furniture'.

85 Patent 293 (1692); *London Gazette*, 2798 (1–5 Sept. 1692); 2813 (24–7 Sept. 1692).

86 Patent 275 (1691); *London Gazette*, 2769 (23–6 May, 1692).

87 M. W. Flinn, 'The travel diaries of Swedish engineers in the eighteenth century as sources of technological history', *T.N.S.*, 31 (1957–9), 100.

88 See below, pp. 128–37.

89 See below, pp. 154–6.

90 *Observations on the utility of patents*, 4th edn (1791), p. 33.

91 *Repertory of Arts*, 8 (1798), pp. 316–19.

92 *The patent, a poem*, pp. 1–2.

93 *Observations on the utility of patents*, pp. 16–17; see also Kenrick, *Address*, p. 43; *Gentleman's Magazine*, 23 (1753), p. 235, and 56(i) (1786), p. 26.

94 *Angliae tutamen*, p. 23. See *H. of C. Jnl*, vol. 11 (1696), p. 595.

95 MacLeod, 'The 1690s patents boom', pp. 562–9.

96 See below, pp. 000–0.

97 P.R.O. SP44.243, p. 334; SP35.26, no. 4; SP34.21, no. 64; SP36.7, fols. 93–5.

98 Aaron Hill, *An account of the rise and progress of the beech-oil invention* (1715), p. 94.

99 B.L. MS Add. 36,140, fol. 13; see also P.R.O. SP44.261, pp. 43–6; patent 701 (1755).

100 MacLeod, 'Patents for invention', pp. 148–9; see above, pp. 25–7.

101 See below, pp. 130–7.

102 B.R.L. MS Wyatt II, fol. 104.

103 Wadsworth and Mann, *Cotton trade*, pp. 441–4.

104 John Blackner, *The history of Nottingham* (Nottingham, 1815), p. 247.

105 *Repertory of Arts*, 9 (1798), pp. 87–96.

106 Robinson and McKie, *Partners in science*, p. 25. See also A. E. Musson and Eric Robinson, *Science and technology in the industrial revolution* (Manchester, 1969), pp. 274–5, 359.

107 Dutton, *Patent system*, pp. 182–3.

108 See below, p. 147, and P.P. 1829, III, p. 441.

109 George Hagar seems even to have secured support in his old age on the strength of a patentable invention: P.R.O. SP44.253, pp. 395–7. For Hagar's shady dealings, see MacLeod, 'Patents for invention', p. 229.

110 Peter Mathias, *The first industrial nation: an economic history of Britain, 1700–1914* (1969), p. 37.

111 See below, pp. 93–5.

112 Houghton, *Collection*, vol. 3, no. 46 (1693).

113 Dubois, *English business company*, p. 12 and *passim*.

114 Dickinson, *Matthew Boulton*, pp. 79–83.

115 B.R.L. MS Wyatt I, fols. 5, 12, 16; patent 562 (1738).

116 W. A. Benton, 'John Wyatt and the weighing of heavy loads', *T.N.S.*, 9 (1928–9), 60–77.

117 Wadsworth and Mann, *Cotton trade*, pp. 427–33.

118 Musson and Robinson, *Science and technology*, p. 323.

119 *Repertory of Arts*, 9 (1798), p. 308. For Dundonald's late-eighteenth-century licensing practices and some early-nineteenth-century examples, see Dutton, *Patent system*, pp. 132–41.

120 See above, p. 67.

121 P.R.O. E134. 25 Geo II, Hil. 2, Lancs, fols. 7, 8.

122 Musson and Robinson, *Science and technology*, pp. 277–8.

123 J. S. Allen, 'The introduction of the Newcomen engine from 1710 to 1733', *T.N.S.*, 42 (1969–70), 169–90; L. T. C. Rolt and J. S. Allen, *The steam engine of Thomas Newcomen* (Hartington, 1977), pp. 69–70.

124 Alan Smith, 'Steam and the City: the Committee of Proprietors of the Invention for Raising Water by Fire, 1715–1735', *T.N.S.*, 49 (1977–8), 5–15.

125 Edward Hughes, 'The first steam engine in the Durham coalfields', *Archaeologia Aeliana*, 4th ser. 27 (1949), 32–43.

126 Patent 449 (1722); Allen, 'Newcomen engine', pp. 223–5, my emphasis; Smith, 'Steam and the City', p. 15.

127 P.R.O. C11.2452.7; C11.2456.21; Wadsworth and Mann, *Cotton trade*, pp. 452–5.

128 Patent 591 (1743); Julia de Lacy Mann, *The cloth industry in the west of England from 1640 to 1880* (Oxford, 1971), p. 292.

129 Patent 180 (1675); Bodl., MS Aubrey 13, fols. 5–6.
130 Lowther to C. Spedding, 10 Dec. 1734, Cumbria R. O. (Carlisle), Lowther MSS.
131 Wadsworth and Mann, *Cotton trade*, p. 490; S. D. Chapman, *The early factory masters* (Newton Abbot, 1967), pp. 73–6.
132 Dutton, *Patent system*, pp. 122–32. See below, p. 142.
133 Patent 652 (1750); N. K. A. Rothstein, 'The London silk industry, 1702–66' (unpubl. M.A. thesis, University of London, 1961), p. 268.
134 Chapman, *Early factory masters*, pp. 23, 34.
135 *H. of C. Jnl*, vol. 26 (1750), pp. 54, 81–2; patent 564 (1738).
136 Cobbett, *Parliamentary history* vol. 8, col. 926; patent 422 (1718).
137 P.R.O. SP35.63, no. 61; patent 488 (1726). Similarly, Richard Fishwick, with his patent for white lead: D. J. Rowe, *Lead manufacturing in Britain: a history* (1983), pp. 33–4, 53 n. 26.
138 George W. Daniels, *The early English cotton industry* (Manchester, 1920), p. 166; Dickinson, *Matthew Boulton*, p. 108; Wedgwood, *Letters*, vol. 2, p. 52.
139 J. R. M. Setchell, 'Henry Hindley & Son, instrument and clock makers of York' (unpubl. B.Litt. thesis, University of Oxford, 1971), pp. 22, 33, 38, 51–6, 63, 104, 116–22, 125, 137. For examples of late-seventeenth-century manufacturers who made, but did not patent, inventions, see MacLeod, 'Patents for invention', pp. 172–4.
140 Beckett, 'Eighteenth-century origin', 61–3. See also S. D. Chapman and S. Chassagne, *European textile printers in the eighteenth century* (1981), p. 82.
141 Beckett, *Coal and tobacco*, pp. 71–2.
142 Ransome, *Implements*, p. 174; G. E. Fussell, *The farmer's tools, 1500–1900* (1952), p. 158.
143 Smiles, *Industrial biography*, pp. 107–8; see T. S. Ashton, *Iron and steel in the industrial revolution*, 4th edn (Manchester, 1968), pp. 55–8.
144 Dickinson, *Matthew Boulton*, p. 51; Mary Walton, *Sheffield: its story and achievement*, 4th edn (Sheffield, 1968), p. 122.
145 Meteyard, *Wedgwood*, vol. 1, p. 289.
146 Bessemer, *Autobiography*, pp. 59–65, 81–3.
147 J. H. Benton, *John Baskerville, type-founder and printer, 1706–1775*, 2nd edn (New York, 1944), pp. 5–7; patent 582 (1742).
148 While 'projector' often had a pejorative overtone, it seems to have been also used neutrally as an alternative for 'undertaker' (in the early-modern sense) or the anachronistic 'entrepreneur'. Thus, for example, Samuel Taylor described himself in patent 453 (1722) as the 'contriver and projector' of his invention, and Joseph Gilmore's affidavit in 1722 spoke of 'the worthy projector': P.R.O. SP44.253, pp. 168–73. See also Dundonald's ironic self-description as a projector, quoted in Dutton, *Patent system*, p. 154.
149 This is examined more closely below, pp. 137–9.

6 Invention outside the patent system

1 Patents have been counted by the industry to which they chiefly related (not by the occupation of the patentee). The percentages here are approximate to the nearest whole number.
2 The metalworking and engine-making trades are considered more fully in chapter 7 below, pp. 130–1, 137–8.
3 Joan Thirsk (ed.), *The agrarian history of England and Wales*, vol. 5 (Cambridge,

1985), pt 2, p. 588, and pp. 533–89 *passim*; E. L. Jones, 'Agriculture, 1700–1800' in Floud and McCloskey, *Economic history*, pp. 78–86; Crafts, *British economic growth*, pp. 38–44.

4 Patents 155 (1668), 159 (1671), 160 (1671).

5 See below, p. 193.

6 I[ethro] T[ull], *The horse-hoing husbandry*, 2nd edn (1733). See G. E. Fussell, *More old English farming books from Tull to the Board of Agriculture, 1731–1793* (1950), pp. 1–4.

7 T[ull], *Horse-hoing husbandry*, p. vii.

8 *By the king's royal letter patent and licence, Charles Baker's treatise for the preventing of smut in wheat* (Bristol, 1797). Authorized publication of an invention in an expensive limited edition was a regular method of rewarding inventors in France: Parker, *Bureau of Commerce*, p. 58.

9 See above, pp. 67–8.

10 Bodl., MS Aubrey 4, fols. 169v–70.

11 Thomas Hale, *A compleat body of husbandry* (1756), p. 474; Fussell, *Farmer's tools*, pp. 153–4.

12 Thirsk, *Agrarian history*, vol. 5, pt 2, pp. 582–3; Fussell, *Farmer's tools*, pp. 22–3, 40–8, 103–4.

13 Fussell, *Farmer's tools*, pp. 99–104.

14 G. E. Mingay, 'The size of farms in the eighteenth century', *Ec.H.R.*, 2nd ser. 14 (1961–2), 469–75, 480–3; S. MacDonald, 'Progress of the early threshing machine', *Agricultural History Review*, 23 (1975), 74–6.

15 G. E. Fussell, *Jethro Tull: his influence on mechanized agriculture* (Reading, 1973), p. 82; idem, *Farmer's tools*, pp. 22–3, 46–8, 104.

16 Fussell, *Farmer's tools*, p. 157; patent 1486 (1785).

17 Ibid., pp. 61–2, 68, 108; Ransome, *Implements*, pp. 29–30.

18 G. E. Mingay (ed.), *Arthur Young and his times* (1975), p. 93.

19 *V.C.H. Suffolk*, vol. 2, p. 283; Fussell, *Farmer's tools*, p. 106.

20 Fussell, *Farmer's tools*, pp. 60, 63; D. R. Grace and D. C. Phillips, *Ransomes of Ipswich: a history of the firm and guide to its records* (Reading, 1975), p. 1; James Cooke, *Cooke's improved patent drill and horse hoe* (1789).

21 William Marshall, *Rural economy of the midland counties*, 2nd edn (2 vols. 1796), vol. 1, p. 106.

22 Fussell, *Farmer's tools*, pp. 156–7; Samuel Smiles, *Lives of the engineers*, ed. L. T. C. Rolt (3 vols., Newton Abbot, 1968), vol. 2, pp. 109–11; MacDonald, 'Threshing machine', p. 66.

23 *A treatise on ploughs and wheel carriages* (Edinburgh, 1784). For seventeenth-century antecedents of this ethic, see Thirsk, *Agrarian history*, vol. 5, pt 2, p. 548.

24 Quoted in *V.C.H. Suffolk*, vol. 2, p. 282. A hundred, at least, of Baldwin's drills are known to have been made and sold, 1792–1804: Fussell, *Farmer's tools*, p. 105.

25 See, for example, Ransome, *Implements*, pp. 184–5.

26 William Borlase, *The natural history of Cornwall* (Oxford, 1758), p. 168; see also T. S. Ashton and J. Sykes, *The coal industry of the eighteenth century*, 2nd edn (Manchester, 1964), p. 12.

27 P. C. Davey, 'Studies in the history of mining and metallurgy to the middle of the seventeenth century' (unpubl. Ph.D. thesis, University of London, 1954), pp. 290–1; Michael Flinn, *The history of the British coal industry, volume 2, 1700–1870: the industrial revolution* (Oxford, 1984), p. 128.

28 Ashton and Sykes, *Coal industry*, pp. 27–31; Flinn, *British coal industry*, pp. 83–7, 90.

29 See, for example, Beckett, *Coal and tobacco*, pp. 68, 74–6; Flinn, *British coal industry*, pp. 74–7, 94–9; William Rees, *Industry before the industrial revolution* (2 vols., Cardiff, 1968), vol. 2, p. 524; *D.N.B.*, sub 'Ralph Allen (1694–1764)'; Ashton and Sykes, *Coal industry*, p. 63; North, *Lives*, vol. 1, p. 176.

30 Beckett, *Coal and tobacco*, pp. 71–4; Flinn, *British coal industry*, pp. 131–6; Ashton and Sykes, *Coal industry*, pp. 48–9.

31 Patent 653 (1750); Ashton and Sykes, *Coal industry*, p. 57.

32 Patents 1660 (1788), 1924 (1792), 2270 (1798); Flinn, *British coal industry*, pp. 103–5; Ashton and Sykes, *Coal industry*, pp. 64, 67.

33 Ashton and Sykes, *Coal industry*, pp. 35, 40; Allen, 'Newcomen engine', pp. 169–90; Flinn, *British coal industry*, pp. 114–28. For the number of engines, see John Kanefsky and John Robey, 'Steam engines in 18th-century Britain: a quantitative assessment', *Technology and Culture*, 21 (1980), 161–86.

34 D. C. Coleman, 'Textile growth' in N. B. Harte and K. G. Ponting (eds.), *Textile history and economic history: essays in honour of Miss Julia de Lacy Mann* (Manchester, 1973), p. 10.

35 See above, p. 92.

36 Coleman, 'Textile growth', pp. 1–12.

37 Mann, *Cloth industry*, pp. 13–14, 286; Bodl., MS Aubrey 2, fol. 64, quoted in Thirsk and Cooper, *Economic documents*, p. 305.

38 See above, p. 92.

39 Wadsworth and Mann, *Cotton trade*, p. 182. For another example, see Mann, *Cloth industry*, p. 302.

40 Coleman, 'Textile growth', p. 9; Peter Thornton, *Baroque and Rococo silks* (1965), pp. 18–19, 23; Wadsworth and Mann, *Cotton trade*, pp. 106–7.

41 For machine-making, see Wadsworth and Mann, *Cotton trade*, p. 493; Musson and Robinson, *Science and technology*, pp. 431–6. For the early concentration of these patents in Lancashire, see below pp. 132–3.

42 Quoted in Wadsworth and Mann, *Cotton trade*, p. 499.

43 Ibid., pp. 496–7; Chapman, *Early factory masters*, pp. 73–6.

44 After the Restoration, private Acts were increasingly substituted for patents as the authorization for schemes involving engineering skills: see T. S. Willan, *River navigation in England, 1660–1750* (1936), pp. 28–30.

45 Ibid., p. 85.

46 The inclined planes and lifts that most of them proposed were rarely built before the 1830s: Baron F. Duckham, 'Canals and river navigation' in Derek E. Aldcroft and Michael J. Freeman (eds.), *Transport in the industrial revolution* (Manchester, 1983), pp. 109–10, 126–7.

47 Paul N. Wilson, '*The waterwheels of John Smeaton*', *T.N.S.*, 30 (1955–7), 25–38; D. S. L. Cardwell, *Technology, science, and history* (1972), pp. 79–84; Musson and Robinson, *Science and technology*, pp. 73–7; C. T. G. Boucher, *John Rennie, 1761–1821* (Manchester, 1963), pp. 30–49.

48 *D.N.B.*, sub 'Charles Labeyle (1705–81)'.

49 Patent 598 (1744); P.R.O. SP36.62, fol. 230; Desaguliers, *Experimental philosophy*, vol. 2, p. 417.

50 Patent 369 (1704); F. Williamson, 'George Sorocold of Derby, a pioneer of water supply', *Jnl Derbys. Archaeological and Natural History Society*, 57 (1937), 44–84.

51 Smiles, *Lives of the engineers*, vol. 1, pp. 319–474 *passim*; vol. 2, pp. 11–222 *passim*; Boucher, *John Rennie*, pp. 78–96; Charles Hadfield (ed.), *Phillips' inland navigation* (Newton Abbot, 1970), pp. 100–4. See also, Musson and Robinson, *Science and technology*, pp. 69–71, on Thomas Hewes.

52 Boucher, *John Rennie*, pp. 111–13. For the millwrighting activities of men famed for their civil engineering, see Jennifer Tann, 'The textile millwright in the early industrial revolution', *Textile History*, 5 (1974), 81–2.

53 Desaguliers, *Experimental philosophy*, vol. 2, pp. 414–16; he was, of course, biased against mere 'men of practice', since he considered a mathematical training to be indispensable.

54 Samuel Smiles (ed.), *James Nasmyth, engineer, an autobiography* (1883), pp. 312–13.

55 A. W. Skempton, 'The engineers of the English river navigation, 1620–1760', *T.N.S.*, 29 (1953–5), 36–50; R. Campbell, *The London tradesman* (1747, repr. Newton Abbot, 1969), pp. 248–9; *Phillips' inland navigation*, p. 100.

56 E. A. Forward, 'The early history of the cylinder boring machine', *T.N.S.*, 5 (1924–5), 36.

57 Smiles, *Industrial biography*, p. 201.

58 H. W. Dickinson, 'Joseph Bramah and his inventions', *T.N.S.*, 22 (1941–2), 173. See also, *H. of C. Jnl*, vol. 53 (1798), pp. 371–2.

59 Dickinson, 'Joseph Bramah', p. 173. Bramah patented a planing machine in 1802 (2652).

60 Rolt, *Tools for the job*, p. 58; H. W. Dickinson, 'The origin and manufacture of wood screws', *T.N.S.*, 22 (1941–2), 80–1.

61 H. W. Dickinson, 'The Taylors of Southampton', *T.N.S.*, 29 (1953–5), 171–2; Carolyn C. Cooper, 'The Portsmouth system of manufacture', *Technology and Culture*, 25 (1984), 213–14.

62 See above, p. 37.

63 Patents 1838 and 1951. See Cooper, 'Portsmouth system', p. 193.

64 Rolt, *Tools for the job*, pp. 83–91.

65 Ibid., pp. 78, and 76–81 *passim*. For similar secrecy, in Bryan Donkin's workshop, see E. S. Ferguson (ed.), *Early engineering reminiscences (1815–40) of George Escol Sellers* (Washington D.C., 1965), pp. 118–30.

66 Rolt, *Tools for the job*, pp. 92–113; Smiles, *James Nasmyth*, pp. 211, 400–39; H. W. Dickinson, 'Richard Roberts, his life and inventions', *T.N.S.*, 25 (1945–7), 125–7.

67 Rolt, *Tools for the job*, pp. 113–21.

68 Dutton, *Patent system*, pp. 72–5.

69 See the description of a special screw made for Matthew Boulton, in Forward, 'Cylinder boring machine', pp. 31–2.

70 P.P. 1829, III, p. 430; see also ibid., pp. 434, 458, 471.

71 See, for example, Josiah Wedgwood's problems in keeping a consignment of Derbyshire stone secret: J. D. Des Fontaines, 'The Society of Arts and the early Wedgwoods', *Jnl of the Royal Society of Arts*, 119 (1970–1), 328.

72 J. K. Crellin, 'Dr James's fever powder', *Trans. of the British Society for the History of Pharmacy*, 1 (1974), 138–40; Rowe, *Lead manufacturing*, p. 5. See also Peter Mathias, *The brewing industry in England, 1700–1830* (Cambridge, 1959), pp. 47–8, 413; Musson and Robinson, *Science and technology*, pp. 339, 343; L. A. Clarkson, 'The organization of the English leather industry in the late sixteenth and seventeenth centuries', *Ec.H.R.*, 2nd ser. 13 (1960–1), 246.

73 John Hutchinson positively wanted to specify his clock's design: see above, p. 73. See also B.L. MS Sloane 4026, fol. 9; P.P. 1829, III, p. 424.

74 A. J. Francis, *The cement industry, 1796–1914: a history* (Newton Abbot, 1977), pp. 20–4.

75 F. Severne Mackenna, *Champion's Bristol porcelain* (Leigh-on-Sea, 1947), pp. 22–4.

76 H. R. Schubert, *History of the British iron and steel industry* (1957), p. 425; A. Raistrick, *Dynasty of ironfounders: the Darbys and Coalbrookdale* (repr. Newton Abbot, 1970), pp. 112–13; Charles K. Hyde, *Technological change and the British iron industry* (Princeton, 1977), pp. 99–100; Clow and Clow, *Chemical revolution*, p. 398; Schofield, *Lunar Society*, p. 97.

77 Musson and Robinson, *Science and technology*, pp. 350–1; Susan Fairlie, 'Dyestuffs in the eighteenth century', *Ec.H.R.*, 2nd ser. 17 (1965–6), 488–510. For an earlier unpatented invention of importance, see S. D. Chapman, 'Enterprise and innovation in the British hosiery industry, 1750–1850', *Textile History*, 5 (1974), 21.

78 E.g. Humphry Perrott, patent 545 (1734); F. Buckley, 'The early glasshouses of Bristol', *Jnl of the Society of Glass Technology*, 9 (1925), 42.

79 See, for example, Clow and Clow, *Chemical revolution*, p. 140. The difficulties of acquiring such knowledge have been stressed in Harris, 'Skills', *passim*.

80 Wedgwood, *Letters*, vol. 2, p. 61.

81 Mathias, *Brewing industry*, pp. xxii–xxiii. This paragraph is based principally on ibid., pp. 13–25, 58–72, 413–14.

82 Ibid., pp. 23, 47–8, 219, 226; *The London and country brewer* (Dublin, 1735), pp. 24–5; *A general description of all trades*, p. 35.

83 *London Gazette*, 2786 (21–25 July, 1692); *London and country brewer*, pp. 8–9.

84 *A general description of all trades*, p. 79.

85 Mathias, *Brewing industry*, pp. 73–5, 94–7; Mitchell and Deane, *Abstract*, pp. 469, 488.

86 Hughes, *Studies*, p. 405; Clow and Clow, *Chemical revolution*, p. 55. The discovery of stronger sources of saline solutions was also a factor in higher productivity. This development is witnessed by Marbury's patent (no. 222) in 1682 for an engine to drain salt pits, after rock salt had been discovered on his lands in Cheshire.

87 William Brownrigg, *The art of making common salt* (1748), p. 55.

88 Richard B. Sheridan, *Sugar and slavery: an economic history of the British West Indies, 1623–1775* (Barbados, 1974), pp. 450, 464–6.

89 Noel Deerr, 'The early use of steam power in the cane sugar industry', *T.N.S.*, 21 (1940–1), 12–15.

90 Weatherill, 'The growth of the pottery industry', pp. 47, 51, 162, 259.

91 Ibid., p. 231.

92 Lorna Weatherill, 'Technical change and potters' probate inventories, 1660–1760', *Jnl of Ceramic History*, 3 (1970), 3–12; idem, *The pottery trade and north Staffordshire, 1660–1760* (Manchester, 1971), pp. 10–23, 33–8; see also Meteyard, *Wedgwood*, vol. 1, pp. 157–61, 165–6; Clow and Clow, *Chemical revolution*, p. 307.

93 V. W. Bladen, 'The Potteries in the industrial revolution', *Econ. Jnl, Economic History Supplement*, 1 (1926), 123–5; Meteyard, *Wedgwood*, vol. 1, p. 290.

94 J. Thomas, 'The pottery industry in the industrial revolution', *Econ. Jnl, Economic History Supplement*, 3 (1934–7), 409.

95 Quoted in S. D. Chapman, 'British marketing enterprise: the changing roles of merchants, manufacturers, and financiers, 1700–1860', *Business History Review*, 53 (1979), 212.

96 Patents 610 (1744), 649 (1749); *V.C.H. Essex*, vol. 2, p. 416.

97 Hugh Tait, 'Bow' in R. J. Charleston (ed.), *English porcelain, 1745–1850* (1965), pp. 42–7; J. V. G. Mallett, 'Chelsea' in ibid., 28–36.
98 Patent 898 (1768); F. Severne Mackenna, *Cookworthy's Plymouth and Bristol porcelain* (Leigh-on-Sea, 1946), pp. 26–32.
99 Meteyard, *Wedgwood*, vol. 1, pp. 338–41; vol. 2, pp. 20–1, 28–9, 200–3; Anthony Burton, *Josiah Wedgwood, a biography* (1976), pp. 85–6, 139–40; Schofield, *Lunar Society*, p. 170.
100 Musson and Robinson, *Science and technology*, pp. 264–78, 305–6, 312.
101 Ibid., pp. 284–7, 308–10.
102 Ibid., pp. 276–7, 308, 322–6.
103 *H. of C. Jnl*, vol. 37 (1780), pp. 914, 916.
104 Richard Padley, 'The beginnings of the British alkali industry', *Birmingham Historical Jnl*, 3 (1951), 64–78; T. C. Barker, R. Dickinson and D. W. F. Hardie, 'The origins of the synthetic alkali industry in Britain', *Economica*, 23 (1956), 167; Musson and Robinson, *Science and technology*, pp. 361–8.
105 Barker et al., 'Alkali industry', p. 168.
106 White, *Sir Edward Coke*, p. 126.
107 Guildhall, MS 2710 II, fol. 81; MS 2710 III, fols. 63, 124, 170, 179–80.
108 Guildhall, MS 8046 II, 7 June 1687; patent 251 (1686).
109 P.R.O. PC2.64, pp. 85, 90; SP44.237, pp. 269–73; patent 254 (1687); H[ale], *An account*, pp. 20–3; idem, *Mill'd lead*, pp. 92–102, 114–15.
110 R.S.A. Guard Book I, no. 82.
111 *H. of C. Jnl*, vol. 26 (1751), p. 292; see Campbell, *London tradesman*, p. 185; J. Lord, *Capital and steam power*, 2nd edn (1966), p. 47.
112 L. A. Clarkson, *The pre-industrial economy of England, 1500–1750* (1971), pp. 80–3, 88–9; idem, 'English economic policy', pp. 150–9; idem, 'Organization of the English leather industry', pp. 245–53; R. Machin, 'The great rebuilding: an assessment', *Past and Present*, 77 (1977), 37–8.
113 Walker, 'The extent of guild control', p. 207.
114 Maurice Daumas, *Scientific instruments of the seventeenth and eighteenth centuries and their makers*, trans. M. Holbrook (1972), pp. 93, 159–66, 173–6, 228–9, 231–4; Campbell, *London tradesman*, pp. 250–1; Chamberlayne, *Angliae notitiae*, 18th edn (1694), pp. 51–2; Cipolla, *Clocks and culture*, pp. 68–70; Taylor, *Mathematical practitioners, passim*; J. Bennet, et al. *Science and profit in 18th-century London* (Whipple Museum, Cambridge, 1985), *passim*.
115 See below, p. 137.
116 Hatcher and Barker, *British pewter*, pp. 138–41, 225–8.
117 See above, pp. 22–4.
118 For the pattern of patenting in papermaking, which again stresses its mechanical aspects, see MacLeod, 'Patents for invention', pp. 195–7.
119 Quoted in Musson and Robinson, *Science and technology*, p. 361; my emphasis.
120 Schofield, *Lunar Society*, pp. 172–4; see also Clow and Clow, *Chemical revolution*, p. 103, for Dundonald's compromise with the Inland Revenue.

7 Patents in a capitalist economy

1 For an example of this in the U.S. Patent Office, see Robert C. Post, '"Liberalizers" versus "scientific men" in the antebellum Patent Office', *Technology and Culture*, 17 (1976), 24–54.
2 The number of patents taken out in more than one name fell from 28 per cent in the period 1660–99 to 11 per cent 1700–49, and 7 per cent 1750–99.
3 George Rudé, *Hanoverian London, 1714–1808* (1971), pp. 56–7.

4 Rudé estimates there were 3,000 to 4,500 resident 'gentle' families and 30,000 families of the 'middling sort' in late-eighteenth-century London: ibid., pp. 48, 58. See also L. D. Schwarz, 'Income distribution and social structure in London in the late eighteenth century', *Ec.H.R.*, 2nd ser. 32 (1979), 258.

5 François Crouzet, *The first industrialists* (Cambridge, 1984), p. 62. See Tables 7.6 and 7.7; and above, pp. 78–9, for gentlemen and amateurs.

6 Geoffrey Holmes, *Augustan England: professions, state and society, 1680–1730* (1982), pp. 166–9; Margaret Pelling, 'Medical practice in early modern England: trade or profession?' in Wilfrid Prest (ed.), *The professions in early modern England* (London, New York and Sydney, 1987), pp. 96–9.

7 I have used Campbell, *London tradesman; A general description of all trades*; Joseph Collyer, *The parent's and guardian's directory* (1761); M. D. George, *London life in the eighteenth century* (repr. 1966), pp. 157–76; T. R. Mandrell, 'The structure and organisation of London trades, wages and prices, and the organisation of labour, 1793–1815' (unpubl. M.Litt. thesis, Unversity of Cambridge, 1968), pp. 38–40, 46–50, 67–8, 85–92.

8 Collyer, *Directory, passim*.

9 These metropolitan trades have been included among the artisans prior to 1740, and among the outworking trades only post 1740, when this new structure became increasingly common.

10 The following discussion deals only with patentees giving addresses in England and Wales, approximately 93 per cent of all patentees in the period 1750–99.

11 F. A. Wendenborn, *A view of England towards the close of the eighteenth century* (2 vols., Dublin, 1791), vol. 1, p. 162; A. L. Beier, 'Engine of manufacture: the trades of London' in A. L. Beier and Roger Finlay (eds.), *The making of the metropolis: London, 1500–1700* (1986), p. 151; Francis Sheppard, *London 1808–1870: the infernal wen* (1971), pp. 158–61.

12 Roger Finlay and Beatrice Shearer, 'Population growth and suburban expansion' in Beier and Finlay, *Making of the metropolis*, p. 45.

13 M. J. Power, 'The social topography of Restoration London' in Beier and Finlay, *Making of the metropolis*, pp. 202–6.

14 See below, p. 154.

15 Power, 'Social topography', pp. 206–12; O. H. K. Spate, 'Geographical aspects of the industrial evolution of London till 1850', *Geographical Jnl*, 92 (1938), 425.

16 Beier, 'Engine of manufacture', p. 152.

17 Ibid., pp. 149, 155.

18 Liliane Perez, 'Les Cadres de l'inventivité en France et en Angleterre au XVIIIe siècle', *Sources*, 1 (1986), 30.

19 Rev. Henry Hunter, *The history of London and its environs*, (2 vols., 1811), vol. 2, pp. 79–81, 118–29.

20 R. J. Hartridge, 'The development of industries in London south of the Thames, 1750–1850' (unpubl. M.Sc. thesis, University of London, 1955), pp. 4–9.

21 Perez, 'Les Cadres de l'inventivité', pp. 31, 33.

22 Adjusting the figures by head of population (in 1801) makes little difference to the picture.

23 E. Buckatzsh, 'The geographical distribution of wealth in England, 1086–1843', *Ec.H.R.*, 2nd ser. 3 (1950), 180–202.

24 Julian Hoppit, 'Risk and failure in English industry, c.1700–1800', (unpubl. Ph.D. thesis, University of Cambridge, 1984), pp. 125–8.

25 Ibid., p. 64.

26 P. J. Corfield, *The impact of English towns, 1700–1800* (Oxford, 1982), p. 11. 'Urban' is defined as populations of 2,500 or more.

252 NOTES TO PAGES 128–33

27 The percentage figures represent the proportion of each county's patents obtained by professed residents of the towns cited, 1750–99.

28 Charles E. Scarse, *Birmingham 120 years ago* (Birmingham, 1896).

29 Only 'productive occupation' (as defined above, p. 117) have been taken in all cases; the vague and general, e.g. chandler, salesman, have been excluded.

30 See above, p. 78.

31 William Hutton, *A history of Birmingham*, 2nd edn (1783, repr. Wakefield, 1976), p. 73; Wendenborn, *View*, vol. 1, p. 164.

32 Prosser, *Birmingham inventors*, p. 4; see also pp. 50, 56.

33 Marie B. Rowlands, *Masters and men* (Manchester, 1975), pp. 148–50.

34 Ibid., pp. 49–53; see also Hutton, *History of Birmingham*, pp. 77–8.

35 Dickinson, *Matthew Boulton*, pp. 45, 61.

36 Hutton, *History of Birmingham*, pp. 75, 83–4, 89–90; Rowlands, *Masters and men*, pp. 23, 30–1, 131–2; Maxine Berg, *The age of manufactures, 1700–1820* (1985), p. 290.

37 Quoted in Eric Robinson, 'Eighteenth-century commerce and fashion: Matthew Boulton's marketing techniques', *Ec.H.R.*, 2nd ser. 16 (1963–4), 42–3.

38 Dickinson, *Matthew Boulton*, pp. 40–55, 61, 108, 113, 140.

39 Prosser, *Birmingham inventors*, pp. 39–40.

40 Clarkson, *Pre-industrial economy*, pp. 88–9.

41 Joseph Hunter, *Hallamshire: the history and topography of the parish of Sheffield in the county of York* (1819), p. 124; David Hey, *The rural metalworkers of the Sheffield region*, University of Leicester, Dept of English Local History, Occasional Papers, 2nd ser. 5 (1972), pp. 14, 52.

42 Hey, *Rural metalworkers*, p. 28; Hunter, *Hallamshire*, p. 127; G. I. H. Lloyd, *The cutlery trades* (1913), p. 143; R. E. Leader, *A history of the Cutlers' Company of Hallamshire* (2 vols., Sheffield, 1905), vol. 1, pp. 71–89.

43 Hey, *Rural metalworkers*, pp. 27, 53; Leader, *Cutler's Company*, vol. 1, p. 73.

44 Hunter, *Hallamshire*, p. 125.

45 Hey, *Rural metalworkers*, p. 59; Walton, *Sheffield*, pp. 118–19.

46 Fitton and Wadsworth, *The Strutts and the Arkwrights*, p. 35.

47 Chapman, 'Enterprise and innovation', pp. 14–16; *Early factory masters*, pp. 34, 37; F. A. Wells, *The British hosiery and knitwear industry: its history and organization*, 2nd edn (Newton Abbot, 1972), pp. 71–2.

48 Chapman, 'Enterprise and innovation', pp. 22–5; Henson, *Framework knitters*, pp. 282–92, 309–10, 341; Blackner, *History of Nottingham*, p. 231.

49 Henson, *Framework knitters*, pp. 276–80.

50 Chapman, *Early factory masters*, p. 29. See also *Felkin's history*, p. 94.

51 Berg, *Age of manufactures*, p. 227.

52 See above, p. 91; W. H. Chaloner, 'The birth of modern Manchester' in C. F. Carter (ed.), *Manchester and its region* (Manchester, 1962), p. 132.

53 Ibid., p. 132; Chapman, 'British marketing enterprise', p. 212.

54 R. G. Wilson, *Gentlemen merchants: the merchant community in Leeds, 1700–1830* (Manchester, 1971), pp. 28–30, 33, 91–2.

55 Chapman, *Early factory masters*, pp. 102–3.

56 John Aiken, *A description of the country from thirty to forty miles around Manchester* (1795, repr. Newton Abbot, 1968), pp. 183–4; S. D. Chapman, 'Fixed capital formation in the British cotton industry, 1770–1815', *Ec.H.R.*, 2nd ser. 23 (1970), appendices B, C, and G; S. Pollard, 'Fixed capital in the industrial revolution in Britain' in François Crouzet (ed.), *Capital formation in the industrial revolution* (1972), pp. 148–9.

57 Wadsworth and Mann, *Cotton trade*, p. 496.

58 W. G. Rimmer, *Marshalls of Leeds, flax spinners, 1788–1886* (Cambridge, 1960), pp. 9, 27, 31, 44; patents 1752 (1790) and 1971 (1793), both in the name of Matthew Murray.

59 Chapman and Chassagne, *European textile printers*, pp. 28, 79–84; Wilson, *Gentlemen merchants*, pp. 42, 46.

60 Walker, 'The extent of guild control', pp. 139–56.

61 Corfield, *Impact*, p. 101; Berg, *Age of manufactures*, pp. 219, 224.

62 Chapman, 'British marketing enterprise', p. 209.

63 Corfield, *Impact*, pp. 90–6.

64 See above, pp. 30, 95. For the categorization of occupations used see above, pp. 117–18.

65 This fall is exaggerated, however, by the exclusion from this analysis of named partners, who were often merchants: see above, p. 116.

66 See below, pp. 139–43.

67 They might more properly be included among the outworking trades (see above, p. 131), which would accentuate the trend being observed here.

68 Corfield, *Impact*, p. 72.

69 Ibid., p. 73.

70 'Musical-instrumentmaker' contains several closely related trades: also, harpsichordmaker, pianomaker, and organbuilder.

71 The other twelve trades were bucklemakers, cabinetmakers, glovers, gunmakers, hosiers, ironmongers, jewellers, 'manufacturers', saddlers, shoemakers, upholsterers, and weavers.

72 E.g. David Wainwright, *Broadwood by appointment* (1982), pp. 53, 55. A quarter of London pianomakers active in the late eighteenth century held patents: Rosamond Harding, *The piano-forte: its history traced to the Great Exhibition of 1851*, 2nd edn (Cambridge, 1978), pp. 402–26.

73 Musson and Robinson, *Science and technology*, pp. 435–9. Again, these are all trades categorized here as 'artisan', which might suggest a further mental deflation of the extent of artisanal patents in the second half of the eighteenth century.

74 Hartridge, 'The development of industries in London', p. 11.

75 See above, pp. 103–5.

76 See above, pp. 78–9.

77 Dutton, *Patent system*, p. 108.

78 Ibid., p. 125.

79 Ibid., p. 113. The figures have been calculated by decade of first patent, which necessitates the inclusion of many patents obtained in the first three decades of the nineteenth century. This also tends to overemphasize the importance of the 'multiple' patentee in the period 1750–99.

80 Cartwright, *A memoir*, pp. 76, 141.

81 Ian McNeil, *Joseph Bramah: a century of invention, 1749–1851* (Newton Abbot, 1968), pp. 30, 51, 57–68, 123.

8 The long-term rise in patents

1 Davies, *Collection*, p. 14.

2 Crafts, 'Industrial revolution', p. 433.

3 Crafts, *British economic growth*, p. 81.

4 Ibid., pp. 82–5.

5 This excludes the lace and hosiery industries.

6 See below, pp. 193–5.

7 Dutton, *Patent system*, pp. 76–9; Dickinson, *Matthew Boulton*, p. 129.

8 Henson, *Framework knitters*, p. 293.

9 See above, pp. 000–00.

10 D. E. C. Eversley, 'The home market and economic growth in England, 1750–80' in E. L. Jones and G. E. Mingay (eds.), *Land, labour and population in the industrial revolution* (1967), pp. 230–1.

11 *Repertory of Arts*, 6 (1797), pp. 359–60, 341–2.

12 *Philosophical Magazine*, 1 (1798), p. 152.

13 Quoted in Dutton, *Patent system*, p. 182; see also ibid., p. 184.

14 Davies, *Collection*, p. 446.

15 See above, p. 000.

16 See above, pp. 000–00.

17 Pollard, 'Fixed capital', pp. 148–9; C. H. Feinstein, 'Capital formation in Great Britain' in Peter Mathias and M. M. Postan (eds.), *The Cambridge economic history of Europe*, vol. 7, pt 1 (Cambridge, 1978), pp. 40–1, 56; Von Tunzelmann, 'Technical progress', p. 151; D. T. Jenkins, *The West Riding wool textile industry, 1770–1835* (Edington, 1975), p. 17.

18 See above, p. 109.

19 Tann, 'Textile millwright', pp. 80–9; Mathias, *Brewing industry*, p. 87.

20 See above, pp. 100–1; Pollard, 'Fixed capital', pp. 149–51.

21 C. H. Feinstein, 'Capital accumulation and the industrial revolution', in Floud and McCloskey, *Economic history*, p. 136.

22 Eversley, 'Home market', pp. 230, 248–50; Crafts, 'Eighteenth century', p. 15; Crafts, *British economic growth*, p. 132; N. McKendrick, 'The consumer revolution of eighteenth-century England' in N. McKendrick, J. H. Plumb, and J. Brewer (eds.), *The birth of a consumer society: the commercialization of eighteenth-century England* (1982), pp. 28–9.

23 T. S. Ashton, 'Some statistics of the industrial revolution in Britain', repr. in Musson, *Science, technology, and economic growth*, pp. 117–18; Dutton, *Patent system*, p. 177.

24 Julian Hoppit, 'Financial crises in eighteenth-century England', *Ec.H.R.*, 2nd ser. 39 (1986), 40–1.

25 MacLeod, 'The 1690s patents boom', pp. 557–62.

26 For example, Walcot, *Sea water made fresh*, p. 1; Hill, *Account*, p. 44; Thomas Baston, *Observations on trade and a public spirit*, 2nd edn (1732), p. 11; *Proposals for subscriptions to a new invention for raising water* (1720?).

27 MacLeod, 'The 1690s patents boom', pp. 568–9.

28 Ashton, *Economic fluctuations*, pp. 115–16.

29 See above, pp. 55–6. Satires of the various projects can be seen in *Catalogue of prints and drawings in the British Museum* (6 vols., 1870), vol. 3, pp. 427–53.

30 Compare Hoppit, 'Financial crises', pp. 48–56, with Figure 8.1.

31 Mann, *Cloth industry*, pp. 29–32, 35, 282–3.

32 Hill, *Account*, pp. 50–65.

33 Mann, *Cloth industry*, p. 284.

34 Ashton, *Economic fluctuations*, pp. 93–4.

35 Hyde, *Technological change*, pp. 44–5; K-G. Hildebrand, 'Foreign markets for Swedish iron in the eighteenth century', *Scandinavian Ec.H.R.*, 6 (1958), 9–11, 34–5.

36 P.R.O. PC1.3.102, fol. 3.

37 Clow and Clow, *Chemical revolution*, p. 66; *H. of C. Jnl*, vol. 26 (1751), pp. 239–41.

38 S.C.L. MS Bagshawe C 493, *passim*; Dossie, *Handmaid to the arts*, vol. 2, p. 238.

39 See above, p. 112.
40 See above, pp. 84–6, 130–2.
41 Doubtless, some of these also had institutional uses and customers: some ovens, for example, were designed specifically for ships, while patentees of washing machines mentioned charitable institutions, the army and navy, as well as 'small and large families'.
42 See above, p. 84.
43 Scientific instruments intended for purely utilitarian ends, navigation for instance, have been excluded as far as possible.
44 Cranfield, *Provincial newspaper*, pp. 12–22, 190–3.
45 See above, p. 103.
46 The idea was not new at this time. Even in 1758 William Bailey, the inventor of one, spoke of 'the machine washing-tubs [which were] some time since much in use': Caroline Davidson, *A woman's work is never done: a history of housework in the British Isles, 1650–1950* (1982), pp. 162–3.
47 J. M. Beattie, *Crime and the courts in England, 1660–1800* (Oxford, 1986), pp. 223–9; patent 2128.
48 Prosser, *Birmingham inventors*, p. 145.

9 The goals of invention

1 M. Blaug, 'A survey of the theory of process innovations' in N. Rosenberg (ed.), *The economics of technological change* (1971), pp. 96–100.
2 Smiles, *Lives of the engineers*, vol. 2, p. 201.
3 R.S.A. Guard Book v, no. 86.
4 Where patentees cited saving time as their goal, this was included under the heading of 'saving capital' if it shortened a process in which little or no labour was used; it was included under 'saving time' where there was ambiguity or where both labour and capital were likely to be saved.
5 Quoted in E. J. T. Collins, 'Harvest technology and labour supply, 1790–1870', *Ec.H.R.*, 2nd ser. 22 (1969), 464.
6 See above, p. 19.
7 P.R.O. SP44.238, p. 247 (1698); SP44.246, p. 162 (1711); Sp44.252, pp. 57–9 (1721).
8 P.R.O. C6.3385(22).
9 Patent 436 (1721).
10 See above, p. 45.
11 P.R.O. SP44.254, pp. 380–1; patent 542 (1733).
12 Thirsk, *Economic policy and projects*, pp. 179–80; see also below, pp. 207, 210–11.
13 See, for example, *An impartial representation of the case of the poor cotton spinners in Lancashire, etc.* [1780]; Adrian J. Randall, 'The philosophy of Luddism: the case of the west of England woolen workers, ca.1790–1809', *Technology and Culture*, 27 (1986), 1–17.
14 *Leeds Mercury*, 5–12 Feb. 1803, quoted in Randall, 'Philosophy of Luddism', pp. 12–13.
15 See, for example, Christopher Morris (ed.), *The journeys of Celia Fiennes* (1949), pp. 257–8; North, *Lives*, vol. 1, pp. 177–8; Desaguliers, *Experimental philosophy*, vol. 1, pp. 67–70; William Pryce, *Mineralogia cornubiensis: a treatise on minerals, mines and mining* (1778), pp. 150–1; and, more generally, *Reflections on various subjects relating to arts and commerce; particularly the consequences of admitting foreign artists on easier terms* (1752), pp. 26–8.

16 Josiah Tucker, *Instructions for travellers* (Dublin, 1758), repr. in Robert L. Schuyler (ed.), *Josiah Tucker: a selection from his economic and political writings* (New York, 1931), pp. 240–1.
17 Savery, *Miner's friend*, pp. 28, 36. See also *Angliae tutamen*, p. 30.
18 P.R.O. SP44.257, pp. 343–5.
19 Patent 202 (1678).
20 R[ichard] H[aines], *Proposals for building in every county, a working-almshouse or hospital* (1677), repr. in *Harleian miscellany*, 2nd edn (1745), vol. 4, pp. 465–6.
21 Ibid., p. 466.
22 Ibid., p. 467.
23 [Daniel Defoe], *Giving alms no charity* (1704), repr. in *A second volume of the writings of the author of The true-born Englishman* (1705), pp. 433–5. Thomas Hobbes was also highly critical of the paternalism behind 'setting the poor to work', where labour was bought cheap: C. B. MacPherson, *The political theory of possessive individualism* (Oxford, 1962), p. 66.
24 Bedwell, patent 508 (1729); Wyatt and Paul, patents 562 (1738), 636 (1748).
25 Patent 230 (1683). See Johann Beckmann, *A history of inventions and discoveries*, trans. William Johnstone (3 vols., 1797), vol. 1, pp. 375–6, for contemporary opposition to mechanical saws.
26 Patent 453 (1723); see also *The London and country brewer*, quoted in Mathias, *Brewing industry*, pp. 39–40.
27 Elizabeth W. Gilboy, *Wages in eighteenth century England* (Cambridge, Mass., 1934), p. 181; François Crouzet, 'Angleterre et France au XVIIIe siècle', *Annales E.S.C.*, 21 (1966), 287–8.
28 Patents 487 (1726), 536 (1732); Meteyard, *Wedgwood*, vol. 1, p. 153.
29 Patent 1187 (1778).
30 Patent 2124 (1796). Kingsley's *Water Babies* (1863) is, of course, ample testimony to its lack of success. See also *Repertory of Arts*, 1 (1794), pp. 93–6; 5 (1796), pp. 249–54, 322–6.
31 Patents 493, 515.
32 B.R.L. MS Wyatt 1, fols. 31–2, quoted in Wadsworth and Mann, *Cotton trade*, p. 417.
33 Ibid.
34 P.R.O. SP36.41, fols. 212–14; patent 562 (1738).
35 See, for example, Thirsk and Cooper, *Economic documents*, p. 295; Joseph Lee, *A vindication of a regulated enclosure* (1656), p. 7; and below, p. 216.
36 See below, pp. 213–15.
37 See Tucker, *Instructions for travellers*, pp. 241; R.S.A. Guard Book v, no. 86; *Reflections on various subjects*, pp. 26–8.
38 Quoted in Clow and Clow, *Chemical revolution*, p. 213.
39 D. C. Coleman and Christine MacLeod, 'Attitudes to new technology: British businessmen, 1800–1950', *Ec.H.R.*, 2nd ser. 39 (1986), 605–9.
40 R.S.L. Classified Papers, III(2), no. 37.
41 B.L. MS Add. 4434, fol. 89.
42 [Daniel Defoe], *A tour through the whole island of Great Britain*, 3rd edn (4 vols. 1742), vol. 3, p. 67.
43 John Smith (ed.), *Chronicon rusticum-commerciale: or, memoirs of wool* (2 vols., 1747), vol. 1, p. 419n.
44 John Dyer, *The fleece, a poem* (1757), bk 3, lines 293–4; see also [Thomas Mortimer], *A concise account of the rise, progress, and the present state of the Society for the Encouragement of Arts, Manufactures and Commerce* (1763), p. 56.

45 *Instructions for travellers*, pp. 241–2; my emphasis. For the renewal of interest in labour productivity among writers of economic treatises see below, pp. 215–17.

46 E. P. Thompson, 'The moral economy of the English crowd in the eighteenth century', *Past & Present*, 50 (1971), 83–99.

47 Cobbett, *Parliamentary history*, vol. 8, col. 927.

48 *The case of the Silk Throwers Company of London* [1732].

49 Cobbett, *Parliamentary history*, vol. 10, col. 792.

50 Ibid., cols. 795–6. For Archer, see Sedgwick, *The House of Commons, 1715–54*, vol. 1, pp. 418–19.

51 Cobbett, *Parliamentary history*, vol. 10, col. 798.

52 Ibid., col. 799.

53 Collier, *Law of patents*, pp. 38–9. The evidence of Table 9.1 casts some doubt on Collier's final point.

54 Coryton, *Treatise*, p. 54; see also Maxine Berg, *The machinery question and the making of political economy, 1815–1848* (Cambridge, 1980), pp. 100–8, 264–7, and *passim*.

55 *Repertory of Arts*, 1 (1794), p. 229.

56 Patent 994 (1771). Such improvements to pumps doubtless gained in attractiveness because of the reductions in manning being achieved through (unpatented) developments in hull design and rigging: Ralph Davis, *The rise of the English shipping industry in the seventeenth and eighteenth centuries* (Newton Abbot, 1962), pp. 71, 74–9.

57 Patent 970 (1770).

58 Patent 1768 (1790).

59 Von Tunzelmann, 'Technical progress during the industrial revolution', p. 161; and see, for example, *An impartial representation of the case*, p. 3.

60 Patent 1838 (1791).

61 Patent 2047 (1795).

62 Crafts, *British economic growth*, pp. 22–3; William Radcliffe, *Origin of the new system of manufacture* (Stockport, 1828), pp. 12–13, 65.

63 S. Pollard, 'Labour in Great Britain' in *Cambridge economic history of Europe*, vol. 7, pt 1, pp. 130–1, 136–7, 145; Ashton, *Economic fluctuations*, p. 167; MacDonald, 'Progress of the early threshing machine', p. 74.

64 Joseph Lowe, *The present state of England* (1822), p. 45; Keith Snell, *Annals of the labouring poor: social change and agrarian England, 1660–1900* (Cambridge, 1985), p. 315.

65 *Repertory of Arts*, 6 (1797), p. 29.

66 *The life of Robert Owen, written by himself*, with an introduction by John Butt (1971), p. 124.

67 See Blaug, 'A survey', p. 103; Nathan Rosenberg, *Perspectives on technology* (Cambridge, 1976), pp. 108–25.

68 *Included* were those labour-saving machines and techniques which contemporaries generally identified as such, e.g. spinning, carding, or threshing machines, and power looms. Even though the particular patentee's aim may have been, say, to make a stronger machine of this type, by improving the machine in any way he was promoting its introduction and thereby the introduction of a labour-saving technology. *Excluded* were machines and techniques whose labour-saving potential was commonly overlooked by contemporaries, *unless* a particular invention would increase its labour productivity further. Thus wind, water, horse, and steam engines were excluded, as were e.g. hand looms, the majority of stocking-frame attachments, sugar mills, the printing press (but not mechanical textile printing).

69 See above, p. 162.

70 Patent 1955.

71 *H. of C. Jnl*, vol. 44 (1794), p. 395. Peter Mathias has queried the extent of leisure preference: *The transformation of England* (1979), pp. 148–67.

72 Rosenberg, *Perspectives*, pp. 117–20.

73 *H. of C. Jnl*, vol. 44 (1794), p. 395.

74 Feinstein, 'Capital accumulation and the industrial revolution', p. 138.

75 Crafts, *British economic growth*, pp. 74–7.

76 Ibid., p. 74.

77 For liquidity preference, see S. D. Chapman, 'Industrial capital before the industrial revolution' in Harte and Ponting, *Textile history and economic history*, pp. 127–8, 137; M. J. Dickenson, 'Fulling in the West Riding woollen cloth industry, 1689–1770', *Textile History*, 10 (1979), 131; and Jennifer Tann, 'The bleaching of woollen and worsted goods, 1740–1860', *Textile History*, 1 (1969), 158.

78 John Cary, *An essay on the state of England* (Bristol, 1695, repr. Farnborough, 1972), pp. 145–8.

79 *Repertory of Arts*, 11 (1799), pp. 168–9; Watts obtained patent 2293 (1799).

80 Patents 385, 573.

81 A. H. John, 'Farming in wartime: 1793–1815' in Jones and Mingay, *Land, labour and population*, p. 28.

82 See also, *Repertory of Arts*, 4 (1796), pp. 25–8; 6 (1797), pp. 311–18.

83 Mitchell and Deane, *Abstract*, p. 455.

84 A new hand-loom was recommended for not merely requiring thirty feet less of timber in its construction but also for taking up less space and thereby making weavers more acceptable tenants ('as some landlords do not care to let their houses to weavers, on account of their breaking the walls'): *Repertory of Arts*, 5 (1796), pp. 322–6.

85 Feinstein, 'Capital formation in Great Britain', pp. 41, 52–6, 74.

86 B. L. Anderson, 'Money and the structure of credit in the eighteenth century', *Business History*, 12 (1970), 95–8, 100.

87 See above, n. 4.

88 Clow and Clow, *Chemical revolution*, pp. 132–9.

89 Ibid., pp. 179–92; Musson and Robinson, *Science and technology*, pp. 251–337; patent 2312 (1799).

90 See above, p. 109.

91 *Repertory of Arts*, 2 (1795), p. 346.

92 Patent 433 (1720). See also patent 1135 (1776).

93 P.R.O. SP36.45, fol. 309; see MacLeod, 'Patents for invention', appendix 2. James Nasmyth stressed the importance of the 'get-at-ability of parts': *James Nasmyth, engineer, an autobiography*, ed. Samuel Smiles (1885), p. 177.

94 Patent 2177 (1797).

95 E.g. Patents 414 (1717), 466 (1724), 476 (1725), 669 (1752).

96 Patent 312 (1693); P.R.O. SP44.252, pp. 77–8, possibly issued as patent 472 (1724).

97 P.R.O. C66.2935(10), C66.3042(8).

98 Patents 348, 653; P.R.O. SP29.101, no. 97; SO3.16, p. 53; SP44.258, p. 248.

99 Patents 356, 449.

100 Patents 513 (1729), 555 (1736); P.R.O. SP44.255, pp. 306–7.

101 Patent 634 (1748); P.R.O. SP36.115, fol. 6. For the cost of coal's part in delaying

diffusion, see H. W. Dickinson, *A short history of the steam engine*, 2nd edn (1963), p. 55; T. R. Harris, 'Engineering in Cornwall before 1775', *T.N.S.*, 25 (1945–7), 115–22. For what seems to have been a precursor of the separate condenser in patent 555 (1736), see B.L. MS Add. 4436, fols. 222–8.

102 Patents 571, 556.

103 See above, p. 35. Renewed interest in steam navigation is marked by 5 patents between 1788 and 1794.

104 Patents 513 (1729), 175 (1674).

105 Patents 407 (1716), 505 (1728); see also Pepys, *Diary*, vol. 1, pp. 272–3.

106 Ashton, *Economic fluctuations*, pp. 8–9; Rowe, *Lead manufacturing*, p. 43.

107 Patents 193 (1677), 208 (1679), 315 (1693), 327 (1693); also P.R.O. SP35.1, no. 61.

108 Patent 567 (1739); P.R.O. SP44.258, pp. 377–9; *Repertory of Arts*, 12 (1800), p. 176.

109 Patent 1997 (1794); also patents 1603 (1787), 1794 (1791); and see Musson and Robinson, *Science and technology*, pp. 67–77.

110 Patents 471 (1724), 609 (1744), 658 (1750); P.R.O. SP44.252, pp. 220–1; see Rex Wailes, 'Horizontal windmills', *T.N.S.*, 40 (1967–8), 128–45.

111 Patent 615 (1745); see Desaguliers, *Experimental philosophy*, vol. 2, p. 537; Rex Wailes, 'Windmill winding gear', *T.N.S.*, 25 (1945–7), 30–1. For other examples and further discussion of this phenomenon of technical change induced by closely competing new technologies, see Rosenberg, *Perspectives*, pp. 202–6.

112 Patents 1484 (1785), 1706 (1789); Rex Wailes, 'Windmills', in Charles Singer, E. J. Holmyard and A. R. Hall (eds.), *A history of technology* (8 vols., Oxford, 1954–84), vol. 3, pp. 100–1.

113 John W. Kanefsky, 'The diffusion of power technology in British industry, 1760–1870' (unpubl. Ph.D. thesis, University of Exeter, 1979), pp. 224–5, 335–6.

114 *Repertory of Arts*, 3 (1795), pp. 401–4.

115 A. E. Musson, 'Industrial motive power in the United Kingdom, 1800–70', *Ec.H.R.*, 2nd ser. 29 (1976), 416–20; Kanefsky, 'Diffusion of power technology', pp. 172, 176, 335–7.

116 Patents 913 (1769); 1298 (1781); Landes, *Unbound Prometheus*, pp. 100–4.

117 *Philosophical Magazine*, 1 (1798), pp. 1–3; patent 2202 (1797).

118 Kanefsky, 'Diffusion of power technology', p. 141.

119 Patent 1306 (1781). For the activities of other steam-engine builders, see Jennifer Tann, 'Makers of improved Newcomen engines in the late 18th century', *T.N.S.*, 50 (1978–9), 181–92; and idem, 'Mr Hornblower and his crew', p. 96–9.

120 Kanefsky, 'Diffusion of power technology', p. 176.

121 P.R.O. SP36.41, fol. 212; patent 562. See also D. T. Jenkins and K. G. Ponting, *The British wool textile industry, 1770–1914* (1982), p. 25; Hills, *Power in the industrial revolution*, p. 19; Wilson, *Gentlemen merchants*, p. 75; and Clow and Clow, *Chemical revolution*, p. 173, on the problem of lack of uniformity in bleached cloth.

122 Patent 440 (1722).

123 Yarranton, *England's improvement . . . the second part*, p. 66; patent 207 to Thomas Harvey in 1679.

124 Patents 854 (1766), 1388 (1783).

125 Patent 1063 (1774); Landes, *Unbound Prometheus*, p. 103. See also Nasmyth, *Autobiography*, pp. 132–3, for the continuing problems arising from the lack of standardization in metalworking.

126 For example, patents 1259 (1780), 1632 (1787), 1687 (1789). The problems arising from ignorance of the exact heat of kilns were discussed by Josiah Wedgwood, in *Repertory of Arts*, 6 (1797), pp. 255–68, 324–38.

127 Patents 409 (1716), 430 (1720), 612 (1745); Desaguliers, *Experimental philosophy*, vol. 2, pp. 557–63.

128 Patent 1492 (1785).

129 See Robert Plot, *The natural history of Staffordshire* (Oxford, 1686), quoted in Thirsk and Cooper, *Economic documents*, pp. 309–11.

130 Flinn, *British coal industry*, pp. 297–311, esp. pp. 308–10.

131 P.R.O. SP36.7, fols. 93–5.

132 For the economics of saltmaking, see Joyce Ellis, 'The decline and fall of the Tyneside salt industry, 1660–1790: a re-examination', *Ec.H.R.*, 2nd ser. 33 (1980), 45–58.

133 Hughes, *Studies*, pp. 407–9.

134 Patent 499 (1728); for the importance of iron imports, see Hildebrand, 'Foreign markets for Swedish iron', pp. 4–15.

135 Patent 529 (1731); P.R.O. SP36.23, fol. 66.

136 Patent 445; see Prosser, *Birmingham inventors and inventions*, p. 5.

137 Hyde, *Technological change*, pp. 25–35, 40–1.

138 Ibid., pp. 53–73.

139 Ibid., pp. 82–92; patents 759 (1761), 794 (1763).

140 Ibid., pp. 88–110. See also Brinley Thomas, 'Escaping from constraints: the industrial revolution in a Malthusian context', *Jnl Interdisciplinary History*, 15 (1985), 732–9.

141 *Repertory of Arts*, 5 (1796), pp. 101–6.

142 Ibid., 6 (1797), pp. 111–18 and 319.

143 Patent 2242 (1798) to Abraham Bosquet. His fears were at least two centuries old, and already beginning to be met by a radical shift – to iron construction.

144 Nasmyth, *Autobiography*, pp. 199–200.

10 Patents: criticisms and alternatives

1 Dutton, *Patent system*, pp. 23–9.

2 R. H. Tawney and Eileen Power (eds.), *Tudor economic documents* (3 vols., 1924), vol. 2, p. 272; Duncan, 'Monopolies under Elizabeth I', pp. 31–2.

3 White, *Sir Edward Coke*, p. 133; Fox, *Monopolies and patents*, p. 182; Dutton, *Patent system*, pp. 22–3.

4 Cobbett, *Parliamentary history*, vol. 8, col. 925.

5 Ibid.

6 Dutton, *Patent system*, p. 28.

7 See above, pp. 11–12; also Getz, 'History of the patentee's obligation', pp. 68–81; and, more generally, Boehm and Silberston, *British patent system*, pp. 1–8.

8 Dutton, *Patent system*, pp. 20–2.

9 See, for example, James Oglethorp's speech in support of Lombe, in Cobbett, *Parliamentary history*, vol. 8, col. 928.

10 See below, p. 192.

11 William Petty, *A treatise of taxes and contributions* (1662), repr. in C. H. Hull (ed.), *The economic writings of Sir William Petty* (2 vols., Cambridge, 1899), vol. 1, pp. 74–5; see also Desaguliers, *Experimental philosophy*, vol. 2, p. 518; Robert Beatson, *An essay on the comparative advantages of vertical and horizontal windmills* (1798), pp. vi–vii.

12 See below, pp. 207–9.

13 Carew Reynell, *The true English interest* (1674), p. 87.

14 *An humble proposal to the parliament of Great Britain* [1702] (Bodl. Theta 665 fol. 142).

15 See Smiles, *Industrial biography*, pp. 61–9.

16 See above, p. 29.

17 Yarranton, *England's improvement . . . the second part*, p. 151.

18 Ibid., pp. 153–4.

19 Ibid., p. 152. See also Matthew Caffyn, *A raging wave foming out his own shame* (1675), p. 20.

20 Andrew Yarranton, *England's improvement by sea and land* (1677), pp. 108–9.

21 *A new discourse of a state subject, called the metamorphosis of Ajax* (1596), p. H2r.

22 Quoted in Raistrick, *Dynasty of ironfounders*, p. 68. See also Stephen Hales, *A description of ventilators* (1743), p. 159.

23 Caffyn, *A raging wave*, p. 6; see also idem, *Envy's bitterness corrected with the rod of shame* (1674), p. 16.

24 Webster, *Great instauration*, pp. 343–6.

25 Ibid., pp. 25, 96–7, 491–505, and *passim*. For some salutary reservations on the hold of Bacon's thought on seventeenth-century science, see Michael Hunter, *Science and society in Restoration England* (Cambridge, 1981), pp. 14–21.

26 Paolo Rossi, *Philosophy, technology and the arts in the early modern era*, trans. Salvator Attanasio, ed. Benjamin Nelson (New York, 1970), pp. 80–7; Webster, *Great instauration*, pp. 333–4.

27 Edgar Zilsel, 'The genesis of the concept of scientific progress', *J.H.I.*, 6 (1945), 331–45; A. C. Keller, 'Zilsel, the artisans and the idea of progress in the Renaissance', *J.H.I.*, 11 (1950), 235–40; Lynn White Jr, 'Cultural climates and technological advance in the middle ages', *Viator*, 2 (1971), 19.

28 Rossi, *Philosophy, technology, and the arts*, pp. 117–21, 163; Webster, *Great instauration*, pp. 326–33; M. E. Prior, 'Bacon's man of science', *J.H.I.*, 15 (1954), 348–55.

29 Approximately twenty fellows secured patents during this period, and another, John Byron, obtained a private Act in 1742 to protect his shorthand method.

30 Roger Hahn, *The anatomy of a scientific institution: the Paris Academy of Sciences, 1666–1803* (1971), pp. 28–30.

31 Patent 143. It covered five new types of carriage or coach, five guns, a powder horn, an engine to break hemp and flax, and a method of dressing it, and a pendulum-regulated watch: P.R.O. SO3.5, pp. 318–19.

32 For example, R.S.L. Classified Papers, III(1), no. 46; A. R. Hall and M. B. Hall (eds. and trans.), *The correspondence of Henry Oldenburg* (13 vols., Madison, Wis., 1965–86), vol. 10, p. 177; B.L. MS Add. 25,071, fol. 115; D. Brewster, 'On Sir Christopher Wren's cypher', *Reports of the British Association for the Advancement of Science* (1859), Notes and Abstracts, p. 34.

33 Hunter, *Science and society*, p. 100; see, for example, Oldenburg, *Correspondence*, vol. 9, pp. 434–5, 493; vol. 10, pp. 3, 42–3, 67, 73–4; vol. 11, pp. 458–75.

34 Oldenburg, *Correspondence*, vol. 11, pp. 184–7; Hooke, *Diary*, pp. 148, 151; and see Richard Waller (ed.), *The posthumous works of Robert Hooke* (1705), p. xxvii.

35 Hooke, *Diary*, pp. 151–86, and *passim*; Oldenburg, *Correspondence*, vols. 11, 12, 13, *passim*; Hunter, *Science and society*, pp. 44–5.

36 Birch, *History*, vol. 4, pp. 86–7. See also A. R. Hall, 'Robert Hooke and horology', *Notes and Records of the Royal Society of London*, 8 (1950–1), 171.

37 Denis Papin, *A new digester, or engine for softening bones* (1681), p. 52. See also Martin Lister, quoted in Oldenburg, *Correspondence*, vol. 8, p. 43.

38 See above, pp. 69–70.

39 Peter, *Truth in opposition*, p. 51. See also Margaret E. Rowbottom, 'The earliest published writing of Robert Boyle', *Annals of Science*, 6 (1950), 380–4; R.S.L. Classified Papers, XI(1), no. 21.

40 R.S.L. Classified Papers, XX, no. 50; Hunter, *Science and society*, p. 57.

41 See below, p. 191.

42 B.L. MSS Add. 4432–5, *passim*; Hunter, *Science and society* pp. 50, 91–8. In the same way, French inventors found the approval of the Académie des Sciences valuable, even without the royal privilège (patent), for advertising their inventions as 'guaranteed by a group of impartial government experts': Hahn, *Anatomy of a scientific institution*, p. 23.

43 I am grateful to Liliane Perez for this information.

44 See below, p. 194.

45 Denis Papin, *A continuation of the new digester of bones* (1687), 'To the Reader'.

46 See above, pp. 13–14.

47 *Reasons humbly offer'd to the consideration of this honourable House, by the Master, Wardens and Assistants of the Company of Clockmakers, of the city of London* (1712), in Guildhall MS 3952, no. 6; see also ibid., no. 13.

48 See above, p. 113.

49 *Reasons offered against the passing of Sir Samuel Morland's bill touching water engines* (1677).

50 *Objections against passing the bill, as desired by the proprietors of the lights now generally used* (1692); see also *H. of C. Jnl*, vol. 10, p. 709.

51 *Reasons humbly offer'd by the jewellers, diamond cutters, lapidaries, engravers in stone, etc. against the bill for jewelled watches* [1704].

52 See above, pp. 18, 185.

53 See above, pp. 60–4; Dutton, *Patent system*, pp. 26–7.

54 Ibid., pp. 36–8.

55 Ibid., pp. 38–41; Robinson, 'James Watt and the law of patents', pp. 118–36.

56 Dalby Thomas, *An historical account of the rise and growth of the West-India collonies* (1690), pp. 45–6. For Dalby Thomas, see Thomas, 'Thomas Neale', p. 395.

57 See above, p. 47.

58 B.L. MS Add. 4433, fol. 122.

59 See above, pp. 52–4.

60 Desaguliers, *Experimental philosophy*, vol. 2, p. viii.

61 *Gentleman's Magazine*, 23 (1753), p. 235.

62 D'Escherny, *Short reflections*, pp. 4–8.

63 J. Spedding, R. L. Ellis, and D. D. Heath (eds.), *The works of Francis Bacon* (14 vols., 1857–74), vol. 3, p. 166.

64 Webster, *Great instauration*, p. 370.

65 Ibid., pp. 370–4.

66 Ibid., pp. 374–5; see also pp. 67–77.

67 Gerrard Winstanley, *The law of freedom*, ed. Christopher Hill (Harmondsworth, 1973), pp. 355–6, 365.

68 Hilda M. Rhodes, 'Literary aspects of inventors, projectors and virtuosi, 1660–1720' (unpubl. M.A. thesis, University of London, 1959), p. 52.

69 *New Atlantis, begun by the Lord Verulam, Viscount St Albans: and continued by R. H. Esquire* (1660), pp. 53–70.

70 Ibid., pp. 53–4.

71 Ibid., p. 55.

72 Ibid., pp. 56–8, 61, 63–6. For the exaltation of the arts of peace over those of war by seventeenth-century natural philosophers, see Richard Foster Jones, *Ancients*

and moderns: a study of the rise of the scientific movement in seventeenth-century England, 2nd edn (St Louis, 1961), pp. 327–8; and Roy S. Wolper, 'The rhetoric of gunpowder and the idea of progress', *J.H.I.*, 31 (1970), 594–8.

73 R. H. *New Atlantis*, pp. 60, 61.
74 Yarranton, *England's improvement . . . the second part*, p. 154.
75 Petty, *Treatise of taxes*, pp. 74–5; see also Savery, *Navigation improv'd*, p. 19.
76 [William Petty], *The advice of W. P. to Mr Samuel Hartlib* (1648), pp. 7, 21.
77 B.L. MS Lansdowne 691, fol. 55.
78 John Bellers, *An essay towards the improvement of physick* (1714), p. 8.
79 Ibid., p. 18. For biographical information, see A. Ruth Fry, *John Bellers 1654–1725, Quaker, economist and social reformer* (1935).
80 George Berkeley, *An essay towards preventing the ruin of Great Britain* (1721), in A. A. Luce and T. E. Jessop (eds.), *The works of George Berkeley, Bishop of Cloyne*, vol. 6 (1953), p. 73. See also Baston, *Observations on trade*, p. 17.
81 Malachy Postlethwayt, *Britain's commercial interest explained and improved* (2 vols., 1757), vol. 2, pp. 424–6.
82 See above, p. 38.
83 Similar rewards were offered by several European governments at this time: A. P. Usher, *A history of mechanical inventions*, 2nd edn (Cambridge, Mass., 1954), p. 324.
84 12 Anne, c.15; repr. in Quill, *John Harrison*, pp. 225–7.
85 Ibid., pp. 35–7, 40–8, 68–9.
86 See above, p. 49.
87 Arthur J. Viseltear, 'Joanna Stephens and the eighteenth-century lithontropics', *Bulletin of the History of Medicine*, 42 (1968), 199–220.
88 Patent 506 (1729); *H. of C. Jnl*, vol. 22 (1732–7), p. 121.
89 Wadsworth and Mann, *Cotton trade*, pp. 443–4, 458; see also Benton, *John Baskerville*, pp. 67–9.
90 Boehm and Silberston, *British patent system*, pp. 25–6.
91 Quoted in Allan, *William Shipley*, p. 10. It was said in 1765 that this proposal suffered in its timing: because of the South Sea Bubble, 'projectors of all sorts were held in general disrepute', [Edward Bridgen], *A short account of the great benefits* (1765), p. 5.
92 R.S.L. Misc. MSS IV, no. 57, quoted in Allan, *William Shipley*, pp. 14–15.
93 Clow and Clow, *Chemical revolution*, pp. 5–6.
94 Enid Gauldie, 'Mechanical aids to linen bleaching in Scotland', *Textile History*, 1 (1969), 134–7. For other initiatives, see Davis D. McElroy, *Scotland's age of improvement: a survey of eighteenth-century clubs and societies* (Washington State University, 1969), pp. 28–9; S. Shapin, 'Property, patronage and the politics of science, the founding of the Royal Society of Edinburgh', *British Jnl for the History of Science*, 7 (1974), 9; *Scots Magazine*, 5 (1743), p. 385.
95 Henry Trueman Wood, *A history of the Royal Society of Arts* (1913), p. 2.
96 Allan, *William Shipley*, p. 16; R.S.A. Guard Book I, no. 120, fol. 4.
97 Wood, *Royal Society of Arts*, p. 2; R.S.A. Guard Book I, no. 120, fol. 5; no. 121, fols. 1–2.
98 Allan, *William Shipley*, pp. 32, 34, 42–57.
99 Rexmond C. Cochrane, 'Francis Bacon and the rise of the mechanical arts in eighteenth-century England', *Annals of Science*, 12 (1956), 144–53. See also the quotation from Bacon's *New Atlantis* on the titlepage of [T.], *Letters on the utility and policy of employing machines to shorten labour* (1780); and the references to Bacon in Kenrick, *Address*, pp. 8–9.

100 Allan, *William Shipley*, p. 67; Wood, *Royal Society of Arts*, pp. 20–1, 28–46.
101 Allan, *William Shipley*, p. 16. An article in the *Gentleman's Magazine*, 25 (1755), p. 126, suggested (with a large dose of hyperbole) that nothing but the Society of Arts was keeping alive 'the flame' of invention.
102 Wood, *Royal Society of Arts*, p. 243.
103 Ibid., p. 244.
104 I am grateful to Liliane Perez for this information.
105 Wood, *Royal Society of Arts*, p. 125.
106 R.S.A. Guard Book I, nos. 120, 121.
107 Bacon, *Works*, vol. 3, p. 165; *The advice of W. P.*, p. 8; R. H. *New Atlantis* (1660), pp. 57–8, 64–6.
108 B.L. MS Lansdowne 691, fol. 56.
109 Allan, *William Shipley*, p. 46.
110 R.S.A. Guard Book I, nos. 61, 68. See also [Bridgen], *Short account*, pp. 8–11.
111 Musson and Robinson, *Science and technology*, pp. 129–30.
112 Quoted in Fitton and Wadsworth, *The Strutts and the Arkwrights*, p. 41.
113 Quoted in Wadsworth and Mann, *Cotton trade*, p. 496.
114 Wood, *Royal Society of Arts*, pp. 125–38, 258; D. Hudson and K. W. Luckhurst, *The Royal Society of Arts, 1754–1954* (1956), p. 102; J. B. Harley, 'The re-mapping of England, 1750–1800', *Imago Mundi*, 19 (1965), 60 2; [Bridgen], *Short account*, p. 12.
115 Des Fontaines, 'The Society of Arts and the early Wedgwoods', p. 329.
116 Hudson and Luckhurst, *Royal Society of Arts*, pp. 124–5.
117 Kenrick, *Address*, pp. 17–18.
118 Ibid., p. 19.
119 Ibid., p. 20. See also Davies, *Collection*, pp. 6–7.
120 *Gentleman's Magazine*, 56 (1786), p. 26.
121 *Observations on the utility of patents*, pp. 18–20.
122 Adam Smith, *An inquiry into the nature and causes of the wealth of nations*, ed. R. H. Campbell, A. S. Skinner, and W. B. Todd (2 vols., Oxford, 1976), vol. 2, p. 754; Getz, 'History of the patentee's obligation', p. 68.
123 Adam Smith, *Lectures on jurisprudence*, ed. R. L. Meek, D. D. Raphael, and P. G. Stein (Oxford, 1978), p. 83.
124 Arnold Plant, 'The economic theory concerning patents for invention', *Economica*, 1 (1934), 40. Bentham made an exception to his general disapproval of premiums in Jenner's case, since he could hope for no reward through commercial exploitation of the discovery. 'The liberality with which the physicians throughout Europe have encouraged a discovery that has lopped off one of the most lucrative branches of their profession, is a most honourable feature in the annals of medicine': Bentham, *Works*, vol. 2, p. 212.
125 Quoted in Marjorie Plant, *The English book trade* (1974), pp. 113–14.
126 *The life and errors of John Dunton, late citizen of London; written by himself in solitude* (1705), p. 257. See also Prager, 'A history of intellectual property', pp. 733, 754, 758.
127 8 Anne, c. 19; Plant, *English book trade*, pp. 99–120, esp. p. 118.
128 Stephen Parks (ed.), *The literary property debate: seven tracts, 1747–1773* (New York and London, 1974).
129 See above, p. 194.
130 P.R.O. SP44.253, pp. 288–9.
131 See below, pp. 202–4.
132 G. R. Rubin and David Sugarman (eds.), *Law, economy, and society: essays in the history of English law, 1750–1914* (Abingdon, 1984), pp. 23–36.

133 Smith, *Lectures on jurisprudence*, p. 11.
134 Cobbett, *Parliamentary history*, vol. 17 (1771–4), cols. 954–1003. For the background to this, see Lieberman, 'The province of legislation determined', pp. 149–52.
135 Cobbett, *Parliamentary history*, vol. 17 (1771–4), cols. 981, 987.
136 Ibid., cols. 974, 982.
137 Sir James Burrow, *Reports of cases adjudged in the Court of King's Bench since the time of Lord Mansfield's coming to preside in it* (5 vols., Dublin, 1785), vol. 4, pp. 2398–9.
138 Kenrick, *Address*, p. 2.
139 Ibid., pp. 4–5, 27–9, 30, 43.
140 *Observations on the utility of patents*, p. 42.
141 Bramah, *A letter to the Rt Hon. Sir James Eyre* (1797), p. 77.
142 Prager, 'A history of intellectual property', p. 756.
143 Davies, *Collection*, p. 434.
144 Its most influential proponent was probably J. R. McCulloch: Dutton, *Patent system*, pp. 17–19.

11 A new concept of invention

1 Lynn Thorndike, *A history of magic and experimental science* (8 vols., New York, 1958), vol. 7, p. 615.
2 Walter E. Houghton, 'The English virtuoso in the seventeenth century', *J.H.I.*, 3 (1942), 62, 70.
3 Thomas Sprat, *The history of the Royal Society of London* (1667), p. 406.
4 Opposition to labour-saving technology was expressed more often in deeds than in print; as is so often the case, those most closely affected left little written trace.
5 L. T. C. Rolt, *The aeronauts: a history of ballooning, 1783–1903*, 2nd edn (Gloucester, 1985), pp. 60–81; Hunter, *History of London*, vol. 1, p. 800; *Gentleman's Magazine*, vols. 53–5 (1783–5), *passim*.
6 The notion of sifting through alternatives to find 'the invention' is encapsulated in Christopher Wren's description of how he invented his double-writing machine: B.L. MS Add. 25,071, fols. 42–3.
7 W. C. Kneale, 'The idea of invention', *Proceedings of the British Academy*, 41 (1955), 85–108.
8 Samuel Johnson, *A dictionary of the English language* (2 vols., 1755), sub 'Invention'. 'Inventor' and 'Inventer', however, both refer primarily to one who produces something new. See also, for example, N. Bailey, *An universal etymological dictionary* (1721); Thomas Dyche and William Pardon, *A new general English dictionary*, 2nd edn (1737).
9 Jones, *Ancients and moderns*, pp. 241–4.
10 W[illiam] Derham, *Physico-theology* (1713), pp. 306–9. For Derham, see W. Coleman, 'Providence, capitalism and environmental degradation: English apologetics in an era of economic revolution', *J.H.I.*, 37 (1976), 27–44, esp. 32. See also [Robert Pitt], *The craft and frauds of physicians expos'd* (London, 1703), pp. 92–4; [Daniel Defoe], *The history of the principal discoveries and improvements* (1727), p. 227. For the idea of the inventor as agent of the divine plan, Hugh Platt, *The jewell house of art and nature* (1594), p. B2v; *Marten Triewald's short description of the atmospheric engine, 1734*, trans. Are Waerland (1928), p. 3. Anthropocentricity tended also to the notion that everything in nature had been put there for man's use: for example, Platt, *Jewell house*, p. 49; Houghton, *Collection*, vol. 6, no. 137.
11 Rhodes, 'Literary aspects', pp. 93–5; for example, [M. Tindall], *A letter to a*

member of parliament (1698), pp. 11, 22; [J. Asgill], *An essay for the press* (1712), p. 4. I owe these references to Mark Goldie.

12 P.R.O. SP32.1, no. 150.

13 Robert Boyle, *The works of the Honourable Robert Boyle*, ed. Thomas Birch (5 vols., 1744), vol. 3, pp. 185–95.

14 Charles Webster, *From Paracelsus to Newton: magic and the making of modern science* (Cambridge, 1982), pp. 52–4.

15 Joseph Glanvill, *Plus ultra* (1668), p. 7; see also Grew, in B.L. MS Lansdowne 691, fol. 56; Papin, *New digester*, preface; Holt, *Artificial stone*, pp. 12, 15.

16 Hales, *Treatise*, p. 3.

17 Hill, *Account*, p. 25. See also a contemporary comment on Thomas Savery, quoted in Rhys Jenkins, 'Savery, Newcomen and the early history of the steam engine', *T.N.S.*, 3 (1922–3), 113–14; and Richard Haines, *Aphorisms upon the new way of improving cyder* (1684), p. 2.

18 Witt Bowden, *Industrial society in England towards the end of the eighteenth century*, 2nd edn (1965), p. 53; and for example, Bodl., MS Aubrey 1, fol. 15.

19 Rossi, *Philosophy, technology and the arts*, ch. 1.

20 Ibid., p. x.

21 Ibid., pp. 15–17, 26–30.

22 George Agricola, *De re metallica* (Basel, 1536), trans. H. C. Hoover and L. H. Hoover (1912).

23 For example, Boyle, *Works*, vol. 3, pp. 186–7; Glanvill, *Plus ultra, passim*.

24 Marjorie H. Nicolson, 'The microscope and the English imagination', *Smith College Studies in Modern Languages*, 16 (1935); and idem, 'A world in the moon', *Smith College Studies in Modern Languages*, 17 (1936); Rhodes, 'Literary aspects', pp. 97–9, 112; B.L. MS Add. 4429, fol. 393.

25 Wolper, 'Rhetoric of gunpowder', p. 598. Henry Power added new manufacturing industries, like sugar-refining and papermaking, to the list: *Experimental philosophy* (1663), p. 190. See also A. C. Keller, 'Kepler, the art of flight and the vision of interplanetary travel as the next great invention', *Procs. XIIIth International Congress for the History of Science, Moscow, 1971* (1974), vol. 12, pp. 72–5.

26 B.L. MS Add. 25,071, fols. 42–3. See also Robert Hooke, *Micrographia* (1665), preface; Mary B. Hesse, 'Hooke's philosophical algebra', *Isis*, 57 (1966), 76–7, 80–1.

27 Contemporary recognition is attested in, for example, Glanvill, *Plus ultra*, p. 104, *et seq.*; Sprat, *History*, p. 403; Boyle, *Works*, vol. 5, p. 336.

28 Boyle, *Works*, vol. 1, pp. 420–583.

29 Ibid., vol. 3, p. 136; Jones, *Ancients and moderns*, pp. 206–21.

30 Boyle, *Works*, vol. 3, p. 162; also vol. 1, p. 463.

31 Ibid., vol. 3, pp. 154–5.

32 See ibid., vol. 3, pp. 155–6; also Glanvill, *Plus ultra*, pp. 22–62; John Arbuthnot, *An essay on the usefulness of mathematical learning* (Oxford, 1701); Robert Dossie, *The handmaid to the arts*, 2nd edn (2 vols., 1764), vol. 1, p. ix; vol. 2, p. 223; L. Trengrove, 'Chemistry at the Royal Society of London in the eighteenth century', *Annals of Science*, 19 (1963), 183–237.

33 Boyle, *Works*, vol. 3, pp. 141–50, 167–9.

34 Ibid., vol. 3, p. 170; see Walter E. Houghton, 'The history of trades', *J.H.I.*, 2 (1941), 49–56.

35 Webster, *Great instauration*, pp. 70–6, 476–9.

36 Rhodes, 'Literary aspects', pp. 78–91.

37 Bacon, *Works*, vol. 3, pp. 247, 385–7; vol. 4, 98–9; Boyle, *Works*, vol. 1, p. 517;

vol. 3, pp. 153–5; Sprat, *History*, pp. 394, 396; Joseph Glanvill, *The vanity of dogmatizing* (1661), p. 179.

38 See above, p. 192.

39 John Houghton, *A collection of letters for the improvement of husbandry and trade* (2 vols., 1681–3), vol. 1, p. 54; see also Maximilian E. Novak, *Economics and the fiction of Daniel Defoe* (Berkeley and Los Angeles, 1962), p. 50.

40 Boyle, *Works*, vol. 3, p. 139.

41 Ibid., vol. 3, p. 168; see also T. H[ale], *An account*, p. lii.

42 Sprat, *History*, p. 392.

43 Ibid., p. 395.

44 Ibid., p. 392.

45 Prior, 'Bacon's man of science', p. 358.

46 R. G. Wilkinson, *Poverty and progress: an ecological model of economic development* (1973) explores (and overemphasizes) this stimulus.

47 [Gabriel Plattes], *A discovery of infinite treasure* (1639), p. 91.

48 It had been raised by the Italian, Botero, in 1589: Joseph A. Schumpeter, *History of economic analysis*, ed. E. B. Schumpeter (1954), p. 254.

49 Ibid., p. 258.

50 Ibid., pp. 259–63; Paul A. Samuelson, *Economics*, 9th edn (Tokyo, 1973), p. 737.

51 Matthew Hale, *The primitive origination of mankind* (1671), pp. 154, 161; Margaret T. Hodgen, 'Sir Matthew Hale and the "method" of invention', *Isis*, 34 (1943), 313–18. See also William Temple, *Observations upon the United Provinces of the Netherlands* (1673), ed. Sir George Clark (Oxford, 1972), p. 109; Charles Davenant, *Discourses upon the public revenue* (1698), in Sir Charles Whitworth (ed.), *The political and commercial works of Charles Davenant* (5 vols., 1771), vol. 1, p. 390; Chamberlayne, *Angliae notitiae*, 3rd edn (1669), p. 61.

52 Houghton, *Collection*, vol. 7, no. 172; see also William Petty, *Political arithmetic* (1690), in Hull, *Economic writings*, vol. 1, p. 256.

53 R. G. Albion, *Forests and sea power: the timber problem of the Royal Navy, 1652–1862* (Cambridge, Mass., 1926), pp. 97–128.

54 An exception was Yarranton, *England's improvement*, pp. 56–63, where he argued that ironmaking actually fostered timber growing. Historians now generally agree with Yarranton in its exoneration: M. W. Flinn, 'Timber and the advance of technology: a reconsideration', *Annals of Science*, 15 (1959), 111–19; Hyde, *Technological change*, pp. 46–7.

55 John Evelyn, *Sylva, or a discourse of forest-trees* (1664); Albion, *Forests and sea power*, p. 131. More generally, see D. C. Coleman, 'Technology and economic history, 1500–1750', *Ec.H.R.*, 11 (1959), 507; and Brinley Thomas, 'Was there an energy crisis in Great Britain in the 17th century?', *Explorations in Economic History*, 23 (1986), 127–37, 141–3.

56 Daniel Defoe, *A plan of the English commerce* (1728), p. 299; see also Bernard Mandeville, *Free thoughts on religion* (1720), p. 331; Houghton, *Collection*, vol. 9, no. 198; Chamberlayne, *Angliae notitiae*, 18th edn (1694), p. 51.

57 Walter Blith, *The English improver improved*, 2nd edn (1652), p. 235; Petty, *Treatise of taxes*, p. 59; Yarranton, *England's improvement*, p. 159; B.L. MS Lansdowne 691, fol. 49.

58 'For I do not call that a real invention which has something before done like it, I account that more properly an improvement': [Daniel Defoe], *An essay upon projects* (1697, repr. Menston, 1969), p. 23.

59 Quoted in Istvan Hont, 'The "rich country–poor country" debate in Scottish classical political economy' in Istvan Hont and Michael Ignatieff (eds.), *Wealth*

and virtue: the shaping of political economy in the Scottish Enlightenment (Cambridge, 1983), pp. 271–315, esp. p. 284.

60 Ibid., p. 287.

61 Ibid., pp. 313–15; James Maitland, Earl of Lauderdale, *An inquiry into the nature and origin of public wealth* (Edinburgh, 1804), p. 299.

62 E. A. Wrigley, 'The process of modernization and the industrial revolution in England', *Jnl of Interdisciplinary History*, 3 (1972), 237–42, 256–7; further developed in 'Continuity, chance and change: the character of the industrial revolution in England' (the Ellen McArthur Lectures, University of Cambridge, 1987).

63 B.L. MS Lansdowne 691, fol. 47; Charles Davenant, *An essay upon the probable methods* (1699), in *Works*, vol. 2, p. 276. See also Defoe, *Plan*, p. 33; Cary, *Essay*, p. 16; Benton, *John Baskerville*, p. 32; Pepys, *Naval minutes* p. 217; Bellers, *Improvement of physick*, pp. 18, 25.

64 Bernard Mandeville, *The fable of the bees, or, private vices, public benefits* (1714), ed. F. B. Kaye (2 vols., Oxford, 1924), vol. 1, pp. 141–5; see also vol. 1, pp. 125, 148, 171; vol. 2, pp. 32, 130.

65 Defoe, *Plan*, pp. 40–2.

66 Ibid., pp. 53–5; Defoe, *Review*, vol. 2, no. 17, p. 66; no. 18, p. 69; no. 20, p. 77; Defoe remarked no difference between wages and labour costs. See also Yarranton, *England's improvement*, p. 106; Berkeley, *Essay*, p. 73.

67 See, for example, Joshua Gee, *The trade and navigation of Great Britain considered* (1729), pp. 5, 13, 31.

68 N[icholas] B[arbon], *A discourse of trade* (1690), pp. 72–3.

69 In 1675 Charles II forbade the wearing of foreign lace in his presence, but this was merely a gesture, not a reshaping of policy, P.R.O. SP29.372, no. 41. See Cary, *Essay*, p. 52; and Samuel Fortrey, *England's interest and improvement*, 2nd edn (1673), in McCulloch, *Tracts*, p. 234.

70 See, for example, Cary, *Essay*, pp. 13, 150; B[arbon], *Discourse*, p. 13; Campbell, *London tradesman*, pp. 115, 143, 171; *A general description of all trades*, p. 195; Dossie, *Handmaid to the arts*, vol. 1, p. vi; Postlethwayt, *Britain's commercial interest*, vol. 2, pp. 400, 411. 'Invention' was often understood simply as a mental capacity, equivalent to 'imagination', or just 'powers of thought', and normally part of everyone's mental equipment. Aubrey, for example, speculated that in north Wiltshire too much dairy produce 'cools their brains, and hurts their inventions', making the local populace phlegmatic and dull: Bodl., MS Aubrey 1, fols. 21, 66.

71 See above, p. 98.

72 Blith, *English improver*, p. d3v. See also J[ohn] W[orlidge], *Systema agriculturae*, 2nd edn (1675), p. c2v.

73 D. C. Coleman, 'Labour in the English economy of the seventeenth century', *Ec.H.R.*, 2nd ser. 8 (1955–6), 287, 292–3.

74 For example, Davenant, *Probable methods*, pp. 184–90; Bellers, *Improvement of physick*, pp. 110–13; Reynell, *True English interest*, p. 70; Fortrey, *England's interest*, p. 219; Berkeley, *Essay*, p. 72; *A letter from a merchant who has left off trade to a member of parliament* (1738), p. 52; B.L. MS Lansdowne 691, pt 4, ch. 2, *passim*;

75 Petty, *Treatise of taxes*, p. 28; J[osiah] C[hild], *Brief observations concerning trade* (1668), p. 68; John Pollexfen, *A discourse of trade, coyn and paper credit* (1697), pp. 155–7.

76 The classic exposition of this is Edgar S. Furniss, *The position of the labourer in a system of nationalism* (Cambridge, Mass. 1920), pp. 94–5, 117–25.

77 See above, pp. 180–1.
78 Houghton, *Collection*, vol. 11, nos. 259, 277; William Petty, *An essay concerning the multiplication of mankind*, 2nd edn (1682), pp. 40–1; Cary, *Essay*, p. 75; Mandeville, *Fable*, vol. 2, pp. 141–5; Francis Hutcheson, *Reflections upon laughter and remarks upon The fable of the bees* (Glasgow, 1750), pp. 48–9, 52.
79 Reynell, *True English interest*, p. av; also Fortrey, *England's interest*, p. 219; Davenant, *Probable methods*, pp. 192, 202.
80 Edgar A. J. Johnson, 'The mercantilist concept of "art" and "ingenious labour"', *Economic Jnl, Economic History Supplement*, 2 (1930–3), 239–45.
81 Blith, *English improver*, p. 5. This was echoed in Houghton, *Letters*, vol. 2, p. 57.
82 Epitomized by John Locke in a philosophical passage in 1677: Lord King (ed.), *The life of John Locke*, new edn (2 vols., 1830), vol. 2, p. 163. See also Lynn White Jr, 'What accelerated technical progress in the western middle ages?' in A. C. Crombie (ed.), *Scientific change: symposium on the history of science, University of Oxford, 1961* (1963), p. 291.
83 [Plattes], *Discovery*, p. 75.
84 Plattes's particular innovations happened to be labour-intensive: ibid., p. 76.
85 Ernest J. Enthoven (ed.), *Life and works of Sir Christopher Wren* (Campden, Glos., 1903), p. 21.
86 Sprat, *History*, p. 400. See also King, *Life of John Locke*, vol. 2, p. 163.
87 Petty, *Political arithmetic*, p. 249.
88 Johnson, 'Mercantilist concept', pp. 246–7.
89 But see Thirsk and Cooper, *Economic documents*, pp. 294–5; and above, p. 161.
90 P. J. Thomas stresses the stimulus afforded to economic reasoning by the controversy over the East India trade, in *Mercantilism and the East India trade* (1963).
91 William Petty, *Verbum sapienti* (1691), in Hull, *Economic writings*, vol. 1, pp. 118–19. See also Sprat, *History*, p. 400; and Bodl., MS Aubrey 2, fol. 67.
92 Jacob Vanderlint, *Money answers all things* (1734), pp. 1–2, 6–8, 21–3, 77–8, 84. At the end of the tract, Vanderlint obstinately parries objections that already too much land is under cultivation and prices so low that farmers are being ruined on a large scale, with reassertion of his 'evidence', putting the blame on abnormally low population levels, not overproduction as such: ibid., pp. 152–6.
93 Ibid., pp. 81–2.
94 Charles Davenant, *An essay on the East India trade* (1697), in *Works*, vol. 1, pp. 100, 102–3, 107. He probably understood 'inventions' more in the sense of new schemes and projects than in the strictly technical sense.
95 [John Houghton], *England's great happiness* (1677), repr. in McCulloch, *Tracts*, pp. 261–2. See also Sprat, *History*, p. 400; Sir Thomas Culpeper, *A discourse shewing the many advantages which will accrue to the kingdom by the abatement of usury* (1668), pp. 8–9.
96 Houghton, *Letters*, vol. 1, p. 52; see also, ibid., pp. 111–19; and *Collection*, vol. 9, no. 200; vol. 15, no. 434; vol. 16, no. 489. Conservative thought was outraged: for example, John Beale's comments on Houghton in a letter to Robert Boyle, 8 July, 1682, in Boyle, *Works*, vol. 5, pp. 508–9. Samuel Fortrey had advocated vanity and excess, but was adamant that only English products should be its object: *England's interest*, pp. 234–5.
97 E.g. Barbon, *Discourse*, pp. 62–4; [Dudley North], *Discourses upon trade* (1691), repr. in McCulloch, *Tracts*, p. 529.
98 *England's great happiness*, p. 260.

99 Houghton, *Collection*, vol. 15, no. 453; see also ibid., vol. 12, nos. 300, 303.
100 Christine MacLeod, 'Henry Martin and the authorship of "Considerations upon the East India trade"', *B.I.H.R.*, 56 (1983), 222–9.
101 *Considerations upon the East India trade* (1701), repr. in McCulloch, *Tracts*, pp. 579–80, 586–7, 598, 608–14.
102 Ibid., p. 589; see also p. 593.
103 Ibid., p. 590; my emphasis.
104 Josiah Tucker in 1755 argued, like Martin, that inventions were the natural outcome of free competition: *Elements of commerce*, p. 124; see also Smith, *Wealth of nations*, vol. 1, pp. 20–2.
105 Cary, *Essay*, pp. 145–7. See ibid., pp. 148–50, for Cary's working out of the thesis that high prices stimulate demand. See also Oliver Lawson Dick (ed.), *John Aubrey's Brief Lives* (1960) p. 191.
106 Defoe, *Giving alms no charity*, p. 428.
107 John Sekora, *Luxury: the concept in western thought* (Baltimore, 1979), pp. 51–109.
108 Rosenberg, *Perspectives*, pp. 141–50. My current research examines the emergence and impact of a specialist capital-goods sector in the eighteenth and nineteenth centuries.
109 *Considerations upon the East India trade*, p. 543.
110 [George Blewitt], *An enquiry whether a general practice of virtue tends to the wealth or poverty, benefit or disadvantage of a people* (1725), p. 15; *Considerations on the bill for a general naturalization* (1748), pp. 10, 20.
111 *Reflections on various subjects*, pp. 25–8.
112 Postlethwayt, *Britain's commercial interest*, vol. 2, pp. 417–21.
113 Tucker, *Instructions for travellers*, p. 241.
114 Sir James Steuart, *An inquiry into the principles of political oeconomy* (2 vols., 1767), vol. 1, pp. 121, 123.
115 Steuart could not conceive of this being the case anywhere in Europe: ibid., pp. 121–2. For the context of Steuart's remarks, see Hont, 'The "rich country–poor country" debate', pp. 296–8.
116 Ibid., p. 295; Tucker, *Instructions for travellers*, p. 241; see also R.S.A. Guard Book v, no. 86.
117 Steuart, *Political oeconomy*, vol. 1, p. 120. See also Dugald Stewart, *Lectures on political economy*, vol. 1, in Sir William Hamilton (ed.), *Collected works* (10 vols., Edinburgh, 1854–60), vol. 8, p. 193.
118 The butt of their scorn was Montesquieu who 'finds fault with water mills, though I do not find that he has made any objection against the use of the plough', Steuart, *Political oeconomy*, p. 119; Tucker, *Instructions for travellers*, p. 242. See also Stewart, *Lectures*, p. 190; David Macpherson, *Annals of commerce, manufactures, fisheries and navigation* (4 vols., 1805), vol. 1, pp. 699–700.
119 [Arthur Young], *Political essays concerning the present state of the British empire* (1772, repr. New York, 1970), pp. 209–19.
120 R. Koebner, 'Adam Smith and the industrial revolution', *Ec.H.R.*, 2nd ser. 11 (1959), 381–91.
121 Lauderdale, *Inquiry*, pp. 286–96; Stewart, *Lectures*, pp. 316–19.
122 Lauderdale, *Inquiry*, p. 164.
123 Ibid., p. 163, 166.
124 Ibid., pp. 348–9. See also Stewart, *Lectures*, p. 196.
125 Lauderdale, *Inquiry*, p. 297. See also Sir Frederic Morton Eden, *The state of the poor* (3 vols., 1797), vol. 1, pp. 441n, 443; Macpherson, *Annals of commerce*, vol. 3, p. 592; Stewart, *Lectures*, p. 192.

126 Lauderdale, *Inquiry*, preface.
127 Berg, *The machinery question*, p. 19, and *passim*.
128 Wadsworth and Mann, *Cotton trade*, pp. 496–7; David L. Wykes, 'The Leicester
    riots of 1773 and 1787: a study of the victims of popular protest', *Trans. Leics.
    Archaeological and Historical Society*, 54 (1978–9), 40–6; C. R. Dobson, *Masters and
    journeymen: a pre-history of industrial relations, 1717–1800* (1980), pp. 160–9.
129 Cary, *Essay*, pp. 145–8; Tucker, *Instructions to travellers*, pp. 240–1; Lauderdale,
    Inquiry, pp. 300–3; Stewart, *Lectures*, pp. 320–1.
130 Iranka Kovacevich, 'The mechanical muse: the impact of technical inventions
    on eighteenth-century neoclassical poetry', *Huntington Library Quarterly*, 28
    (1964–5), 266–7, 273–5; Francis D. Klingender, *Art and the industrial revolution*,
    3rd edn, ed. Arthur Elton (1972), pp. 43–56, 66–90.
131 *European Magazine*, vol. 11 (1787), 364–7. See also, for example, *Marten Triewald's
    short discourse*, pp. 50–1.
132 *Considerations on the bill for a general naturalization*, pp. 17–18. See also Gee, *Trade and
    navigation*, p. 10; Tucker, *Instructions for travellers*, p. 241; A[dam] Anderson, *An
    historical and chronological deduction of the origin of commerce* (2 vols., 1764), vol. 2, p.
    284; Macpherson, *Annals of commerce*, vol. 3, pp. 75–6.
133 Tucker, *Instructions for travellers*, p. 240.
134 [T.], *Letters on the utility and policy*, pp. 21–2.
135 Hutton, *History of Birmingham*, p. 93.
136 A recent television advertisement proclaimed, as a truism, 'no nation has ever
    been as inventive as the British'. Jewkes et al. found, however, 'no convincing
    evidence to support the present popular view that the British are "good at"
    invention but "bad at" development. Indeed, in other countries, the opposite is
    often believed': John Jewkes, David Sawyers, and Richard Stillerman, *The
    sources of invention*, 2nd edn (1969), p. 181n.
137 [T.], *Letters on the utility and policy*, p. 16. It is salutary to remember that self-
    justificatory statements are made in similar terms in the present century: see, for
    example, Winston Churchill, in *The Times* of 7 Aug., 1945, and others, quoted in
    Paul Chilton, 'Nukespeak: nuclear language, culture and propaganda' in
    Crispin Aubrey (ed.), *Nukespeak: the media and the bomb* (1982), pp. 99–100.
138 King, *Life of John Locke*, vol. 1, p. 162.
139 Bramah, *A letter*, pp. 77, 83.
140 Smith, *Lectures on jurisprudence*, p. 347; my emphasis.
141 *Observations on the utility of patents*, p. 42.
142 Eden, *State of the poor*, vol. 1, p. 442n. See also Kovacevich, 'Mechanical muse',
    p. 275.
143 Stewart, *Lectures*, p. 196; my emphasis.
144 *Report from the committee on Dr Cartwright's petition respecting his weaving machine*, P.P.
    1808, II, p. 140.
145 Malcolm I. Thomis, *Responses to industrialization: the British experience 1780–1850*
    (Newton Abbot, 1976), p. 17; Jasper Wilson [James Currie], *A letter, commercial
    and political*, 3rd edn (1793), p. 7; criticized by George Chalmers, *An estimate of the
    comparative strength of Great-Britain*, new edn (1794), pp. xxiii–xxiv; Macpherson,
    Annals of commerce, vol. 4, pp. 78–80.
146 See above, pp. 197–9.
147 Cobbett, *Parliamentary history*, vol. 17, col. 999.
148 Kenrick, *Address*, p. 2; *Observations on the utility of patents*, pp. 9, 45.

Bibliography

Manuscript sources

London:

Public Record Office	ADM1	SO1
	C6–12	SO3
	C66	SP29
	E126	SP30
	E134	SP34
	PC1	SP35
	PC2	SP36
		SP44

British Library	Additional MSS
	Lansdowne MSS
	Sloane MSS

Guildhall Library	Clockmakers Company MSS
	Glass Sellers Company MSS
	Joiners Company MSS
	Weavers Company MSS

Victoria and Albert Museum	MS 86.JJ.8

Royal Society of London	Record Books (RBC)
	Journal Books
	Classified Papers

Royal Society of Arts	Guard Books I–V
	Minute Books I–II

Wellcome Institute	MS 3013

Outside London:

Berkshire County Record Office	Hartley Russell MSS
Birmingham Reference Library	Wyatt MSS

Cumbria County Record Office (Carlisle)   Lowther MSS

Edinburgh, University Library   MS La.II.311
    Scottish Record Office   'Calendar of Scottish patents
                                    and specifications, 1712–
                                    1812'
                                    MS GD1.500.72

Oxford, Bodleian Library   Aubrey MSS
                                    Rawlinson MSS

Sheffield City Library   Bagshawe MSS

Government reports and official papers

Report from the committee on Dr Cartwright's petition respecting his weaving machine, Parliamentary Papers 1808, II.

Report from the select committee on the law relating to patents for invention, Parliamentary Papers, 1829, III.

Calendar of State Papers Domestic.

Calendar of State Papers Venetian.

Calendar of Treasury Books.

Report of the Deputy Keeper of the Public Records, vol. 2 (1841).

Works published before 1850 and published documents

Agricola, George, *De re metallica*, Basel, 1536, trans. H. C. Hoover, and L. H. Hoover, 1912.

Aiken, John, *A description of the country from thirty to forty miles round Manchester*, 1795, repr. Newton Abbot, 1968.

Anderson, A[dam], *An historical and chronological deduction of the origin of commerce*, 2 vols., 1764.

Angliae tutamen: or, the safety of England, 1695.

Arbuthnot, John, *An essay on the usefulness of mathematical learning*, Oxford, 1701.

[Asgill, J.], *An essay for the press*, 1712.

Aubrey, John, *John Aubrey's Brief Lives*, ed. Oliver Lawson Dick, 1960.

B[arbon], N[icholas], *A discourse of trade*, 1690.

Bacon, Francis, *The works of Francis Bacon*, ed. J. Spedding, R. L. Ellis, and D. D. Heath, 14 vols., 1857–74.

Bailey, N. *An universal etymological dictionary*, 1721.

Baker, Charles, *By the king's royal letters patent and licence, Charles Baker's treatise for the preventing of smut in wheat*, Bristol, 1797.

Baskerville, John, *Letters of the famous eighteenth-century printer, John Baskerville of Birmingham*, ed. Leonard Jay, Birmingham, 1932.

Baston, Thomas, *Observations on trade and a public spirit*, 2nd edn, 1732.

[Baxter, Richard], *Reliquiae Baxterianae*, ed. Matthew Sylvester, 1696.

Beatson, Robert, *An essay on the comparative advantages of vertical and horizontal windmills*, 1798.

Beckmann, Johann, *A history of inventions and discoveries*, trans. William Johnston, 3 vols., 1797.

Bellers, John, *An essay towards the improvement of physick*, 1714.

Bentham, Jeremy, *The works of Jeremy Bentham*, ed. John Bowring, 11 vols., Edinburgh, 1843.

Berkeley, George, *An essay towards preventing the ruin of Great Britain*, 1721, repr. in *The works of George Berkeley, Bishop of Cloyne*, ed. A. A. Luce and T. E. Jessop, vol. 6, 1953.

Birch, Thomas, *The history of the Royal Society of London*, 4 vols., 1756.

Blackner, John, *The history of Nottingham*, Nottingham, 1815.

Blackstone, William, *Commentaries on the laws of England*, 4 vols., Oxford, 1765–9.

[Blewitt, George], *An enquiry whether a general practice of virtue tends to the wealth or poverty, benefit or disadvantage of a people*, 1725.

Blith, Walter, *The English improver improved*, 2nd edn, 1652.

Borlase, William, *The natural history of Cornwall*, Oxford, 1758.

Boyle, Robert, *The works of the Honourable Robert Boyle*, ed. Thomas Birch, 5 vols., 1744.

Bramah, Joseph, *A letter to the Rt Hon. Sir James Eyre, Lord Chief Justice of the Common Pleas*, 1797.

[Bridgen, Edward], *A short account of the great benefits*, 1765.

Brownrigg, William, *The art of making common salt*, 1748.

Burrow, Sir James, *Reports of cases adjudged in the court of King's Bench since the time of Lord Mansfield's coming to preside in it*, 5 vols., Dublin, 1785.

Byfield, Timothy, *The artificial spaw, or mineral waters to drink*, 1684.

Byfield, Timothy, *A short but full account of the rise, nature, and management of the small-pox*, 1711.

Caffyn, Matthew, *Envy's bitterness corrected with the rod of shame*, 1674.

Caffyn, Matthew, *A raging wave foming out his own shame*, 1675.

Campbell, R. *The London tradesman*, 1747, repr. Newton Abbot, 1969.

Carpmael, William, *The law of patents*, 1832.

Carpmael, William, *Law reports of patent cases*, 3 vols., 1843–[52].

Cartwright, Edmund, *A memoir of Edmund Cartwright*, ed. Kenneth G. Ponting, Bath, 1971.

Cary, John, *An essay on the state of England*, Bristol, 1695, repr. Farnborough, 1972.

The case of the Silk Throwers Company of London [1732].

Chalmers, George, *An estimate of the comparative strength of Great-Britain*, new edn, 1794.

Chamberlain, John, *The letters of John Chamberlain*, ed. N. E. McLure, 2 vols., Philadelphia, 1939.

Chamberlayne, Edward, *Angliae notitiae; or the present state of England*, 3rd edn, 1669; 18th edn, 1694.

Chambers, Ephraim, *Cyclopaedia: or, an universal dictionary of arts and sciences*, 5th edn, 2 vols., 1741.

Charles II, *By the king, a proclamation for the prohibiting the importation of glass plates, July 1664*, 1664.

Charles II, *By the king, a proclamation prohibiting the importation of blue paper*, 1666.

C[hild] J[osiah], *Brief observations concerning trade*, 1668.

Clarendon, Edward Hyde, 1st Earl of, *The history of the rebellion and civil wars in England*, 3 vols., Oxford, 1702–4.

Cobbett, William (ed.), *The parliamentary history of England*, 36 vols., 1806–20.

Coke, Edward, *The third part of the institutes of the laws of England*, 4th edn, 1669.

Collier, John Dyer, *An essay on the law of patents for new inventions*, 1803.

Collyer, Joseph, *The parent's and guardian's directory*, 1761.

Considerations on the bill for a general naturalization, 1748.

Cooke, James, *Cooke's improved patent drill and horse hoe*, 1789.

Culpeper, Sir Thomas, *A discourse, shewing the many advantages which will accrue to this kingdom by the abatement of usury*, 1668.

Davenant, Charles, *An essay on the East India trade*, 1697, repr. in Sir Charles Whitworth (ed.), *The political and commercial works of Charles Davenant*, 5 vols., 1771, vol. 1.

Davenant, Charles, *Discourses upon the public revenue, and on the trade of England*, 1698, repr. in *Works*, vol. 1.

Davenant, Charles, *An essay upon the probable methods of making a people gainers in the balance of trade*, 1699, repr. in *Works*, vol. 2.

Davies, John, *A collection of the most important cases respecting patents of invention and the rights of patentees*, 1816.

[Defoe, Daniel], *An essay upon projects*, 1697, repr. Menston, 1969.

[Defoe, Daniel], *Giving alms no charity* [1704], in *A second volume of the writings of the author of The true-born Englishman*, 1705.

[Defoe, Daniel], *The Review*, ed. A. W. Secord, 22 vols., New York, 1938.

[Defoe, Daniel], *The history of the principal discoveries and improvements*, 1727.

[Defoe, Daniel], *A plan of the English commerce*, 1728.

Defoe, Daniel, *A tour through the whole island of Great Britain*, 3rd edn, 4 vols., 1742.

Derham, William, *Physico-theology: or, a demonstration of the being and attributes of God, from his works of creation*, 1713.

Dering, Sir Edward, *The parliamentary diary of Sir Edward Dering, 1670–1673*, ed. Basil Duke Henning, New Haven, 1940.

Desaguliers, J. T., *A course of experimental philosophy*, 2 vols., 1734–44.

Dickens, Charles, 'A poor man's tale of a patent' in *Household words*, vol. 2 (19 Oct. 1850), repr. in *Reprinted pieces*, 1925.

Dickens, Charles, *Little Dorrit*, 1855–7.

D'Escherny, David, *A treatise of the causes and symptoms of the stone*, 1755.

D'Escherny, David, *Short reflections upon patents*, 1760, appended to *An essay on fevers*, 1760, and to *An essay on the small pox*, 1760.

Dossie, Robert, *The handmaid to the arts*, 2nd edn, 2 vols., 1764.

Dunton, John, *The life and errors of John Dunton, late citizen of London; written by himself in solitude*, 1705.

Dyche, Thomas and William Pardon, *A new general English dictionary*, 2nd edn, 1737.

Dyer, John, *The fleece, a poem*, 1757.

[Eaton, Robert], *An account of Dr Eaton's styptick balsam*, 1723.

Eden, Sir Frederic Morton, *The state of the poor*, 3 vols., 1797.

Edgeworth, Richard Lovell, *Memoirs of Richard Lovell Edgeworth*, ed. Desmond Clarke, 2 vols., Shannon, 1969.

Evelyn, John, *Sylva, or a discourse of forest-trees*, 1664.

Evelyn, John, *The diary of John Evelyn*, ed. E. S. de Beer, 6 vols., Oxford, 1955.

Fiennes, Celia, *The journeys of Celia Fiennes*, ed. Christopher Morris, 1949.

Fortrey, Samuel, *England's interest and improvement*, 2nd edn, 1673, repr. in McCulloch (ed.), *Tracts*.

Fowke, John, *John Fowke of Nightingale Lane, Wapping, London, engineer . . .* [1726?].

Francis, Richard, *Maxims of equity*, 1727.

Gee, Joshua, *The trade and navigation of Great-Britain considered*, 1729.

A general description of all trades, 1747.

Glanvill, Joseph, *The vanity of dogmatizing*, 1661.

Glanvill, Joseph, *Plus ultra*, 1668.

Godfrey, Ambrose, *An account of the new method of extinguishing fires by explosion and suffocation*, 1724.

Grew, Nehemiah, *A treatise of the nature and use of the bitter purging salt* [trans. Francis Moult], 1697.

H[aines] R[ichard], *Proposals for building in every county, a working-alms-house or hospital*, 1677, repr. in *Harleian miscellany*, 2nd edn, 1745, vol. 4.

Haines, Richard, *Aphorisms upon the new way of improving cyder*, 1684.

Hale, Matthew, *The primitive origination of mankind*, 1671.

H[ale], T[homas], *An account of several new inventions and improvements now necessary for England*, 1691.

H[ale], T[homas], *The new invention of mill'd lead, for sheathing of ships against the worm*, 1691.

Hale, Thomas, *A compleat body of husbandry*, 1756.

Hales, Stephen, *A description of ventilators*, 1743.

Hales, Stephen, *A treatise on ventilators*, 1758.

Harrington, John, *A new discourse of a state subject, called the metamorphosis of Ajax*, 1596.

Henson, Gravenor, *The civil, political and mechanical history of the framework knitters*, Nottingham, 1831, ed. S. D. Chapman, Newton Abbot, 1970.

Hill, Aaron, *Proposals for raising a stock of one hundred thousand pounds*, 1714.

Hill, Aaron, *An account of the rise and progress of the beech oil invention*, 1715.

H.M.C. 7th Report, *House of Lords Manuscripts*.

H.M.C. new series, vol. 2, *House of Lords Manuscripts*.

Holt, Richard, *A short treatise of artificial stone*, 1730.

Hooke, Robert, *Micrographia*, 1665.

Hooke, Robert, *The diary of Robert Hooke, M.A., M.D., F.R.S., 1672–1680*, ed. Henry W. Robinson and Walter Adams, 1935.

Hooke, Robert, *The posthumous works of Robert Hooke*, ed. Richard Waller, 1705.

H[ooke?], R[obert?], *New Atlantis, begun by the Lord Verulam, Viscount St Albans, and continued by R. H. Esquire*, 1660.

[Houghton, John], *England's great happiness*, 1677, repr. in McCulloch, *Tracts*.

Houghton, John, *A collection of letters for the improvement of husbandry and trade*, 2 vols., 1681–3.

Houghton, John, *A collection for improvement of husbandry and trade*, 12 vols., 1692–8.

An humble proposal to the parliament of Great Britain [1702] (Bodl. Theta.665, fol. 142).

Hunter, Rev. Henry, *The history of London and its environs*, 2 vols., 1811.

Hunter, Joseph, *Hallamshire: the history and topography of the parish of Sheffield in the county of York*, 1819.

Hutcheson, Francis, *Reflections upon laughter and remarks upon The fable of the bees*, Glasgow, 1750.

Hutton, William, *A history of Birmingham*, 2nd edn, Birmingham, 1783, repr. with introduction by C. R. Elvington, Wakefield, 1976.

An impartial representation of the case of the poor cotton spinners in Lancashire, etc., [1780].

Jacob, Giles, *A new law dictionary*, 9th edn, 1772.

Johnson, Samuel, *A dictionary of the English language*, 2 vols., 1755.

Kenrick, W. Ll.D. *An address to the artists and manufacturers of Great Britain*, 1774.

Lauderdale, James Maitland, Earl of, *An inquiry into the nature and origin of public wealth*, Edinburgh, 1804.

Lee, Joseph, *A vindication of a regulated inclosure*, 1656.

A letter from a merchant who has left off trade to a member of parliament, 1738.

Locke, John, *The life of John Locke*, ed. Lord [Peter] King, new edn, 2 vols., 1830.

The London and country brewer, Dublin, 1735.

Lowe, Joseph, *The present state of England*, 1822.

Luttrell, Narcissus, *The parliamentary diary of Narcissus Luttrell, 1691–1693*, ed. Henry Horwitz, Oxford, 1972.

McCulloch, J. R. (ed.), *A select collection of early English tracts on commerce*, 1856, repr. Cambridge, 1954.

Macpherson, David, *Annals of commerce, manufactures, fisheries and navigation*, 4 vols., 1805.

Mandeville, Bernard, *The fable of the bees: or, private vices, public benefits*, 1714, ed. F. B. Kaye, 2 vols., Oxford, 1924.

Mandeville, Bernard, *Free thoughts on religion*, 1720.

Marshall, William, *Rural economy of the midland counties*, 2nd edn, 2 vols., 1796.

[Martin, Henry], *Considerations upon the East India trade*, 1701, repr. in McCulloch, *Tracts*.

[Mortimer, Thomas], *A concise account of the rise, progress, and the present state of the Society for the Encouragement of Arts, Manufactures and Commerce*, 1763.

[North, Dudley], *Discourses upon trade*, 1691, repr. in McCulloch, *Tracts*.

North, Roger, *Lives of the Norths*, ed. Augustus Jessop, 3 vols., 1870.

Objections against passing the bill, as desired by the proprietors of the lights now generally used, 1692.

Observations on the utility of patents, and of the sentiments of Lord Kenyon respecting that subject, 4th edn, 1791.

Oldenburg, Henry, *The correspondence of Henry Oldenburg*, ed. and trans. A. R. Hall and M. B. Hall, 13 vols., Madison, Wis., 1965–86.

Oldmixon, John, *The history of England during the reigns of King William and Queen Mary, Queen Anne, King George I*, 1735.

Owen, Robert, *The life of Robert Owen, written by himself*, ed. John Butt, 1971.

Papin, Denys, *A new digester or engine for softening bones*, 1681.

Papin, Denys, *A continuation of the new digester of bones*, 1687.

Parkes, Joseph, *A history of the court of Chancery*, 1828.

Parks, Stephen (ed.), *The literary property debate: seven tracts, 1747–1773*, New York and London, 1974.

The patent, a poem, by the author of The graces, 1776.

Pepys, Samuel, *The diary of Samuel Pepys*, ed. R. Latham and W. Matthews, 11 vols., 1970–83.

Pepys, Samuel, *A descriptive catalogue of the naval manuscripts in the library at Magdalene College, Cambridge*, ed. J. R. Tanner, 4 vols., Navy Record Society, 1903–23.

Pepys, Samuel, *Samuel Pepys' naval minutes*, ed. J. R. Tanner, Navy Records Society, 1926.

Peter, Josiah, *Truth in opposition to ignorant and malicious falsehood*, 1701.

P[etty], W[illiam], *The advice of W. P. to Mr Samuel Hartlib*, 1648.

Petty, William, *A treatise of taxes and contributions*, 1662, repr. in C. H. Hull (ed.), *The economic writings of Sir William Petty*, 2 vols., Cambridge, 1899.

Petty, William, *An essay concerning the multiplication of mankind*, 2nd edn, 1686.

Petty, William, *Political arithmetic*, 1690, repr. in Hull, *Economic writings*.

Petty, William, *Verbum sapienti*, 1691, repr. in Hull, *Economic writings*.

Phillips, John, *A general history of inland navigation, foreign and domestic*, 5th edn, 1805, repr. as Charles Hadfield (ed.), *Phillips' inland navigation*, Newton Abbot, 1970.

[Pitt, Robert], *The crafts and frauds of physick expos'd*, 1703.

Platt, Hugh, *The jewell house of art and nature, conteining divers rare and profitable inventions*, 1594.

[Plattes, Gabriel], *A discovery of infinite treasure*, 1639.

Plot, Robert, *The natural history of Oxfordshire*, Oxford, 1676.

Plot, Robert, *The natural history of Staffordshire*, Oxford, 1686.

Pollexfen, John, *A discourse of trade, coyn and paper credit*, 1697.

Postlethwayt, Malachy, *Britain's commercial interest explained and improved*, 2 vols., 1757.

Power, Henry, *Experimental philosophy*, 1663.

Proposals for subscriptions to a new invention for raising water, [1720?].

Pryce, William, *Mineralogia cornubiensis: a treatise on minerals, mines, and mining*, 1778.

Radcliffe, William, *Origin of the new system of manufacture*, Stockport, 1828.

Ransome, J. Allen, *The implements of agriculture*, 1843.

Reasons humbly offer'd by the jewellers, diamond-cutters, lapidaries, engravers in stone etc. against the bill for jewelled watches, [1704].

Reasons humbly offer'd to the consideration of this honourable House, by the Master, Wardens and Assistants of the Company of Clockmakers, of the city of London, 1712.

Reasons offered against the passing of Sir Samuel Morland's bill touching water engines, 1677.

Reflections on various subjects relating to arts and commerce; particularly the consequences of admitting foreign artists on easier terms, 1752.

Reynell, Carew, *The true English interest*, 1674.

Roberts, Lewes, *The treasure of traffike, or a discourse of forraigne trade*, 1641.

Savery, Thomas, *Navigation improv'd, or the art of rowing ships of all rates in a calm*, 1698.

Savery, Thomas, *The miner's friend, or, an engine to raise water by fire*, 1702.

Scarse, Charles E. *Birmingham 120 years ago*, Birmingham, 1896.

Sellers, George Escol, *Early engineering reminiscences (1815–40) of George Escol Sellers*, ed. Eugene S. Ferguson, Smithsonian Institute, Washington D.C., 1965.

Shaw, Simeon, *History of the Staffordshire potteries*, 1829, repr. Newton Abbot and Wakefield, 1970.

Small, James, *A treatise on ploughs and wheel carriages*, Edinburgh, 1784.

Smith, Adam, *An inquiry into the nature and causes of the wealth of nations*, Edinburgh, 1776, ed. R. H. Campbell, A. S. Skinner, and W. B. Todd, 2 vols., Oxford, 1976.

Smith, Adam, *Lectures on jurisprudence*, ed. R. L. Meek, D. D. Raphael, and P. G. Stein, Oxford, 1978.

Smith, John (ed.), *Chronicon rusticum-commerciale: or, memoirs of wool*, 2 vols., 1747.

[Smith, Sir Thomas], *A discourse on the commonweal of this realm of England, attributed to Sir Thomas Smith*, ed. Mary Dewar, Charlottesville, 1969.

Sprat, Thomas, *The history of the Royal Society of London*, 1667.

Steuart, Sir James, *An inquiry into the principles of political oeconomy*, 2 vols., 1767.

Stewart, Dugald, *Lectures on political economy*, vol. 1, in Sir William Hamilton (ed.), *The collected works of Dugald Stewart*, 10 vols., Edinburgh, 1854–60, vol. 8.

Switzer, Stephen, *An universal system of water and water-works, philosophical and practical*, 1734.

[T.], *Letters on the utility and policy of employing machines to shorten labour*, 1780.

Tawney, R. H., and Eileen Power (eds.), *Tudor economic documents*, 3 vols., 1924.

Temple, William, *Observations upon the United Provinces of the Netherlands*, 1673, ed. Sir George Clark, Oxford, 1972.

Thirsk, Joan, and J. P. Cooper (eds.), *Seventeenth century economic documents*, Oxford, 1972.

Thomas, Dalby, *An historical account of the rise and growth of the West-India collonies*, 1690.

[Tindal, M.], *A letter to a member of parliament*, 1698.

Triewald, Marten, *Marten Triewald's short description of the atmospheric engine published at Stockholm, 1734*, trans. Are Waerland, 1928.

Tucker, Josiah, *The elements of commerce and the theory of taxes*, 1755.

Tucker, Josiah, *Instructions for travellers*, Dublin, 1758, repr. in Robert L. Schuyler (ed.), *Josiah Tucker: a selection from his economic and political writings*, NY, 1931.

T[ull], I[ethro], *The horse-hoing husbandry*, 2nd edn, 1733.

Vanderlint, Jacob, *Money answers all things*, 1734.

Vox et lacrimae Anglorum; or, the true Englishmen's complaints to their representatives in parliament, 1668.

Walcot, H[umphry], *Sea water made fresh and wholesome*, 1702.

Webster, Thomas, *Reports and notes of cases on letters patent for inventions*, 1844.

Wedgwood, Josiah, *Letters of Josiah Wedgwood*, ed. Katherine Farrar, 3 vols., Manchester, 1973.

Wendenborn, F. A. *A view of England towards the close of the eighteenth century*, 2 vols., Dublin, 1791.

Wilson, Jasper [James Currie], *A letter, commercial and political addressed to the Rt Hon. William Pitt*, 3rd edn, 1793.

Winstanley, Gerrard, *The law of freedom*, ed. Christopher Hill, Harmondsworth, 1973.

W[orlidge], J[ohn], *Systema agriculturae*, 2nd edn, 1675.

Wren, Christopher, *Life and works of Sir Christopher Wren*, ed. Ernest J. Enthoven, Campden, Glos., 1903.

Yarranton, Andrew, *England's improvement by sea and land*, 1677.

Yarranton, Andrew, *England's improvement by sea and land . . . the second part*, 1681.

[Young, Arthur], *Political essays concerning the present state of the British empire*, 1772, repr. New York, 1970.

Newspapers and journals

European Magazine
The Gentleman's Magazine
The London Gazette
The Philosophical Magazine
Post Man
Repertory of Arts and Manufactures
Scots Magazine

Works published after 1850

Adams, Robert M. 'In search of Baron Somers' in Perez Zagorin (ed.), *Culture and politics from Puritanism to the Enlightenment*, Los Angeles and London, 1980.

Albion, R. G. *Forests and sea power: the timber problem of the Royal Navy, 1652–1862*, Cambridge, Mass., 1926.

Allan, D. G. C. *William Shipley, founder of the Royal Society of Arts*, 1968.

Allen, J. S. 'The introduction of the Newcomen engine from 1710 to 1733', *T.N.S.*, 42 (1969–70), 169–90.

Anderson, B. L. 'Money and the structure of credit in the eighteenth century', *Business History*, 12 (1970), 85–101.

Andrews, Charles M. *British committees, commissions, and councils of trade and plantations, 1622–1675*, Baltimore, 1908.

Ashton, T. S. 'The discoveries of the Darbys of Coalbrookdale', *T.N.S.*, 5 (1924–5), 9–14.

Ashton, T. S. *The industrial revolution, 1760–1830*, Oxford, 1948.

Ashton, T. S. *Economic fluctuations in England, 1700–1800*, Oxford, 1959.

Ashton, T. S. *Iron and steel in the industrial revolution*, 4th edn, Manchester, 1968.

Ashton, T. S. 'Some statistics of the industrial revolution in Britain', repr. in A. E. Musson (ed.), *Science, technology and economic growth in the eighteenth century*, 1972.

Ashton, T. S. and J. Sykes, *The coal industry of the eighteenth century*, 2nd edn, Manchester, 1964.

Baker, R. *New and improved . . . inventors and inventions that have changed the modern world*, 1976.

Barker, T. C., R. Dickinson, and D. W. F. Hardie, 'The origins of the synthetic alkali industry in Britain', *Economica*, 23 (1956), 158–71.

Baugh, Daniel, *British naval administration in the age of Walpole*, Princeton, 1965.

Baynes, Ken, and Francis Pugh, *The art of the engineer*, Guildford, 1981.

Beattie, J. M. *Crime and the courts in England, 1660–1800*, Oxford, 1986.

Beckett, J. V. 'The eighteenth-century origins of the factory system: a case study from the 1740s', *Business History*, 19 (1977), 55–67.

Beckett, J. V. *Coal and tobacco; the Lowthers and the economic development of west Cumberland, 1660–1760*, Cambridge, 1981.

Beier, A. L. 'Engine of manufacture: the trades of London' in A. L. Beier and Roger Finlay (eds.), *The making of the metropolis: 1500–1700*, 1986.

Bennet, J. et al., *Science and profit in 18th-century London*, Whipple Museum, Cambridge, 1985.

Benton, J. H. *John Baskerville, type-founder and printer, 1706–1775*, 2nd edn, New York, 1944.

Benton, W. A. 'John Wyatt and the weighing of heavy loads', *T.N.S.*, 9 (1928–9), 60–77.

Berg, Maxine, *The machinery question and the making of political economy, 1815–1848*, Cambridge, 1980.

Berg, Maxine, *The age of manufactures, 1700–1820*, 1985.

Bessemer, Sir Henry, *An autobiography*, 1905.

Bimson, Mavis, 'References to John Dwight in a seventeenth-century manuscript', *Trans. English Ceramic Circle*, 4 (1959), pt 5, 10–12.

Bladen, V. W. 'The Potteries in the industrial revolution', *Economic Jnl, Economic History Supplement*, 1 (1926), 117–30.

Blaug, M. 'A survey of the theory of process innovation' in N. Rosenberg (ed.), *The economics of technological change*, 1971.

Boehm, Klaus, and Aubrey Silberston, *The British patent system: i, administration*, Cambridge, 1967.

Booker, Peter J. *A history of engineering drawing*, 1963.

Boucher, C. T. G. *John Rennie, 1761–1821*, Manchester, 1963.

Bowden, Witt, *Industrial society in England towards the end of the eighteenth century*, 2nd edn, 1965.

Brace, Harold W. *History of seed crushing in Great Britain*, 1960.

Brewster, D. 'On Sir Christopher Wren's cypher', *Reports of the British Association for the Advancement of Science*, 1859.

British Museum, *Catalogue of prints and drawings in the British Museum*, 6 vols., 1870.

Brown, P. S. 'Medicines advertised in eighteenth-century Bath newspapers', *Medical History*, 20 (1976), 152–68.

Bryson, W. H. *The equity side of the Exchequer*, Cambridge, 1975.

Buckatzsch, E. 'The geographical distribution of wealth in England, 1086–1843', *Ec.H.R.*, 2nd ser. 3 (1950), 180–202.

Buckley, Francis, 'The early glasshouses of Bristol', *Jnl Society of Glass Technology*, 9 (1925), 36–61.

Burton, Anthony, *Josiah Wedgwood, a biography*, 1976.

Campbell, Lord John, *The lives of the Lord Chancellors*, 8 vols., 1845–69.

Cardwell, D. S. L. *Technology, science and history*, 1972.

Carswell, John, *The South Sea Bubble*, 1960.

Chaloner, W. H. 'The birth of modern Manchester' in C. F. Carter (ed.), *Manchester and its region*, Manchester, 1962.

Chapman, S. D. *The early factory masters*, Newton Abbot, 1967.

Chapman, S. D. 'Fixed capital formation in the British cotton industry, 1770–1815', *Ec.H.R.*, 2nd ser. 23 (1970), 235–66.

Chapman, S. D. 'Industrial capital before the industrial revolution' in N. B. Harte and K. G. Ponting (eds.), *Textile history and economic history: essays in honour of Miss Julia de Lacy Mann*, Manchester, 1973.

Chapman, S. D. 'Enterprise and innovation in the British hosiery industry, 1750–1850', *Textile History*, 5 (1974), 14–37.

Chapman, S. D. 'British marketing enterprise: the changing roles of merchants, manufacturers, and financiers, 1700–1860', *Business History Review*, 53 (1979), 205–33.

Chapman, S. D. and S. Chassagne, *European textile printers in the eighteenth century*, 1981.

Charleston, R. J. (ed.), *English porcelain, 1745–1850*, 1965.

Chilton, Paul, 'Nukespeak: nuclear language, culture and propaganda' in Crispin Aubrey (ed.), *Nukespeak: the media and the bomb*, 1982.

Cipolla, Carlo, *Clocks and culture*, 1967.

Clapham, J. H. *The economic history of modern Britain*, 3 vols., Cambridge, 1926–38.

Clark, Sir George, *A history of the Royal College of Physicians of London*, 3 vols., Oxford, 1966.

Clark-Kennedy, A. E. *Stephen Hales, D.D., F.R.S., an eighteenth-century biography*, Cambridge, 1929.

Clarke, Desmond, *The ingenious Mr Edgeworth*, 1965.

Clarkson, L. A. 'The organization of the English leather industry in the late sixteenth and seventeenth centuries', *Ec.H.R.*, 2nd ser. 13 (1960–1), 245–53.

Clarkson, L. A. 'English economic policy in the sixteenth and seventeenth centuries: the case of the leather industries', *B.I.H.R.*, 38 (1965), 149–62.

Clarkson, L. A. *The pre-industrial economy of England, 1500–1750*, 1971.

Clay, Christopher, *Public finance and private wealth: the career of Sir Stephen Fox, 1627–1716*, Oxford, 1978.

Clayton, Muriel, and Alma Oakes, 'Early calico printers around London', *Burlington Magazine*, 96 (1954), 135–8.

Clow, Archibald, and Nan L. Clow, *The chemical revolution: a contribution to social technology*, 1952.

Cochrane, Rexmond C. 'Francis Bacon and the rise of the mechanical arts in eighteenth-century England', *Annals of Science*, 12 (1956), 137–56.

Coleman, D. C. 'Labour in the English economy of the seventeenth century', *Ec.H.R.*, 2nd ser. 8 (1956), 280–95.

Coleman, D. C. *The British paper industry, 1495–1860: a study in industrial growth*, Oxford, 1958.

Coleman, D. C. 'Technology and economic history, 1500–1750', *Ec.H.R.*, 2nd ser. 11 (1958), 506–14.

Coleman, D. C. 'Textile growth' in N. B. Harte and K. G. Ponting (eds.), *Textile history and economic history: essays in honour of Miss Julia de Lacy Mann*, Manchester, 1973.

Coleman, D. C. *The economy of England, 1450–1750*, Oxford, 1977.

Coleman, D. C. and Christine MacLeod, 'Attitudes to new technology: British businessmen, 1800–1950', *Ec.H.R.*, 2nd ser. 39 (1986), 588–611.

Coleman, W. 'Providence, capitalism and environmental degradation: English apologetics in an era of economic revolution', *J.H.I.*, 37 (1976), 27–44.

Collins, E. J. T. 'Harvest technology and labour supply, 1790–1870', *Ec.H.R.*, 2nd ser. 22 (1969), 453–73.

Cooper, Carolyn C. 'The Portsmouth system of manufacture', *Technology and Culture*, 25 (1984), 182–225.

Corfield, P. J. *The impact of English towns, 1700–1800*, Oxford, 1982.

Coryton, J. *A treatise on the law of letters patent*, 1855.

Crafts, N. F. R. 'The industrial revolution in England and France: some thoughts on the question "Why was England first"', *Ec.H.R.*, 2nd ser. 30 (1977), 429–41.

Crafts, N. F. R. 'The eighteenth century: a survey' in Roderick Floud and Donald McCloskey (eds.), *The economic history of Britain since 1700: volume 1, 1700–1860*, Cambridge, 1981.

Crafts, N. F. R. *British economic growth during the industrial revolution*, Oxford, 1985.

Craig, Sir John, *The Mint: a history of the London Mint from A.D.287 to 1948*, Cambridge, 1953.

Cranfield, G. A. *The development of the provincial newspaper*, Oxford, 1962.

Crellin, J. K. 'Dr James's fever powder', *Trans. British Society for the History of Pharmacy*, 1 (1974), 136–43.

Crouzet, François, 'Angleterre et France au XVIIIe siècle', *Annales E.S.C.*, 21 (1966), 254–91.

Crouzet, François, *The first industrialists*, Cambridge, 1984.

Cunningham, W. *The growth of English industry and commerce*, 3rd edn, 3 vols., Cambridge, 1896–1903.

Daniels, George W. *The early English cotton industry*, Manchester, 1920.

Daumas, Maurice, *Scientific instruments of the seventeenth and eighteenth centuries and their makers*, trans. M. Holbrook, 1972.

Davidson, Caroline, *A woman's work is never done: a history of housework in the British Isles, 1650–1950*, 1982.

Davies, D. Seaborne, 'The early history of the patent specification', *L.Q.R.*, 50 (1934), 86–109, 260–74.

Davis, Ralph, *The rise of the English shipping industry in the seventeenth and eighteenth centuries*, Newton Abbot, 1962.

Davis, Ralph, 'The rise of protection in England, 1689–1786', *Ec.H.R.*, 2nd ser. 19 (1966), 306–17.

Deane, Phyllis, *The first industrial revolution*, Cambridge, 1965.

Deerr, Noel, 'The early use of steam power in the cane sugar industry', *T.N.S.*, 21 (1940–1), 11–21.

Des Fontaines, J. D. 'The Society of Arts and the early Wedgwoods', *Jnl of the Royal Society of Arts*, 119 (1971), 327–31, 407–10.

Dewhurst, Kenneth, *The quicksilver doctor: the life and times of Thomas Dover, physician and adventurer*, Bristol, 1957.

Dickenson, M. J. 'Fulling in the West Riding woollen cloth industry, 1689–1770', *Textile History*, 10 (1979), 127–42.

Dickinson, H. W. *Matthew Boulton*, Cambridge, 1937.

Dickinson, H. W. 'The origin and manufacture of wood screws', *T.N.S.*, 22 (1941–2), 79–89.

Dickinson, H. W. 'Joseph Bramah and his inventions', *T.N.S.*, 22 (1941–2), 169–86.

Dickinson, H. W. 'Richard Roberts, his life and inventions', *T.N.S.*, 25 (1945–7), 123–37.

Dickinson, H. W. 'The Taylors of Southampton: their ships' blocks, circular saws and ships' pumps', *T.N.S.*, 29 (1953–5), 169–78.

Dickinson, H. W. *A short history of the steam engine*, 2nd edn, 1963.

Dickson, P. G. M. *The financial revolution in England: a study in the development of public credit, 1688–1756*, 1967.

Dobson, C. R. *Masters and journeymen: a pre-history of industrial relations, 1717–1800*, 1980.

Doorman, G. *Patents for invention in the Netherlands*, trans. Joh. Meijer, The Hague, 1942.

Dubois, Armand Budington, *The English business company after the Bubble Act, 1720–1800*, New York, 1938.

Duckham, Baron F. 'Canals and river navigation' in Derek E. Aldcroft and Michael J. Freeman (eds.), *Transport in the industrial revolution*, Manchester, 1983.

Dutton, H. I. *The patent system and inventive activity during the industrial revolution*, Manchester, 1984.

Earle, Peter, *The wreck of the Almiranta: Sir William Phips and the search for the Hispaniola treasure*, 1979.

Edwards, Rhoda, 'London potters *circa* 1570–1710', *Jnl of Ceramic History*, 6 (1974), 1–141.

Ehrman, John, *The navy in the war of William III, 1689–1697*, Cambridge, 1953.

Ellis, Joyce, 'The decline and fall of the Tyneside salt industry, 1660–1790: a re-examination', *Ec.H.R.*, 2nd ser. 33 (1980), 45–58.

Entwistle, E. A. 'The Blew Paper Warehouse in Aldermanbury, London', *Connoisseur*, 125 (1950), 94–8.

Eversley, D. E. C. 'The home market and economic growth in England, 1750–80', in E. L. Jones and G. E. Mingay (eds.), *Land, labour and population in the industrial revolution*, 1967.

Fairlie, Susan, 'Dyestuffs in the eighteenth century', *Ec.H.R.*, 2nd ser. 17 (1965–6), 488–510.

Feinstein, C. H. 'Capital formation in Great Britain' in Peter Mathias and M. M. Postan (eds.), *The Cambridge economic history of Europe*, vol. 7, pt 1 (Cambridge, 1978).

Feinstein, C. H. 'Capital accumulation and the industrial revolution' in Roderick Floud and Donald McCloskey (eds.), *The economic history of Britain since 1700: volume 1, 1700–1860*, Cambridge, 1981.

Felkin, William, *Felkin's history of the machine-wrought hosiery and lace manufactures*, ed. S. D. Chapman, Newton Abbot, 1967.

Finlay, Roger, and Beatrice Shearer, 'Population growth and suburban expansion' in A. L. Beier and Roger Finlay (eds.), *The making of the metropolis: 1500–1700*, 1986.

Fitton, R. S. and A. P. Wadsworth, *The Strutts and the Arkwrights, 1758–1830*, Manchester, 1958.

Flinn, M. W. 'The travel diaries of Swedish engineers in the eighteenth century as sources of technological history', *T.N.S.*, 31 (1957–9), 95–109.

Flinn, M. W. 'Timber and the advance of technology: a reconsideration', *Annals of Science*, 15 (1959), 109–20.

Flinn, M. W. *The history of the British coal industry, volume 2, 1700–1830: the industrial revolution*, Oxford, 1984.

Forward, A. E. 'The early history of the cylinder boring machine' *T.N.S.*, 5 (1924–5), 24–38.

Foster, Elizabeth Read, 'The procedure of the House of Commons against patents and monopolies, 1621–1624' in W. A. Aiken and B. D. Henning (eds.), *Conflict in Stuart England: essays in honour of Wallace Notestein*, 1960.

Fox, Harold G. *Monopolies and patents: a study of the history and future of the patent monopoly*, Toronto, 1947.

Francis, A. J. *The cement industry, 1796–1914: a history*, Newton Abbot, 1977.

Frumkin, Maximilian, 'Early history of patents for invention', *T.N.S.*, 26 (1947), 47–55.

Fry, A. Ruth, *John Bellers 1654–1725, Quaker, economist and social reformer*, 1935.

Furniss, Edgar S. *The position of the labourer in a system of nationalism*, Cambridge, Mass., 1920.

Fussell, G. E. *More old English farming books from Tull to the Board of Agriculture, 1731–1793*, 1950.

Fussell, G. E. *The farmer's tools, 1500–1900*, 1952.

Fussell, G. E. *Jethro Tull: his influence on mechanized agriculture*, Reading, 1973.

Garner, F. H. 'John Dwight, some contemporary references', *Trans. English Ceramic Circle*, 1 (1937), pt 5, 30–7.

Gauldie, Enid, 'Mechanical aids to linen bleaching in Scotland', *Textile History*, 1 (1969), 129–57.

George, M. D. *London life in the eighteenth century*, 1966.

Getz, L. 'History of the patentee's obligation in Great Britain', *Jnl of the Patent Office Society*, 46 (1964), 68–81.

Gibbs, F. W. 'Bryan Higgins and his circle' in A. E. Musson (ed.), *Science, technology, and economic growth in the eighteenth century*, 1972.

Gilboy, Elizabeth W. *Wages in eighteenth century England*, Cambridge, Mass., 1934.

Girtin, T. *The mark of the sword: a narrative history of the Cutlers Company, 1689–1975*, 1975.

Gittens, L. 'Soapmaking and the excise laws, 1711–1853', *Industrial Archaeology Review*, 1 (1976–7), 265–75.

Godfrey, Eleanor S. *The development of English glassmaking, 1560–1640*, Oxford, 1975.

Godfrey, Richard T. *Printmaking in Britain*, Oxford, 1978.

Gomme, A. A. 'Date corrections of English patents, 1617–1752', *T.N.S.*, 13 (1932–3), 159–64.

Gomme, A. A. 'Patent practice in the 18th century: the diary of Samuel Taylor, threadmaker and inventor, 1722–3', *T.N.S.*, 15 (1934–5), 209–24.

Gomme, A. A. *Patents of invention: origin and growth of the patent system in Britain*, 1946.

Goodison, Nicholas, *English barometers, 1680–1860*, 1969.

Gordon, J. W. *Monopolies by patents, and the suitable remedies available to the public*, 1897.

Grace, D. R. and D. C. Phillips, *Ransomes of Ipswich: a history of the firm and a guide to its records*, Reading, 1975.

Griffenhagen, George, *Medicine tax stamps worldwide*, Milwaukee, 1971.

Griffiths, D. 'The exclusion of women from technology' in Wendy Faulkner and Erik Arnold (eds.), *Smothered by invention: technology in women's lives*, London and Sydney, 1985.

Hahn, Roger, *The anatomy of a scientific institution: the Paris Academy of Sciences, 1666–1803*, 1971.

Hall, A. R. 'Robert Hooke and horology', *Notes and Records of the Royal Society of London*, 8 (1950–1), 167–77.

Harding, H. *Patent Office centenary*, 1952.

Harding, Rosamond, *The piano-forte: its history traced to the Great Exhibition of 1851*, 2nd edn, Cambridge, 1978.

Harley, C. K. 'British industrialization before 1841: evidence of slower growth during the industrial revolution', *Jnl Econ. Hist.*, 42 (1982), 267–89.

Harley, J. B. 'The re-mapping of England, 1750–1800', *Imago Mundi*, 19 (1965), 56–67.

Harris, J. R. *Industry and technology in the eighteenth century: Britain and France*, Birmingham, 1972.

Harris, J. R. 'Skills, coal and British industry in the eighteenth century', *History*, 61 (1976), 167–82.

Harris, T. R. 'Engineering in Cornwall before 1775', *T.N.S.*, 25 (1945–7), 111–22.

Hatcher, John, and T. C. Barker, *A history of British pewter*, 1974.

Hesse, Mary B. 'Hooke's philosophical algebra', *Isis*, 57 (1966), 67–83.

Hewish, John, *The indefatigable Mr Woodcroft*, 1982.

Hey, David, *The rural metalworkers of the Sheffield region*, Leicester University, Dept of English Local History, Occasional Papers, 2nd ser. no. 5 (1972).

Hildebrand, K-G. 'Foreign markets for Swedish iron in the eighteenth century', *Scandinavian Economic History Review*, 6 (1958), 3–52.

Hills, Richard L. *Power in the industrial revolution*, Manchester, 1970.

Hinton, R. W. K. 'The decline of parliamentary government under Elizabeth I and the early Stuarts', *Cambridge Historical Jnl*, 13 (1957), 116–32.

Hodgen, Margaret T. 'Sir Matthew Hale and the "method" of invention', *Isis*, 34 (1943), 313–18.

Holdsworth, William, *A history of English law*, 17 vols., 1922–72.

Holmes, Geoffrey, *Augustan England: professions, state, and society, 1680–1730*, 1982.

Hont, Istvan, 'The "rich country–poor country" debate in Scottish classical political economy' in Istvan Hont and Michael Ignatieff (eds.), *Wealth and virtue: the shaping of political economy in the Scottish Enlightenment*, Cambridge, 1983.

Hoppit, Julian, 'Financial crises in eighteenth-century England', *Ec.H.R.*, 2nd ser. 39 (1986), 39–58.

Houghton, Walter E. 'The history of trades', *J.H.I.*, 2 (1941), 33–60.

Houghton, Walter E. 'The English virtuoso in the seventeenth century', *J.H.I.*, 3 (1942), 51–73, 190–219.

Hudson D. and K. W. Luckhurst, *The Royal Society of Arts, 1754–1954*, 1956.

Hughes, Edward, *Studies in administration and finance, 1558–1825*, Manchester, 1934.

Hughes, Edward, 'The first steam engine in the Durham coalfield', *Archaeologia Aeliana*, 4th ser. 27 (1949), 29–45.

Hulme, E. Wyndham, 'The history of the patent system under the prerogative and at common law', *L.Q.R.*, 12 (1896), 141–54.

Hulme, E. Wyndham, 'On the consideration of the patent grant, past and present', *L.Q.R.*, 13 (1897), 313–18.

Hulme, E. Wyndham, 'The history of the patent system under the prerogative and at common law: a sequel', *L.Q.R.*, 16 (1900), 44–56.

Hulme, E. Wyndham, 'On the history of patent law in the seventeenth and eighteenth centuries', *L.Q.R.*, 18 (1902), 280–8.

Hulme, E. Wyndham, 'Privy Council law and practice of letters patent for invention from the Restoration to 1794', *L.Q.R.*, 33 (1917), 63–75, 181–95.

Hunter, Michael, *Science and society in Restoration England*, Cambridge, 1981.

Hyde, Charles K. *Technological change and the British iron industry*, Princeton, 1977.

Jenkins, D. T. *The West Riding wool textile industry, 1770–1835*, Edington, 1975.

Jenkins, D. T. and K. G. Ponting, *The British wool textile industry, 1770–1914*, 1982.

Jenkins, Rhys, 'The protection of inventions during the Commonwealth and Protectorate', *Notes and Queries*, 11th ser. 7 (1913), 162–3.

Jenkins, Rhys, 'Savery, Newcomen and the early history of the steam engine', *T.N.S.*, 3 (1922–3), 96–118.

Jewitt, Llewellyn, *The ceramic art of Great Britain*, 2 vols., 1878.

Jewkes, John, David Sawyers, and Richard Stillerman, *The sources of invention*, 2nd edn, 1969.

John, A. H. 'Farming in wartime: 1793–1815' in E. L. Jones and G. E. Mingay (eds.), *Land, labour and population in the industrial revolution*, 1967.

Johnson, Edgar A. J. 'The mercantilist concept of "art" and "ingenious labour"', *Economic Jnl, Economic History Supplement*, 2 (1930–3), 234–53.

Jones, E. L. 'Agriculture, 1700–1800' in Roderick Floud and Donald McCloskey (eds.), *The economic history of Britain since 1700: volume 1, 1700–1860*, Cambridge, 1981.

Jones, J. R. *The revolution of 1688 in England*, 1972.

Jones, Richard Foster, *Ancients and moderns: a study of the rise of the scientific movement in seventeenth-century England*, 2nd edn, St Louis, 1961.

Kanefsky, John, and John Robey, 'Steam engines in 18th-century Britain: a quantitative assessment', *Technology and Culture*, 21 (1980), 161–86.

Keller, A. C. 'Zilsel, the artisans and the idea of progress in the Renaissance', *J.H.I.*, 11 (1950), 235–40.

Keller, A. C. 'Kepler, the art of flight and the vision of interplanetary travel as the next great invention', *Procs. XIIIth International Congress of the History of Science, Moscow 1971*, 1974, vol. 12.

Kellett, J. R. 'The breakdown of gild and corporation control', *Ec.H.R.*, 2nd ser. 10 (1957–8), 381–94.

King, Henry C. *The history of the telescope*, 1955.

Klingender, Francis D. *Art and the industrial revolution*, 3rd edn, ed. Arthur Elton, 1972.

Kneale, W. C. 'The idea of invention', *Proceedings of the British Academy*, 41 (1955), 85–108.

Koebner, R. 'Adam Smith and the industrial revolution', *Ec.H.R.*, 2nd ser. 11 (1959), 381–91.

Kovacevich, Ivanka, 'The mechanical muse: the impact of technical inventions on eighteenth-century neoclassical poetry', *Huntington Library Quarterly*, 28 (1964–5), 263–81.

Kuznets, Simon, 'Inventive activity: problems of definition and measurement' in Richard R. Nelson (ed.), *The rate and direction of inventive activity*, Princeton, 1962.

Landes, David S. *The unbound Prometheus: technological change and industrial developments in western Europe from 1750 to the present*, Cambridge, 1969.

Leader, R. E. *A history of the Cutlers' Company of Hallamshire*, 2 vols., Sheffield, 1905.

Lindert, P. H. 'English occupations, 1670–1811', *Jnl Econ. Hist.*, 40 (1980), 685–712.

Lipson, E. *The economic history of England*, 3 vols., 1934.

Lloyd, G. I. H. *The cutlery trades*, 1913.

Lord, John, *Capital and steam power, 1750–1800*, 2nd edn, 1966.

McCloskey, D. N. 'The industrial revolution, 1780–1860: a survey' in Roderick Floud and Donald McCloskey (eds.), *The economic history of Britain: volume 1, 1700–1860*, Cambridge, 1981.

MacDonald, S. 'Progress of the early threshing machine', *Agricultural History Review*, 23 (1975), 63–77.

McElroy, Davis D. *Scotland's age of improvement: a survey of eighteenth-century clubs and societies*, Washington State University, 1969.

McKendrick, N. 'The consumer revolution in eighteenth-century England' in N. McKendrick, J. H. Plumb, and J. Brewer (eds.), *The birth of a consumer society: the commercialization of eighteenth-century England*, 1982.

Mackenna, F. Severne, *Cookworthy's Plymouth and Bristol procelain*, Leigh-on-Sea, 1946.

Mackenna, F. Severne, *Champion's Bristol porcelain*, Leigh-on-Sea, 1947.

McKie, D. 'James, Duke of York, F.R.S.', *Notes and Records of the Royal Society of London*, 13 (1958), 6–18.

MacLeod, Christine, 'Henry Martin and the authorship of "Considerations upon the East India trade"', *B.I.H.R.*, 56 (1983), 222–9.

MacLeod, Christine, 'The 1690s patents boom: invention or stock-jobbing?', *Ec.H.R.*, 2nd ser. 39 (1986), 549–71.

MacLeod, Christine, 'Accident or design? George Ravenscroft's patent and the invention of lead-crystal glass', *Technology and Culture*, 28 (1987), 776–803.

Macpherson, C. B. *The political theory of possessive individualism*, Oxford, 1962.

McNeil, Ian, *Joseph Bramah: a century of invention, 1749–1851*, Newton Abbot, 1968.

Machin, R. 'The great rebuilding: a reassessment', *Past & Present*, 77 (1977), 33–56.

Maddison, R. E. W. 'Studies in the life of Robert Boyle, F.R.S.; part ii, salt water freshened', *Notes and Records of the Royal Society of London*, 9 (1952), 196–213.

Malament, Barbara, 'The "economic liberalism" of Sir Edward Coke', *Yale Law Jnl*, 76 (1967), 1321–58.

Mann, Julia de Lacy, *The cloth industry in the west of England from 1640 to 1880*, Oxford, 1971.

Mathias, Peter, *The brewing industry in England, 1700–1830*, Cambridge, 1959.

Mathias, Peter, *The first industrial nation: an economic history of Britain, 1700–1914*, 1969.

Mathias, Peter, 'Skills and the diffusion of innovation from Britain in the eighteenth century', *T.R.H.S.*, 5th ser. 25 (1977), 90–113.

Mathias, Peter, *The transformation of England*, 1979.

Matthews, Leslie G. *History of pharmacy in Great Britain*, Edinburgh and London, 1962.

Meteyard, Eliza, *The life of Josiah Wedgwood*, ed. R. W. Lightbourn, 2 vols., 1970.

Minchinton, W. E. *The British tinplate industry, a history*, Oxford, 1957.

Mingay, G. E. 'The size of farms in the eighteenth century', *Ec.H.R.*, 2nd ser. 14 (1961–2), 469–88.

Mingay, G. E. (ed.), *Arthur Young and his times*, 1975.

Mitchell, B. R. and Phyllis Deane, *Abstract of British historical statistics*, 2nd edn, Cambridge, 1971.

Mumford, Lewis, *Technics and civilization*, 1934.

Musson, A. E. (ed.), *Science, technology and economic growth in the eighteenth century*, 1972.

Musson, A. E. 'Industrial motive power in the United Kingdom, 1800–70', *Ec.H.R.*, 2nd ser. 29 (1976), 415–39.

Musson, A. E. *The growth of British industry*, 1978.

Musson A. E. and Eric Robinson, *Science and technology in the industrial revolution*, Manchester, 1969.

Nasmyth, James, *James Nasmyth engineer, an autobiography*, ed. Samuel Smiles, 1883.

Nef, J. U. 'The progress of technology and the growth of large-scale industry in Great Britain, 1540–1640', *Ec.H.R.*, 1st ser. 5 (1934), 3–24.

Nicolson, Marjorie H. 'The microscope and the English imagination', *Smith College Studies in Modern Languages*, 16 (1935).

Nicolson, Marjorie H. 'A world in the moon', *Smith College Studies in Modern Languages*, 17 (1936).

Nockolds, Harold, *The Coachmakers: a history of the Worshipful Company of Coachmakers and Coach Harness Makers, 1677–1977*, 1977.

Novak, Maximilian E. *Economics and the fiction of Daniel Defoe*, Berkeley and Los Angeles, 1962.

Padley, Richard, 'The beginnings of the British alkali industry', *Birmingham Historical Jnl*, 3 (1951), 64–78.

Parker, Harold T. 'French administrators and French scientists during the Old Regime and the early years of the Revolution' in Richard Herr and Harold T. Parker (eds.), *Ideas in history, essays presented to Louis Gottschalk*, Durham, N.C., 1965.

Parker, Harold T. *The Bureau of Commerce in 1781 and its policies with respect to French industry*, Durham, N. Carolina, 1979.

Paulinyi, Akos, 'Revolution and technology' in Roy Porter and Mikulas Teich (eds.), *Revolution in history*, Cambridge, 1986.

Pelling, Margaret, 'Medical practice in early modern England: trade or profession?' in Wilfrid Prest (ed.), *The professions in early modern England* (London, New York and Sydney, 1987).

Perez, Liliane, 'Le "Privilège", source d'histoire économique et révélateur d'une politique au XVIIIe siècle' in F. Caron (ed.), *Les Brevets: leur utilisation en histoire des techniques et de l'économie*, Table Ronde, C.N.R.S. 1984, Paris, 1985.

Perez, Liliane, 'Les Cadres de l'inventivité en France et en Angleterre au XVIIIe siècle', *Sources*, 1 (1986), 29–39.

Plant, Arnold, 'The economic theory concerning patents for invention', *Economica*, 1 (1934), 30–51.

Plant, Marjorie, *The English book trade*, 1974.

Plummer, Alfred, *The London Weavers Company, 1600–1970*, 1972.

Pocock, J. G. A. 'Early modern capitalism: the Augustan perception' in E. Kamenka and R. Neale (eds.), *Feudalism, capitalism and beyond*, 1975.

Pole, William (ed.), *The life of Sir William Fairbairn, Bart.*, 1877, repr. Newton Abbot, 1970.

Pollard, S. 'Fixed capital in the industrial revolution in Britain' in François Crouzet (ed.), *Capital formation in the industrial revolution*, 1972.

Pollard, S. 'Labour in Great Britain' in Peter Mathias and M. M. Postan (eds.), *The Cambridge economic history of Europe*, vol. 7, pt 1 (Cambridge, 1978).

Post, Robert C. '"Liberalizers" versus "scientific men" in the antebellum Patent Office', *Technology and Culture*, 17 (1976), 24–54.

Power, M. J. 'The social topography of Restoration London' in A. L. Beier and Roger Finlay (eds.), *The making of the metropolis: 1500–1700*, 1986.

Prager, Frank D. 'A history of intellectual property from 1547 to 1787', *Jnl of the Patent Office Society*, 26 (1944), 714–19.

Prager, Frank D. 'Examination of inventions from the middle ages to 1836', *Jnl of the Patent Office Society*, 46 (1964).

Price, William Hyde, *The English patents of monopoly*, Harvard Economic Studies, vol. 1, 1906.

Prior, M. E. 'Bacon's man of science', *J.H.I.*, 15 (1954), 348–70.

Prosser, R. B. *Birmingham inventors and inventions*, Birmingham, 1881.

Quill, Humphrey, *John Harrison, the man who found longitude*, New York, 1966.

Raistrick, Arthur, *Dynasty of iron founders: the Darbys and Coalbrookdale*, repr. Newton Abbot, 1970.

Randall, Adrian J. 'The philosophy of Luddism: the case of the west of England woolen workers, ca.1790–1809', *Technology and Culture*, 27 (1986), 1–17.

Rees, William, *Industry before the industrial revolution*, 2 vols., Cardiff, 1968.

Rimmer, W. G. *Marshalls of Leeds, flax spinners, 1788–1886*, Cambridge, 1960.

Robinson, Eric, 'Eighteenth-century commerce and fashion: Matthew Boulton's marketing techniques', *Ec.H.R.*, 2nd ser. 16 (1963–4), 39–60.

Robinson, Eric, 'James Watt and the law of patents', *Technology and Culture*, 13 (1972), 115–39.

Robinson, Eric and Douglas McKie, (eds.), *Partners in science: letters of James Watt and Joseph Black*, 1970.

Rolt, L. T. C. *Tools for the job: a short history of machine tools*, 1965.

Rolt, L. T. C. *The aeronauts: a history of ballooning, 1783–1903*, 2nd edn, Gloucester, 1985.

Rolt, L. T. C. and J. S. Allen, *The steam engine of Thomas Newcomen*, Hartington, 1977.

Rosenberg, Nathan, *Perspectives on technology*, Cambridge, 1976.

Rosenberg, Nathan, *Inside the black box: technology and economics*, Cambridge, 1982.

Rossi, Paolo, *Philosophy, technology and the arts in the early modern era*, trans. Salvator Attanasio, ed. Benjamin Nelson, New York, 1970.

Rostow, W. W. *How it all began: origins of the modern economy*, 1975.

Rowbottom, Margaret E. 'The earliest published writing of Robert Boyle', *Annals of Science*, 6 (1950), 376–89.

Rowe, D. J. *Lead manufacturing in Britain: a history*, 1983.

Rowlands, Marie B. *Masters and men*, Manchester, 1975.

Rubin, G. R. and David Sugarman (eds.), *Law, economy and society: essays in the history of English law, 1750–1914*, Abingdon, 1984.

Rubinstein, W. D. *Men of property: the very wealthy in Britain since the industrial revolution*, 1981.

Rudé, George, *Hanoverian London, 1714–1808*, 1971.

Rushen, Percy C. *The history and antiquities of Chipping Camden, in the county of Gloucester*, Woodbridge, 1899.

Sachse, William Lewis, *Lord Somers: a political portrait*, Manchester, 1975.

Samuel, Raphael, 'The workshop of the world: steam power and hand technology in mid-Victorian Britain', *History Workshop*, 3 (1972), 6–72.

Samuelson, Paul A., *Economics*, 9th edn, Tokyo, 1973.

Schechter, Frank Isaac, *The historical foundation of the law relating to trade-marks*, Columbia Legal Studies, vol. 1, New York, 1925.

Schmookler, Jacob, *Invention and economic growth*, Cambridge, Mass., 1966.

Schofield, Robert E. *The Lunar Society of Birmingham*, Oxford, 1963.

Schubert, H. R. *History of the British iron and steel industry*, 1957.

Schumpeter, Joseph A. *History of economic analysis*, ed. E. B. Schumpeter, 1954.

Schwarz, L. D. 'Income distribution and social structure in London in the late eighteenth century', *Ec.H.R.*, 2nd ser. 32 (1977), 250–9.

Scott, William R. *The constitution and finance of English, Scottish and Irish joint-stock companies to 1720*, 3 vols., Cambridge, 1912.

Scoville, Warren C. 'The Huguenots and the diffusion of technology', *Jnl of Political Economy*, 60 (1952), 294–311.

Sedgwick, Romney (ed.), *The House of Commons, 1715–1754*, 2 vols., 1970.

Sekora, John, *Luxury: the concept in western thought*, Baltimore, 1979.

Shapin, Steven, 'Property, patronage and the politics of science: the founding of the Royal Society of Edinburgh', *British Jnl for the History of Science*, 7 (1974), 1–41.

Shaw, W. A. *Letters of denization and acts of naturalization for aliens in England and Ireland*, The Publications of the Huguenot Society of London, vol. 18 (1911), vol. 27 (1923).

Sheppard, Francis, *London 1808–1870: the infernal wen*, 1971.

Sheridan, Richard B. *Sugar and slavery: an economic history of the British West Indies, 1623–1775*, Barbados, 1974.

Singer, Charles, and E. A. Underwood, *A short history of medicine*, 2nd edn, Oxford, 1962.

Skempton, A. W. 'The engineers of the English river navigation, 1620–1760', *T.N.S.*, 29 (1953–5), 36–50.

Smiles, Samuel, *Industrial biography: iron workers and tool makers*, ed. L. T. C. Rolt, Newton Abbot, 1967.

Smiles, Samuel, *Lives of the engineers*, ed. L. T. C. Rolt, 3 vols., Newton Abbot, 1968.

Smith, Alan, 'Steam and the City: the Committee of Proprietors of the Invention for Raising Water by Fire, 1715–35', *T.N.S.*, 49 (1977–8), 5–20.

Snell, Keith, *Annals of the labouring poor: social change and agrarian England, 1660–1900*, Cambridge, 1985.

Spate, O. H. K. 'Geographical aspects of the industrial evolution of London till 1850', *Geographical Jnl*, 92 (1938), 422–32.

Stander, S. 'Eighteenth-century patent medicines', *History of Medicine*, 7 (1976).

Supple, B. E. *Commercial crisis and change in England, 1600–1642*, Cambridge, 1959.

Tann, Jennifer, 'The bleaching of woollen and worsted goods, 1740–1860', *Textile History*, 1 (1969), 158–69.

Tann, Jennifer, 'Fuel saving in the process industries during the industrial revolution: a study in technological diffusion', *Business History*, 15 (1973), 149–59.

Tann, Jennifer, 'The textile millwright in the early industrial revolution', *Textile History*, 5 (1974), 80–9.

Tann, Jennifer, 'Makers of improved Newcomen engines in the late 18th century', *T.N.S.*, 50 (1978–9), 181–92.

Tann, Jennifer, 'Mr Hornblower and his crew: Watt engine pirates at the end of the 18th century', *T.N.S.*, 51 (1979–80), 95–105.

Taylor, E. G. R. *The mathematical practitioners of Hanoverian England, 1714–1840*, Cambridge, 1966.

Thirsk, Joan, *Economic policy and projects: the development of a consumer society in early modern England*, Oxford, 1978.

Thirsk, Joan, (ed.), *The agrarian history of England and Wales*, vol. 5, Cambridge, 1985.

Thomas, Brinley, 'Escaping from constraints: the industrial revolution in a Malthusian context', *Jnl Interdisciplinary History*, 15 (1985), 729–53.

Thomas, Brinley, 'Was there an energy crisis in Great Britain in the 17th century?', *Explorations in Economic History*, 23 (1986), 124–52.

Thomas, P. J. 'The pottery industry in the industrial revolution', *Economic Jnl, Economic History Supplement*, 3 (1934–7), 399–414.

Thomas, P. J. *Mercantilism and the East India trade*, 1963.

Thomis, Malcolm I. *Responses to industrialization: the British experience, 1780–1850*, Newton Abbot, 1976.

Thompson, E. P. 'The moral economy of the English crowd in the eighteenth century', *Past & Present*, 50 (1971), 76–136.

Thorndike, Lynn, *A history of magic and experimental science*, 8 vols., New York, 1958.

Thornton, Peter, *Baroque and rococo silks*, 1965.

Trengrove, L. 'Chemistry at the Royal Society of London in the eighteenth century', *Annals of Science*, 19 (1963), 187–237.

Tookey, Geoffrey W. 'Patents and public policy under the British common law' in Association Internationale pour la Protection de la Propriété Industrielle, *Venetian patent law*, Milan, 1974.

Usher, A. P. *A history of mechanical inventions*, 2nd edn, Cambridge, Mass., 1954.

Victoria County History, Essex, vol. 2.

Victoria County History, Suffolk, vol. 2.

Viseltear, A. J. 'The last illness of Sir Robert Walpole', *Bulletin of the History of Medicine*, 41 (1967), 195–207.

Viseltear, A. J. 'Joanna Stephens and the eighteenth-century lithontropics', *Bulletin of the History of Medicine*, 42 (1968), 199–220.

Von Tunzelmann, G. N. 'Technical progress during the industrial revolution' in Roderick Floud and Donald McCloskey (eds.), *The economic history of Britain since 1700: volume i, 1700–1860*, Cambridge, 1981.

Wadsworth, A. P. and J. de L. Mann, *The cotton trade and industrial Lancashire, 1600–1870*, repr. Manchester, 1965.

Wagner, Donald O. 'Coke and the rise of economic liberalism', *Ec.H.R.*, 1st ser. 6 (1935–6), 30–44.

Wailes, Rex, 'Windmill winding gear', *T.N.S.*, 25 (1945–7), 27–35.

Wailes, Rex, 'Horizontal windmills', *T.N.S.*, 40 (1967–8), 125–45.

Wailes, Rex, 'Windmills' in Charles Singer, E. J. Holmyard, and A. R. Hall (eds.), *A history of technology*, 8 vols., Oxford, 1954–84, vol. 3.

Wainwright, David, *Broadwood by appointment*, 1982.

Walton, Mary, *Sheffield: its story and achievements*, 4th edn, Sheffield, 1968.

Weatherill, Lorna, 'Technical change and potters' probate inventories, 1660–1760', *Jnl of Ceramic History*, 3 (1970), 3–12.

Weatherill, Lorna, *The pottery trade and north Staffordshire, 1660–1760*, Manchester, 1971.

Weatherill, Lorna, and Rhoda Edwards, 'Pottery making in London and Whitehaven in the late-seventeenth century', *Post Medieval Archaeology*, 5 (1971), 160–81.

Webster, Charles, *The great instauration: science, medicine and reform, 1626–1660*, 1975.

Webster, Charles, *From Paracelsus to Newton: magic and the making of modern science*, Cambridge, 1982.

Wells, F. A. *The British hosiery and knitwear industry: its history and organization*, 2nd edn, Newton Abbot, 1972.

Welsh, Charles, *A bookseller of the last century*, 1885.

White, Lynn, Jr. 'What accelerated technical progress in the western middle ages?' in A. C. Crombie (ed.), *Scientific change: symposium on the history of science, University of Oxford, 1961*, 1963.

White, Lynn, Jr. 'Cultural climates and technological advance in the middle ages', *Viator*, 2 (1971), 171–202.

White, Stephen D. *Sir Edward Coke and 'The grievances of the commonwealth', 1621–1628*, Chapel Hill, 1979.

Wilkinson, R. G. *Poverty and progress: an ecological model of economic development*, 1973.

Willan, T. S. *River navigation in England, 1600–1750*, 1936.

Williamson, F. 'George Sorocold of Derby, a pioneer of water supply', *Jnl Derbys. Archaeological and Natural History Society*, 57 (1937), 44–84.

Wilson, Paul, 'The waterwheels of John Smeaton', *T.N.S.*, 30 (1955–7), 25–48.

Wilson, R. G. *Gentlemen merchants: the merchant community in Leeds, 1700–1830*, Manchester, 1971.

Wolper, Roy S. 'The rhetoric of gunpowder and the idea of progress', *J.H.I.*, 31 (1970), 589–98.

Wood, Sir Henry Trueman, 'The inventions of John Kay, 1704–70', *Jnl of the Royal Society of Arts*, 60 (1911–12), 73–86.

Wood, Sir Henry Trueman, *A history of the Royal Society of Arts*, 1913.

Woodcroft, Bennet, *Chronological index of patents of invention*, 2 vols., 1854.

Woodcroft, Bennet, *Subject-matter index, made from titles only of patents of invention, from March 2, 1617, 14 James I to October 1, 1852, 16 Victoriae*, 2 vols., 1854.

Woodcroft, Bennet, *Alphabetical index of patentees of inventions*, 1854, repr. 1969.

Wrigley, E. A. 'The supply of raw materials in the industrial revolution', *Ec.H.R.*, 2nd ser. 15 (1962), 1–16.

Wrigley, E. A. 'The process of modernization and the industrial revolution in England', *Jnl of Interdisciplinary History*, 3 (1972), 225–59.

Wykes, David L. 'The Leicester riots of 1773 and 1787: a study of the victims of popular protest', *Trans. Leics. Archaeological and Historical Society*, 54 (1978–9), 39–50.

Young, J. H. 'Proprietors of other days', *Chemist and Druggist*, 106 (1927), 831–4.

Zilsel, Edgar, 'The genesis of the concept of scientific progress', *J.H.I.*, 6 (1945), 325–49.

Unpublished theses

Davey, P. C. 'Studies in the history of mining and metallurgy to the middle of the seventeenth century', Ph.D. thesis, University of London, 1954.

Duncan, G. D. 'Monopolies under Elizabeth I', Ph.D. thesis, University of Cambridge, 1976.

Hartridge, R. J. 'The development of industries in London south of the Thames, 1750–1850', M.Sc. thesis, University of London, 1955.

Hoppit, Julian, 'Risk and failure in English industry, c.1700–1800', Ph.D. thesis, University of Cambridge, 1984.

Kanefsky, John W. 'The diffusion of power technology in British industry, 1760–1870', Ph.D. thesis, University of Exeter, 1979.

Lieberman, David, 'The province of legislation determined: legal theory in eighteenth-century Britain', Ph.D. thesis, University of London, 1980.

MacLeod, Christine, 'Patents for invention and technical change in England, 1660–1753', Ph.D. thesis, University of Cambridge, 1983.

Mandrell, T. R. 'The structure and organisation of London trades, wages and prices, and the organisation of labour, 1793–1815', M.Litt. thesis, University of Cambridge, 1968.

Rhodes, Hilda M. 'Literary aspects of inventors, projectors and virtuosi, 1660–1720', M.A. thesis, University of London, 1959.

Rothstein, N. K. A. 'The London silk industry, 1702–66', M.A. thesis, University of London, 1961.

Setchell, J. R. M. 'Henry Hindley & Son, instrument and clock makers of York', B.Litt. thesis, University of Oxford, 1971.

Thomas, J. H. 'Thomas Neale, a seventeenth-century projector', Ph.D. thesis, University of Southampton, 1979.

Walker, Michael J. 'The extent of the guild control of trades in England, c.1660–1820; a study based on a sample of provincial towns and London Companies', Ph.D. thesis, University of Cambridge, 1986.

Weatherill, Lorna, 'The growth of the pottery industry in England, 1660–1815', Ph.D. thesis, University of London, 1981.

Index

Academia del Cimento, 186
Académie des Sciences, 41, 47, 186, 189, 262 n. 42
achromatic lenses, 70
Acts of Parliament: confirming patents, 16–17, 49, 60, 72–3, 82, 232 n. 1; for engineering schemes, 247 n. 44; rewarding inventors, 31, 38, 49, 60, 193, 196
advertising, 85–7
agricultural implements, 98–100, 129, 168, 169
agriculture: patents for, 97, 101, 168; productivity of, 6, 144, 212; unpatented innovations, 98–100
Albemarle, 2nd Duke of (Christopher Monck), 28
Alberti, Girolamo (Venetian ambassador), 26, 228 n. 36
Albion Mills (London), 104, 176, 219
alkali manufacture, 89, 111–12, 114, 153
Allen, John, 175
Angell, Justinian, 84
Annual Register, 147
apprentices, 13, 18, 118
apprenticeship, 66
Archer, Henry, 166–7
Ardesoif, Charles, 231 n. 102
Argand, Aimé, 72, 78
Arkwright, Richard, 71, 78, 89, 92, 103, 133, 162, 189, 221
Artificers, Statute of (1563), 12, 113
artisans, 118, 121, 133–5, 137; emigration of, 33
Ashton, Samuel, 50, 82
Astbury, John, 71
atmospheric engine, 7, 28, 91, 101–2, 175, 218–19, 221
Aubrey, John, 102, 268 n. 70
Auriol, John, 29

Bacon, Francis, 183, 185–6, 190, 194, 195, 204–6, 261 n. 25, 263 n. 99
Bacon, Joseph, 82
Baddeley, Richard, 88, 179
Bailey, William, 225 n. 46
Baker, Charles, 98
Baker, John, 77
Baker, Walter, 59, 86, 235 n. 74
balance of trade, theories, 31–2
Baldwin, Henry, 100
Ball, John, 100
balloons (hot-air and hydrogen), 202
Baltic, trade with, 32
bankruptcies, 125
Barbon, Nicholas, 210
Barlow, Robert, 53
Bashforth, John, 67–8
Bashforth, William, 67–8
Baskerville, John, 71, 95, 219
Batchelor, John, 93, 238 n. 44
Bath and West Society, 195
Bayly, Lewis, 29–30, 229 n. 66
Beale, John, 269 n. 96
Becker, Andrew, 81
beech oil, 16–17, 88
bee hives, 92
Bellers, John, 192
Bellingham, John, 25, 26
Benson, Thomas, 77, 164
Bentham, Jeremy, 44, 264 n. 124
Bentham, Samuel, 44, 105, 147, 168
Bentley, Thomas, 196
Berkeley, George, Bishop of Cloyne, 192
Berthollet, Claude Louis, 111
Bertie, Philip, 86
Berty, Francisco, 11
Bessemer, Henry, 77, 95
Betton, Michael, 59
Betton, Thomas, 59
Betts, William, 162

Hornblower, Jonathan, 71, 73, 174
hosiery industry, 60–1, 131–2, 143, 154
Houghton, John, 208, 213, 215, 269 n. 96
Howard, Charles, 82
Howard, Sir Philip, 27, 35, 49, 51, 58–9
Hulls, Jonathan, 77, 175
Hume, David, 209
Hunter, Joseph, 131
Huntsman, Benjamin, 7, 94, 131
Hurd, Edward, 86
Hutchinson, John, 73, 198
Hutton, Thomas, 45–6
Hutton, William, 130, 219
Huygens, Christian, 186
Hyde, Lawrence, Earl of Rochester, 28

immigrants, *see* patentees, immigrant
import substitution, 12, 27–8, 31, 109
improvement, 188, 209, 210, 267 n. 58;
  national reputation for, 208, (*see also*
  invention national reputation for);
  patenting of, 13, 14, 18, 62, 67–8, 145–6
indigo, 27
industrial espionage, 54, 108
industrial revolution, 156–7
industrialization, 5–6, 62, 125
industries: propensity to patent, 97–114;
  protection of, 32–3; *see also under individual
  industries*
ingenuity, promotion of, 209, 210
Inglis, Alexander, 23
instrumentmaking, 70, 97, 113, 143
intellectual property, 31, 67, 197–9, 221
invention: concepts of, 145, 198–9, 201–22;
  definitions of, 61–2, 65–8, 209, 210, 221,
  267 n. 58, 268 n. 70; diffusion of, 5–6,
  183, 194–5; economic context of, 205–6,
  207–9, 214, 216–17; ethic of
  communicating, 100, 187–8; folk-lore of,
  204; goals of, 158–81; interest in, 145,
  199–200; investment in, 77, 88, 90, 93,
  193–4; measurement of, 1–2, 4–5, 7, 144;
  national reputation for, 219, 271 n. 136,
  (*see also* improvement, national reputation
  for); promotion of, 182–95, 200, 220–1;
  property in, 198–9; sources of, 206,
  270 n. 104; unpatented, 7, 8, 93–4, 97–
  114; *see also* capital-saving inventions;
  fuel-saving inventions; labour-saving
  inventions; process inventions; product
  inventions; technical change; technology
'invention industry', 4, 75, 79, 139–41
inventors: amateur, 78–9; definition of,
  265 n. 8; as designers, 210; heroic image
  of, 3, 220–1; motivation of, 7, 159;

professional, 79, 92, 135, 139–43; rewards
  for, 31, 38, 60, 190–6, 221; and Royal
  Society, 187; in trade, 79, 93–5
Ireland, 8, 76, 194–5
iron industry: coal-burning, 234 n. 39;
  imports, 260 n. 134; and patents, 28, 30,
  46, 52–3, 57, 145, 153, 179; and timber
  scarcity, 208, 267n
Irwin, James, 87

Jackson, Benjamin Habakkuk, 86–7
Jamaica, 28, 110
James I, 14–15
James II, 21, 43
James, Robert, 59, 62–3, 86, 107
Jeffreys, George, Chief Justice, 68
Jennens, Sir William, 77
Jenner, Edward, 193, 264 n. 124
Jewellers, Company of, 188
Jewes, Daniel, 77
Johnson, Moses, 65, 66
Joiners, Company of, 59, 112–13
joint-stock companies, 55–6, 151
Jones, Sir William, 62
judiciary, 31, 48, 58–74, 145, 167; *see also
  under individual judges*

Kay, John, 53, 60, 63, 66, 92, 102, 161,
  164, 193, 234 n. 58
Keir, James, 61, 89, 114, 147
Kenrick, W., Ll.D., 196, 199
Kent, 128, 129
Kenyon, Lord Chief Justice, 87

Labeyle, Charles, 104
labour: costs, 171, 209–10, 212; deskilling,
  168, 177–8, 180–1; division of, 210–11,
  216; leisure preference, 158, 171,
  258 n. 71; relief of, 211; shortages, 99,
  211; shortages, 99, 168–9, (in
  Netherlands, 208); underemployment,
  211, 214; *see also* employment
labour-saving inventions, 158, 159–73,
  180–1, 201, 202, 210–18, 219, 257 n. 68
labour theory of value, 210
laissez-faire, see government
Lancashire, 124, 125, 133, 139
Lauderdale, 8th Earl of (James Maitland),
  209, 216–17
Le Blon, James Christopher, 55–6
Leach, Sir Simon, 29
leather industry, 82, 97, 113, 168, 173, 174
Lee, Edward, 176
Lee, William, 226 n. 16
Leeds, 129, 133, 134

Murray, Matthew, 106, 253 n. 58
musical-instrumentmaking, 97, 143

nail-making machines, 168
napping engine, 29
Nasmith, John, 49, 50
Nasmyth, James, 104–5, 106, 180–1, 258 n. 93, 259 n. 125
National Debt, 30, 54, 152
Neale, Thomas, 30, 79, 81
neo-platonism, 203, 219–20
Netherlands, 41, 47, 208
New Atlantis (1660), 187, 191
Newcomen, Thomas, 7, 28, 218–19; *see also* atmospheric engine
Newell, Henry, 12
Newsham, Richard, 48, 66, 70, 95, 153
North, Francis, *see* Guildford, Baron
Northey, Sir Edward, 38, 45, 48, 54, 236 n. 99
Northumberland, 101, 124
Norwich, 16, 129, 133, 134
Nottingham, 88, 124, 125, 128, 129, 131–2, 154

occupational health, 164
Oglethorp, James, 260 n. 9
Oldenburg, Henry, 43, 186
opportunity costs, 212–14
Ordnance Office, 36–8, 231 n. 105
Owen, Robert, 169

Painter Stainers, Company of, 59, 83, 112–13
Palmer, Sir Geoffrey, 46
Pantin, Lewis, 104
Pantoune, Robert, 198
paper industry, 32–3, 46, 114, 250 n. 118, 266 n. 25
Papin, Denis, 187
parliament: attacks on monopolies, 14–17; attitudes to labour-saving inventions, 166–7; select committee on patents (1829), 42, 50, 62, 78, 232 n. 131, 237 n. 29; *see also* Acts of Parliament; premiums
Parrott, Stonier, 91
partnerships, 55–6, 77, 88, 90, 116, 250 n. 2
Passman, John, 175
Patent, The, a poem (1776), 87
patent agents, 40
patent law, 14, 48, 58–64, 66–7, 145, 167; *see also* common law; equity courts; Monopolies, Statute of; *under individual cases*
patent medicines, *see* proprietary medicines

Patent Office, 1, 2
patent rolls, 10, 41, 44
patent system: awareness of, 77–8, 145, 146–7, 157; criticisms, 182–90; defences, 196–200, 222; development, 1, 40–57, 80; economic consequences, 4; historiography, 3–4; a misnomer, 1; positive feedback in, 95, 147; subject to government interests, 38–9
patentees: courtiers, 14–15, 16, 25–30, 43, 82–3, 95, 134; female, 9, 52, 105; financial burden on, 77; gentleman, 116, 117, 121; immigrant, 28, 82, 95, 102; in London, 118–25, 128, 129, 137, 139, 143; motivation of, 7, 75–96; occupations of, 116–18, 121–4, 134–9; places of residence of, 116–17; prejudice against, 58, 72, 145; in the provinces, 124–34, 143; and reform of patent system, 182, 188–9, 200; in trades, 84, 87, 134–5, 143, 153; types of, 78–9, 95, 117, 152
patents: affidavit, 42, 48, 53–4; applications lapsed and rejected, 42, 45, 76; caveats, 43–4, 89, 147, 195–6; clusters of, 87, 137, 152–6; conditions placed on, 12; consideration, 13, 14, 44–5, 49, 61, 158; cost of, 76–7, 146, 188; disclosure of secret, 13–14, 42, 49, 182, 183, 185, 187–8, 193; disincentives to seeking, 75–8, 124–5; enforcement of, 58–74, 78, 92, 98; examination, 41, 223 n. 4; geographical distribution of, 77, 115, 118–34; infringement of, 58, 60–2, 64–6, 68–72, 73; insecurity of, 72–3, 78, 188–9; Italian influence on, 11; justification of, 13, 182–4, 196–200; non-obstante, 42, 82; origins of, 10–11; procedure for obtaining, 40–1, 42, 76; property in, 89; publication of, 43–4, 50, 58, 146; registration, 2, 41, 51; rents for, 20–1, 28, 228 n. 12; revocation of, 59–60; sale of, 92–3, 142; scrutiny of, 12, 41–8, 189, 190, 229 n. 43; statistics (interpretation of, 2, 5–7, 115, 144, 156–7, 158; long-term rise in, 144–57; and political crises, 38; short-term fluctuations in, 145, 151–6); uses of, 7, 74, 75–96, (heterodox, 80, 81–8; orthodox, 80, 88–93, 107); *see also* licensing; monopolies; specification
patronage, 24–30, 54, 80
Paul, Lewis, 63, 89, 90, 164–5, 166, 177, 193
Paulden, Thomas, 25
Payne, John, 30, 52–3, 88, 178
pearlashes, *see* potashes
Peck, Philip, 194